Blairsville High School Library

P9-EER-581

DATE DUE

DEC 1 4 1973			
GAYLORD			PRINTED IN U.S A.

The
Price of
Vigilance

The Price of Vigilance

By
Joan M. Jensen

RAND MCNALLY & COMPANY   Chicago · New York · San Francisco

Blairsville High School Library

Copyright © 1968 by Rand McNally & Company
Copyright 1968 under International Copyright Union by
Rand McNally & Company
All Rights Reserved
Library of Congress Catalog Card Number 68-30929
Printed in the United States of America by
Rand McNally & Company
First Printing, October, 1968

Contents

Illustrations

*"The study of error . . .
serves as a stimulating
introduction to
the study of
truth."*

Walter Lippman

Introduction

Following the sinking of the British steamer *Lusitania* in 1915, President Woodrow Wilson dispatched several notes of protest and warning to the German government. His tone became sterner after the torpedoing of the French cross-channel passenger ship *Sussex* in 1916. To Wilson's notes Theobald von Bethmann-Hollweg, Germany's Chancellor, at first reacted by opposing his country's U-boat campaign, contending that it was likely to bring about American intervention in the European war.

Generals Hindenburg and Ludendorff did not view the possibility with the same alarm. They argued that military considerations, not political implications, must shape their strategy. "We are counting on the possibility of war with the United States and have made all preparations to meet it. Things cannot be worse than they are now," Hindenburg maintained. Ludendorff was sure that the United States could supply no more shipping or war matériel or financial assistance to the Allies than had already been provided; and American troops could not be dispatched in sufficient numbers to become a determining factor for more than six months. By that time England would be crushed.

Thus out-voted, on January 1, 1917, Bethmann finally withdrew his opposition, and the Kaiser ordered resumption of unrestricted submarine warfare, bringing to an end attempts to settle peacefully his government's quarrel with the United States.

The two years of diplomatic quarreling between the United States and Germany were two years of indecision on the part of President Wilson over how neutrality could be maintained. In the first months of the war, it was simple enough, but as the European war reached a stalemate, each belligerent attempted to promote disaffection among its enemies, to forestall action by neutrals which might be helpful to the other side, and to bring new allies to their aid. In such an atmosphere, it was inevitable that the United States, the largest neutral nation, should become the arena for many preliminary skirmishes.

The Germans were determined to encourage immigrants from India and Ireland living in the United States to work for the independence of their homelands from Great Britain. By blocking munitions shipments from the United States and by agitating to keep America out of the war, the Irish and East Indians (Indians from India) could contribute to England's defeat. Germany courted them. The English were equally determined to encourage Czechs, Yugoslavs, and Poles in the United States to work against Austria and Germany, to keep the munitions coming, and to bring the United States into the war.

President Wilson could not decide what to do about the activities of German and British agents. He could have ignored their machinations, of course, but many Americans argued that the federal government should purge the country of these foreign intriguers and punish their domestic sympathizers. If the President were to act, he would have to obtain the sanction of Congress through the enactment of new laws or risk Congressional conflict by acting without its approval.

Wilson's Attorney General, Thomas Watt Gregory, maintained that the Justice Department could take no action because the agents were not violating federal law. The courts had held that the treason statute covered all those "owing allegiance to the United States," including foreigners domiciled in the United States; but activities of spies and saboteurs in peacetime did not come under the definition of treason— waging war or giving aid and comfort to the enemy.

Criminal statutes enacted during the Civil War applied to seditious conspiracy, insurrection, and rebellion, not to the activities of persons acting individually. Congress passed a bill during a Japanese war scare in 1911 "to prevent the disclosure of national defense secrets," but none of the European agents were interested in that type of espionage. Article 82 of the United States Articles of War dealt specifically with "spies" but could be used only where an individual was found "lurking" about military fortifications or reservations. No federal law prohibited espionage or even sabotage outside military zones, and these zones consisted solely of bases during peacetime.

In 1917 only two neutrality laws applied to activities within the United States. One prohibited the enlisting of men to fight in a foreign army against a nation with which the United States was at peace; the other prohibited organizing a military expedition against a nation with which the United States was at peace. Few men were so careless as to violate these laws. Most of the activities of the Germans labeled "intrigues" by the British were not, therefore, violations of any laws whatever.

In the absence of federal authority to act against the "German intrigues," Gregory counseled that nothing be done to adversely affect Wilson's policy of neutrality. Early in 1915 a young German reservist attempted to destroy the Canadian Pacific Railroad bridge between Canada and the United States and took refuge in Maine. When Canada asked for his extradition, Gregory said at a Cabinet meeting, "Better keep him in Maine and avoid international trouble." As evidence of the activities of other German aliens came to light, however, some Cabinet members urged that action be taken despite the risk. Secretary of the Treasury William McAdoo suggested that all suspected German agents be rounded up and sent back to Germany, to which Gregory retorted that he did not have sufficient evidence to engage in such a roundup.

Gregory asked Congress for legislation to deal with the problem. In December, 1915, even President Wilson urged Congress to enact pending laws to "save the honor and self-respect of the nation" from persons who "poured the poison of disloyalty into the very arteries of our national life ... who have sought to bring the authority and good name of our government into contempt, to destroy the industries ... for their vindictive purposes ... to debase our politics to the uses of foreign intrigue." They were "infinitely malignant," Wilson had said; only new laws could purge the country of their "corrupt distempers."

But Congress did not respond to Wilson's plea. Illinois Representative Frank Buchanan, organizer of a committee to oppose munitions manufacturing, had been indicted for conspiracy in restraint of trade. He thereupon accused the Bureau of Investigation of interfering with labor under the guise of maintaining neutrality. Such suspicions fed a growing distrust of prosecutions undertaken by the Justice Department, and additional legislation which would have strengthened the hand of Attorney General Gregory in dealing with "intrigues" was sidetracked in the House. In May, 1916, when Gregory again urged Congress to pass the needed legislation, that body remained unmoved. Even when Germany resumed unrestricted U-boat warfare, many congressmen still feared that the proposed laws, if enacted, would be used by the executive branch to stifle criticism of President Wilson's policies. Thus measures which Gregory had been requesting for over a year had not been enacted.

When Congress refused to act, Gregory also refused to act. He ruled that his Bureau of Investigation agents had no legal right to investigate activities that were not violations of federal law. In Cabinet meetings, Secretary of the Treasury William McAdoo had indicated that he felt the government should not be prevented from acting against "German intrigues" merely by a lack of federal authority. So when Secretary of State William Jennings Bryan decided that German diplomats should be investigated for possible espionage, he requested and received President Wilson's permission to use, not Bureau of Investigation agents, but members of the Secret Service.

Before 1916 the Secret Service was far better known than the Bureau of Investigation, the agency which was later to become the powerful FBI. Established within the Treasury Department during the Civil War to track down counterfeiters, the Secret Service had been given the job of protecting the President. Until 1908 it had remained the major federal investigating force.

The War Department had hired Pinkerton detectives for military intelligence during the Civil War, rather than establish its own force; and in 1870, when the Justice Department was created by Congress, it, too, hired private detectives as investigators. However, in 1893, after the Homestead Massacre in which Pinkerton men gunned down striking workers, Congress had passed a law forbidding departments of the federal government to contract with private detectives, and the Justice Department had begun the practice of borrowing Secret Service agents from the Treasury Department.

This arrangement had worked satisfactorily until Theodore Roosevelt's Attorney General, Charles Bonaparte, put Secret Service agents on the trail of a land fraud—and the trail ended at the doors of Congress. A representative and a senator, both from Oregon, were convicted of conspiracy to defraud. Indignant at being investigated by agents of the executive branch of the government, Congress passed a law in 1908 prohibiting the Justice Department from borrowing Secret Service agents, at the same time refusing to give the Attorney General his own investigating force. Undaunted, President Roosevelt simply ordered Bonaparte to hire agents and pay the cost out of general funds allocated to the Justice Department.

By 1909 the Bureau had, indeed, been organized, but it would be several years before its investigative function within the Department of Justice would be taken seriously enough for Congress to appropriate funds for its effective operation. Congress had ignored the 1909 display of executive power for a whole year. Then in 1910, when reformers pushed through the White Slave Act, the prospect of stamping out commercialized vice in America so fascinated congressmen that they voted a specific appropriation so that the Justice Department could enforce the Act vigorously. With this tacit approval, the Bureau began to grow, reaching a strength of 100 agents by 1914. During 1915 the Justice Department spent $14,000 investigating violations of neutrality laws, but it could not do much more to increase its influence while Attorney General Gregory limited its investigations strictly to violations of federal law.

Secretary of the Treasury William McAdoo felt no similar compunctions about the activities of his department's Secret Service. The most politically ambitious of Wilson's Cabinet members, he responded immediately to Bryan's invitation to engage in counterespionage. McAdoo hoped to become Secretary of State should Bryan resign in opposition to Wilson's stern policy toward Germany, and he was anxious that information which might be used to discredit German diplomats be gathered. He assigned a number of agents to work with the New York City police to keep watch on diplomatic offices there.

McAdoo, as it happened, was disappointed in his hope to become Secretary of State. But when Bryan did resign as expected, the new Secretary, Robert Lansing, indicated an interest in continuing the work of the Secret Service agents. In fact, Lansing was willing to do much more than Bryan had done in publicizing the suspicious activities of German diplomats. New York papers soon began to give wide publicity to "German intrigues."

The first spectacular exposé came in August, 1915, after Secret Service agent Frank Burke stole the briefcase of German Commercial Attaché Heinrich Albert. In the briefcase were propaganda plans which, although they did not violate any American law, would certainly serve to convince Americans of German treachery and strengthen support for the Administration's hardening stance toward Germany.

After a hurried conference with President Wilson, his advisor Colonel Edwin M. House, and Secretary of State Lansing, McAdoo gave the papers to Frank I. Cobb of the *New York World* for publication. Headlines announcing propaganda plots immediately stirred public concern about German agents in the United States. These headlines also aroused Attorney General Gregory and his chief spy-catcher, A. Bruce Bielaski, neither of whom had known about the theft of the briefcase.

The morning after publication, Bielaski sent his agent to the office of the *World* to demand the original papers and to ask how they were obtained. Gregory told reporters that there were no laws under which he could prosecute the German propagandists; propaganda was not illegal. The whole affair left the public with the impression that German agents were intervening in America's domestic affairs and that the Justice Department was helpless to stop them.

September, 1915, saw a second exposé of "German intrigues." This time British intelligence agents took papers from James J. Archibald, a friend of Austrian diplomats in the United States, and turned them over to Secretary of State Lansing. The papers contained plans to persuade Austro-Hungarian subjects to quit working in American munitions plants. Again the actions called for were not illegal, so Lansing had McAdoo turn the evidence over to the newspapers rather than to Attorney General Gregory. Publication of the plans in the *New York World* increased American indignation over foreign interference in domestic affairs. Three months later President Wilson approved the publication of papers relating to various other schemes, some aimed at stopping the export of munitions to the Allies and others suggesting intrigues between Germans and Mexican revolutionaries. Apparently Wilson hoped these revelations would push Congress into support for his military preparedness program. Instead, their publication brought only criticism of Attorney General Gregory for failing to catch and prosecute German spies.

The Attorney General consistently maintained that no federal laws had been violated. He called upon the states to prosecute German aliens under state laws, at the same time protesting against the activity of the Secret Service in investigating these aliens. It soon became evident that discord existed within the Administration. Secret Service and Bureau of Investigation agents were battling among themselves in an effort to find evidence against the Germans and to claim the credit for exposing spies. At first Gregory denied the existence of a conflict, but after a Cabinet meeting held specifically to discuss the issue, he admitted to reporters that the State Department had appointed counselor Frank Polk to coordinate investigations so that there was no duplication of effort, and to make specific assignments where conflict had occurred.

Meanwhile, Wilson and the State Department continued to use the Secret Service for investigations of unpopular activities which did not involve actual violations of federal law. Not until July, 1916, did Congress agree to expansion of the Bureau of Investigation. Then it appropriated funds to allow the Bureau to investigate matters not constituting federal offenses if the State Department requested such investigations. Apparently this action was to permit the Bureau of Investigation to probe the cause of a munitions explosion which rocked Black Tom Island in New York Harbor earlier that month. There was no conclusive evidence that German saboteurs had been responsible, but many Americans were convinced that only Germany would be interested in blocking munitions shipments to the Allies. With this precedent Gregory allowed his Bureau to extend its investigations more and more into German activities. By the end of 1916 the Justice Department had spent $64,000 in investigations of war-related activities of aliens and citizens and had enlarged the Bureau of Investigation to include 300 agents.

After the war, reformer Robert LaFollette would write that Gregory was a reactionary, that he had been "an evil influence" in the suppression of free speech, that his repressive laws had been "the conception of a fifteenth century mind," and that he had allowed his "Secret Service thugs" to terrorize the public. But in 1916 Gregory had an impressive record of liberalism.

When the slight but distinguished-looking Texas lawyer entered the Cabinet in 1914, he was known mainly as the man who had convinced Colonel House to support Wilson's nomination in the 1912 Democratic convention. James C. McReynolds, whom Gregory replaced as Attorney General, had managed to antagonize both the Cabinet and the Congress. Gregory's deft handling of the troubled politics of the Justice Department, on the other hand, helped gain the support of liberals, those reformers without whom Wilson could not have been reelected in 1916. Gregory vigorously pushed antitrust prosecutions and encouraged Chief Bielaski of the Bureau of Investigation to investigate violations of such reform legislation as the White Slave Act. Liberals also applauded many of his appointments. For example, he pleased California progressives by naming Annette Abbott Adams as the first woman Assistant United States Attorney, an appointment which McReynolds had indignantly blocked. To the post of United States Attorney for Massachusetts he appointed George W. Anderson, a liberal Democrat who had crusaded for reform with Louis Brandeis. Then in March, 1916, he suggested that Wilson appoint Brandeis Associate Justice of the Supreme Court. To those who objected that Brandeis was a radical, Gregory replied, "One radical in nine is not such a bad thing on the Supreme Bench."

Wilson asked Gregory to take a place beside Brandeis on the Supreme Court when Charles Evans Hughes resigned to campaign for the presidency in 1916, but Gregory declined because of his deafness (even with a hearing aid he had difficulty following conversation). Instead, he campaigned for Wilson's reelection; then, with victory assured, asked to leave the Cabinet and return to private practice. Wilson insisted he stay. And so the quiet, soft-spoken Texan, who chain-smoked small black cigars and liked to tell jokes, remained in the Justice Department.

Once Gregory decided to remain, he resolved to assert the supremacy of his department in counterespionage investigations. By February, 1917, he had established the Bureau of Investigation firmly within the Department and had encouraged its director to investigate all suspected sabotage and espionage. Since the Post Office Department's investigating force was concerned only with mail frauds, and since neither the Army nor the Navy had any field force at the time, opposition to this upstart organization came mainly from the Secret Service, which considered its own ancient lineage and experience sufficient license to catch spies.

Bielaski had no intention of being shunted aside by the Secret Service. When he had entered the Justice Department in 1907, a boyish-looking dark-haired investigator with a pugnacious chin and a tip-tilted nose, he had been the butt of office humor for the indefatigable energy exhibited in long walks and garden work before breakfast, in baseball, boxing, running, and rowing long after his exhausted stenographers had gone home. It also imbued his work with resourcefulness and a spirit of experimentation that won him the position of Chief of the Bureau of Investigation after only five years.

By February 1, 1917, the day Germany resumed unrestricted submarine warfare, Chief Bielaski had asserted his claim to all counterespionage investigations but had not yet won his battle against the Secret Service. The next day, in Chicago, an event occurred which was to give him a new weapon in his struggle.

The Volunteers

A portly middle-aged man marched up the steps of the Justice Department in Chicago, entered the old building, and told the clerk he wanted to talk to the official in charge of federal investigations. He gave his name as Albert M. Briggs, vice-president of Outdoor Advertising, Incorporated, and was admitted to the office of Superintendent Hinton D. Clabaugh. Once inside, Briggs went straight to the point. Nineteen years before, he had volunteered to go to Cuba when war with Spain seemed imminent. Now war with Germany seemed imminent, and he wanted to volunteer again for the Army but was physically unfit. Could he not at least recruit a volunteer organization to help with investigations of Germans, he asked. The superintendent thanked him for the offer and said he would think it over.

The parsimony of the legislature still made it difficult for Bielaski to compete with the Secret Service, and men like Clabaugh were loud in their complaints about their lack of equipment and manpower. The superintendent of the Chicago office had already voiced his discontent to local businessmen over the difficulty of investigating breaches of neutrality laws under these handicaps. A week before Briggs's visit, Clabaugh had told him that cases were piling up and that the Bureau could do nothing about them. Many investigations were already underway, such as one into the mysterious explosion aboard the steamship *Eastland,* believed to be the result of German sabotage. Now he had requests to investigate East Indian radicals for conspiring with German agents to send arms and men to India to foment rebellion against England. While attorneys within the Justice Department kept sending new cases to him, each day's mail also brought requests from private citizens to investigate German aliens suspected of other violations of federal laws.

Clabaugh had only fifteen detectives to cover the states of Illinois, Wisconsin, and Minnesota. Funds to hire and equip agents were limited. He had no automobiles—his agents had to chase suspects by streetcar. Briggs had already offered to get ten or twenty good, quiet men—with cars—who would work without pay, taking time from their business affairs or from their leisure to assist the Bureau. Clabaugh had accepted the offer and had used a few of Brigg's business friends to chauffeur detectives. Now the advertising man wanted permission to enlist other volunteers.

Briggs's idea for organizing volunteers was not new, of course. Following a tradition which began with the Sons of Liberty during the Revolution, Americans had organized into groups to fight enemies of the community, and there was strong precedent in Illinois for such a voluntary group to combat subversion. Over fifty years earlier, in the summer of 1862, a group of northern patriots had met in Pekin, Illinois, there to pledge absolute and unqualified loyalty to the government and unswerving support of its efforts to suppress the southern rebellion. They organized themselves as the Union League. Republican officials had encouraged the League, and it had spread throughout the state. Within a year, national headquarters were set up in Washington, and other groups had been formed in Philadelphia, New York, Baltimore, Boston (where Ralph Waldo Emerson became an enthusiastic member), and even in the frontier towns of San Francisco and Los Angeles. Illinois, with fifty thousand members, remained the stronghold of the Union League.

Those were exciting days, when Union Leaguers believed southern sympathizers to be organizing the so-called "Chicago Conspiracy" to foment uprisings throughout the Midwest and liberate tens of thousands of Confederate prisoners of war, then use them as the nucleus for new armies that would sack Chicago and sweep through the middle border states, spreading death and destruction. Undercover agents working for Republican Governor Louis Morton claimed to have discovered the plot. Prison camps were reinforced, and members of the Knights of the Golden Circle, an organization of suspected southern sympathizers, were arrested. Meanwhile, patriots cried, "Eternal vigilance is the price of liberty." They labeled the election of 1864 a battle between "despotism and freedom" and marched to the polls to vote for the Union party and against treason. The Knights of the Golden Circle disintegrated. The League, which had forwarded to Washington reports on Knights of the Golden Circle and others believed to be disloyal, flourished through the reconstruction era, then lingered on into the Gilded Age as a refuge of aging patriots. Although vigilantism found its home in the West in the nineteenth century, the idea that volunteers must organize when they considered the community to be in danger had deep roots in the Midwest.

Clabaugh needed no specific authorization from the Bureau of Investigation in Washington to utilize civilian volunteers on investigations, for that practice was not really new, either. In 1912 the Bureau had embarked upon its first crusade, that against the white slave traffic, under the banner of the Bureau's new chief. At that time Bielaski had encouraged Clabaugh and other superintendents to ask waiters, socialites, and members of various organizations to eavesdrop on private conversations and to forward tips to Bureau offices if their suspicions were aroused. Many prosecutions had resulted from these tips. From using volunteers against organized vice to using them against conspiracy to commit espionage and sabotage was an easy transition.

For Hinton D. Clabaugh, at least, it seemed perfectly consistent with Bureau practice. To a man born and raised in Alabama, the idea of groups of men working regularly with local police could not have been foreign, either, for such groups had operated in the South to help control the Negro since antebellum days. Yet Clabaugh was not sure that the Chicago police and community leaders would want federal investigators to call upon such a force, one which might disrupt the local system of law enforcement. Consequently, before accepting Briggs's offer, Clabaugh called the Chief of Police and a group of other prominent Chicagoans into conference.

On February 3, President Wilson told Congress he had severed diplomatic relations with Germany. The next day newspapers announced that the first United States ship had been torpedoed by a German submarine. Like the rest of the nation, Chicago expected immediate sabotage on the home front. Clabaugh called Briggs. An organization of volunteers would be of very great help to the Department, Clabaugh said, suggesting that the businessmen start by putting a fleet of automobiles at the disposal of his agents. Briggs told Clabaugh a free taxicab service would be organized within days.

Meanwhile, Congress was still questioning the motives of the Justice Department in requesting new counterespionage legislation. The reservations were aptly expressed by Theodore Roosevelt, who wrote to Senator Henry Cabot Lodge after the Senate had passed thirteen measures requested by Gregory and while the House was considering them, "I am told that the so-called 'Spy' bill that was just passed by the Senate would not really interfere with spies but would forbid all criticism of the President." Lodge assured him that it would not, and that the legislation was much needed. Attorney General Gregory even appealed to other Cabinet members for support, sending letters to Postmaster General Burleson and Secretary of the Treasury McAdoo with the lament, "It seems to me that my Department and I have about exhausted our resources in trying to advance these measures." But the House remained adamant, and the session ended without their passage.

In November, 1916, Gregory had started turning over evidence to the state attorney generals, asking them to prosecute acts of violence under state laws. When in March, 1917, the Council of National Defense asked him what the Justice Department could do to defend the country against overt acts by enemy agents and the possible destruction of industrial centers, he had replied bitterly, "Nothing." The rebuffs of Congress made it more likely that he would turn increasingly to state officials and to volunteers to counteract the expected sabotage.

A few weeks after his February visit, Briggs reappeared at Clabaugh's office and announced that a group of Chicago businessmen had seventy-five automobiles they wished to turn over to the Justice Department. He suggested that most of these be transported to other cities for the use of Bureau offices; four would be retained for Chicago, several sent to New York and Washington, D. C. Clabaugh reached for a sheet of paper, quickly scrawled the proposal, and ordered his secretary to wire the offer to Washington. Then he took another sheet, wrote a brief note introducing Briggs to his Chief, A. Bruce Bielaski, and asked his volunteer to report to Washington to discuss the offer in person.

When Briggs arrived in Washington a few days later, it was a city divided. President Woodrow Wilson was rapidly moving from a policy of "preparedness" to one of "armed neutrality." Congress, rent with factions, refused to move with him. The House had easily passed the President's bill to arm merchant ships, but the "little group of willful men" in the Senate who saw strings of war attached were filibustering it to death. Finally, on March 1, Wilson tried his last means of persuasion: He made public the text of a telegram, intercepted by British Intelligence, from German Foreign Secretary Arthur Zimmermann to the German ambassador in Washington, proposing an alliance with Japan and Mexico against the United States should this country enter the war. The revelation inflamed the public but left the "willful" senators unmoved. When Congress adjourned on March 3, all possibility of congressional support for Wilson's defense policy died. If Wilson wanted the United States to remain neutral but armed, he would have to establish that policy by means of executive orders.

While Wilson experimented with using the press to gain public support for his diplomatic and national defense policies, approving McAdoo's publicity campaigns against German diplomats and recalcitrant senators, Gregory continued to oppose that strategy. He specifically asked the State Department to do nothing to publicize the case involving East Indians accused of collaborating with Germans in an attempt to foment rebellion in India. However, Secret Service agents, working with British agents and the New York police department, either received secret orders from the State Department to proceed or they disobeyed orders. They arrested the East Indian suspects and released a story to the *New York Times* about a great conspiracy, directed from Berlin, between the Indians and German aliens. These arrests were only the prelude to a countrywide roundup of aliens who were taking advantage of American neutrality to plot on American soil against the allies, the *Times* predicted. The arrests brought a strongly worded note of protest from the Justice Department to the State Department on March 16.

Meanwhile, in Washington, Bielaski considered the gift of automobiles Briggs had offered. A bit skeptical about the motives of posterman Briggs, Bielaski telegraphed Hinton Clabaugh, "Wire immediately whether acceptance offer automobiles would be used as advertisement in any way. Believe Congress opposed to any advertisement feature." "Specifically stated to the contrary," Clabaugh reassured him.

If Bielaski actually discussed this proposed gift with any members of Congress, there is no record of the conversation. He may not have asked the approval of Attorney General Gregory either, for Gregory believed Bielaski to be a master sleuth and usually gave him free rein in the Bureau. Moreover, Gregory had already advised President Wilson to go ahead and arm the merchant ships by executive order; equipping the Bureau with automobiles to make it more effective in trailing German agents would only be consistent. At any rate, Bielaski accepted the gift, and Briggs returned to Chicago, his mission accomplished.

The brief visit to the Bureau of Investigation only convinced Briggs that the Justice Department could not meet the crisis without volunteer help. Publication of the Zimmermann telegram intensified public fear of espionage, sabotage, and invasion. The number of letters and telegrams reaching the Bureau quadrupled during the first two months of 1917, and the Bureau had to borrow clerks from three other departments to sort the incoming mail. Federal officials around the country were demanding more special agents for investigations, but the Bureau had none to spare. Bielaski had already increased the number of men in the field from three hundred to four hundred and had asked local police officials to detail additional men to work under these agents. In Washington, his force was putting in long hours and making little headway against the volume of cases reported.

The situation gave Briggs another idea. Within two weeks after his return to Chicago, he had formulated a plan to build his local volunteer regiment into a nationwide army which would work directly under the Bureau of Investigation. On March 14, he was back in Clabaugh's office with the draft of a third proposal.

Its Purpose: A volunteer organization to aid the Bureau of Investigation of the Department of Justice.

The Object: To work with and under the direction of the Chief of the Bureau of Investigation, of the Department of Justice, or such attorney or persons as he may direct, rendering such service as may be required from time to time.

Membership: This organization is to be composed of citizens of good moral character who shall volunteer their service and who may be acceptable to your Department.

Construction: It is proposed that national headquarters be established either in Washington, or perhaps, Chicago, because of its geographical location, and that branch organizations be established in such cities as your Department may direct.

Finances: It is proposed that headquarters organization and branch organizations shall finance themselves either by outside subscriptions or by its members.

Control: It is proposed that each unit of this organization shall be under the control of the Government but will report to and be under the direction of the nearest Department of Justice head-quarters.

Clabaugh sent the plan to Bielaski—and waited.

No immediate encouragement came from Bureau Chief Bielaski. Three days passed while American merchant ships put into effect Wilson's March 12 decision to inaugurate "armed neutrality." On the fourth day three American merchant ships were sunk by German torpedoes. On the fifth day Bielaski wired a terse reply to Clabaugh: "Briggs should be encouraged in organization association. Be glad to talk with him about matter."

Germany's submarine offensive had now settled the diplomatic issue for Gregory. He no longer believed the United States could or should stay out of the European war. But it would take some time for him to mobilize the home front defenses, and in the meantime, Bielaski's suggestion to use more volunteers seemed one way to make sure that Secret Service incursions into spy-hunting territory would not continue.

War seemed inevitable; the only question remaining was when. The Cabinet meeting of March 20, the most momentous Wilson ever called, marked the last divide between peace and war. The President began with a statement, that he was disinclined to make the final break with Germany, and a request for advice. One after another the Cabinet members solemnly rendered their verdict:

Secretary of Commerce William C. Redfield: Declare war.

Secretary of Labor William B. Wilson: Germany had already "made war upon this country."

Postmaster General Albert Burleson: The nation is already at war.

Secretary of Agriculture David F. Huston: A state of war already exists.

Secretary of the Navy Josephus Daniels: There is no other course; armed neutrality cannot be effective. Having tried patience, there is "no course open to us except to protect our rights on the seas."

Secretary of the Treasury William McAdoo: Immediate war, for the German government represents "every evil in history."

Secretary of the Interior Franklin K. Lane: The public is indignant against the Germans.

Secretary of War Newton D. Baker: Recent outrages show the Germans do not intend to modify their policy of inhumanity and lawlessness.

Secretary of State Robert Lansing: German agents in the United States have "seriously menaced our national safety." Under peacetime statutes the President is powerless, and Germany is a "menace to the national safety of this country and of all other countries with liberal systems of government."

And Attorney General Gregory: It is useless to delay. The possibility of peace with Germany is a thing of the past: Congress should be assembled as soon as possible; all necessary legislation must be enacted. And action as aggressive as possible should be pursued toward Germany. German intrigues, the departure of German reservists, and the helplessness of the Department under existing laws increase the danger with every day's delay.

Wilson expressed no concern about the effect war might have on civil liberties or democracy at home, nor did anyone else present. Foreign entanglement was the issue, not its domestic consequences. Lansing remembered the President as cool and unemotional when he said, after the last Cabinet member had spoken, "Well Gentlemen, I think there is no doubt as to what your advice is. I thank you." A brief discussion followed regarding preparation of war legislation to be submitted to Congress when it convened. Lansing noted after the meeting, "No one could be sure that he [Wilson] would echo the same opinion and act accordingly." Wilson told Lansing he would not issue the call to Congress that day; he wanted to sleep on it.

On the same day that the Cabinet agreed on war, Bielaski gave Hinton Clabaugh his approval for a volunteer organization. However, the Bureau superintendent in Chicago was to handle the preliminaries confidentially and cause no apprehension among aliens as to their fair treatment: "No arrests should be caused, except after consultation with the federal authorities, in order that there may be no confusion," Clabaugh wired Briggs, who was in New York on business. A few hours later Briggs replied, "Great news." He had an appointment to see Bielaski in Washington in two days.

When Briggs arrived in Washington on March 22, newspapers were announcing that Wilson had called Congress back into session two weeks early. This meant war.

Bielaski accepted Briggs's plan for a nationwide organization exactly as originally proposed to Clabaugh and asked him to establish units immediately in cities with high alien populations. Notices went out the same day to Bureau agents across the country announcing that Briggs was forming "a volunteer committee or organization of citizens for the purpose of co-operating with the department in securing information of activities of agents of foreign governments or persons unfriendly to this Government, for the protection of public property, etc." The organization was to supply information and to assist in securing information, but it was to be kept "as confidential as practicable." Bielaski informed his agents, as Clabaugh had warned Briggs, that no arrests were to be caused by these volunteers "except after consultation with the Federal authorities." Bielaski's notices officially launched the new experiment in internal security.

Back in Chicago, Albert Briggs assumed the title of General Superintendent and began marshalling his volunteer army. Headquarters were at the Peoples Gas Company, in rooms donated by Samuel Insull, the Chicago public utilities magnate. Briggs selected as second in command Thomas B. Crockett, handsome swashbuckling descendant of the famous frontiersman, who had impressed Briggs with his martial bearing. The title the group chose for their home front army was "American Protective League," a name once used by a secret patriotic organization in Maryland and still used in 1917 by an insurance company in Illinois.

Recruiting began. Old friends of Briggs in New York and New Jersey, in Missouri and Wisconsin, received calls and letters. Former Chicago residents who had strayed as far west as San Diego heard the call to arms. Briggs rushed to New York, where he found a young lawyer willing to head a division. In Milwaukee he met with members of the Wisconsin Defense League and arranged for one of their number, John Stover, to head an APL unit there. In St. Louis, too, he outlined his plan to interested businessmen.

Briggs told his volunteers to form "Secret Service Divisions" which would work under cover in industries and public utilities and keep aliens under surveillance. He outlined a quasi-military organization of chiefs, captains, lieutenants, and squads of operatives, units to be established throughout the financial, industrial, and business life of each city. Each chief was to enlist a number of responsible persons in each bank, business house, or industrial concern of importance, with the sworn duty to report any disloyalty, industrial disturbance, or other matter "likely to injure or embarrass" the Government of the United States.

A man "high up in the organization, preferably one of the executive officers," should serve as captain in each firm. He would in turn select as lieutenants "a reliable man in each department, preferably a superintendent, foreman, or other man filling a responsible position in his department." Lieutenants were then to suggest "names of several trusted employees in each department," citizens of legal age who "on account of their long service and general character can be relied upon to be loyal in the service of the country and of the employer." These names would then be forwarded to each APL chief, who would call in the officers to take an oath to defend the Constitution, as if they were being inducted into the Regular Army.

Officers were also to have badges, Briggs promised, "to be worn concealed by the members of our organization and only shown in cases where it is necessary to establish the operative's identity where important government investigation is being made." Operatives selected from the ranks of employees were not to receive badges, however, nor were they to be informed of the organization of the League. They were to be assigned numbers, and they were to provide their officers with information helpful to their country—and to their employer.

The coverage of northern California industries by the APL offers a good example of the organization in action. Working through the Bureau of Investigation agent in San Francisco, APL chief H. R. Basford set up a secret organization in the telephone and telegraph companies, meat packing plants, gas and electric industries, and in the railroads and oil fields. The general agent of the San Joaquin Light and Power Corporation acted as chief of one APL unit, and the superintendent of the Southern Pacific Railroad was one of his captains. All captains knew each other and knew the names of all lieutenants; lieutenants knew only the names of other lieutenants and the general scheme of organization. Operatives knew nothing of the APL. They knew only that a superior wanted to obtain information about their fellow employees. "These men are in every case purely operatives working for the benefit of their own companies by whom they are employed and know nothing of any organization," Basford explained. Briggs offered operatives that almost irresistible bait: a chance to be important and "on the inside" by playing detective, by being a labor spy, or as labor organizers would have termed it, to be a "fink."

Once organized, the chiefs were to contact the nearest "Government agent" and to inform the local police of their presence, "so that the Chief of Police may instruct his officers fully in reference to our organization so that the badge will be recognized by the police in cases where such recognition is desired." Briggs assured his volunteer chiefs that they would find the local chiefs of police glad to work with his men "wherever their assistance may be necessary in forwarding the interests of the Government."

By early April, hundreds of these mobilization orders had poured from the Chicago headquarters. Letters went out to a people expecting violence. Frightened by journalistic sensationalism, many Americans believed that a declaration of war would transform the United States into a battlefield, with every one of the million resident German aliens an agent of the Kaiser. Mexicans in league with Germany would march north, retake Arizona and New Mexico, and cut off California from the rest of the country. Japanese would then land on the Pacific Coast and invade California. In the East, German submarines would shell New York. Sabotage would be particularly widespread in the heavily industrialized Northeast. Spies, of course, were believed to be operating everywhere.

The War Department heightened the alarm by alerting American troops along the Mexican border and authorizing commanding generals in all departments to "sternly repress acts committed with seditious intent" and to protect "public utilities" essential to the war. General Pershing was still in command of the troops which had just been withdrawn from Mexico after a futile chase of Pancho Villa. He deployed detachments to guard power plants in Louisiana, Texas, Oklahoma, New Mexico, and Arizona. National Guard regiments were ordered to Buffalo and Detroit to prevent sabotage. In Connecticut, General Leonard Wood asked the governor to help him protect railroad bridges against sabotage by enemy aliens, and the governor called up two companies of reserves. From Illinois, Major General Thomas H. Barry called upon the governor of Michigan to protect the locks at Sault Ste. Marie and the international bridge and railroad. Governor Frank O. Lowden of Illinois called up two companies of militiamen to guard bridges and plants against property damage by German sympathizers, and his Adjutant General released United States government-owned rifles and ammunition to private industries. The nation, in short, was triggering its hysteria.

On March 25, Wilson sent the first call for troops to the governor of New Jersey, and at the same time these federalized National Guards began to move, the War Department imposed secrecy on all military activities and asked newspapers to exercise voluntary censorship. In the news blackout which followed, reason gave way to fantasy, and rumor ran riot.

In Milwaukee, a citizen's committee met with the district attorney, state officials, and plant managers and requested that Brigadier General Charles King mobilize his forces to protect the city from German spies. Although no plant manager would admit that he feared for his own plant, all asked that a regiment of the Wisconsin National Guard be placed on stand-by at the Fair Grounds. The chief of police insisted that there was no danger. The governor agreed, as did the state Adjutant General. Consequently, General King told the citizen's committee that he could not send troops.

But the restraint of the Wisconsin governor was unusual. More typically, the governors succumbed to the war hysteria along with the people of their states. California provided one of the most extreme examples of the surrender of the American people to irrationality. When soldiers moved into place to guard railroad tunnels in the mountains, Bakersfield power plant owners decided to surround their plants, pipe lines, and reservoirs with barbed wire fences charged with high-power electric current. The United States Attorney in San Francisco threw a police guard around his own home, armed himself, and advised Californians to do likewise. "The secret service men tell me I had better protect myself," one pro-war educator from southern California told Ray Lyman Wilbur, president of Stanford University, whereupon Wilbur contemplated the purchase of a six-shooter. Movie producer Cecil B. DeMille offered the city of Los Angeles a troop of seventy-five studio men armed with a machine gun, rifles, and ammunition, while in San Diego a private rifle club mobilized itself as the Cabrillo Rifles and prepared to protect the city from invasion. There was absolutely no evidence that either Japan or Mexico knew about the Zimmermann proposal—except through American newspapers—or that either government would accept the German invitation to war against the United States. Nevertheless, Pacific Coast racists had talked for so long about the "yellow peril" and the threat of a Japanese invasion that conservatives and progressives alike prepared for actual hand-to-hand combat.

In this atmosphere even California reformers who should have been wary of a counterespionage organization within industries welcomed the APL volunteers as a reasonable alternative to barbed wire and machine guns. At a time when labor was just beginning to reach for a larger share in shaping—and enjoying—the American economy, conservative businessmen were delighted to have such a secret network to inform them of the activities of workers. They set about selecting officers and operatives even as California congressmen boarded trains to return to Washington for a special message from the President of the United States.

California Senator Hiram Johnson was one of a very few legislators who regarded the activities in his home state as pure hysteria. From Washington he wrote to one constituent in disgust, "The bunk about military preparedness, guarding the mountain passes, protecting the coast highways, repelling the invader from our soil, suffering no profane hands to touch us, and the like, has gotten over, apparently in California, not alone with the stand-pat press but with most of our own." But everywhere those who raised a word of warning or sounded a note of skepticism were being shouted down.

In Washington, Secretary of War Newton D. Baker was also being shouted down for his lack of concern about the danger from enemy aliens. On March 27 he objected to Secretary of State Lansing's unequivocal statement that Mexico was teeming with spies. He also recommended to Gregory that no enemy aliens be arrested or interned except for actual commission of crime. Unfortunately, Charles Warren, Gregory's adviser in the Justice Department, vigorously disagreed with Baker's suggestion. Warren himself had previously objected to arrests by Secret Service men before evidence justifying prosecution had been collected. Now he urged Gregory to resurrect the old 1798 Alien Enemies Act and use it against sixty-three aliens whom he felt should not be at large if Congress declared war. In a memorandum to Gregory, Warren wrote, "There are many dangerous leaders and plotters in New York and elsewhere of whom we have no absolute evidence, at present, of having committed a Federal crime but yet who would be very dangerous if left at large." Gregory got up from a sickbed to carry Warren's fears to the Cabinet meeting of March 30.

At that Cabinet meeting President Wilson responded to rumors of a German in the White House cellar by saying yes, there was an inoffensive German employed to tend fires. The President concluded, "I'd rather the blamed place should be blown up than to persecute inoffensive people." Although no record exists of the conversation that followed, it was apparently at this point that Gregory announced he was encouraging volunteers to collect information on "foreign governments or unfriendly aliens." Cabinet members raised no objections to his proposal; indeed, it seemed preferable to sending troops to every section of the country that was insisting upon federal protection. Apparently at this same meeting the arrest of enemy aliens who had committed no crimes was also agreed to tacitly.

The first steps were being taken which could lead to the persecution, not only of Wilson's "inoffensive German," but of dissenters and citizens as well. Wilson said that in his war message he wished to attack "the miasma of German enemies," and he asked the Cabinet whether he could safely trace it to the German embassy. Gregory replied that certain men convicted in New York for crimes against the country had been paid by German consuls. Secretary of the Treasury

McAdoo broke in to add that all the crimes of the Germans should be set forth "to arouse and stir the people." McAdoo needed no encouragement for his stand, but Warren's fears had convinced a skeptical Gregory, and Gregory's fears, in turn, influenced the Cabinet and President Wilson.

The essential weapons for the home front war had now been selected and approved, though Congress had not yet assembled, nor had the President presented his request for a declaration of war. The basic assumption that the nation was crawling with disloyal Germans and the decision to intern indiscriminately on the basis of that fear had been made. In the months that followed, the implications of this compromise of the fundamental American ideal—innocent until proven guilty—would be spun out. Attorney General Gregory was explicit in a hastily written note to the Solicitor General the day following the Cabinet meeting: "There are a very large number of German citizens in this country who are dangerous and who are plotting trouble, men from whom we must necessarily expect trouble promptly of a sinister sort."

The task of distinguishing between the innocent and the guilty was a task for the Justice Department's Bureau of Investigation. Bielaski promptly passed the responsibility on to his volunteers, but not without cautioning them that innocent Germans must not be victimized. In a letter to Briggs dated April 2, 1917, the chief relayed the Administration's concern—very genuine on the part of Wilson and the Department—that innocent persons might lose their lives or suffer damage at the hands of mobs or irresponsible individuals. Such acts, Bielaski wrote, would be a "serious blot upon the name of this country." Therefore he requested that the League add "the protection of peaceful aliens" to the protection of property and investigation of violations of federal neutrality laws as "an important patriotic duty."

Although the Justice Department alerted the public to the danger of spies, it did not publicly voice concern about attacks on innocent people. Unfortunately, too, it was only Wilson's alarm over spies, not his concern for peaceable enemy aliens, that found expression in his war message to Congress on April 2. Instead of making an effort to dissipate the growing national hysteria, he added to the people's fears. To justify the United States' involvement in the war, the President marshaled the legal argument that German submarine warfare violated the nation's freedom of the seas and threatened its security; the moral argument that Americans must make the world safe for democracy; and then appended a third justification, that

Germans posed a threat to internal security through espionage and sabotage. Americans of the progressive age, nourished on the accusations of reformers that conspiracies abounded among "malefactors of great wealth," found this fear of subversion easier to understand than either the legal or moral arguments. Espionage was the fruit of autocracy, Wilson told the hushed audience.

"Self-governed nations do not fill their neighbor states with spies or set the course of intrigue to bring about some critical posture of affairs which will give them an opportunity to strike and make conquest . . . from the very start of the present war [the German government] has filled our unsuspecting communities and even our offices of government with spies and set criminal intrigues everywhere afoot against our national unity of counsel, our peace within and without, our industries, and our commerce . . . it is now evident that its spies were here even before the war began . . . that the intrigues which have more than once come perilously near to disturbing the peace and dislocating the industries of the country have been carried on at the instigation, with the support, and even under the personal direction of official agents of the Imperial Government accredited to the Government of the United States . . . that it meant to stir up enemies against us at our very doors the intercepted note of the German Minister to Mexico City is eloquent evidence."

As Wilson stood there accusing Imperial Germany, he little realized that he himself, at the Cabinet meeting of March 30, had tacitly endorsed an organization which could field a legion of spies larger than any autocrat had ever dreamed of. By the time Congress responded to his speech with the Declaration of War against Germany, almost a hundred branches of the American Protective League were in process of being formed; Briggs predicted he would have over six thousand units by the end of April. When Wilson signed the Declaration of War at 1:00 P.M. on April 6, the volunteer home front army was already in arms.

Into the Lists of Honor

America was now officially at war. Along the home front the volunteers waited for the expected German spy attack. Sabotage like that at Black Tom and Kingsland would certainly be widespread, they thought. But nothing happened. An explosion did occur at the Eddystone Ammunition Corporation in Chester, Pennsylvania, whereupon an APL unit was hastily organized. It rushed about looking for German spies but could find no evidence of sabotage. Apparently carelessness, inexperience, or hostility of laborers toward employers had been the cause.

Factory owners were quick to see the benefit of the APL investigations, however, even if they turned up no spies. In Pennsylvania, industrialists gladly subsidized the APL by contributing fifty dollars a month. It is obvious now that Germany was not prepared to launch a widespread sabotage campaign in April, 1917; yet the likely presence of spies had become irrelevant. Employers wanted protection from labor. They would have preferred federal troops, but when those could not be obtained, most settled for the APL.

The American Protective League, having sprung full-armed from the head of Albert Briggs, had no precedents—only an improvised organizational structure and a lot of zeal to guide it. Not surprisingly, abuses of authority soon came to light. In a very early Michigan case, APL volunteers and Bureau of Investigation special agents working together actually subverted the authority of the United States Attorney, the federal official to whom they should have been subordinate. At the Ford Motor Plant in Highland Park, Michigan, a Bureau of Investigation agent and a Leaguer collaborated in having the local police arrest a German alien employee, probably a union organizer, who had been found with photographs, blue prints, and drawings of the plant. When notified, the United States Attorney refused to become involved and had the man released. The persistent investigators appealed to the state district attorney; he wanted no part in the case either. Finally, by threatening that the company would have the man prosecuted for larceny, the agent and Leaguer persuaded the police department to rearrest the man, and the United States Attorney recommended internment. The man was interned as a dangerous enemy alien, although he had neither violated any federal law nor posed any threat to internal security.

The War Department knew what was going on. "The trouble in all this business," complained General Barry, commander of federal troops in the Midwest, to Secretary of War Baker, "is that just so long as plant owners, state and local authorities can get the National Government to do what *they* ought to do, just so long will they pass it up to the National Government." Factory owners would claim that a strike was about to be called, then demand protection of federal troops. "We have been alive to all these situations, as we will continue to be," the general contined, "and if owners of corporations who are howling for protection will do their part and howl less, and if city and state authorities do likewise, there will be no trouble."

General Barry's experience in St. Louis confirmed him in his evaluation of the dangers of responding to every owner's request for troops. In East St. Louis, two regiments of Illinois militiamen had been called in to defend plants against sabotage. Labor groups had complained that the troops were being used to break a strike against the Aluminum Ore Corporation. Then on May 6, 1917, the United States Attorney in St. Louis demanded that federal troops be called in to avert a strike. General Barry refused to send them across the river. Martial law had not been declared, and the governor of Missouri had not requested the troops, so Barry suggested the Justice Department investigate the strike. "I believe the preventive throwing of United States troops into such strike situations will do more harm than good as nothing is calculated to agitate strikers more than the premature use of United States troops," the general wrote to Attorney General Gregory.

This fear of being drawn into industrial disputes led the War Department to veto a proposal by Gregory for a national police force under the War Department. The War College refused to support such a plan, and Secretary of War Baker accepted their view. Instead, Baker suggested that Gregory could perhaps establish a force of armed marshals under his own department to guard plants.

Gregory might have used his federal marshals as an alternative to the APL, but he did not want to accept the responsibility of paying, training, and disciplining thousands of new federal officers. He might have considered another alternative, that of simply refusing the demands of industrialists for protection, but this alternative was not considered by the Wilson Administration; no one questioned that protection of war plants was the responsibility of the federal government. That APL volunteers might serve as labor spies seems not to have occurred to Gregory and Baker, either. Gregory had inordinate faith in the motives of the Americans rushing to offer their services to the government. He still believed "men of good executive capacity" would volunteer "from purely patriotic motives."

Thus the failure of spies and saboteurs to materialize did not alter Gregory's determination to keep the APL on guard, and he made no move to disband it. Instead, on May 3 Bielaski urged Briggs to hold the League together, even though there was no work for some units to do. The organization would be a "source of comfort and assistance to us," he said.

By May, "comfort and assistance" had come to mean more than plant protection; it included enforcement of the new conscription bill.

The unpopularity of the National Conscription Act passed during the Civil War had convinced President Wilson that a new system must be evolved. Civil War conscription in the North had been administered from the War Department by a Provost Marshal General, through district provost marshals charged with enrolling male citizens in assigned areas. This draft system had broken down almost immediately after conscription was begun in New York on July 11, 1863. In fact, so intense had been the sentiment against it that rioting had erupted in which an estimated three hundred people were killed, many more wounded, and two million dollars' worth of property destroyed during four days of violence. Police, militia, and federal troops had quelled the disturbance; but when the draft resumed a month later, the city was under heavy guard.

Enoch A. Crowder, Judge Advocate
General, 1911–1918; Provost
Marshal General, 1917–1919

John Lord O'Brian, Director of
the War Emergency Division of the
Justice Department, 1917–1919

Wide World Photo

A. Bruce Bielaski, Chief, Bureau
of Investigation of the Justice
Department, 1912–1919

Thomas Watt Gregory,
Attorney General, 1914–1919

While still a professor, Wilson had written in his *History of the United States* that the New York draft riots of the nineteenth century "were to linger in the recollection many a long year like an ugly nightmare." Now, as President, he did not wish to provoke such opposition again. Even after the Cabinet had decided for war, the President, Secretary of the Navy Josephus Daniels, and Secretary of War Baker had refused to support conscription. "Why introduce Prussianism to fight Prussianism?" Daniels had asked, speaking for them all.

If Wilson remembered the failure of the Civil War draft and feared the introduction of compulsory service, the men in the War Department felt differently. Volunteers in the Spanish American War had proven so undisciplined and uncontrollable that as early as 1916 Chief of Staff Hugh L. Scott, in a report to the Secretary of War, had stated, "The volunteer system in this country in view of the highly organized, trained and disciplined armies that our possible opponents possess, should be relegated to the past." Even Theodore Roosevelt, so enthusiastic about his Rough Riders in the Spanish American War, had supported this view during the preparedness campaign of 1915 and 1916, affirming, "We ought to demand from all alike the same service."

But as war seemed imminent in February, 1917, Roosevelt began to press for permission to take a volunteer unit to France. And as Roosevelt persisted, the reluctance of Baker and Wilson to conscript faded. Military advisers pointed to England as an example of the disruptive effects on industry and agriculture of indiscriminate enlistment, and Baker capitulated on March 29. By the time Wilson delivered his war message, the volunteer principle had been abandoned. He announced that the 500,000 men needed should be chosen "upon the principle of universal liability to service." As Wilson left the platform, he turned to his cousin FitzWilliam McMaster Woodrow and said, "Thank God for Abraham Lincoln." To his cousin's query why, he replied, "I won't make the mistakes that he made." But there were many new ones still to be made.

A model draft bill had been ready for Wilson since early February. According to Enoch Crowder, then Judge Advocate General of the Army, Wilson called Secretary Baker one evening shortly after breaking diplomatic relations with Germany to say that by ten o'clock the following morning he wanted to have a bill which would call every young man into service, the provision to be used only when the supply of volunteers had been exhausted. Crowder did most of the actual drafting of the conscription bill himself.

The son of a poor Union soldier from Missouri, Crowder had gone to West Point because that was the only way to satisfy his craving for books and to obtain an education. Assigned to Fort Brown, Texas, he had studied law; then in 1895, after fighting Indians in the West and reorganizing the student reserve batallions at the University of Missouri, he joined the Judge Advocate's office. During the next sixteen years he served in the Philippines, participated in the military government of Puerto Rico, and, during the second intervention in Cuba of 1908, supervised the elections and headed the advisory law commission which drafted most of the organic laws for the Cuban republic. In 1911, he had become Judge Advocate General, top legal officer for the Army.

Now an irascible bachelor of fifty-eight with a capacity for incessant work, this stern officer with his bristle-brush moustache and close-cropped hair had earned a name for himself in the War Department. Louis B. Wehle, later a New Dealer, then assistant to Secretary Baker, recalled watching Crowder dictating to his secretary one day. Suddenly the general crumpled up a letter and shouted, "I won't answer the _ _ _ _ man! Spells my name Chowder!" His bad temper, according to Wehle, was perhaps exceeded only by his speed, efficiency, originality, and boldness. Felix Frankfurter, who joined the Judge Advocates Office as a young reserve corps major in 1914, considered Crowder "one of the best professional brains" he had ever encountered. Crowder had no hobbies, no pastimes, and no recreations. His office was similarly stripped of nonessentials. It had no files, no reference books, no memorandum pads, only a small stack of red tags lettered EXPEDITE. "All velvet over shimmering steel," ran one comment.

The system Crowder developed to administer the draft could also be so described, although he called it "supervised decentralization." Consciously termed "selective service" rather than "conscription" by the Congress which enacted it into law, it rested on the assumption that America was "essentially a nation founded upon local self-government," that under the dual federal-state system each man had two centers of interest, loyalty, obligation, and devotion, and therefore federal coercion would be most palatable if achieved through the machinery of state and local governments. Under the statute drawn by Crowder, the President could empower any federal, state, or local officer or agent to enforce the Act, with emphasis on the role of civilian appointees.

The only aspect of the plan which Crowder had not yet worked out when he received Baker's hurried request for a bill was how to or-

Blairsville High School Library

ganize the registration itself. The War College had suggested the Post Office districts be used, but Crowder felt this would be slow and cumbersome. A visiting Congressman offered him no sympathy. "If we can arrange for every man to vote on one day why can't it be managed for every man to register in one day?" With that comment, the last obstacle was overcome. The young men, Crowder decided, would register in their voting precincts with volunteer draft boards. The next morning, Wilson received the bill. Later, Crowder would chuckle over how his bill came back from the President blue-pencilled like a freshman's theme; but Wilson accepted his plan and the theory behind it.

The complex facts of modern social organization seemed to demand government control, which in turn could result in a specialized and devitalizing bureaucracy. This draft law would forestall that evil. Draft officials were not mere government functionaries, they were volunteers who would implement government control without undue interference in the affairs of private citizens. So it seemed in theory, anyway. And once Wilson accepted the theory, the notion that voluntary service at home was somehow pure became a permanent part of the American ideology.

On April 7, Wilson had issued a statement in support of Crowder's plan, but even its depiction as the red-white-and-blue American way did not make the draft bill popular in the House of Representatives. Fiorello La Guardia, then a newly-elected representative from New York, remembered later that opponents of the bill included the Speaker of the House, the Majority Leader, the chairman and the second ranking member of the House Military Affairs Committee. Chairman Hubert S. Dent of Alabama demanded retention of the old volunteer system. Fellow Alabama Congressman George Huddleston warned of "this great shadow of militarism that overhangs the land." Other southerners in the House told newsmen that they opposed conscription because large numbers of Negroes trained to handle arms might return to the South after the war and cause trouble. Secretary of War Baker appeared before the Committee to urge quick action, but still the members stalled. They wanted to know why conscription was necessary; if the word "conscription" could not be changed to "personal obligation to service"; and why volunteers could not still be used. Finally, after a week of wrangling, on April 16 the House Military Affairs Committee took an informal vote. Nine members were opposed, eight in favor.

Wilson talked to the Democratic leaders. They told the President that although other war legislation would present no problem, opposition among the Democrats to conscription was strong. Speaker of the House Clark even vacated his chair to take the floor and speak of the American volunteer as one of the "glories of the Republic." But it was clear that the Administration would be willing to use Republican support to push the measure through.

Thus it was left for Bavarian-born Republican Julius Kahn of San Francisco, member of the conservative wing of the party, to introduce the Administration's bill in the House, while the Democrats on the committee issued a majority report favoring amendments which would allow the volunteer principle to be continued. In the Senate, Republican George Chamberlain, former governor of Oregon, steered his Committee on Military Affairs into a majority endorsement of the bill, leaving the Democrats to report a minority bill embodying amendments to use volunteers. By April 26, passage of the bill seemed so certain that Crowder moved into the old Land Office building and began work on secret preparations for the printing of draft registration forms to be mailed to state governors, who were to supervise registration through their adjutant generals. This was three days after Wilson had promised Britain's Balfour Commission that one and a half million American soldiers would be on the Western Front before the end of 1918.

Wilson used the occasion of the dedication of the Red Cross building on May 12, 1917, to sound a last blast in favor of the draft bill with the pronouncement, "This is no war for amateurs. This is no war for spontaneous impulse." He meant on the battle front. On the home front, amateurs and spontaneous impulse would be relied upon to ensure a steady supply of military professionals. It was a job ready-made for the rear echelon warriors, the APL.

Six days later, Wilson signed the Selective Service Act into law. The War Department announced that it would decline the volunteer services of Theodore Roosevelt and said that the first professionals, the American Expeditionary Force under Major General John J. Pershing, would sail for France soon. On May 22, Crowder became Provost Marshal General in charge of conscription. The way was now clear for the APL volunteers—almost. Only Secretary of the Treasury McAdoo stood in their path.

In his war proclamation of April 6 President Wilson, acting under the old Alien Enemies Act of 1798, had imposed restrictions on enemy aliens as the Justice Department had advised. He followed this move with authorization for the arrest of over sixty enemy aliens on presidential warrants. Policing of restrictions on enemy aliens (presumably including any German agents in the United States) was to be the responsibility of the Justice Department. Gregory, thinking this would put an end to Treasury Department competition in spy-hunting, had Wilson sign a formal order to the effect that the Justice Department should enforce provisions of the proclamation.

McAdoo was not ready to get out of the spy-catching business, however. Nine days later he ordered the chief of the Secret Service to begin investigating violations covered by Wilson's proclamation. Then he suggested to the President the expansion of the State Department's system of coordinating and comparing investigations and reports assigned to the Secret Service and to the Bureau of Investigation. The government, he argued, needed a special bureau in the State Department or in the Treasury Department to investigate both international and domestic problems growing out of the war, an agency independent of existing intelligence groups, so that it could eliminate "crossing wires." To head this new office, McAdoo recommended his old friend Robert Woolley, who had directed publicity for the Democratic Party in 1916 before joining the Treasury Department as director of the United States Mint. Clearly, McAdoo intended to dominate this central intelligence agency, perhaps to use its findings for political purposes.

This proposal, copies of which McAdoo sent to Secretary of State Lansing, Attorney General Gregory, and Postmaster General Burleson, brought immediate objections from Burleson. But McAdoo, still intent on the new bureau, simply advised Wilson to eliminate the Post Office Department's investigating force from the executive plan and allow his Secret Service men and the agents of the Bureau of Investigation to report to the director of the proposed new force.

Gregory's reaction, as one might have expected, was like Burleson's, an immediate negative. "There is, to my mind, not the slightest overlapping of authority so far as the three branches of the secret service are concerned," Gregory wrote Wilson. There had been no trouble on cases unrelated to the war, none whatsoever with the Post Office. "I regret that such a condition has not existed so far as the Secret Service of the Treasury is concerned," he went on, reminding Wilson of the embarrassment caused the Bureau of Investigation by Treasury Department operatives during the neutrality period. He also brought up more recent complaints from agents in Detroit, Indianapolis, and New York that Secret Service men were continuing to intrude into "other matters exclusively delegated to the Department of Justice."

In some cases, not only had Secret Service men refused to give the Bureau information they had collected, but they had handed out press releases implying that their department was in charge of work actually delegated to the Justice Department. The State Department clearing-house was working fine on diplomatic and international matters, he said, but he objected to using Woolley as a director because Woolley had no connection with the State Department and no experience with its problems. "As conditions develop," Gregory concluded, "new machinery may become necessary, but it seems to me we are in danger of creating too much machinery, and so far as I can observe, the Bureau of Investigation of the Justice Department is carefully and wisely handling the large problems on its hands, and I see no need at this time for making any change in the plan of operations."

Nor was Wilson prepared to endorse a unified counterespionage agency. On April 11 he had used Gregory's very words in writing to Secretary of War Baker, "We are in danger of creating too much machinery." And two days after receiving Gregory's letter, he assured the public in a statement on the food law that they had nothing to fear from the establishment of a wartime food administration: It was composed of volunteers and therefore could not become a per-manent bureaucracy.

During the first weeks of Wilson's war administration, the phrase "danger of creating too much machinery" had become somewhat a watchword for protecting the ideal of limited government. Instead of following Lincoln's example and using his powers as Commander-in-Chief to expand the executive branch in wartime, thus swelling the federal payroll, Wilson chose to build a separate temporary bureaucracy, manned by volunteers, which could then be quickly dismantled after the war. Gregory had counseled him that utilizing volunteers for "a dollar a year" was perfectly constitutional.

Like Wilson, Gregory wanted above all else to keep civilians in control of the war administration. This attitude necessitated support for legislation broadening the federal courts' jurisdiction over civilian wartime activities, which meant that the Justice Department would have greater responsibilities than ever before. Given his intention of enforcing wartime legislation as vigorously as he had enforced earlier reform legislation, Gregory faced the choice of expanding the Bureau of Investigation by developing a highly organized and carefully trained cadre of agents or of relying more and more on volunteers. There was little time to recruit and train a professional force and little in-

The American Protective League badges

clination on the part of Bielaski to do so. Moreover, Gregory had already agreed with Wilson that "too much machinery" should not be created. His drive for expanded jurisdiction had collided with the ideal of a restricted bureaucracy. If then, he still wished to rebuff the sallies of the Secret Service in the increasingly popular game of "I Spy," he had no alternative but to accept Bielaski's volunteers.

Gregory followed up his letter to Wilson with one directly to Mc-Adoo complaining about the interference of Secret Service agents. He enclosed a copy of the formal order Wilson had given him confirming the jurisdiction of the Justice Department in enforcing the enemy alien proclamation. McAdoo immediately ordered his Secret Service men off the job and dropped his proposal for a central intelligence agency. To add to the confusion, letters began to arrive at Secret Service headquarters from men requesting enrollment in a "Secret Service" called the American Protective League.

Late in April, William Flynn, head of the Treasury Department's Secret Service, protested to Bielaski against the APL's using the official title of his treasury agents. The Justice Department's only reply was an announcement in the Administration's *Official Bulletin* three weeks later that it had accepted the offer of the APL to aid in protecting the United States "against sedition and other acts inimical to the general welfare."

Gregory's announcement and Flynn's complaints led Secretary of the Treasury McAdoo to lodge an official complaint with President Wilson in mid-May. It was unfortunate, McAdoo wrote, at a time when it was particularly necessary to avoid stirring up internal discord, "that a miscellaneous horde of so-called Secret Service operatives be loose upon the country to pry into the business of peaceful citizens. . . . I greatly fear that if this new organization of volunteer detectives and Secret Service operatives is allowed to continue to exist, suspicion will be engendered among our people, smoldering race antagonisms will burst into flame, and the melting pot of America will be a melting pot no longer, but a crucible out of which will flash the molten lead of suspicion and dissension."

Had McAdoo only wanted to get rid of the APL, he should have ended his letter there. But he went on to defend his Secret Service agents and to push once again for his pet project, a central intelligence agency. Not only did McAdoo argue that APL use of the term "Secret Service" had caused public confusion; he also asserted that to discontinue use of the Secret Service would be "contrary to the public welfare, and absolutely dangerous." With his letter McAdoo sent an

APL badge and organizational literature bearing the "Secret Service" title. He observed that "abuses of authority" had resulted because "no direct control [was] exercised by any responsible official of the Government in Washington." In conclusion, he claimed that his proposal for a Bureau of Intelligence would assure cooperation and efficiency in place of this loose organization of private citizens scattered over the country.

Wilson might have acted decisively in regard to McAdoo's warning had it come separately from the central intelligence agency plan. In the context, however, McAdoo's complaints appeared to arise chiefly from a long-standing feud between two Cabinet members and to be linked to a proposal of which Wilson disapproved. Thus, Wilson opposed the plan for the new agency to replace the APL and stepped aside to let the two Cabinet officers settle the squabble over the "Secret Service" title themselves—but not before he had shown McAdoo the letter in which Gregory had implied that the Treasury Department was intentionally interfering with the work of the Justice Department and attempting to absorb its functions.

But McAdoo was not to be banished so summarily from the home front war. After reading Gregory's letter with growing indignation, he retorted to Wilson, "The Attorney General's letter contains so many erroneous statements that I must reply to it at the first opportunity. . . . The Treasury case in this respect is overwhelming; I only need to find a moment to prepare the answer. . . . Let me say that I don't care three straws about the organization of the Bureau of Intelligence; it was merely a suggestion which I thought would find ready acceptance on the part of the other Departments." Then he launched a full-scale probe into the activities of the APL.

Within two weeks McAdoo had collected enough evidence against the APL to send a formal protest to Gregory. "I cannot believe that you have personally sanctioned the formation and the activities of this private association," McAdoo began. "The scheme is fraught with the gravest danger of misunderstanding, confusion and even fraud, and in the public interest I am sending you my serious protest against the continuation under its present designation."

Furthermore, McAdoo continued, by allowing the APL to use the Secret Service trademark, the Justice Department had armed a private organization with a "power the very existence of which in private hands is detrimental to the public interest and the public service. The government cannot escape responsibility for their activities whatever they may be," McAdoo lectured Gregory. "With this statement of my views before you," he concluded, "permit me to request that steps be taken at once to check the activities of this organization under a name to which it has no right and the use of which is fraught with so much danger to the public and the government." To ensure that his brief received Gregory's attention, he sent a copy to President Wilson along with a sample of the APL badge and a protest against its "harmful possibilities." He also observed that the League seemed quite similar to the Sons of Liberty, a vigilante group responsible for many injustices during the American Revolution.

Wilson's attempt to avoid a decision on the League had failed. McAdoo had effectively shifted the responsibility for determining whether or not the APL should be killed right back where it belonged. In a note to Gregory, Wilson finally admitted that the APL appeared dangerous and queried, "I wonder if there is any way in which we could stop it?"

Wilson's note could not have come at a better time to insure the continuance of the APL. Gregory was growing more apprehensive as the day for the first draft registration approached. No one in the administration could be sure how the young men of America would react to being conscripted into the Army. Organized opposition began to appear. Where it did, the Justice Department quickly closed in with its APL volunteers. Thirty persons were arrested for obstructing the draft before it had even been put into effect. Rumors spread that large numbers of young men were leaving the country, and President Wilson announced on June 1 that fugitives would be prosecuted upon their return. Gregory asked Briggs to call out all members of the APL to be on hand at polling places when registration got underway on June 5. Briggs promised that eighty thousand plainclothesmen would be at the garages, stores, houses, pool halls, and clubs where the young men were to enroll.

The Census Bureau had come up with a figure of 10,264,867 males in the United States between the ages of twenty-one and thirty-one who would be required to register. The War Department estimated that about 600,000 of these had already volunteered, leaving more than 9,500,000 who were expected to appear. Aliens were to register in exactly the same way as citizens. APL members were to assist in answering the questions of the registrants—especially aliens, many of whom could not even read English—and to give them assistance in filling out forms. Other members were to watch for anyone attempting to persuade men not to register and to call police to arrest persons observed in such activity.

On the morning of June 5, 1917, APL men pinned their badges inside their coats and went to work. They intended to see that, as Wilson had promised, this would be "a great day of patriotic devotion and obligation," that all young men were enrolled in the "lists of honor."

Confusion, not opposition, was what most APL volunteers encountered that day. Men who objected to the draft on principle simply stayed away from their local boards. In west Texas one man was shot, allegedly for trying to avoid conscription, but there were no pickets and no uprisings. Most men signed up quietly; immigrants were assisted in filling out their cards. All received small registration certificates to prove that they had complied with the law. At 9:00 P.M. the registration polls closed, and Leaguers dispersed to await further orders.

Wilson, Gregory, and Baker waited in Washington for the returns from the registration polls with as much anxiety as if the figures represented election returns. This was the first real test of how well the American people would accept the President's war plans, and in the absence of open demonstrations, the only way to determine acceptance was to compare census figures for each state with registration totals. Within forty-eight hours almost all the registration lists had been assembled in Washington, but the administration had to wait for two weeks before the census and registration statistics could be compared.

Whether the lack of resistance on June 5 indicated that the APL had been effective in enforcing conscription, or whether opponents of the draft had simply not bothered to register, no one yet had any way of knowing. In the interval, Gregory asked Bielaski for particulars on which to base a reply to McAdoo's complaints about the APL.

Bielaski did not know of all the APL activities, of course, but he certainly must have had reports from his own Bureau agents as well as from the Secret Service; it was his responsibility to know what his subordinates were doing. Yet when Gregory asked him about the APL, he maintained that there had been no complaints so far, that members had been very circumspect, and that the APL was the largest, best organized, and most effective of his volunteer groups.

Best organized? Perhaps. But neither APL members nor Bureau agents were sure exactly what the relationship of the League to the federal government was to be. The inevitable result was that the volunteers and agents did pretty much as they wished. Not only did members refer to themselves as Secret Service agents, but apparently, as in Philadelphia, they actually reported to and worked for Secret Service operatives. In many cases, even when they were working for the Bureau of Investigation they referred to it as the Secret Service, thus evidencing their own confusion, a confusion that made possible even greater irresponsibility. Sometimes an APL member—like the one who felt the agent was too young and lacked experience—would refuse to work with the local Bureau personnel. Sometimes it was an agent who refused to work with the APL member. One chief wrote to Briggs in April, "There has always been a question in my mind just how welcome we are with the different Government agents . . . ."

But such qualms were rare. Expansion of the League continued as great numbers of men, many too old to be drafted, flocked to enlist in the APL. Clabaugh estimated that "about one million" volunteers had applied for work with the Bureau of Investigation by early May. Of course he exaggerated; but recruits ranged from such influential men as former Secretary of War Lindley M. Garrison, who volunteered to head an APL section in New York, to hundreds of men already engaged in detective work. In Detroit, the former Commissioner of Police formed the APL unit and became its chief. In Ellsworth, Kansas, the proposed chief recommended a subordinate, "a natural born genius for this kind of work," who had previously worked with local sheriffs.

Often the APL simply absorbed groups already working for local law enforcement agencies. In Syracuse, New York, a Municipal Guard of two hundred men, having police powers and operating under cover for the Mayor's Committee of Home Defense, joined, with the police department, en masse. In Utica, it was the Oneida County Home Defense Committee which merged with the APL; in Jamestown, the Manufacturers Association; in Rochester, a volunteer group already working for United States Marshal John D. Lynn.

The mayor of East Orange, New Jersey, who had recruited a group of ninety operatives in 1916, enrolled them all in the APL. In San Francisco, the Midway Oilfields Protective Committee, a local self-appointed organization of businessmen and oil property superintendents, became a part of the APL unit. A small group of Negroes in North Carolina were enrolled to check on possible disaffection among members of their own race. Where local organizations for counter-espionage already existed, as Briggs explained to the Los Angeles chief, the APL was "suggesting to such organizations that they join hands with us and become a branch of this National organization . . . ."

It was natural that APL members drawn from groups already working with the local police should continue to perform their old duties after becoming involved in federal investigations. In Chicago, for example, the APL reported to the District Attorney of Cook County any instances of desecration of the flag, a state offense. In Rock Island, Illinois, members investigated routine cases for the county sheriff.

Although chiefs were encouraged to take an oath of loyalty and secrecy, their subordinates were not even constrained by this formality. Briggs urged the chiefs to obtain financial support from "influential individuals or corporations of your community who usually are the ones most benefited in a property sense by the protection afforded by our organization." At the same time that he told members the Justice Department did not want them to arm themselves or make arrests, he suggested they apply to local police, who would probably give them permission to go armed. Many members had already received the power to arrest from local police. Perhaps the note from one semiliterate member in Los Angeles most eloquently summed up the problem of discipline when he wrote to APL headquarters, "I am not shure of how much athority I have. Do I have power to arrest also cary a weapon."

For the Leaguer, the APL badge became his federal authority. Approved by Bielaski and available to officers of the League for seventy-five cents, this was the insignia that so angered Secretary McAdoo. It looked official and proclaimed its owner to be a member of the Secret Service; and members quickly discovered that a slight wave of the badge could both unlock information ordinarily considered confidential and quiet a suspect's qualms about accompanying an APL member to League headquarters to be questioned. If there were no suspects handy, the badge could always be used to obtain free admittance to theaters, subways, and parking lots. Some members who joined the Army even took their badges along to camp and proceeded to investigate officers and men. The public naturally assumed that these men were agents of the Secret Service of the Treasury Department. Soon chiefs were ordering flocks of badges and peddling them to members at whatever price they pleased.

The kinds of abuses on the part of individual zealots were most clearly reflected in bulletins instructing members as to their conduct. Some orders sent out by the Chicago division illustrate the tendencies with which APL chiefs had to contend.

Bulletin: Certain recent occurrences make it necessary to issue further instructions to captains in the matter of arrests and deportment of operatives ... No captain, lieutenant, or operative has the power to arrest.

Bulletin: Captains will instruct their lieutenants and through them all members of their squads that members are not privileged through membership in the organization to carry fire arms or other weapons forbidden by law, and that the carrying of such weapons at any time is entirely upon the responsibility of the individual.

Bulletin: Under no circumstances shall [lieutenants and members] state they are members of the "Secret Service Department of the United States" ... members are not Secret Service Officers of the United States. It is absolutely necessary that members understand this to avoid confusion, and any possible charge at any time against any member through inadvertence of impersonating a government official.

Bulletin: No captain, lieutenant, or operative shall participate in any way in the commission of any offense against the law, or induce anyone to commit such offense, for the purpose of securing evidence or information. No dictagraphs shall be installed, telephone wires tapped, or similar methods employed without specific authority therefor. Members will be held to strict accountability for their acts and are permitted in no respect to violate the law upon their own account. No interviews with persons under investigation shall be held by appointment of captains, lieutenants, or operatives in their private offices, but all interviews and examinations must be held in the Federal Building.

Neither Bielaski nor Briggs had a complete list of the names of operatives and officers enlisted in this growing army of counterspies. Briggs was supposed to authorize the establishment of new units and commission chiefs, but captains began to organize their own units without his knowledge. For example, one enterprising Los Angeles member started a unit in Santa Barbara for a friend who wanted to become a counterspy. Briggs had to ask the Los Angeles chief to investigate a Latin Protective League in Phoenix to see if it was another of these bastard units. In fact, the situation was much worse than even McAdoo imagined.

Gregory nevertheless sent his defense of the APL to McAdoo on June 12. He reminded the Treasury Secretary that the Cabinet as a whole had approved the policy of using APL volunteers, and he argued that the League had provided valuable assistance in coping with wartime problems. He reiterated what Bielaski had said, that the APL was the largest and best-organized of a number of volunteer groups being used by the Bureau of Investigation. He insisted that the Justice Department had received no complaints about the League and that he had been unable to uncover any instance of members' claiming government status. Two days later, Gregory also answered Wilson's query about the League, repeating substantially what he had told McAdoo. "I am sure you will agree with me that it should be encouraged and that its work is not subject to any real criticism," he concluded.

As Wilson read Gregory's defense of the APL, Congress was debating an Espionage Act which would incorporate the laws which Gregory had been asking for since 1915. Passage of the bill would, of course, set in motion even more investigations by the Bureau of Investigation. If Wilson did not insist on disbanding the APL, Gregory and Bielaski could use the volunteers to enforce this legislation, as well as the draft law. The Espionage Act, even its censorship provisions, had Wilson's complete support; and unless the President considered the danger to civil liberties inherent in an extralegal force to be an overriding concern, it did not seem likely he would order the volunteers disbanded.

McAdoo's complaints had worried Wilson, but they had not worried him enough to cause him to intervene over Gregory's objections. His very reluctance to coerce the American people with federal instruments left the way open for more coercion less carefully controlled. The alternative, trusting the entire population to be loyal, was scarcely considered. Once Gregory had refused the claims of the Treasury Department, there seemed no choice but to use the APL. If civil libertarians or reformers had voiced opposition, Wilson might have been more insistent that the League be abolished. But there was no opposition in June, 1917.

Indeed, in the early days of war, reformers seemed too caught up in the excitement of making the world safe for democracy to give careful attention to undemocratic measures at home. They joined conservatives in demanding unqualified patriotism. For example, Senator Albert Beveridge, a militant reformer, had announced that when the United States entered the war there must be "only one competition—the competition of patriotism." A few days after the declaration of war, William Stephens, the man California reformers had helped elect governor, declaimed, "Lack of patriotism must be made odious. There can be no laggards in this national crisis. There can be no neutrality where our own country is involved." The first war issue of the *New Republic* went so far as to boast that liberals and intellectuals were responsible for the entrance of the United States into the war. Even old Henry Adams wrote in surprise from retirement in Washington that it was the first time he had been with the majority on any question. Everywhere American liberals expected the crisis of war to obliterate factions in American society, not to perpetuate them, as McAdoo had predicted the APL might do. To the few antiwar irreconcilables like literary radical Randolph Bourne, it was "a bitter experience to see the unanimity with which the American intellectuals [had] thrown their support to the use of war technique in the crisis in which America found herself."

Under the circumstances, Crowder's plan was an experiment which reformers were willing to try. "The engine of conscription is autocratic, unfair, and ruthless," a *New Republic* editorial began, but then it went on to denounce the alternative of a recruiting campaign as no less ugly and much more wasteful. "When a democracy goes to war it is compelled for the emergency to lay aside much of its own character," the editor rationalized; any decision as to the wisdom of the war itself had to be deferred. "Whether war against Germany was wise will not be finally settled until the peace conference is over," and in the meantime war presented an opportunity to use terrible means to accomplish great ends. "We have still to see whether we can make the end justify the means," the editorial concluded. Most reformers were willing to wait and see.

Moreover, the same day that Wilson received Gregory's defense of the APL, the President gave evidence that he was still more concerned about spies than about civil liberties. In a Flag Day address in Washington, he again publicly indicted the Imperial German government for continuing to carry on "sinister intrigue" in America, in places "high and low," through "agents and dupes." Wilson's words troubled Lincoln Colcord, Washington correspondent for the *Philadelphia Public Ledger*, who asked Colonel House privately "if he had not noticed a trace of imperialism, a certain appeal to emotionalism, a false note," in the President's Flag Day speech. House agreed with Colcord but denied the possibility that Wilson was losing some of his liberalism. House told Wilson that he fully approved of the speech, and then noted in his diary that it was "a proper indictment of Germany." The next day Wilson signed the Espionage Act into law.

Introduction of the Espionage Act in Congress, with its provisions for censorship, had caused the first alarm on the part of men sensitive to civil liberties. However, their success in having the clause stricken despite Wilson's opposition seemed to lull them into a false sense of security, acquiescence in its passage, and disregard of the policies evolving for its enforcement. As late as August, John Dewey could still write in the *New Republic* that he was not "specially concerned" that "liberty of thought and speech" would "seriously suffer," that he could not "arouse any genuine distress on this score." He was mainly concerned lest the ill-considered attempts to repress discussion and criticism lead Americans to miss "the great experience of discovering the significance of American life by seeing it reflected into a remaking of the life of the world." With such support as this from leading intellectuals, and in the absence of public criticism of his administrative policy of law enforcement, it is not surprising that Wilson based his decision regarding the APL more on trust in Gregory's regard for civil liberties than on McAdoo's fears that the APL was dangerous. After the war, Gregory would claim of Wilson that "he gave me a free hand in the handling of my department, and I do not recall a single instance in which he failed to support my policies and views."

Nevertheless, McAdoo's complaint to the Justice Department did bring change. Ironically, however, it touched off a reshuffling in the Bureau of Investigation which resulted, not in dissolution of the League, but in its official recognition by the Justice Department. The back-street mistress was about to become the morganatic wife.

Until June, the American Protective League had been only a volunteer group working with the Bureau of Investigation, its claim to being a "Secret Service Division" having been concocted by Briggs to make the League sound official. But shortly after the passage of the Espionage Act on June 15, Bielaski called Albert Briggs back to Washington to discuss reorganization of his secret army. Bielaski asked if Briggs could stop the distribution of the "Secret Service" badges and notify members that they were in no way connected with the Secret Service of the Treasury Department. He asked if prospective members could be investigated before enrolling them in the League and if they could appear before a notary public to swear to uphold the Constitution. He asked whether the APL chief could persuade members not to exhibit credentials "except in the necessary performance" of their duty nor to disclose information collected in their work to any but government officials or authorized APL officers. Bielaski further asked if Briggs could supply a master list of all captains, lieutenants, and chiefs. If Briggs could meet these conditions, the Justice Department would allow the APL to work for it. If these requirements could be met, Bielaski was not only willing to allow the APL to continue, he was willing to give it even more authority, and he would see that it received recognition as an official secret service force working for the Justice Department alone.

The terms having been agreed to, Bielaski planned to select APL chiefs in key units in large cities and commission them as special agents in the Bureau of Investigation. These chiefs would then set up APL investigation bureaus in League offices, completely separate from the regular Bureau offices in the federal buildings and out of sight of the United States attorneys. Branches would then be reorganized, unsuitable members dropped, and members told not to refer to themselves as Secret Service men or to the League as a secret service. These APL divisions could then become centers of counterespionage from which the Bureau of Investigation could deploy private citizens actually engaged in ferreting out subversion for the federal government.

"The matter of Government recognition is now settled," Briggs wrote happily to the Chicago APL chief on June 29. "Chief Bielaski this morning definitely approved the enclosed form." The enclosed form bore the words "Organized with the Approval and Operating Under the Department of Justice of the United States." This endorsement was to appear on all letterhead stationery and on new commission cards which members would receive to replace their badges. The Chicago division dutifully began to inform members as to the relation of the League to the Justice Department: "It is not connected with the Secret Service of the United States. . . . The Secret Service of the United States is under the Department of the Treasury. . . . It is under Secretary of the Treasury McAdoo, and is separate and distinct from the Bureau of Investigation of the Department of Justice, which is under Attorney General Gregory. Members will therefore understand that they are not members of the 'Secret Service.' "

While Bielaski regrouped his legions, McAdoo was gone from Washington on a tour to drum up support for a Liberty Loan drive. When he returned, he appeared at first to have lost all interest in the APL, to be intent only upon stamping out "German inspired" opposition to the Liberty Loan. McAdoo had visited with J. F. McGee of the Minnesota Commission of Public Safety, who was advocating that publications opposing the Liberty Loan be suppressed as "seditious." On his return to the capital, McAdoo sent McGee's views on to Gregory with a note saying, "The publications he enclosed are of such a seditious nature that I felt the matter should be drawn to your personal attention."

Then McAdoo found out that Bielaski was merging the Bureau of Investigation with the APL and planning to keep the Secret Service out of home defense. This information rekindled his opposition to Gregory's burgeoning power. On June 12, Congress had passed an appropriation bill authorizing the President to use Secret Service men "without reference to existing limitation" if he judged "an emergency exists which requires such action." McAdoo, his previous proposal of a central bureau of intelligence dead, now suggested that Wilson allow Treasury men to work with the Army and Navy in setting up their own intelligence bureaus.

McAdoo attacked Gregory for relying on Bielaski's judgment in allowing the APL to continue to operate. He was patronizing. "The Attorney General is a fine fellow," he wrote, "and you know how genuinely attached I am to him. He is, like the rest of us, overwrought with heavy responsibilities, and I cannot believe that he has been able to go fully into the record of his own Bureau in this matter or he would not have shown such sensitiveness on the subject. In all of the departments we are, of necessity, obliged to rely greatly upon our subordinates, and they do not always steer us right."

McAdoo did not suggest that Secret Service Chief Flynn head up the new bureau. He left that for others. A few chosen New York newspapers announced that the government was considering a merger of all its detective forces, whereupon United States Marshal Thomas D. McCarthy, who had worked with the Secret Service in New York and opposed the continuance of the APL, wired Wilson's secretary, Joseph Tumulty, recommending the appointment of Chief Flynn: "His appointment would be met with favor all over the nation as he is regarded as America's greatest detective."

To further his campaign against the APL, McAdoo raised the specter of spies in the State Department. Chief Flynn had been investigating State Department employees suspected of being German sympathizers, and McAdoo warned Wilson that the situation would remain dangerous as long as the United States had no central intelligence agency. "This serves to emphasize the importance of my previous suggestion to you for the organization of a strong Bureau of Intelligence to deal with situations of this character and with the general spy system in the United States."

McAdoo brought up the topic of spies again when the Cabinet met on July 6. Gregory, who three months earlier had also been fearful of German espionage, now damned the talk as "hysteria." It was to his advantage to argue that there was no danger and that his department had the defenses well secured at home. It was to Mc-Adoo's advantage to argue that, on the contrary, the danger of German espionage was grave indeed.

Three days later McAdoo was back at his desk writing to Secretary of War Baker, urging that he set up a more effective intelligence organization. Wilson received a copy and another warning: "The German spy system is highly organized and is operating efficiently. I have no hysterical notions about it, but I think it ought to be extirpated with a strong hand. The country is much aroused about the German spy activities. What you said on this subject in your Flag Day speech made a great impression. I earnestly hope that you will soon take action to make more effective the secret service agencies of the government, so that the dangerous activities of German agents and sympathizers in this country may be more effectively dealt with."

McAdoo was right. Wilson's comments had made an impression on the country; they had convinced the people that the Administration was alarmed. On July 4, news had also been released that General Pershing's Expeditionary Force had been fired on by U-boats and had found European harbors mined. Alarm spread. Some members of Congress helped it along. Senator Chamberlain, Chairman of the Senate Military Affairs Committee, singled out the Navy Department as a nest of German spies and urged that they be found and executed. Senator Ben Tillman, Chairman of the Senate Naval Affairs Committee, stated unequivocally, "I have no doubt spies are in our departments. I want to see the German devils ferreted out and hanged."

The *Pittsburgh Leader* spoke of a German spydom and insisted the government "must uncover the system and wipe it out." The *New York Tribune* added that enemy aliens interned at Ellis Island could easily give information to spies. The *New York Evening Post* announced with approval the arrest of a "quartet of spies." Only the *Springfield Republican* warned that "a spy-hunting people would present a deplorable spectacle in this country, for in a panic of suspicion we should inevitably commit many grievous wrongs. It is a business to be handled with firmness and decision, but also with great care and discretion by experienced secret-service men."

Obviously, Wilson did not agree with Gregory that the fear of espionage was all hysteria, for he wrote the Attorney General, "I am writing now to ask if you would be generous enough to cooperate with the Secretary of the Treasury and Mr. Polk in working out for me a plan for the cooperation of these services into which we can all enter with spirit and effect. I am genuinely in need of counsel in this matter and am sure, that you three can compound a plan which will be worth acting upon."

Nor did Wilson agree with the *Springfield Republican,* for he did not insist that the APL be banned. Instead, his opposition to the APL disintegrated, and McAdoo's plan backfired.

Indeed, some coordination was evolving, but certainly not the kind McAdoo favored. Bielaski assured Gregory that there was no need for a unified agency, that he was in daily touch with Naval Intelligence, Army Intelligence, and the State Department, and that he was receiving reports from them in return. He claimed that he had secret agents in every arsenal and factory that held war contracts. Gregory again accepted his subordinate's assurances and refused to work with McAdoo on any new scheme. By mid-July, Bielaski had convinced Gregory and Gregory had convinced Wilson that McAdoo's plan for abolition of the APL and substitution of Secret Service agents coordinated by a central intelligence agency was not necessary.

Meanwhile, official recognition by the Justice Department brought further growth to the APL. After one month of government recognition, the number of League units had more than doubled, from four hundred in early June to over nine hundred by the end of July. Since no German spies could be found, the APL turned its attention to an organization which conservative businessmen had long considered a menace and which, because of its opposition to the war, was now being accused of being in sympathy with the German cause. The APL found its new enemy in the Industrial Workers of the World.

Soldiers of Darkness

Chicago APL members were well acquainted with the Wobblies, as the Industrial Workers of the World had come to be called, for the IWW had established their headquarters in that city in 1905. From Chicago, these dissident laborers had distributed literature advocating the overthrow of capitalism and the establishment of a socialistic society. They had directed strikes to improve working conditions and increase wages all the way from Goldfield, Nevada, to Lawrence, Massachusetts. The war which Wilson claimed would make the world safe for democracy was, according to the IWW, a war which would make the world safe for "predatory capitalists," a scheme of the Wall Street plutocrats, a purely imperialistic struggle in which they wanted no part. Their strikes, their criticism of the system would go on despite the war.

To APL businessmen, this sentiment was treason, and they lost little time in abandoning cold spy trails for the warm traces of radicals. One of the Chicago APL captains, Thomas Gowenlock, boasted later that the most valuable work of the sleuths had not been tracking down enemy aliens at all, but "breaking up the activities of labor agitators and anarchists."

Gowenlock formed a "flying squad" composed of fifteen picked Leaguers and fifteen city police, including two of the "toughest members of the bomb squad," as a first move in the attack against the IWW. These "soldiers of darkness," as Gowenlock affectionately called them, began by trailing IWW leaders. Then, growing more eager, they began to infiltrate closed meetings. One APL member passed as a reporter for an IWW newspaper and boldly took notes of everything said; others eavesdropped by wiretapping. Leaguers impersonating workers contributed to fund-raising drives and agitated against the war. Operatives working openly broke up meetings called to oppose the war. At an auditorium on the west side of Chicago, where Wobblies had assembled to hear their leaders denounce the capitalistic war, Leaguers roughed up the speakers, placed them under arrest, and took them to jail. At a Grant Park rally of five thousand men and women gathered to hear antiwar speeches, Gowenlock jumped up on the platform and grabbed one of the speakers. When other IWW leaders rushed to the speaker's defense, Leaguers had them arrested and locked up for disturbing the peace.

As soon as Congress passed the draft law, the APL could increase its attack on all labor radicals opposed to the war under the guise of enforcing federal law. In Cincinnati, for example, APL undercover agents joined a socialist organization. Discovering circulars opposing the draft were to be handed out, the agents confiscated them and had the men who were to distribute them arrested on a charge of conspiracy to oppose the draft. In another case, three employees of the Ford plant in Highland Park, Michigan, having been arrested for conspiring to oppose the draft, made the mistake of appealing to the Ford Motor Company for an investigation, maintaining that they had not distributed antidraft pamphlets as the police claimed. The company simply turned over their letter of appeal to an undercover APL member working in the plant. He in turn sent it to the United States Attorney, who passed it on to the district attorney, who promptly lost it. Meanwhile, the employees waited hopefully in jail for company help which never came.

When the federal order came for young men to register for the draft, the APL had yet another excuse for antilabor activities. IWW leaders had advised their followers that concerted opposition to registration would only divert members from needed organizational activities, but each member was free to decide for himself whether or not to register. When a group in Rockford, Illinois, declined to register and scheduled an all-day picnic at a local park to publicize their position, the chief of the Rockford APL called Superintendent Clabaugh and gave him the facts. Clabaugh ordered the chief to have authorities arrest all IWW members who had not registered. The local police found only three.

The IWW were enraged. They held meetings; they lodged protests. Then several hundred began a mile-and-a-quarter march to the jail to demand release of the three prisoners. The sheriff refused, ordering the marchers to disperse. When they refused, 135 were jailed.

It did not take long for the IWW to realize that the federal government was cooperating with businessmen and corporations in an attempt to crush their dissent and their organizing activities. Because the APL was a secret organization, however, IWW leaders could not determine exactly what was happening. They suspected that some of their own most violently antiwar members might actually be *agents provocateurs.* They knew they were being trailed, that their meetings were being watched, but they believed the undercover agents were either private detectives working for local companies or genuine government operatives. The result of the harassment was to make leaders more hostile to the war effort and to the federal government itself.

Involvement on the part of the Leaguers varied with their personal hostility toward labor. In some towns, APL units remained on the fringe of this battle between the government and the IWW. In Tulsa, Oklahoma, for example, private company detectives provided all the reports on the IWW to the United States Attorney, while local APL members watched without interest. In contrast, Philadelphia Leaguers seized IWW membership lists and succeeded in having fifty members dismissed from defense plants. South Dakota APL members joined with Home Guards and other vigilante groups to clear IWW laborers from the wheat fields near Aberdeen on the pretext that the radicals planned to burn the crop. One Leaguer boasted, "The methods adopted by this branch of the APL have proved efficacious"; and the United States Attorney approvingly dubbed this zealous group "the Ku Klux Klan of the Prairies." As a result of this South Dakota purge, the Minneapolis IWW called a strike; but by this time, there were more draft regulations to use against the IWW.

Two weeks passed between the first draft registration and Secretary of War Baker's report to the Cabinet that registration had exceeded census estimates. North Carolina, for example, had produced 106 men for every one hundred men expected. Despite this excess in agricultural states like North Carolina, states like Oregon and Washington in which violent conflict existed between labor and industry had produced only 60 percent of the expected number. The governor of Washington brushed the matter off with the explanation that the census figures had been padded, but the Justice Department felt that the only way to be sure was to find the men who had not registered. The law provided for one year imprisonment for nonregistrants, and Gregory was determined to impose the penalty. To do so, however, he first had to find the men.

There was little guidance from European precedent in locating draft evaders. England had adopted the practice of letting military men raid theaters, football fields, parks, and other public places, where they demanded evidence of exemption, then held civilians at local police stations, coining the euphemism "virtual arrest" to hedge the constitutional issues. The results of this use of press gangs had been meager compared to the annoyance caused and the criticism provoked. The practice was soon discontinued.

In the United States, such an experiment was never tried because it did not fit in with the theory of nonmilitary enforcement of conscription. Wilson wanted to reduce contact between civilians and military authorities as much as possible, especially since it was evident by the summer of 1917 that the military was being drawn into labor disputes and that many civilians were anxious to use federal military power to defend their own economic interests. As long as the job of hunting draft dodgers remained in civilian hands, Wilson seemed unconcerned about who did the hunting. It was up to Attorney General Gregory to decide how enforcement could be implemented. On July 3, he mobilized the Justice Department, and Bielaski ordered his agents to make a "prompt, thorough, and countrywide search" for nonregistrants.

This directive gave the APL the opening it needed to continue harassment of the IWW. During July twelve hundred draft investigations were made on the south side of Chicago where the IWW was particularly active. Investigation inevitably led to false arrests. Anyone who could not produce a registration certificate was told to go to the Federal Building. Anyone who refused to go was taken. In Minnesota, where Leaguers were given police powers by the sheriff, hundreds of IWW's were rounded up and deposited in jail. By the end of July, the jails were full of men trying to prove that they were ineligible for the draft, yet the APL went right on staging roundups. Due process was being ignored. No warrants had been issued for arrests. Sometimes Bureau of Investigation agents filed complaints for violation of the Selective Service Act; sometimes they used local ordinances which allowed men to be held for twenty-four hours pending investigation of alleged crime. Usually they simply allowed the men to be held illegally.

The draft law provided one year imprisonment for failure to register. But the Justice Department in Washington wanted to be lenient. It seemed wasteful to go to the expense of prosecuting each nonregistrant when Crowder needed men. United States attorneys were given the freedom to decide whom to prosecute and whom to release after forced registration.

The attorneys relied upon local draft boards for advice, boards that had insisted they had a right to determine who had evaded the law. Nonregistrants, the boards claimed, might be willful or nonwillful; perhaps the men had not understood regulations and needed only to be persuaded to register. Of almost 6,000 nonregistrants the APL helped to round up during the summer and fall of 1917, one third were declared nonwillful, allowed to register, and to remain free until called up by draft boards. The other 4,000 were prosecuted by the Justice Department for evading the draft.

Political friends were, of course, never prosecuted. In practice, Crowder's "supervised decentralization" was already being twisted to partisan purposes, just as the Civil War draft had been. The Republican governor of Pennsylvania was busily packing his state's boards with party hacks who were expected to protect young men of the proper political persuasion. The Republican governor of New York was doing the same; so was the Republican governor of Indiana. So it seemed to Democrats who could not place their own politicos on the exemption boards. In the South, where there was only one party, feuds broke out between Democratic factions. Everywhere laborers were being passed over when boards were being selected. Finally Secretary Baker decreed that representatives of labor must sit on local draft boards, but only the most conservative were selected, and the persecution of radical labor organizers went on.

Invariably, radicals found not to have registered were prosecuted to keep them from organizing strikes. The United States Attorney in St. Paul, Alfred Jacques, later explained how he had arrested over a hundred IWW leaders and "prevented an IWW strike in the mining regions of Minnesota in the summer of 1917." He explained, "I thought it a good idea to keep these IWW aliens so busy defending prosecutions for failure to register that they would not have time to plot against the industrial interests of Northern Minnesota." The IWW's who had been arrested in Rockford, Illinois, were treated in the same manner.

These government prosecutions sanctified the claims of businessmen that IWW radicals were primarily responsible for any opposition to the war effort. Even racial violence came to be explained away as resulting from IWW agitation.

War production speedups had already begun to draw Negroes up the Mississippi to the North. For many southern Negroes, East St. Louis, Illinois, was the first stop. There employers had shown a willingness to hire them and to ignore the protests of white workers. Proper domestic intelligence might have alerted Wilson to the kindling of racial animosity by competition for wartime jobs. But the APL was the only intelligence force working within industries, and their interests were not necessarily identical with the government's interests. As employees or friends of industrialists, their concern was to prevent strikes, not to report their possible causes.

Animosity over competition from the Negro existed in other parts of the North. In Schenectady, one Jewish-Austrian labor leader threatened to call a strike because a war industry wanted to employ a single Negro student. The New York APL sent a Jewish member up as troubleshooter. He lectured his co-religionist on the Fourteenth Amendment and the Constitution and convinced him to call off the strike.

In the Midwest, the problem was not that simple. In East St. Louis, the APL had also worked to avert a strike called to protest the hiring of Negro workers, but the workers were not convinced that opposition to their strike was based on a selfless desire to win the war. Soldiers, on duty ostensibly to guard against sabotage, appeared to be working for private companies. The local police force was negligent and inadequate. The local politicians were corrupt. All the elements necessary for a riot were present. On July 2 the most violent race riot since Civil War Reconstruction days swept East St. Louis.

Such an event should have drawn from the President a condemnation of violence at home, if not in defense of civil liberties, at least because it was a force for disunity and a deterrent to the war effort. Not a word of condemnation came from Wilson following the riots, however, riots in which nine whites and thirty-nine Negroes were killed. Illinois militiamen brought in to quell the disturbance were seen by witnesses to shoot at and beat Negroes, loot their houses, and stand by while white men bludgeoned, burned, and killed others. The *New York Evening Mail* carried a cartoon with the question: "Mr. President, Why Not Make America Safe for Democracy?" Theodore Roosevelt condemned the appalling "infamies imposed on colored people." Even business leaders in East St. Louis called for an investigation by a federal grand jury under the United States Judge for the Northern District of Illinois, Kenesaw Mountain Landis. But newspapers blamed the whole episode on efforts of the IWW to stir up racial unrest.

In Bisbee, Arizona, members of the Citizens Protective League and the Workmen's Loyalty League had decided a little old-fashioned vigilante action was the best way to rid their town of any working-class troublemakers. At a joint meeting they concluded that the time had come for action; the sheriff of Cochise County was there, but he didn't offer any opposition. They proceeded to nominate Jack Greenway, an aging Rough Rider, to lead the attack. The APL never admitted any official connection with these vigilante groups, but they were the type of groups which Briggs had been encouraging to join hands with his national organization, and later the APL reported one thousand IWW investigations for Cochise, Arizona. If members did not participate, neither did they try to stop the vigilantes or to warn the Justice Department. Nor did the Military Intelligence officer stationed in Arizona warn the War Department. Instead he sent the chief of the Military Intelligence a report claiming that the IWW was being financed by German money and that large funds had been deposited in Arizona banks to hire lawyers to defend IWW members being prosecuted under local laws for antiwar activities.

On July 10, vigilantes rounded up sixty-five IWW's. Stuffing them into a boxcar, the mob sent the boxcar across the California border and told the sheriff there to do what he wished with the occupants. Gregory ordered an investigation of the IWW the next day to see if German agents were supplying them with money, but he made no move to investigate the activities of the vigilantes. When no rebuke came from the federal government, the mob brazenly rounded up twelve hundred IWW and laborers and sundry townspeople suspected of collaborating with them and repeated the deportation process, sending boxcars into the New Mexico desert. What would happen to the people locked in the boxcars the vigilantes didn't care.

This time Wilson was forced to act. He sent federal troops to care for the Arizona refugees, telling the governor of Arizona that he looked upon such action as a "great danger" to be viewed with "grave apprehension" and warning that "a very serious responsibility is assumed when such precedents are set."

At the Cabinet meeting of July 13, discussion of the menace of the IWW replaced talk of German spies. Gregory advised Wilson that the federal government could not properly take action against them because no federal statute had been violated. Three days passed. The Cabinet met again. Once more the members discussed the IWW, concluding that it was not "an imminent danger."

Nevertheless, the following day Bielaski and Gregory alerted special agents and United States attorneys throughout the country that the IWW was definitely dangerous. The organization, Bielaski told his agents, was "taking advantage of the needs of the country occasioned by the war to advance its own interests utterly without regard for the welfare of the people as a whole." He asked for complete information on their plans, organization, finances, and leaders. While echoing Bielaski's words, Gregory warned attorneys to remember that IWW members were entitled to the full protection of the law and that oppressive and illegal methods dealing with them should be discouraged. Reporters were told only that the rumors of German financing had not yet been proven. At the same time, they were told that the Justice Department would go ahead with an investigation into the East St. Louis race riots.

Western governors now began to harry the Administration about the IWW. The day after Gregory ordered his investigation, George L. Bell, executive officer of the California Committee of Immigration and Housing, swept to Washington with a demand from the governors of eight western states that the federal government put all IWW's in concentration camps because they were hindering war work. Wilson replied that American citizens could not be imprisoned without a trial. (Later, in World War II, Japanese-American citizens did not receive such consideration.) Californian Franklin K. Lane, Secretary of the Interior, thought Bell's plan a good one, but it found little favor among other Cabinet members. Instead, after the July 20 Cabinet meeting, Wilson endorsed the secret investigation of the IWW which Gregory had already ordered.

United States Attorney Charles Karch in St. Louis felt that if the Justice Department investigated the IWW for subversion it could also investigate local authorities for violation of civil rights. He advised Gregory that the federal government had jurisdiction under both the 1866 Civil Rights Act, which guaranteed Negroes security of their persons and property, and the 1870 statute aimed originally at the Ku Klux Klan, prohibiting conspiracy to violate rights and privileges guaranteed by the Constitution and federal law. If evidence could be procured showing that local authorities had failed to perform duties required of them because the people involved were Negroes, then there was a basis for a federal grand jury investigation.

Karch assured Gregory that the violence against the Negroes and the consequent denial of their constitutional prerogatives and immunities were directly due to state action, and that both he and Judge Landis favored an investigation. But by the time the attorney's letter reached Gregory, Wilson had ordered the Justice Department off the case, declaring there was no evidence of violation of federal law. On July 27, Gregory instructed the St. Louis attorney to close the case. Judge Landis, who had told Karch privately that he believed there was ample basis for an inquiry under the 1870 law, now told reporters that he questioned whether the riot was a proper subject for federal judicial inquiry.

It must have been reassuring for Representative L. C. Dyer of Missouri to hear that although the Justice Department was assisting the state in efforts to restore tranquility, no facts had been turned up to indicate violation of federal statutes. Conditions might develop justifying federal action, Wilson told Dyer, but in fact there was now little chance that the federal government would intervene.

Representatives of the National Association for the Advancement of Colored People who called at the White House were refused permission to see Wilson. An Illinois Military Board of Inquiry submitted a report to the Adjutant General vindicating the conduct of the commanding general, who had arrived in East St. Louis in a seersucker suit and straw hat and had stayed in City Hall while his men perpetrated outrages on Negroes and refused to arrest white terrorists. The Board concluded that troops had been insufficient and inexperienced and could have done nothing to save the victims. A congressional investigation called in mid-October received no support from the Justice Department; Gregory refused a request for information in his files. The Administration had washed its hands of the matter.

Instead of defending civil liberties, the Administration turned its attention back to enforcing conscription. American mobilization could not be halted pending a solution of problems in Europe. General Nivelle's *grande offensive,* promised as a decisive blow, had ended indecisively. Demoralized French soldiers had mutinied on May 20— some refused to attack, others would not go into the trenches, two regiments at Soissons wanted to march on Paris. All offensive action by the French ceased while Nivelle's replacement, General Pétain, pacified the rebellious troops. *"J'attends les Américans et les tanks,"* he announced.

On July 20, 1917, in a giant lottery in the Senate Office Building, officials had drawn black capsules providing key numbers which, when matched to numbers on registration certificates, determined who would go to the front. Although less than a million men were needed, General Crowder and Secretary Baker decided to call three million for examinations on the assumption that a third would be disqualified for physical reasons and another third would be exempted as aliens or because they had dependent relatives. Thus, three million men were summoned, and when many of them did not respond, the APL turned from hunting nonregistrants to hunting registrants who had not appeared for their physicals. On July 27, Bielaski ordered his agents to put APL volunteers on the track of these men.

Meanwhile, the Administration had kept the IWW issue alive. A week after Bell's appearance in Washington, the Minnesota Commission of Public Safety had taken up the campaign against the Wobblies, asking for more prosecutions rather than internment. There was not yet "sufficient ground for federal jurisdiction," Gregory replied.

Determined to change Gregory's stand, John Lind, an ex-governor of Minnesota and head of the Commission of Public Safety, called Hinton Clabaugh to Minneapolis to discuss the "crisis." Lind suggested that IWW leaders in Chicago might be arrested to demoralize the rank and file, and Clabaugh agreed. His files were already bulging with APL reports on the dangerous potentials of the IWW, reports he felt indicated that members could be charged with conspiracy and with hindering efficient prosecution of the war. He recommended deporting alien leaders under provisions of the Immigration Act, charging they were anarchists. Lind was delighted with Clabaugh's suggestion and turned over to him all the information collected by his Safety Commission on the activities of the IWW in Minneapolis. "If IWW organize agricultural workers, crops will be wasted and lost, lumber industry paralyzed," Lind warned Gregory by telegram. Then he offered to send the counsel for his Commission, Ambrose Tighe, to Washington with Clabaugh to confer with the Attorney General.

Clabaugh's suggestion, that the conspiracy statute be used to prosecute IWW members whose activities individually were not illegal, was not new to the Justice Department in July, 1917. Using that method to suppress labor radicals was new, however, since previously it had been used mainly against aliens for activities during the neutrality days. It had been used first to prosecute the German Consul in San Francisco, Franz Bopp, then to prosecute the East Indian revolutionists accused of conspiring with the Germans to ship arms for a rebellion against the British in India. San Francisco had been the scene of the action against the East Indian conspirators; Chicago was to be the center for the prosecution of the IWW conspirators. Clabaugh was eager to go to work.

But Gregory was not ready to go along. He dispatched a curt reply to Lind asking for more information on which to base the prosecution. He explained that if labor unrest called for emergency action, the governor of the state should first telegraph the President, and then the United States Attorney in Minneapolis should telegraph the Justice Department. Troops could then be called to quell any violence. Prosecutions could not be used to avert a strike that was only threatened.

Lind sent his lawyer on alone to Washington to present the Minnesota Commission's case. Governor Burnquist of Minnesota telegraphed Gregory that he would defer an appeal to the President until after Gregory had talked to the Minnesota lawyer, Ambrose Tighe.

When Tighe arrived in Washington, he carried reams of material collected through the Commission's sixty Pinkerton detectives and Clabaugh's APL members. Tighe claimed the material proved conspiracy, but his first interview did not convince Gregory that a federal statute had been violated by the IWW. Tighe then appealed to Minnesota Senator Knute Nelson. It was while Tighe talked to the senator that the President discussed the IWW crisis with his Cabinet. Bill Haywood, the one-eyed ex-miner who led the IWW, had dispatched a telegram to Wilson warning that unless Wobblies who had been driven out of Bisbee and left in the desert by the local vigilantes were returned, strikes would be called in the western mines. Wilson was indignant at the threat but said Haywood only wanted to be a martyr. "What shall I do?" he asked his advisers. They suggested he refer the problem to Secretary of Labor W. B. Wilson and Attorney General Gregory.

When Tighe returned to Gregory's office on the afternoon of July 31, he found the Attorney General had completely reversed his stand against federal intervention in a matter strictly the responsibility of the states. The Justice Department now accepted the principle that achieving the immediate paralysis of IWW activities by arresting the leaders was more important than their ultimate conviction. Tighe wired Governor Burnquist that everything was "satisfactorily arranged"; the department would send a criminal expert to Chicago, make investigations, and start prosecutions. A conference was scheduled in Chicago for the following Sunday with Gregory's special assistant, William C. Fitts. The *New York Times* announced confidently that the government was expected to act against the IWW because they were involved in a German plot.

On Sunday, August 4, Fitts met with Clabaugh, Attorney Tighe, Chicago Police Chief Schuettler, and a member of the Minnesota Commission. Clabaugh and Schuettler were in complete agreement with the Minnesota men. The American Protective League had already convinced them that the Industrial Workers of the World should be destroyed. They were also certain that if the Bureau of Investigation and the APL concentrated all their energies on the dissenting laborers, conspiracy could be proven. Clabaugh volunteered to lead the task of collecting information throughout the country for this purpose.

A few days after the Sunday meeting, Clabaugh opened a secret office in Chicago some distance from the Federal Building. There he installed a corps of special agents whom he ordered to work closely with the APL in systematically collecting evidence against the IWW. His superior, Bielaski, agreed to instruct agents in all parts of the United States to forward copies of reports involving IWW activities to Clabaugh's special office.

Leaguers and agents now began to pry into IWW affairs with a vengeance. They contacted detective agencies, company detectives, and city police officers to ask for reports on IWW activities, old or new. They uncovered a mass of information on earlier IWW activities but nothing indicating violation of federal laws. Not even undercover agents and *agents provocateurs* could turn up the kind of evidence necessary to build a case. Just five years earlier San Diego had been the scene of a violent six-month fight—IWW members on one side, vigilantes and police on the other—over a municipal ordinance which had closed up what IWW orators regarded as a sort of Hyde Park. Yet neither the young lawyer who headed the APL unit nor the federal agents in that border city could find evidence of illegal activities. Elsewhere agents were equally unsuccessful. APL members recruited from major mining companies in Butte, Montana, could provide no evidence either. IWW's had caused no violence in Butte, had broken no laws; they were not a menace to the government.

Despite their failure to find damaging evidence against the IWW,

Bielaski was properly appreciative of his volunteers. In mid-August he wrote to Briggs that the League had "rendered exceptionally effective service not only in seeing that the registration was accomplished in a smooth and satisfactory manner, but that those who did not register have been properly dealt with." His approval gave Leaguers a sanction to continue their business as usual.

Efforts to locate "disloyal" draft dodgers, generally identified with the IWW, gave rise to renewed violence. Using the vigilante symbol of the old frontier days, "3-7-77," new bands of vigilantes began to terrorize IWW members still brave enough to advocate strikes openly. The vigilantes were able to frighten into silence everyone but Frank Little, a labor organizer and opponent of the war. When they couldn't intimidate him, they simply took him out and murdered him, leaving a note with the grave dimensions—3 feet by 7 feet by 77 inches—pinned to his body.

Radical newspapers called vigilantism a plot to crush the IWW. A few reform sheets suggested that lynchings would not solve the problem, that it was one calling for some sort of federal mediation between laborers and industry. But western newspapers were almost unanimous in asserting that the federal government should have taken action against the IWW. The *Seattle Times,* for instance, advocated concentration camps for all who would hamper wartime industry and promote "unjustifiable dissension." Montana newspapers expressed pride in the vigilantes' action. Western men shoot first and ask questions afterward, was their boast.

In eastern Oklahoma, a man was arrested as a draft opponent. Newspapers claimed he was an IWW sent from Chicago to stir up draft resistance among the farmers. The man had not been sent by the Chicago IWW; in fact, he had already been expelled from the IWW for criminal activities. Nor did the farmers need artificial whipping up. A socialist Working-Class Union had flourished among the debt-ridden farmers of western Arkansas and eastern Oklahoma in 1914, but as prosperity marked the years following the opening of the European war, socialism had lost ground, and Socialists had been voted out of office. Five men had been arrested at Seminole, Oklahoma, for resisting the draft, but only one Working-Class Union man had been arrested at nearby Holdenville for circulating antidraft literature. During July, however, city draft boards had managed to push the Union into greater opposition to the draft through arbitrary arrests of men who had not registered. Sons of farmers were almost never exempted from service, and farmers who could not replace laborers saw chances for wartime profits disappear. By late July, the farmers' unhappiness was evident in the counties of Seminole and Pottawatomie. But as usual, discontent was attributed to machinations of the IWW. Arrest of one former IWW seemed proof enough to those looking for a weapon against the radicals.

Then on August 3, an embattled farmer ran up a red flag in his yard near Wewoka, Oklahoma. Townspeople didn't know exactly what it meant, but it looked dangerous. Out in the farmland, farmers were said to be destroying crops, killing livestock, and congregating by the hundreds. They planned to march on Washington, some said, even now getting ready by gorging themselves on barbecued beef and green corn. Merchants were sure the farmers were planning resistance to the draft—probably sabotage, as well. Besides, the crops destroyed and livestock killed had been mortgaged to the merchants. Groups of vigilantes formed and rode out to disperse the farmers.

On August 6, twenty-six of the farmers arrested were identified by newspapers as members of the IWW. The press assured the citizenry that this farm revolt was actually an IWW conspiracy to oppose the draft. Caught in the vigilante dragnet were all known Socialists who had formerly held office or run for office. Whether or not they were in any way connected with what was now being called "the Green Corn Rebellion," the charge of IWW conspiracy stuck. Vigilantes took over, with the help of the Oklahoma Home Guards; there were gun battles and deaths. One twenty-five-year-old school teacher who had applied for officer's training school and was on the way to take his exam failed to halt his car at the command of a group of Home Guards. He was gunned down.

Wholesale arrests continued. By August 10, county jails in the southeastern part of the state were crowded to capacity, the overflow being taken to the state prison. Newspapers branded everyone involved as IWW conspirators, and the editor of the Wewoka *Capital Democrat* advocated that the four hundred and fifty prisoners be put in federal prison or made to mount a "federal scaffold." Men were held for days without hearings and with no formal charges against them while United States Attorney W. P. McGinnis trumpeted that if evidence proved sufficient, he would ask for the death penalty. He announced that nearly three hundred men would be brought before the federal grand jury on the charge of draft resistance and that eight IWW leaders would be charged with conspiracy. The "Green Corn Rebellion," newspapers shrilled, was part of a nationwide IWW conspiracy.

In other western towns, mayors were asking for federal troops to quell incipient labor disputes. According to law, only the President could determine the need for federal troops, but during the April spy scare, regional army commanders had been ordered by Secretary of War Baker to respond to requests from local officials for troops; and although these orders had been altered on May 29, some commanders continued to send troops in whenever mayors decided to have them around. In San Jose, California, for instance, the mayor asked for and received a detachment of troops from the commanding general in California.

Nor was such extremism confined to the West. On August 10, the governor of Ohio had to telegraph the commanding general of the central department asking him not to respond to requests from mayors in Ohio cities where labor unrest was occurring.

Meanwhile, army intelligence officers attached to command posts diligently collected information on IWW activities and asked the War Department not to withdraw federal troops from areas where the IWW was organized. The presence of troops in an area gave Military Intelligence officers an excuse to meddle in civilian affairs, for probing local radical labor activities was justified as protecting the military bases. Such intrusion spread disaffection among men eligible for the draft, however; if being a soldier meant becoming a strike breaker, many young men were not interested.

Suppression of widespread opposition to the draft now eclipsed all concern for the right of American citizens. Bielaski was urging the APL to exert even greater efforts to round up men who had failed to appear for their physical examinations. Crowder announced that such men would be automatically accepted for service and should be jailed if they refused to report for induction. Drafted men who failed to report were to be considered deserters who could be arrested summarily, either by law enforcement agents or by civilians upon the order of a military officer. Once more, however, boards claimed the right to determine treatment of these young men. If they judged the man to be a willful deserter, he could be turned over immediately to the military police to be taken to the nearest camp as a prisoner. There he could be examined by the commander, who could recommend he be sent on to a mobilization camp or tried for desertion. Any man found guilty of desertion could be sent to a disciplinary battalion. It was an easy way to get rid of men suspected of being labor radicals. On the other hand, if the local board found he was a nonwillful deserter, the man could be examined and freed to await his call. Local boards sent the Bureau of Investigation lists of men to arrest. The APL went to work, and in the excitement of preparing the young men for shipment to cantonments on September 3, 1917, its activities were hardly noticed.

Now racial violence broke out anew. Distrust between Negro soldiers and white civilians in Illinois had been growing ever since May, 1917, when twenty-one Negro soldiers had been accused of assaulting a white woman. The APL at Rockford had been called in by Major General Charles H. Martin to secure confessions from the Negroes, and fifteen of the twenty-one had been court-martialed. The convictions had been "principally due to your able and efficient service," General Martin said in thanking the APL. On August 25, another incident touched off a bitter clash between police, townspeople, and Negro soldiers stationed in Houston, Texas. The city was placed under martial law by the governor, and the Negro troops involved were arrested. Texas congressmen now demanded all Negro troops be withdrawn from the state. Four days later, Secretary of War Baker ordered that no Negro draftees should be called up. More confusion. More alarms.

In the confusion, the western governors stepped up demands for suppression of the IWW. Governor Stewart of Montana wired the President that work was almost at a standstill in the state because of the IWW who had terrorized workers and closed down all the copper mines. He asked that the Council of National Defense assign fifty detectives to get enough evidence on the IWW to put twenty-five of their most active leaders in jail. Other western governors urged the federal government to keep all investigations secret. Arizona Representative Carl Hayden sent the President a suggestion, made by the Jerome Industrial Peace League, that the IWW be declared an outlaw organization so that the vigilantes could take care of them. The Council of National Defense voted to ask Wilson to appoint an investigating commission. Wilson felt that publicity would only aid the IWW cause and quietly appointed Chief Justice J. Harry Covington of the Supreme Court of the District of Columbia to investigate. Big Bill Haywood invited Covington to inspect the mine union's Chicago files.

At Clabaugh's secret headquarters, however, APL men and Bureau of Investigation agents continued their search for evidence. Chicago APL members boldly publicized the fact that they were working for the Justice Department. One member told newsmen that the APL covered every city, town, and hamlet in every section of the United

States, that it had a membership of 200,000, and that a million men, including bank presidents, railroad executives, judges, lawyers, and other captains of industry, were sending intelligence reports and making investigations for the Justice Department. Bielaski, who had just issued commissions as Bureau of Investigation special agents to more APL chiefs, meanwhile maintained the myth of complete separateness when inquiries reached him in Washington. "The members of this League have no official connection with the Government," he wrote to men who wanted to know more about the status of this volunteer organization they were being asked to join, "they cooperate with agents of this Department in investigating improper activities on the part of alien enemies or German sympathizers."

Bielaski, in an interview with a Massachusetts reporter, boasted of his practice of using the services of patriotic volunteers. "The American public is the most intelligently patriotic body on the face of the earth to-day," he assured the man from the *Springfield Union*. "It hasn't had hysteria. It hasn't run wild—save in a few exceptional instances." The interviewer was impressed. Calm, implacable, energetic, was how he described Bielaski. Recently a subordinate had urged him to take a vacation, the admiring reporter wrote. "What's the use?" was the chief's reply. "I don't need it."

Gregory bore up less well under the pressure. "Why do they [the governors] not come to me?" he complained at the Cabinet meeting of August 31. His agents were trailing leads, but they needed concrete evidence before seeking indictments. He assured his attorneys privately that patriotic volunteers were on the job upholding the government, watching the disloyal, and reporting on disloyal utterances. There was no need for precipitous action. He himself planned to start a short vacation on September 4, the day after the first carloads of future doughboys were scheduled to leave for southern cantonments.

At least one voice counselled prudence amid all these alarms. George W. Anderson, the Massachusetts reformer, wrote that he had evidence that private detective agencies were circulating, among employers, extreme statements by IWW and Socialist agitators. Agencies often planted their own operatives in business firms. Then these men posed as Anarchists and Socialists, gained admission to movements, and became proponents of wild and extreme ideas in their efforts to entrap labor agitators. Some employers were hysterically scared, said Anderson; others were willing to use the detectives to discredit the labor movement, and most refused to face the fact that they were really "silent partners in one of the meanest games ever played in any economic controversy." He warned that the federal government should be careful to keep within the law in its prosecutions and not be made an unwilling, vicious partner in the labor spy racket.

In the War Department, another Massachusetts reformer, Felix Frankfurter, was working out a plan to ensure domestic peace by attempting to identify IWW leaders and to distinguish between them and other dissatisfied unionists whom employers were accusing of being IWW members. Given the facts, the government could then mediate grievances of more moderate groups, isolate the IWW, and so render them impotent. On September 4, he presented his plan to Secretary Baker, suggesting that Sidney Hillman be sent as a special investigator. His plan, he told Baker, had the support of Justice Brandeis and the most disinterested students of the labor movement in government service.

Judge Covington had just returned from his investigation in the West and was preparing to report his findings to Wilson. Gregory left for Magnolia, Massachusetts, where he planned to visit Colonel House before heading north into the Maine woods for his vacation. In Chicago, Clabaugh and his volunteers worked on. Clabaugh wired agents in all parts of the country asking for the names of IWW leaders. Then he ordered arrest warrants and dispatched secret orders to agents and APL members to raid IWW offices at precisely 2:00 P.M. Chicago time on Thursday, September 5, 1917.

At the appointed hour, Bureau of Investigation agents and APL members struck. In Chicago, guards were thrown around IWW headquarters on Madison Street while it was ransacked. Then raiders moved down the street to the Socialist party headquarters and repeated the process. An IWW print shop was visited next. Raiders went to the private residences of Bill Haywood and other Wobbly leaders, where they confiscated everything which related to IWW affairs. Haywood and Ralph Chaplin were dragged off to the Federal Building for interrogation. Chaplin, who was brought in handcuffed while Haywood was being questioned, later described the confusion accompanying the arrests. After about an hour of checking and rechecking of the prisoners, the United States Marshal read the warrant for their arrests, explaining that it had just arrived and apologizing for not having served it individually at the time of arrest, as specified by law.

Twenty other IWW offices were raided in the West and as far south as New Orleans. In Salt Lake City, raiders confiscated two thousand pictures of Frank Little, the Wobbly lynched a few weeks before in

Montana. In Spokane, they seized two strongboxes. Everywhere, they carted away boxes and bundles of IWW literature and arrested Wobbly leaders.

The next morning, newspapers headlined a "country-wide" plot by the IWW to destroy wheat and corn crops, disorganize the mining industry, and generally disrupt the home front war effort. The Justice Department in San Francisco described the material confiscated there as "treasonable literature." Detroit agents said they had confiscated a bomb which could have destroyed a battleship. Cleveland agents reported they had found a dangerous-looking grayish powder. There was no doubt among federal officials that German spies figured in the conspiracy against the government and the people, according to the *New York Times*.

In Chicago an additional four Socialist publishing houses were raided. As a result of the raids, a spokesman for the Chicago office of the Justice Department announced, not a single IWW, Anarchist, or Socialist publication was being printed in the country. Excellent, replied a *New York Times* editor: "Sedition must stop. The country must protect itself against its enemies at home. The Government has made a good beginning."

Gregory kept a bold face when reporters rushed up to Magnolia to quiz him about the raids. "I was convinced that we were warranted in taking such action as this," he told reporters. "The raids will be followed quickly by indictments if we find anything to warrant them." But when pressed to characterize particular offenses, he was vague. "Sedition," he replied, covering his embarrassment at not knowing what his subordinates were doing.

In fact, no one in the Justice Department seemed to know precisely what the charge was against the IWW. George Anderson immediately dashed off another letter to the Justice Department asking just what the legal nature of the proceedings directed or advised by the Department had been, what charges had been made, and what evidence adduced. The evidence, replied Assistant Attorney General William L. Frierson, "is of such a varied character and is so great in mass that this Department cannot give you any summary of it."

Indictments of members of the Socialist party were to be based on conspiracy to violate the Espionage Act, while those against the IWW members were to be based on conspiracy to prevent by force the execution of the laws of the United States. Meanwhile, APL lawyers in Chicago were feverishly sorting out the evidence, helping the United States Attorney to construct a case which might hold up before the grand jury. The raids had been only a fishing expedition. They hoped somewhere in the mass of letters, pamphlets, and lists to find enough evidence to convince a grand jury that indictments should be brought. Considering that newspaper headlines had already branded the arrested men dangerous conspirators, it didn't have to be very convincing evidence. By now it was generally accepted that grand juries had a patriotic duty to support the actions of the Justice Department.

It took over three weeks for the APL lawyers to piece together a story of conspiracy. On September 28, 166 IWW members were indicted. Wobblies asked Clarence Darrow to defend them as he had defended labor radicals Eugene Debs, Bill Haywood, and John J. McNamara. Darrow later was to work for the IWW, but in 1917 he sent word that he was too busily engaged in Washington on "war work."

The *Literary Digest*, in summing up reaction to the raids, accurately noted that the American press did not appear to regard the raids as "one of those tyrannical persecutions of the downtrodden, such as our Republic was founded to prevent." The *Chicago Daily News* echoed the nationwide conspiracy theory; the *Grand Rapids News* found the "strong arm of the law" eminently fitting treatment; the *Louisville Times* said "no national achievement could have awakened the pride and the interest" that the raids had kindled in the people; the *Portland Oregonian* described the raids as the government taking its knife in hand at the right moment to operate on the IWW, an operation which gratified "every loyal American heart." It therefore took daring for a newspaper such as the *Detroit Free Press* to counsel: "There is need for prudence on the part of the representatives of the Department of Justice—all the more need, perhaps, because any tendency to go beyond their actual authority is likely to be condoned by public opinion. In the wholesale onslaught there may be disregard of Constitutional and statutory provisions, unless Washington uses expert generalship, and . . . the country cannot afford to have its Constitutional safeguards overridden in order to catch the seditious or the criminal, nor are extra-legal methods necessary. It is hoped that while the Government proceeds vigorously in routing what has all the stigmas of a widespread and pernicious plot against the United States and its people, the authorities will take a little extra care just at this time in proceeding strictly within the limits allowed by the basic law. In the end the clean-up will be more complete and more permanent for such care."

Even pro-Administration liberals hesitated to criticize. "If such a conspiracy is established, the country will have reason to be grateful to the Department of Justice for its trenchant vigor in striking down a national peril," said a *New Republic* editor, before going on to hint that action on the part of unpatriotic employers who harassed laborers as in the Bisbee deportations might also be a peril. Conspiracies to harass the government by reckless and disloyal fomenting of strikes should be put down with a "strong hand," but raids should be used with the utmost discrimination, the editorial continued. Still, the editor went on, the Department of Justice had given "refreshing evidence that at least one arm of the Government has a clear-cut labor policy." This may have been a hint that the War Department do something to put Frankfurter's plan into action, but it certainly was no vigorous defense of civil liberties.

Radicals were a bit more explicit in their criticism than were liberal reformers. "My law-abiding neck gets very warm under its law-abiding collar these days at the extraordinary violations of fundamental laws which are being put over," Walter Nelles wrote to Max Eastman, Socialist editor of *The Masses*. At the urging of Nelles, the American Union Against Militarism had already sent a long bill of particulars against the Justice Department to Wilson, charging that Department agents had broken up meetings of conscientious objectors and were bringing criminal charges against persons engaged in lawful opposition to the draft law.

Wilson went to Gregory with the complaint, and, as usual, Gregory went to Bielaski. Noting that his agents were accused of breaking up meetings in Chicago, Bielaski went to Clabaugh. The offenders had been APL men, Clabaugh admitted to Bielaski. But, he continued, there was so much work for his regular agents that he needed the help of the volunteers and could not afford to lose their support. Once again Bielaski accepted the excuse and once again made his defense of the APL to Gregory. And once again Gregory accepted that defense.

Gregory replied to Wilson's inquiries about the charges of the American Union Against Militarism on September 13 with a complete exoneration of his volunteers and the Bureau of Investigation. "While some few isolated instances of excess of zeal are shown," Gregory said, the charges relating to matters coming under his jurisdiction were "without substantial merit." In Chicago, the only rebuke Clabaugh delivered was to his own agents. Reports had reached him that agents referred to Leaguers as "voluntary detectives" and "greenhorns." Such "slurring or insulting remarks, with reference to any member of the American Protective League, will result in the immediate suspension and possible dismissal from the service of the person making it," he warned. In the face of this defense of the APL, civil libertarians backed down. The AUAM did little further in defense of civil liberties because their members feared retaliation for their accusations.

Wilson did take the time to write to Max Eastman on September 18 with an apology for the actions of the Administration regarding opposition to the war. "I can only say that a line must be drawn and that we are trying, it may be clumsily but genuinely, to draw it without fear or favor or prejudice," Wilson said. But within a few weeks, the President had reverted to distrust of criticism and was urging Gregory to prosecute the editor of *The People's Counselor* for treason, because, he said, "one conviction would probably scotch a great many snakes."

For the next year APL lawyers in Chicago lent Clabaugh their support and encouragement while he prepared evidence in the case against the IWW conspirators. But the trial was anticlimactic. In reality, the September raids had already crushed the dissident organization, providing the first major victory for the home front army. League members had been disappointed to find no spies, but the victory over the labor radicals rekindled their enthusiasm for battle. They now needed a new enemy.

Secretary of State Lansing provided it by releasing a batch of documents to the press, including a letter from German Ambassador von Bernstorff in which he had requested authority from his government to influence Congress through American pacifist organizations. What organizations? No one knew. And since no one knew, everyone could join the game of denouncing his enemies. Congressmen accused each other. Anyone who had opposed the war or any of the Administration's war measures was now suspect. "SPIES ARE EVERYWHERE," shrilled the *New York Tribune*.

In what Lewis Mumford called the "fumy" atmosphere of war, the "patriotism complex" was being born. By fall, the doctrine of the single, indivisible nation was being preached, the cult of the united front assembled, and a "patriotic" inquisition, with imprisonment and torture of "heretics," was being advocated. All pacifists were traitors, all patriots, chivalrous heroes who went about slaying the dragon of spydom. "During the war," Mumford recalled, "men were sent to jail for their convictions; they were asked to lecture upon patriotism for their suspicions."

Had reformers not been so anxious to influence the Administration from within, to help guide the war, they might have been quicker to grasp the true significance of the ruthless suppression of the IWW dissent and more critical of the Justice Department's tactics. Certainly conservatives were quick to seize opportunities to suppress dissenters once dissent was labeled treason. Said the *New York Times,* "If Germany was spending money to organize disloyalty within the United States when she was at peace with us, she most certainly did not become high-minded and stop it the moment she went to war with us." The *Times* pursued this logic further. Germany would no longer purchase strikes and dynamite factories; she would aim at creating a false public opinion in favor of laying down our arms. "When we find a movement in the United States which duplicates the moves from Berlin, it is safe to assume that Germany is backing it in the same way in which she backed other movements . . . on former occasions." "What the nation demands," said the *Cleveland Plain Dealer,* "is that treason, whether thinly veiled or quite unmasked, be stamped out."

The new definition of treason spread. At a dinner given by the Authors' Club at Princeton, a speaker argued that anyone who put destructive material into the minds of American citizens by urging them to be disloyal or recalcitrant should be shot like a saboteur. According to this simple analogy—so serviceable that it would still be in use fifty years later—these men were obstructing the Ship of State in the same way saboteurs would jam the machinery of a ship; they imperiled the unity, welfare, and success of the country. "Upon conviction, shooting will be too honorable a punishment to inflict upon such criminals," he went on, for they imperiled the lives of loyal citizens and the safety of the Republic. "A man who by speech or action endeavors to impede America's efficiency in this righteous war should be judged by the law, and if convicted, promptly hung."

George Harvey, conservative editor of the *North American Review,* a one-time supporter who had been soured by Wilson's domestic reforms, spoke for those who applauded the suppression of dissent. "We regard with profound satisfaction and a most buoyant heartening the President's vigorous action against the IWW and other disloyal troublers of the land. Thank God for what has already been done, though late, and let us pray that the good work will go unsparingly on." Then he offered his wartime definition of treason: Treason, said Harvey "is anything which hampers our Government in its prosecution of the war. It is anything which impairs the efficiency of our military establishment or deprives it of necessary supplies. It is also anything which is designed to embarrass our relations with our allies, or to injure them." The trustees of Columbia University agreed. They dismissed professors James McKeen Cattell, Henry Wadsworth Longfellow Dana, and Leon Fraser for traitorous activities.

Dana, a professor of literature, had encouraged students to oppose conscription when the Selective Service bill was before Congress. Cattell, a psychology professor, had criticized military preparedness before the war, opposed entry of the United States into war, and then petitioned three congressmen to support pending legislation which would exempt conscientious objectors from combat service abroad. Both men had previously criticized the administration of the university and its trustees; so when Congressman Julius Kahn protested about Cattell to President Nicholas Murray Butler, the latter took the opportunity to rid the university of the presence of these dissenters by charging them with treason and sedition. Leon Fraser, who had formerly worked for Butler as a peace propagandist and made the mistake of continuing his pacifist work after the declaration of war, was also dismissed. "If colleges and universities are not to become breeding grounds of radicalism and socialism," the *New York Times* proclaimed, "it must be recognized that academic freedom has two sides, that freedom to teach is correlative to the freedom to dispense with poisonous teaching," that universities were responsible to "sane public opinion" which held them accountable for "errors of indulgence to the teachers of false doctrines sheltering themselves behind the shibboleth of academic freedom." Historian Charles Beard resigned in protest the following week, asserting that "opinions cannot be changed by curses or bludgeons."

Here was a cause upon which members of the academic community might have built some guidelines for Wilson and the Justice Department. At least they might have done some probing into the uses to which patriotism was being prostituted; into how, with lip service to the goal of unity, old defenses against arbitrary interference in the life of individuals were being torn down.

John Dewey, who had witnessed the dismissal of his colleagues at Columbia, at least made a try. "Treason," he wrote, had become "every opinion and belief which irritates the majority of loyal citizens." The reason, he said, might be that loyalty was being solicited into paths of bigotry to accomplish private ends, that "would-be leaders and noisy leagues" were helping to promote disunion through distrust, and that "bigots of patriotism" were causing intolerance. Or, he went on, possibly there was another reason: Perhaps intolerance was merely the result of Americans' being new to war, of their being eager beginners; perhaps getting into war had upset their equilibrium. He preferred the latter interpretation, that intolerance was only a deviation from the path of democracy. He concluded that "some of our intolerance to diversity of opinion and our willingness to suppress the civil liberties of democracy is merely part of the rush to mobilization which, thank heaven, had to be improvised because of our historic and established antimilitarism." Positive achievement, he felt confident, would restore sanity to the American people.

Meanwhile, however, Dewey did caution liberals who believed in the war to be "more aggressive than they have been in their opposition to those reactionaries who also believe in war—and who believe that loud denunciation of treason on sight is the best way to regain a political prestige of hate badly discredited . . . let the liberal who for expediency's sake would passively tolerate invasions of free speech and action, take counsel lest he be also preparing the way for a later victory of domestic Toryism."

A month earlier, as Dewey had complacently written that there was nothing to fear for freedom of speech, the APL was preparing its IWW raids. Now, as he cautioned liberals to be on guard, the APL was again on the march. It was preparing for total war against those who still insisted on their right to dissent.

The Bounty Hunters

In the fall of 1917, the nature of America's involvement in World War I changed. Seventeen thousand Russian soldiers, tired of war and responsive to the Bolshevik peace campaign, had to be disarmed by the Allies and shipped homeward to ports on the Black Sea. Italians were mauled by Austro-German forces at Caporetto. The British were being slaughtered in Flanders. Heretofore, Wilson had clung to the hope that Americans would not fight in large numbers in Europe. Industrial mobilization, yes. In fact, his complicity in the suppression of labor radicals stemmed at least in part from his fear that otherwise they might seriously slow the process.

Now, however, he faced the prospect of ordering large numbers of American troops sent overseas immediately to replace the disaffected Russians and to reinforce the crumbling English lines. Possibly war might even have to be declared on Austria-Hungary so that American troops could fight in Italy. American military forces would play a decisive role in Europe soon. There would be no way to escape the general slaughter.

This was the first war in which young American men had no choice about participating. Even under Civil War conscription, a substitute could be bought, but Crowder's plan of conscription included all—rich and poor, alien and citizen, pacifist and jingoist. It was inevitable that there would be men who opposed the draft on principle, men who evaded it for selfish reasons, and men who found the new regimentation incomprehensible. Crowder would brook no opposition, however, nor were most Americans prepared to make distinctions among opponents of the draft. Any man who objected became a deserter in popular terminology, just as any man who opposed war measures became a traitor. Behind the popular confusion, as usual, lay indecisiveness on the part of the federal government as to where to draw the line in punishing these men. And as usual, the APL was willing to become the chief instrument in drawing the line.

Provost Marshal Crowder gave the APL an added incentive. During the Civil War, any man who failed to report for service had been treated as a deserter, and Crowder adopted the same policy in September of 1917, but to this he added a unique twist. State governors were advised not only that any man who failed to report for duty could be declared a deserter, but that the War Department would pay a bounty of fifty dollars for his delivery to the nearest army camp. If the man was inducted, the fifty dollars came out of his first paycheck. If the deserter was prosecuted instead, the War Department footed the bill. Posters soon began to appear throughout the country reading: "$50.00 REWARD for the Arrest and Delivery of John Doe DESERTER FROM THE ARMY OF THE UNITED STATES, who was drafted into the National Army ... and having failed to so report, is now charged with being a deserter from the Army of the United States."

The Justice Department, realizing that Bureau of Investigation agents might utilize their jobs to profit by the bounty directly or arrange to have someone outside the Department collect it, issued a bulletin warning them against either practice. But APL members could collect the reward. So, too, could state and county officials who were also perfectly free to work in collaboration with the APL. Moreover, neither the Justice Department nor the War Department had made clear exactly who was a deserter.

At first special agents interpreted "deserter" to mean anyone who had not appeared for his physical. Then in October, 1917, when the War Department realized how many men had not reported, it narrowed the term to mean only men who, having qualified physically, had not reported for military duty.

Draft boards could overcome this new restriction easily enough, however. A man who did not register could be automatically reclassified from "delinquent" to "deserter." As for a man who had not appeared for his physical, his local board could order him to camp. If he did not then report for mobilization, he could be labeled a deserter, subject to military law, with a fifty-dollar price on his head. As Crowder himself said, "Delinquency might ripen into desertion."

To Crowder's rule that a deserter could be summarily arrested by any civilian merely on order of a military officer the Justice Department added the provision that any state or local law enforcement officer or any Bureau of Investigation agent could arrest a deserter without a warrant. Once this principle was accepted, every man could be considered a possible deserter, free game for the APL.

It was still up to the local boards to determine whether individual men were willful or nonwillful deserters and whether they should be sent to army camps to face court-martial or just kept on the eligible list. Since local boards did not often distinguish between conscientious objectors and mere draft dodgers, men with religious or philosophical convictions against war could be delivered up for court-martial; and under the bounty system almost four thousand conscientious objectors, most of them native born, were sent to camps where they often became the objects of sadistic attacks by other soldiers.

Treatment of these conscientious objectors varied with the attitude of the commanding generals. A man like General Leonard Wood at Camp Funston, who considered conscientious objectors frauds, refused even to consider complaints against mistreatment. Generally, military officer or any Bureau of Investigation agent could arrest a deserter tried by courts-martial, only one was acquitted. The rest received sentences ranging from months to life imprisonment. One—a Socialist—was even sentenced to death.

Punishment decreed by the United States military for these men was more extreme than in either England or Germany; it gave the newly formed National Civil Liberties Bureau (later the American Civil Liberties Union) its first cause célèbre. NCLB leaders—among them Norman Thomas, Roger Baldwin, John Nevin Sayre, Lucille Millner—appealed to the War Department for an investigation of the treatment of conscientious objectors.

When word reached Secretary of War Baker in December of the treatment being meted out to conscientious objectors, he decreed that all men who had personal scruples against war—not just those few religious sects, like the Mennonites, already recognized as legitimately exempt from making war—would be considered conscientious objectors and segregated in camps. As a former pacifist, Baker took a personal interest in the fate of the conscientious objectors and reviewed all court-martial proceedings. Although about twelve hundred men were sent to prison for refusing any form of military service, most C.O.'s were furloughed to farms. None were executed, and none of the long sentences were carried out.

Whenever Baker intervened, treatment would improve. When he did not, or after he had, subordinates subverted his policies. And Crowder's system went on. Outside the camps, the draft boards continued their devious ways. From the beginning, the burden of proof was on the young man to show that he had complied with the law. APL men adopted the illegal practice of stopping a man, asking for his registration card, and detaining him while local boards checked their records. But what complaints did arise were directed for the most part against the draft boards, not the APL.

Late in October, Bielaski asked the League to help investigate members of draft boards themselves. By December APL reports had convinced Wilson that the draft organization was being used for political purposes. To continue to leave the draft machinery under state control seemed to increase the danger of favoritism and inequity in its application and partisanship in its purpose, something Wilson had earlier specifically condemned in his analysis of the enforcement of Civil War conscription.

It was clear by now that the haste and ruthlessness with which the first mobilization had been conducted had been entirely unnecessary. The War Department could not process and train competently all the men rushed to cantonments. Throughout the summer, the Department had operated under a cloak of secrecy while Secretary Baker fed the public with optimistic but vague speeches about the great progress underway. Now the truth was being sent home from camp in every recruit's letters: Many men had neither arms nor equipment with which to train. Epidemics of measles and pneumonia were sweeping through the tent camps. The War Department halted the draft while, with the encouragement of Congress, it investigated the training program.

At the same time, Gregory began to grope toward a more efficient organization of the Justice Department. He decided to establish a War Emergency Division which would be responsible for the enforcement of all war-related legislation and would keep a tighter reign on the energetic Bielaski, his agents, and the volunteers. The Justice Department was not to be led into raids as it had been in September.

To head the new division, Gregory brought in John Lord O'Brian, a progressive Republican from Buffalo who had been United States Attorney in New York and had gained a reputation as an expert in constitutional law. O'Brian later said he was brought into the Justice Department to strengthen the civilian arm of the government in securing the internal safety of the country, and to coordinate war work. But O'Brian entered the Justice Department unheralded. Gregory made no public announcement of this buttressing of civil law, nor did he outline O'Brian's duties.

One of O'Brian's first jobs was to decide what the future relationship of the APL should be to the Justice Department. After the war, O'Brian would say he was opposed to the use of volunteer spies in peacetime; but in 1917 the country was at war, and its army of home front defenders was already in the field, headed by a volunteer commander anxious to move his headquarters to Washington.

With the IWW raids over, Briggs had begun to look around for a new target. Invitations came from several federal departments, including one to work with Herbert Hoover in tracking down violators of the food laws. But the most attractive offer came from Colonel Ralph Van Dieman, head of the Military Intelligence. He asked that the APL help with the increasing number of investigations assigned to his section by the War Department involving the civilian population. Van Dieman was willing to bestow a commission on whoever headed the Washington office and to use this man for liaison between the War Department and the APL. It was this proposed move which O'Brian had to consider almost as soon as he arrived in Washington.

Briggs had already discussed Van Dieman's proposition with Chicago APL chief Daniel Frey and his associate, Victor Elting. After considerable debate, the three men decided to form a triumvirate, each of them to be equal in power as a national director. They would move the APL headquarters to Washington and command the ever-growing army from there. Once in Washington, they could establish relations with all the federal departments and offer their services to all.

Frey, a young advertising executive, agreed to accept the responsibility for liaison with the War Department—and the commission—while Elting, a successful Chicago attorney, was to manage the new office. Briggs planned to spend most of his time in the field, where he could direct the formation of new APL units and inspect old ones. Before moving east, however, Frey and Elting took a quick trip to Washington to obtain the approval of the Justice Department and to request that they be allowed to set up their offices within the Bureau of Investigation. For that, they needed an interview with O'Brian.

O'Brian had already asked Bielaski for a complete report on his volunteers when Frey and Elting arrived in Washington early in November. The APL, Bielaski estimated, now had over twelve hundred separate city units, all organized geographically and by industries, according to an elaborate organizational plan developed by Frey and Elting for the Chicago division and imposed on all other cities at the beginning of August. Frey brought to Washington copies of the Chicago handbook of regulations, which he had distributed to all members; he brought copies of the bulletins with which he had lectured members on proper conduct; and he brought an impressive organizational manual containing street maps of each Chicago division, complete with lists of captains and lieutenants. Frey and Elting proposed to O'Brian that this tightly organized system worked out for Chicago be expanded to the rest of the divisions and that the national headquarters of the APL be turned into a policy-making unit rather than simply an organizing bureau.

Almost against his will, O'Brian was impressed by the two dapper Chicagoans and their organizational plan. Briggs, somewhat a salesman type, might be suspected of not being able to manage such a far-flung organization as proposed; but these two men were impressive in appearance and background. Frey, a native of Denver, Colorado, had been in art and advertising with the *Chicago Evening Post* and now headed his own advertising company, a business he described as "producing ideas, copy and illustrations for magazines, newspapers, national advertisers, advertising agencies and book publishers." Eminently successful in this advertising venture, at thirty-one he was already established comfortably, both financially and socially. He belonged to the Chicago Press Club, the Navy League, the Red Cross, the Masons, and the Republican Party. He came to Washington with letters of introduction to Mark Sullivan, then with *Collier's Weekly*, and to Walter Lippmann, Assistant Secretary of War. Somewhat boyish in appearance, Frey had a youthful enthusiasm which he had directed toward organizing and marshaling his Chicago division and which he now promised to channel toward making the national League more efficient.

National Headquarters,
American Protective League,
Washington, D.C.

National Directors,
American Protective League
Left to right:
Charles Daniel Frey,
Albert M. Briggs,
Victor Elting

Frey's associate, Victor Elting, was probably the man who most impressed O'Brian. A New Yorker like O'Brian, Elting had been born in Yonkers, attended Columbia University, and then received his law degree from the University of Michigan. Drawn to Chicago by the prospects of the growing industrial center, he had opened a law office there in 1892 and in the years before the war had combined his law practice with civic reform activities. He was Chairman of the Board of Trustees of the Chicago School of Civics and Philanthropy, trustee of the Bureau of Public Efficiency, director of the National Housing Association, president of the City Homes Association, and a director of the Winnetka State Bank. Like Frey, he belonged to a host of clubs and the Republican Party. Always impeccably dressed, restrained, precise in speech and writing, he lent an air of respectability to the volunteer army and promised responsibility.

With these men now commanding the APL—and they gave the impression that they were definitely in command—any opposition O'Brian might have had to the use of volunteer spies disappeared. He did, however, block the directors' plan to move into the Justice Department, and he insisted on certain reforms.

Although the APL was to remain affiliated with the Justice Department, O'Brian wanted it entirely separated administratively from the Bureau of Investigation. Members were not to be enrolled as special agents of the Bureau, and special agents were no longer to head city APL units. The three national directors were to assume complete responsibility for the internal affairs of the League. They were to attempt to retrieve as many "Secret Service" badges as possible and see that members no longer used them. All recruiting literature and office stationery with these words was to be destroyed. Members were to be instructed carefully about their status as purely voluntary workers who had no federal power and who must not attempt to usurp any. Arrests were not to be made. The volunteer soldier on the home front was to secure information and to transmit it to the Bureau of Investigation, nothing else. Although the branches were to have considerable autonomy, individual members were to be subject to firmer control. Thus reformed, the APL was to be allowed to set up camp in Washington and to expand throughout the rest of the country.

Such reforms seemed to reflect a trend within the Administration. Both Wilson and Colonel House appeared willing to listen more readily to complaints about the treatment of radicals. Liberals outside the government claimed November as a month in which Wilson showed more interest in civil liberties. "I think I see in the words and acts from Washington already some effect of my appeal for more tolerance, less 'patriotism,' " Lincoln Steffens wrote to his wife on November 1, 1917, although he still classed Gregory, Burleson, and McAdoo as "war-mad."

On November 12, Wilson issued his first warning against mob violence, one which liberals had waited for since the July race riots in East St. Louis. "I have been very much distressed, my fellow citizens," Wilson told an American Federation of Labor convention at Buffalo, "by some of the things that have happened recently. The mob spirit is displaying itself here and there in the country," he said, comparing the mobs to Anarchists as a manifestation of "the unwillingness to cooperate." His words reassured some.

But not all. A careful analysis of Wilson's speech led Walter Nelles to rightly observe that although Wilson had condemned those taking law into their own hands, he had been silent on the question of free discussion versus suppression of dissent. He made no promises regarding the Administration's future action when he denounced lawlessness on the part of citizens.

Indeed, little consolation could be drawn by civil libertarians or radicals from the President's pronouncements. The *Official Bulletin*, published by the federal government to inform the country about wartime policies, continued to print telegrams, letters, and rumors accusing German officials of engaging in propaganda, espionage, and sabotage. The State Department released more documents; the Navy Department added reports of suspected sabotage. McAdoo sent letters regularly to Gregory containing rumors of disloyalty. The Postmaster General suppressed socialist and radical magazines. In Illinois the People's Council, which had been formed to oppose conscription and suppression of civil liberties in wartime, was driven out of existence by troops of the Illinois National Guard, with Justice Department agents participating.

On November 21 the Attorney General delivered a bitter denunciation of Germany and said of disloyal men, "May God have mercy on them for they need expect none from an outraged people and an avenging government."

And with Gregory's blessing, the APL continued in its own role of avenger. Frey and Elting were delighted with the new arrangements and called a meeting of the seventy-five hundred Chicago members to solicit funds for financing the move to Washington. They invited Lieutenant Sousa to bring down his Great Lakes Naval Training Station Band. They cautioned members to maintain absolute secrecy about the meeting and promised prominent speakers. To encourage participation, Frey dispatched a bulletin telling them, "The assistance and information furnished by [the APL] in connection with the registrations and violations of the draft law have alone fully justified its existence."

In his speech to the assembled members Frey elaborated the theory of the APL. Beginning with the statement that "espionage is repugnant to the American people," he went on to argue that this very repugnance was the reason the government was depending on the loyal volunteers of the APL, who he estimated now numbered 250,000. Reviewing his trip to Washington, he emphasized the friendly welcome both he and Elting had received at the Justice Department and asked for a hundred thousand dollars to finance the League. Having obtained pledges totaling seventy-five thousand dollars, he and Elting and Briggs packed their bags and moved to Washington.

It was late November when the APL directors set up their headquarters in the capital. Gregory welcomed the volunteers with a letter to Briggs terming the APL a "most valuable auxiliary to the Bureau of Investigation." Bielaski added his greetings in an official letter of praise for their past work. In his *Annual Report* to Congress, Gregory discussed the importance of the work of the APL, asserting that membership was carefully guarded, that only leading men in each community were admitted, that they took no decisive action, only reported on situations in their localities, and that they were entirely self-supporting.

Thus with praise and plaudits, the APL established a beachhead in Washington. Headquarters were in an old baroque building on I Street. Frey received his army commission. With his volunteers marshaled in force, Gregory could now challenge the continuation by the Secret Service of security investigations.

Gregory was more firmly convinced than ever that the Secret Service should withdraw from the home front war. Recently, William Bayard Hale had complained to Wilson that Secret Service agents had used rough and brutal tactics and attempted to seduce his secretary. After an investigation by his Bureau agents, Gregory concluded that Secret Service agents had indeed been at fault. Moreover, he discovered that the Secret Service had carved out quite a bit of investigative territory for themselves. To their State Department work they had added investigations for the Bureau of War Risks and for Herbert Hoover's Food Administration. Bureau of Investigation agents on the trail of violators of food regulations in Chicago discovered eight

Secret Service men investigating the same case. Upon inquiry by the Justice Department, Hoover confirmed that agents from the Treasury Department had been very active in these investigations. He apologized for the confusion, for being "so little informed about the borderland of the two fields of activities." It seemed to him, however, that a solution could be found if the Justice Department would only discuss the problem with the Treasury.

That was precisely what Gregory's animosity toward McAdoo rendered him incapable of doing. Instead of going to McAdoo directly, Gregory gathered together all the information on the Secret Service investigations and complained at the Cabinet meeting of November 16. The need for cooperation was evident, but no one could offer a solution satisfactory to the belligerents.

The Cabinet did apparently agree that Gregory should compromise on the issue of food-hoarding investigations, for the Justice Department ordered its men off the job in December. In the future, APL rumors of food-hoarding would be reported to Bureau agents, who would pass the reports on to Secret Service men.

But sanctioning this small field of operation did not satisfy McAdoo, who managed to regain Wilson's attention with his repeated demands for coordination. "I was a bit distressed by the discussion in Cabinet the other day," Wilson wrote to McAdoo two days later. "It made me feel derelict in not having sought a remedy at the time you suggested it, though I must say I am still in doubt as to what the best remedy is." At the same time, Wilson forwarded a report on the Hale complaint against the Secret Service.

In reply, McAdoo protested that the attitude of the Secret Service had been "scrupulously correct," that it had not intentionally encroached on territory of the Bureau of Investigation. Jealousy, he stated, was not a factor in his work. To withdraw the Secret Service from wartime investigations, he warned Wilson, would be "very hurtful to the public interest." Instead, he volunteered to devise a plan for more effective coordination of investigations.

Gregory continued his attack, writing to McAdoo on November 28 that Secret Service agents had interfered with Bureau of Investigation work. McAdoo replied curtly that he was looking into the matter; then two days later he forwarded a complaint about a New York counterfeit suspect who had escaped and asked for any facts relating to the Secret Service. A week later Gregory admitted to McAdoo that two assistant United States attorneys in New York had bungled that case: one had been reprimanded, the other, asked to resign.

Meanwhile, Wilson's attention was diverted from the battle between his Cabinet members by matters of greater import. His conviction was growing that the United States must declare war on the Austro-Hungarian Empire, although Secretary of State Lansing admitted on November 20, 1917, that the United States did not have "a very strong case against Austria so far as hostile acts are concerned." It seemed to Lansing to come down "very largely to a matter of having at large and free to act a very considerable body of Austrian subjects in this country."

A week later, Alexander Konta, a Hungarian nationalist, forwarded Wilson a long indictment of Austrian participation in espionage activities. The sympathizers of Germany, Konta said, "were perhaps more dangerous to our welfare" than even the German aliens because they plotted under the "cloak of non-enemy nationality," while the United States was powerless to punish these "maldoers," and thus the defenses at home were left in "dangerous insecurity." He urged that Wilson risk injustice to loyal Austro-Hungarians rather than allow disloyal ones to pursue their "nefarious activities" unmolested. Wilson thanked journalist Frank I. Cobb, who had forwarded Konta's letter: "It concerns a matter which has deeply concerned me and I am mighty glad to have this detailed discussion of it in all its aspects."

Four days later, Wilson asked for a declaration of war against the Austro-Hungarian Empire. Congress complied quickly, thereby adding several million new enemy aliens and potential spies to the home front battle.

The first action of the Justice Department, after it had arrested Austro-Hungarians suspected of being potentially dangerous, was to instruct its Bureau agents as to the status of the APL. Implementing O'Brian's new regulations, the Bureau of Investigation ordered superintendents to stop the volunteers from making illegal arrests and to strip APL men of any commissions they still held as special agents. Clabaugh dutifully sent a formal note to Frey: "I beg respectfully to remind you that no member of the American Protective League has any authority to arrest or detain any person or take any action whatsoever which involves governmental activity." And Frey dutifully warned members: "You have not the right to stop a man and ask to see his registration card, nor to detain him, or to cause him any inconvenience whatsoever . . . you are not to apprehend, or in any way disturb, or inconvenience, a possible deserter, but report your suspicions or such information as you may have to Mr. Clabaugh, and upon his request, should he so desire, you will complete your investigation, turning over the information gathered for such action as Mr. Clabaugh may deem necessary." In the future, according to General Bulletin No. 3 to all members: "No member of the League will stop and interview any persons upon the street, or elsewhere in connection with registration or other matters, unless he is working on a specific investigation properly assigned to him."

Members were incredulous to learn that they actually had no federal authority. Some wrote to the Justice Department to see if the report was really true. Bear in mind, O'Brian replied to one, "that members are not Government officers and are not officially connected with this Department." But, of course, such warnings had been issued before. Most Leaguers continued to conduct themselves much as they had in the past. In New York, APL'ers visited Roger Baldwin, head of the NCLB, in January and told him they were federal agents. When Baldwin protested to Bielaski, the Bureau chief replied that members had no right to represent themselves as Justice Department employees. It made little difference what O'Brian or Bielaski might say, however; they continued to recognize the APL as their auxiliary.

The directors did not collect the APL badges; they simply ordered operatives not to use them "except when approaching one who cannot read English." They ordered members not to use the new credentials to secure exemption from laws and ordinances. Moreover, loss of identification cards would be regarded "as evidence of the unfitness of such member to possess such credentials." They asked members to destroy all old "Secret Service" letterhead stationery. Where members had obtained the franking privilege, it was withdrawn. Meanwhile, Bielaski recruited new men who had legal training, linguistic knowledge, or investigating experience to replace the discharged APL members as special agents.

Such half-hearted attempts at reform satisfied Gregory. He was now ready to recommend to all volunteer groups who asked for investigative jobs that they contact the APL and apply to it for recognition. He intended to have the APL and the Bureau of Investigation monopolize the defense of the home front.

Gregory had yet to convince the Treasury Department, however. Chief William Flynn, head of the Secret Service, began the year 1918 by launching a publicity campaign to compel the consolidation of intelligence forces which McAdoo had requested and which many Americans were convinced was necessary. To dramatize his position Flynn resigned, calling in reporters and telling them he had not received the cooperation of the Justice Department. "Discord Forced Flynn out of the Secret Service," read one headline the following day. The *New York Times,* under the banner "Seek Co-ordination of Secret Services," announced that "the Government has suffered to a considerable extent as a result of jealousies which have arisen in the secret services." It claimed that the Secret Service had conducted all the IWW investigations while the Bureau of Investigation had taken the credit, and concluded, "That this announcement did not please the Secret Service is well known in Government circles." Assistant Attorney General Charles Warren clipped the items and sent them to Gregory, suggesting he make a public denial of the "misstatements" to prevent "great public misapprehension." Before the Attorney General could do so, McAdoo followed up the publicity with another denunciation of the APL.

McAdoo now emphasized the danger of the APL to the government as well as to the citizen. He had no special interest in whether a German spy was caught by a special agent of the Department of Justice, a Secret Service operative, a Post Office Department inspector, or any other investigating agent, McAdoo told Gregory. He was interested only in seeing that German spies were caught. McAdoo explained that he had not pursued his plan for coordination because Gregory had objected so strenuously and had criticized the Secret Service.

He insisted that Secret Service agents be allowed to investigate violations of wartime legislation and that a central intelligence bureau be established to delegate investigations among the various intelligence groups in the federal government. Evidence of need for this bureau, he argued, was the continued use of the APL by the Justice Department. As for the APL, McAdoo went on, "I am frank to say that if I were a German spy I should want nothing better than the opportunity of joining this organization, getting one of its 'Secret Service' badges, and carrying on my nefarious activities under the guise of this organization." Many abuses had arisen out of the "unfortunate situation created by this voluntary organization." McAdoo concluded, "No voluntary organization should in my opinion be entrusted with power of this character, which can be irresponsibly exercised with resultant injustices of the gravest sort to the people."

McAdoo's idea for a central intelligence agency was now receiving considerable support both within and outside the Wilson Administration. A precedent had been set when criticism of other departments had led Wilson to consolidate and centralize the direction of industrial mobilization. Colonel House urged Wilson to continue this centralization and develop a real "war machine." Even Justice Louis Brandeis believed a central intelligence bureau to be an absolute necessity.

McAdoo's indictment of the APL and Flynn's much-publicized resignation had little effect in the Justice Department, however. Bielaski, reading to Elting extracts of the letter Gregory received from McAdoo, assured the APL director that McAdoo was greatly mistaken regarding the League, having received all his information from the Secret Service. Gregory, for his part, told O'Brian, "I am not disposed to continue to quarrel with the Treasury Department about details. . . . I must at the same time in a general way at least express my non-acquiescence in a number of the propositions [Mc-Adoo] has advanced to sustain certain activities of the Secret Service of the Treasury."

While opposing expansion of the Secret Service, Gregory continued to encourage expansion of the APL by mergers with patriotic groups throughout the country. Quietly, the APL began plans to absorb one of the largest such groups in the country, the American Defense Society.

Among the national organizations devoted to stamping out "disloyalty," none had better financial and political backing than the ADS. Formed with the support of Theodore Roosevelt, Leonard Wood, and a group of wealthy Republicans who had pledged their fortunes to the pursuit of preparedness in 1914, the ADS had led the movement for "one hundred percent Americanism." With Theodore Roosevelt as its honorary president and former Attorney General Charles J. Bonaparte as one of the honorary vice-presidents, the ADS always retained the aura of a "Roosevelt-first society" while it preached America first. But as the war went on, it became increasingly ambitious in its self-appointed internal security functions.

The ADS had begun its Americanism campaign with anti-German propaganda, publishing a series of pamphlets, one by Harry Elmer Barnes, then a graduate student of history at Columbia University. It went on to oppose the teaching of German in city schools. It joined a drive for teachers' loyalty oaths, attempted to have Robert La-Follette excluded from the Senate for his antiwar sentiments, crusaded for closure of all German-owned insurance companies in the United States, and enrolled high school students in a Junior ADS. At the end of August, 1917, it had inaugurated an American Vigilance Patrol aimed at putting an end to "seditious street oratory" by having city police arrest speakers on charges of disorderly conduct.

Former Assistant Attorney General James M. Beck, who headed

the antidisloyalty committee, had the assistance of a publicity committee which included Irwin S. Cobb, Hamlin Garland, and Cleveland Moffett. Most members of this committee were also members of the Vigilantes, an organization of writers formed in 1916 to urge assistance to England and France and enlarged in 1917 to present their version of the war issues to the American public. With such experts directing the publicity for its crusades, the ADS had become even more enthusiastic about spy-catching. In November, 1917, it advertised in *Vogue* magazine, asking readers to write or bring in reports of German activities. One of the activities of the society, an ADS official told Military Intelligence officer Nicholas Biddle, was to put a stop to all German influence in America. "We are to have another Secret Service Organization," Biddle had written to his chief, Colonel Van Dieman, after seeing the *Vogue* advertisement. Judging from the illustrous names, it appeared to be a highly patriotic organization he admitted, but added, "The power of these volunteer organizations to do harm is tremendous, and it would seem to me advisable that some steps be taken either to curb or control their activities."

His misgivings were well-founded. From Boston came a complaint to the War Department that the ADS was forming new branches which could be set up by anyone who wanted to report disloyalty in their section and who had a dollar for the membership fee. In a small city in upstate New York, one member began to solicit from businessmen a "federal protection tax."

Van Dieman went to Bielaski to ask if the ADS was working with him or with some other regular government agency, but Bielaski confessed his ignorance. Soon after, Bielaski instructed Frey and Elting to arrange for a conference with ADS leaders to discuss possible absorption of the ADS by the APL, and Frey reported to co-director Briggs that the Justice Department was "doing everything they could to kill the American Defense Society's activities wherever they were interfering with the League." Briggs replied, "I think it is very wise to suggest disbanding while they still have something to disband."

Roosevelt, who kept in close touch with the ADS, defended organized vigilance on the part of nongovernmental groups and felt the APL was too closely identified with the Justice Department. "There are sound arguments both for and against tying up the volunteer vigilance work directly and closely with the Federal government," he wrote to L. B. Hayes. "On the whole I think the arguments against have most weight," he went on, because the work "against the soap-box anarchist and pro-German agitator was undertaken precisely because the

Government was not acting in the matter." Furthermore, the New York police department had told him "of the limitations of the national Government's work along this line."

Limitations, as defined by Roosevelt, were such things as allowing Thorstein Veblen to remain at large after publication of *An Inquiry into the Nature of Peace,* in which Veblen said that the patriotic spirit never rose "to the consummate pitch of enthusiastic abandon except when bent upon some work of concerted malevolence," and that its net contribution to the modern world was "obscuration, distrust, and retardation at every point where it touches the fortunes of modern mankind." An ADS member had reported Veblen to the Society, whereupon Roosevelt wrote to ADS official Richard Hurd, "I quite agree with him that Mr. Thorstein Veblen ought to be in jail. Is there anything that our Society can do in the matter?"

Despite their vaunted independence, the ADS had a yen to share the quasi-official status enjoyed by the APL. Plans for the conference with the APL directors went forward despite Roosevelt's opposition. The Washington representative of the ADS, George Garver, told Elting that his organization "did not regard it necessary to confer with Colonel Roosevelt about it." The conference was scheduled for January 28.

Flynn chose this moment to turn his criticism of the Justice Department into a partisan attack on the Administration. In an interview with the Republican *New York Sun* on January 18, he again advocated unification of all intelligence activities. The *Sun* editorialized, "The evident laxity of the Department of Justice in dealing with the enemy is, we believe, another subject of grave concern, especially in view of what the enemy is doing abroad."

Theodore Roosevelt, in Washington to lend support to critics of the War Department, opened his doors to Flynn, who told the former President that the government needed a unified bureau because German agents were destroying property and jeopardizing lives. That was all Roosevelt needed to hear. He wrote a public letter to Senator George Chamberlain of Oregon, Chairman of the Committee on Military Affairs, endorsing the proposal for a centralized intelligence bureau. The ADS broke off negotiations with the APL to follow the Roosevelt bugle, protesting against the inefficiency and disorganization of the intelligence bureaus and complaining that the Secret Service had been ordered to stop running down German spies, even though other bureaus were undermanned.

Tension rose still higher when C. S. Thompson, an ADS officer, made the astounding announcement that the War Department had already put to death fourteen enemy spies. Provost Marshal General Crowder immediately denied the charge, but the public refused to believe the denial. The ADS announcement only seemed to confirm the suspicions of thousands of Americans already feeding on spy stories dispensed by federal, state, and local governments, and by patriotic organizations. To add to the confusion and conflict among departments, other Administration critics affirmed that the Justice Department had allowed known German spies to remain at large.

Most notorious of the concoctors of spy stories was Australian-born John Rathom, editor of the *Providence* [Rhode Island] *Journal,* who printed a daily warning in his newspaper: "Every German or Austrian in the United States unless known by years of association, should be treated as a spy." In January he had accused the War Department of appointing rabid pacifists—some German—to important posts. Gathering up some of his best spy stories, which he had published during the neutrality period in cooperation with British Intelligence agent Captain Guy Gaunt, he now prepared a series of articles for the *World's Work,* the first of which appeared simultaneously with the ADS spy announcement under the title "Germany's Plots Exposed: The German Spy System from the Inside."

For the first time, the Justice Department decided to act positively against the men who were circulating fake spy stories. The day after Thompson's allegation hit the pages of the *New York Times,* the United States Attorney for New York went up to the offices of the ADS to question Thompson, and three days later he was hailed before a grand jury to prove his tales. On February 9, the grand jury branded them as untrue and based on rumors. Thompson resigned; the APL conference with the ADS was cancelled. ADS official George Garver admitted to Elting that his men had been "very much upset recently" over the episode, but he promised to reinstate arrangements for the conference.

At the same time that Gregory countered Thompson's claims, he also called Rathom before the grand jury in New York to have him questioned about his writings. The Attorney General labeled Rathom's spy stories "pure and unadulterated fabrications," many "outrageously untrue," and threatened to have him indicted for perjury if he lied. Rathom agreed to sign a statement admitting that a number of his stories were without foundation and promised not to repeat them if the Justice Department would not seek an indictment. "I consider Rathom utterly unworthy of belief," Gregory wrote later to the editor of the *Christian Herald* in Boston, "and the most charitable construction which can be put upon his performances is that along certain lines he is mentally deranged."

Yet the public continued to chase phantom spies. Even ex-President William Howard Taft lent his prestige to the spy scare by recommending a firing squad for spies and plotters in a speech before the Congress of National Service. Gregory attempted to counteract the new scare with assurances that the government's defenses were well guarded because he had the cooperation of civilian volunteers. But, as usual, his persecution of dissenters continued. At the very time the Justice Department was attempting to halt the circulation of false spy stories, it was tarring the American radicals Emma Goldman and Alexander Berkman with the brush of espionage.

Emma Goldman and Alexander Berkman had organized a No-conscription League in May, 1917. After a series of protest meetings against the draft, the two were indicted for conspiring to induce men subject to the Selective Service Act to oppose it. In June the Justice Department raided their New York offices, confiscated their records, and hustled them off to jail. While out on bail pending an appeal to the Supreme Court, Goldman toured the country speaking for the "new-born hope" exemplified by Russia. A Greek-American employed as chauffeur, janitor, and handyman by her friends Agnes Inglis and Edith Kern, whom she visited in Ann Arbor, Michigan, was an undercover member of the APL. He attended her meetings, distributed radical pamphlets and literature, and at the same time forwarded to the APL daily reports which the League, in turn, forwarded to the Justice Department. By the time the Supreme Court affirmed the lower court's conviction of Berkman and Goldman in January, 1918, the Justice Department was determined to quell their attempts to gain support for the Bolsheviks. The two were placed under arrest.

When in February, 1918, radicals began to demand the release of Berkman and Goldman, the Justice Department rekindled the spy hysteria in an attempt to defend its own course of action. O'Brian remembered having seen, somewhere in the testimony introduced into a trial in New York involving violations of neutrality acts by East Indians, a letter allegedly written from Amsterdam by the revolutionist Har Dayal to Berkman. "It has occurred to me that [the letter] might be of very great value just now," O'Brian wrote to United States Attorney John C. Knox, "because of the agitation in

Russia as well as here, arousing sympathy for Emma Goldman among the Bolsheviki element. If the letter had a distinctly German taint," O'Brian continued, "and would in any way tend to connect her up even indirectly with the German activities you can readily see that it might have just now extraordinary value."

Knox dug several letters out of the files and sent them on to Washington. O'Brian certainly must have known that he was engaging in just the type of smear campaign that was already inflaming public sentiment and endangering the civil liberties he claimed to be upholding. The United States Attorney in San Francisco was just finishing up the government's case against the East Indians accused of conspiring with German spies to violate United States neutrality. Daily, across the country, newspapers carried the outrageous claims of this over-eager San Francisco prosecutor, who even credited German gold with having built an Indian temple erected in 1905. Yet the Justice Department chose this moment to hand over the letters to George Creel for publication in the *Official Bulletin*, along with a letter from Gregory charging that Goldman and Berkman were "apparently working in conjunction with German spies in foreign countries."

That was all that was needed to spur on the spy scare. The same day that the *Official Bulletin* carried the letters, a *New York Times* headline affirmed, "Berkman in Ring of German Spies." Several days later when Rabindranath Tagore, the Nobel Prize-winning Indian poet, arrived in New York, the *Times* linked his name with German espionage plots on the basis of testimony published by the government in San Francisco. As the Justice Department added to the mounting hysteria, O'Brian went calmly about planning his campaign against the Secret Service.

All the pressure from outside the Administration did not put an end to the vendetta between the Secret Service and the Bureau of Investigation and its volunteers. Under the leadership of O'Brian, the Justice Department now formulated and put into practice a new plan of coordination that would reassert its own supremacy on the home front, restrict the Secret Service, and thus insure that the expansion of the APL would go forward.

O'Brian and Ralph Van Dieman, head of the Military Intelligence, met to work out the details. They decided that O'Brian would write an unofficial letter to all the intelligence services asking them to confer informally at his office three days later. Ostensibly, the meeting was to air the fears of Van Dieman over the possibility of spies returning from Mexico, and to consider establishing a zone at the border from which aliens would be barred. In fact, it was a movement to eliminate the Secret Service from the home front war. The army men proposed weekly meetings in the Justice Department, whereupon the representative of the Secret Service said that since his force had been limited to a definite field, he saw no reason to return. The following Wednesday at 5:00 P.M., the heads of the intelligence services met again, this time without the Secret Service representative. None of the other groups had any objection to the APL. Indeed, they encouraged its continuation; and the Secret Service, McAdoo's squad, was out of the action.

Gregory called the commanders of his volunteer army into conference shortly thereafter to discuss the criticism directed at the League by the Secret Service. He told them that the League was constantly the object of vicious attacks and asked them if they had discontinued issuing badges and eliminated the words "Secret Service" from their literature. The directors assured him that these instructions had been carried out. But since members needed proper identification, the directors asked permission to submit a design for a new badge. Previously, O'Brian had objected to any credentials which would carry the words "United States Department of Justice" and had told the directors that he did not think Gregory would approve a new badge. On February 8, however, disregarding all the objections McAdoo had raised, O'Brian and Gregory both approved a badge to read "Cooperating with the United States Department of Justice."

In a letter to McAdoo, Gregory suggested that another conference among representatives of State, Treasury, and Justice could easily work out any remaining conflicts. McAdoo's reply to Gregory on February 14 was conciliatory but by no means represented surrender of his position. "I quite agree with you that nothing will be accomplished by further discussion of the past and shall close that phase of the matter," he said. Then, after assuring Gregory that Secret Service men could still legally be assigned to investigative functions for other departments, he suggested that representatives of all intelligence services meet with his assistant George R. Cooksey on March 1. A week later, the *New York Times* again aired plans for establishing a central bureau or clearinghouse for coordination of the Secret Service and other agencies. McAdoo, it appeared, was not yet ready to give up.

On March 1, O'Brian met with Cooksey of the Treasury Department to discuss coordination and invited him to join in the next general conference on intelligence matters. Cooksey frankly stated his aim to O'Brian at this meeting: that his highly trained Secret Service agents be utilized in war work, either through a new agency or through a central clearinghouse. O'Brian explained that the Army was already acting as a clearinghouse. As soon as Cooksey had gone, however, O'Brian warned Gregory in a memorandum, "It is obvious that when the representatives meet in conference next Wednesday the chief question will be whether the other services are willing to adopt some plan by which the Treasury Secret Service will have its powers broadened and be put on an even footing with the War, Navy and Justice Departments."

The meeting took place as planned on March 6. Representatives from the Army, Navy, State, Labor, Post Office, Justice, and Treasury assembled, O'Brian chairing the meeting. O'Brian offered the delegates two alternatives. One plan was to create a central bureau of intelligence, with a director appointed by and responsible to the President, all intelligence agencies to be subordinate to this director. This was the plan advocated by the newspapers, by McAdoo, and by the National Security League, an organization founded before the war to promote military preparedness. The second plan was to create a clearinghouse, without a central bureau, which would simply compare reports and assign investigations. Bielaski and O'Brian shrewdly refused comment on the first plan, leaving it to the spokesmen for the Army and Navy to argue against it. All but the Secret Service men thought that such a plan would interfere with their own work.

The second plan was then discussed, and the clearinghouse arrangement already functioning in the Army was reviewed. Reports dealing with "war intrigue" were being sent to the Military Intelligence for indexing and classification. Thus if the Military Intelligence was to receive copies of all reports, that office could discover duplication of effort. The Secret Service representative vigorously opposed this procedure, arguing that it was of no benefit unless Secret Service agents could be "set free and engage in war work generally." The rest of the representatives said this was not their concern but should be settled by McAdoo and Gregory. Thus outmaneuvered, the Secret Service representative could do nothing but acquiesce to another meeting with O'Brian to discuss extension of the jurisdiction of the Secret Service. The other men all agreed to continue their regular meetings, regardless of what the Treasury Department and the Justice Department decided.

Without support from any of the other departments involved, the move to expand the Secret Service counterespionage activities was permanently doomed. Even McAdoo seemed to lose interest in his subordinates after this showdown in O'Brian's office. Gregory wrote once more to McAdoo informing him of the weekly conferences, and McAdoo said he would send a subordinate to discuss details of any proposed agreement with the Justice Department; but he no longer discussed the establishment of a central intelligence agency nor did he demand withdrawal of the APL from the home front war. With McAdoo's capitulation, the threat to the League's existence from within the Wilson Administration ended. The demand for a central intelligence agency was not to be revived for another thirty years. Gregory had won his battle to keep the volunteers in the field.

Had Wilson considered reversing his earlier opposition to unification, the support of Roosevelt and the Republican-oriented ADS for the plan would probably have induced him, for partisan reasons, to hold to his original decision. Establishing a unified intelligence agency might have confirmed the claims of his critics that conflict did exist and that the government had not been active enough in countering the espionage and sabotage activities of German spies. But by remaining silent, he had also allowed militarists to muster support for another plan.

By April, the principle of military jurisdiction over suspected spies, wherever they might be—despite the fact that civilians would be liable to investigation by army and navy personnel—had gained powerful support throughout the country. Proponents of this extension of military authority felt that greater efficiency would result. They saw inefficiency, not militarism, as the prime danger to democracy.

This movement presented a new threat to the APL, for if the military take-over succeeded, the League would not be needed. The men of the Military Intelligence, such recent allies, now replaced the Secret Service as prime competitors of the Bureau of Investigation for the glory of catching German spies.

Prompt Trials, Quick Hangings

On March 16, 1918, the Soviet Congress ratified the Treaty of Brest-Litovsk, sealing the end of the war between Russia and Germany. With the threat of a two-front war removed, Germany attacked with renewed energy in the West, at La Fère and Arras, and deep discouragement spread through the United States. This state of affairs gave the militarists their opportunity to push for extension of control on the home front, and they lost no time in doing so.

Fortunately for the life of the APL, plans for a central intelligence agency and complaints against volunteers were submerged beneath a new wave of spy hysteria sweeping the country based, strangely enough, on the complaint by militarists that the government had not shot enough spies.

In Europe there was never any contest between military and civil authorities for jurisdiction in espionage cases as there was in America. In Austria, for example, in the first week of war the Reichsrat had put into force a War Service Act which transferred jurisdiction in all offenses such as treason, sedition, espionage, and sabotage from the civil courts to military courts. England had passed the Defense of the Realm Act just as quickly, a bill which allowed both alien and subject accused of spying anywhere in the British Empire to be tried under military law.

In the early months of the war, the English tried one Carl Hans Lody by court-martial for espionage. He was convicted and shot. The following year the Russians hanged a Colonel Myasoedev as a spy. In October, 1915, the Germans executed British nurse Edith Cavell for helping Allied prisoners to escape from German prison camps. In 1917, the French joined in by executing the Dutch Mata Hari, charging that she fraternized with French officers, giving military information thus obtained to the Germans. In early 1918, France had just condemned Bolo Pasha to be executed as a traitor. In short, executions occurred at close enough intervals to convince Europeans that their governments were on the job.

American militarists waited impatiently for the government to find a spy and execute him. Critics of the Wilson Administration clamored for more vigorous action. Spy tales, spread by those who criticized the Justice Department for not acting ruthlessly enough, were reinforced by the Administration's own stories, published to convince the nation that the federal government was on guard.

A deluge of letters to senators demanded that the military be given more control over spies. Oklahoman Robert L. Owen, Democratic leader in the Senate, as well as Senators John H. Bankhead of Alabama, John W. Weeks of Massachusetts, and Duncan U. Fletcher of Florida, all went to the Administration with telegrams, letters, protests, and demands during the first two weeks of January. They asked Gregory for guidance in drafting bills which would defend the country against espionage and sabotage.

Gregory had asked Congress for a Sabotage Act in 1917, and such a bill had passed the Senate on April 9, 1917. But after a first reading in the House, members had turned their attention to the Selective Service Act and the Espionage Act. The Sabotage Act had died. Now many senators suggested that war zones be created around defense plants and that the military be given jurisdiction in these areas. Their suggestions, coupled with harassment and pressure for a central intelligence agency and distraction over the serious illness of his mother, had placed Gregory under great strain. As had been his practice, the Attorney General went to Charles Warren for advice on the bills, asking him to draft a reply to the proposal of Senator Weeks for more stringent legislation dealing with sabotage.

Charles Warren was no ordinary legal clerk. A descendant of the Warren family of Revolutionary fame, he had graduated from Harvard

Law School and had practiced with Moorfield Storey in Boston. He had served as private secretary to the Massachusetts governor in 1893, and he numbered among his friends Henry Cabot Lodge and others of the pro-English Rooseveltian circle. He had urged prosecutions of persons charged with anti-British activities in the United States during the neutrality period and had gained Gregory's admiration for his drafting of neutrality and wartime legislation, particularly for the ingenuity with which he had drawn upon the old Alien Enemies Act of 1798. It was Warren, too, who had convinced Gregory that German aliens must be arrested, even though they had violated no federal statutes.

The advent of O'Brian into the Justice Department had removed almost all administrative duties from Warren, and since there had been little new legislation to formulate, he had been more or less left to himself. He had found time, for example, to research a paper describing congressional attacks on Lincoln in 1861–63 and to write an article for the *Yale Law Journal*, "What is Giving Aid and Comfort to the Enemy?" in which he argued that aliens, like citizens, were punishable under the treason statute and thus were liable to the death sentence. In 1922 he was to win the Pulitzer Prize for the best book on American history, and in 1926, to write two volumes on the Supreme Court which Oliver Wendell Holmes termed "first rate," at least for a man who did not have a "superior and penetrating intellect."

For a man working within the civil branch of the government, Warren had an amazing disdain for the judicial process when it came to disloyalty. In 1943, he would maintain that German war criminals were entitled to no court hearings whatsoever because they were already guilty of "barbarous crimes against civilization." In World War I, he had not advanced quite this far; he advocated trials for all, but they should be military.

When Gregory asked Warren to draft the letter to Senator Weeks, therefore, Warren refused, saying he felt the whole matter of sabotage should be handled by the War Department and that until it was, outrages and constant destruction of war material would continue. "One man shot, after court-martial," he told Gregory, "is worth a hundred arrests by this Department." Turning to another assistant, John W. Davis, Gregory received a similar response: "I am with Mr. Warren in believing that the trial and execution of a spy under one or the other of these statutes would be wholesome."

Under the influence of Warren and Davis, Gregory's commitment to civil courts seemed momentarily to falter, for he wrote to O'Brian,

"I am disposed to think that the power to handle by court-martial should be given in cases where munitions or supplies for the Army and Navy are produced, or where ships conveying munitions and troops are injured or blown up."

But O'Brian was not convinced. The day after receiving Gregory's request, O'Brian lunched with Elting at the Cosmos Club and indicated that he opposed the enactment of any further laws regarding disloyalty. He referred Elting to Senator Beveridge's *Life of Marshall* for a full discussion of the first sedition law in American history and the reasons for its repeal. He maintained that the right of free speech must be preserved during the war and that the restrictions of the Espionage Act were adequate.

O'Brian's attitude stiffened Gregory's resistance to new legislation. Replying to Senator Bankhead, who had advocated establishment of war zones around shipbuilding plants, Gregory used O'Brian's arguments to warn that such zones, once established, would come under the control of military officers and courts; the military would have the power to define offenses, and military courts would both try and punish civilians as well as military personnel. Such provisions would arouse the hostility of labor and do infinite harm. Besides, he concluded, Military Intelligence had set up a Plant Protection Section, and guards and patrols had already been established around war plants.

But by now the demand for executions had become a part of the war rhetoric. What the country needed, Representative Julius Kahn of California told a Hotel Astor audience, was "a few prompt trials and a few quick hangings."

Gregory continued to oppose the war zone bills. To Senator Weeks he wrote, "Our regular criminal courts and judicial machinery are in full force and operation, and there have been thus far no developments which would lead to the conclusion that they are not or will not remain equal to the emergency. Any further extension of the jurisdiction of military tribunals or of military procedure at this time would be inexpedient and of doubtful constitutionality." And in yet a third letter, also in response to the bill affecting shipbuilding plants, Gregory stated flatly that the proposed bill would be "disastrous in disrupting business organization" and cause "great uneasiness and apprehension" among unskilled laborers in the shipyards. "Apart from the question of the constitutionality of any such proposed legislation," Gregory wrote to Senator Morris Sheppard, "I feel that it would be inexpedient."

A few days later, President Wilson answered in similar vein a suggestion of Senator Owen. "I must frankly say, my dear Senator, that my present opinion is that it would be a very serious mistake to put our own citizens under court-martial, for I think it would make an impression with regard to the weakness of our ordinary tribunals which would not be justified."

Wilson was less sure about enemy aliens, however, and Gregory suggested a new sabotage act to deal with willful injury to, or destruction of, war supplies. Gregory promised Senator Weeks a draft of the statute. At the same time, he began work on an amendment to the Espionage Act of 1917 which would give his department greater latitude in prosecuting men accused of "disloyalty" and allow the courts to inflict harsher penalties.

Secretary Baker, feeling that he had successfully reformed the War Department after the congressional criticism of January, left the country secretly on February 27 for a tour of the war front. In his absence, militarists within Congress joined hands with members of the Military Intelligence in an attempt to give the Army jurisdiction over all spies so that some could be found and shot.

What weakened the Wilson Administration's resolve to defend civil liberties was the conviction that although there might not be widespread espionage by foreign agents, disloyalty was still rampant and had to be extirpated. In March, Wilson seized the whole of Dutch shipping in American waters, some 700,000 tons, thus signaling his willingness to engage in total economic war. For the moment, he seemed willing to go further on the home front, as well. In private letters, he confessed he was "keenly alive" to "the insidious dangers" of pro-German activity. He personally asked Gregory to prosecute a hundred workmen who had been discharged from a defense plant for allegedly puncturing gas masks, to which Gregory replied that if the facts could be established, he would ask for indictments for treason.

At Gregory's insistence, two measures were introduced into Congress to give him even broader powers over allegedly disloyal activities. On March 4, 1918, Edwin Y. Webb, Chairman of the House Judiciary Committee, introduced an amendment to the Espionage Act which was speedily passed by the House and referred to the Senate. The old sabotage bill, forgotten in the discussion of the first Espionage Act, was also exhumed. Amended so that nothing in the act should be construed as outlawing strikes, it passed the House on March 6.

Now Gregory and Wilson were caught in a dilemma: how to convince the Senate that the administration needed more legislation, while at the same time allaying any fear that the Justice Department was not doing an adequate job. To complicate the situation, pre-election mania was rising to join spy hysteria.

Pressure from patriots came just at the time when senators were beginning to put up their political weathervanes to see which way the autumn winds would blow. Letters like one Senator W. A. Smith received and forwarded to the Justice Department were typical. A Flint, Michigan, lawyer complained that the United States Attorney in Detroit was "too timid" to prosecute "German whelps," and that "political harlots" were using the local draft boards for political favoritism. "Are we going to be compelled to put up with this sort of thing?" the lawyer demanded. "If there is no use of trying to do anything and our people in authority are more interested in the political rumblings than in the welfare of the nation, then I want to know it because I am in favor of organizing a Vigilance Committee and hanging these degenerate political whelps to lamp-posts rather than to permit them to go on debauching the young men who are subject to draft."

The demand that spies be found and shot became louder, mingling inextricably with pressure to stamp out all criticism and opposition to the war. By the time Gregory's two bills had been returned to conference committees and reported out once again, the newspapers were ablaze with news of German successes along the Western Front. Had Baker been in the United States he might have countered the demand to do something at home. In his absence, the conviction spread that the activities of German agents and pro-German sympathizers on the home front had somehow been responsible for reverses on the battlefield thousands of miles away. That conviction metamorphosed American patriotism into a vicious and vindictive attack on dissenters.

Elected and appointed officials who should have worked to allay the public's fears instead encouraged excesses with their own political rhetoric. Representative Kahn, the Republican who had introduced the draft bill in the House and had proposed prompt hanging for those who raised "a seditious or traitorous voice," elaborated: "We must make an example of these people and do it quickly. . . . The man in this country who denounces this war to-day, with his country in the war, has no business on American soil. The man who refused to contribute a dollar to buy a Liberty Bond and support our boys in the Army . . . is a traitor to our country . . . he should be whipped out of the country by the scourge of public opinion." Senator Warren G.

Harding, who had previously scored the Administration for drumming up support for the Liberty Loan, now claimed that the government had not done enough. In a Baltimore address under the auspices of the National Council of Defense, he demanded the death penalty for spies. In a speech to the Chamber of Commerce of Muskogee, Oklahoma, William Howard Taft again urged that spies be shot, and the next day, several hundred miles away from Muskogee, near the town of Collinsville, Illinois, a responsive crowd of vigilantes lynched Frederick Praeger, a German-American Socialist who had opposed the war.

The country looked to Washington for approbation or repudiation of this act of violence. Wilson was silent. After a Cabinet discussion on April 5, Gregory condemned the act but told newsmen the federal government could do nothing; the state of Illinois would have to handle any prosecution. The next day, Wilson made a speech emphasizing not restraint, but force.

In the face of the federal government's refusal to take a strong stand against such outrages, intemperate outcries against dissenters increased. Among those clamoring for more action were members of the APL. "In my humble judgement, it is high time to shut the mouths of the pro-Germans," a North Carolina member complained to the special agent in Knoxville, arguing that the Justice Department was nullifying "the work of patriots." Others wrote directly to Briggs complaining that the lack of action on the part of the Justice Department was making the APL a laughing stock. "If this thing is to be treated as a farce by Department of Justice Agents, I don't care to be connected with it," affirmed one. Following the Praeger incident, a Collinsville Leaguer wired Senator Lee Overman, head of the Senate Judiciary Committee, "Our convictions are very clear that the Government itself must share in the responsibility as long as it pursues the present tender policy with respect to offending alien enemies and disloyal citizens." United States attorneys flooded Senator Overman with telegrams expressing fear of widespread violence if Congress did not act immediately. Gregory urged that the revisions of the Espionage Act be rushed through Congress in time for the start of a new bond sale on Monday, April 8. Overman obliged by calling for full Senate debate on the pending espionage and sabotage bills.

As with later debates on internal security legislation in 1950, the April 6, 1918, debate in the Senate revealed the carelessness with which matters intimately related to civil liberties could be treated during an election year. True, some members of the Progressive party who had earlier counseled moderation in enacting espionage laws still opposed bills to broaden the definition of sedition. Hiram Johnson pointed out that under the proposed amendment to the espionage law, now being called a sedition bill, legitimate criticism of the Administration could be punished and freedom of speech curtailed. Miles Poindexter of Washington argued that state laws were perfectly adequate for any sabotage which took place. But the hour for reason was past. Moderate Democrats, led by Senator Overman, were joined by a group of usually moderate Republicans in supporting Gregory's measures.

Republican conservatives not only endorsed the bills as necessary, but were willing to go further. Henry Cabot Lodge, raising the specter of a defenseless America, turned again to the old fund of spy stories fabricated in part by the discredited Rathom and to the so-called espionage activities reported during the neutrality period. Lodge painted a picture for his fellow senators of a country overrun with German spies who dynamited factories, started great fires, attempted to destroy railroad bridges, poisoned food, and mixed glass with flour in bread. Other agents, he claimed, furnished the German government with information injurious to the American government. Lodge conjured the mirage known in World War II as "the fifth column," a combination of unprincipled spies and saboteurs working to bring military defeat through clandestine warfare on the civilian population. "The criminals who put a bomb on a ship or blow up a factory and destroy innocent lives according to my idea have been treated altogether too delicately," Lodge declaimed. "The only way, in my opinion, to put an end to those criminal activities of organized German agents and spies is to treat them as spies and agents of that kind always have been treated in time of war—try them by court-martial and shoot them. Germany does not hesitate to do that."

The vista of espionage and sabotage presented by Lodge successfully held the attention of the Senate long enough for Senator Chamberlain, a self-styled committee of one on the conduct of the war, to present the militarists' argument that the Army should have jurisdiction over all spies. Republican Senator Albert Fall protested that only spies on military reservations could be subject to court-martial, and on this note of conflict the Senate adjourned on Friday night, April 5, without passing the bills. By Monday, Charles Warren had supplied a document to reconcile the differences of Chamberlain and Fall. Warren had remained sullenly silent during the controversies of the early spring. Now this Assistant Attorney General in a Democratic administration sent Republican critics a brief arguing that the military should have jurisdiction over all spies. Coupled with his brief was a model bill revising the Eighty-second Article of War—which limited such jurisdiction—to allow this change.

In his brief, Warren explained how the article had originated in the Continental Congress of 1776, how it had been revised several times during the nineteenth century, had been gradually expanded to include citizens and certain other civilians, and finally had been incorporated into the 1916 act of Congress. The main question of interpretation, according to Warren, was just what constituted the zone of operations in modern war, the area in which the military had control over spies. Traditionally, zones of operations had been considered fortifications, posts, quarters, or encampments of armies, or areas in the immediate vicinity. The new definition recently advanced by Judge Advocate General Crowder declared the entire country a war zone on the theory that modern means of communication and transportation made it necessary. "In time of war, spies are within the jurisdiction of military tribunals," Crowder stated flatly. Warren agreed.

Warren marshaled all the historical precedent he could find to bolster Crowder's opinion, even citing the execution of a French spy by William III in 1695. But the main line of his argument was contemporary, not historical: "Changed conditions of modern warfare have altered the forms of danger to the armies. It is now not only the disguised enemy agent seeking information within the lines, but also the destructive enemy agent engaging in acts of violence upon industrial property, who may constitute a source of disaster to the armed forces."

With a brief of this type coming out of the Justice Department and prosecutions proceeding in all parts of the country, it is little wonder that civil libertarians were dismayed. "While the administration is full of liberals, they unfortunately are not in the two departments which enforce this war legislation, namely, the Post Office Department and the Department of Justice," Roger Baldwin of the NCLB wrote to Harold Evans on April 13.

Gregory chose to defend his department rather than civil liberties. Intent upon saving the Justice Department from additional adverse criticism, he ignored Warren's insubordination at first. He called in David Lawrence of the *New York Evening Post* and asked him to prepare an article for the *Saturday Evening Post* to offset criticism of the Justice Department for lack of activity. To build up confidence,

Gregory suggested a story about the APL that would emphasize that its 250,000 members were on guard for the government throughout the United States. The article was expected to reach two and a half million subscribers and was to be read by that many more, thus telling five or six million people the APL story.

The directors of the APL were delighted. Frey and Elting began to collect material for Lawrence and had several interviews with him. At the same time, they sent out letters to their own members asking them to exercise a "steadying influence" in their communities. Each member, Elting told one APL chief, was "the center of a zone of influence and should do his best to impress upon the people of his community the fact that the strong arm of the Government is at work." He encouraged chiefs to publicize the fact that their divisions all over the country were watching out for enemies.

Since the article by Lawrence could not be scheduled before July, Gregory also planned to make a series of public speeches on the same theme, denouncing alarmist spy stories and calling attention to the protective work of the APL. At Bridgeport, Connecticut, on April 10 he assured citizens that the country was not honeycombed with German spies, that there was no foundation for the stories that German spies had been released or paroled, and that gas masks had not been willfully made defective. He branded as false the story that fifty million dollars' worth of property had been destroyed by enemy aliens. Above all, he told the audience that 400,000 officials and citizens guarded the nation's domestic life.

The same day that Gregory made this speech at Bridgeport, the Senate passed the sedition bill without the antistrike measure demanded by the House, thus necessitating another conference committee session. Gregory, seeking to influence Congress, continued to write letters for publication in which he asked for the legislation as a weapon against "flagrant disloyalty." To his credit, he also reiterated that reports of poisoned food and water had not been substantiated and that the Bureau of Investigation had absolutely no evidence that glass or poison had ever been maliciously placed in food supplies. For the first time, he pointed out that accidents could happen even in wartime; that not every mistake, every fire, every explosion was necessarily the result of foreign intrigue or the work of domestic sympathizers. Yet the Democratic-dominated House still balked at passing his legislation. Perhaps, looking to the past, Democrats envisioned this sedition bill being used the way the 1798 act had been used in the 1800 campaign by Jefferson and Madison, as a political issue. Consequently, the House and Senate were able to agree on only the sabotage bill, which went to Wilson for his signature on April 16. Debate on the sedition bill churned on.

Gregory continued to alternate his pleas for passage with assurances that his department was already doing an adequate job under existing laws. In a speech on April 16 before the Executive Committee of the American Bar Association, he pleaded for the lawyers' help in stemming the rise of lawlessness in the country. Explaining that he had over 200,000 APL members in more than 1,000 communities, he went on to condemn the bloodthirsty demands for executions. "From every section of the country comes up the cry that the disloyal and seditious should be tried by military courts and promptly shot. It is hardly conceivable how lawyers acquainted with the three great guarantees of our Constitution and the decisions of our courts can contend that civilians should be tried at a time when our civil courts are performing their proper functions, and when our country is not being subjected to invasion or rebellion." Shortly thereafter he published an article on disloyalty and treason in which he promised, "I shall not be half measured in undertaking the control of those who persist in their disloyalty and schemings against the Government and its purposes." However, current and proposed legislation would be adequate to punish crimes being committed, he asserted in the article, which appeared first in the *Official Bulletin,* then in four law journals.

In private letters, Gregory used less rhetoric and more sarcasm. To T. V. Taylor, he wrote, "There is quite a deal of hysteria in the country about German spies. If you will kindly box up and send me from one to a dozen I will pay you very handsomely for your trouble. We are looking for them constantly, but it is a little difficult to shoot them until they have been found."

While the Attorney General continued to assert that the disloyal were being prosecuted, that he had thousands of men under constant surveillance, and that new legislation would "strengthen the hands" of the Justice Department, most of his talk was drowned out by headlines giving details of the execution of Bolo Pasha, the Frenchman accused of accepting German money to finance "defeatist propaganda" in the French press. Journalists began to talk about "American Boloism," an epithet applied by the *Peoria Transcript* to "meddlers with public opinion." The *Richmond Journal* wistfully mourned the passing of the "boiling-in-oil period" of reprisal for traitors. The *Christian Science Monitor* reminded its readers that in his war message to Congress in

April of 1917, Wilson had referred to the net of German espionage and treason.

The April, 1918, mood of crisis jolted O'Brian into a stronger defense of civil liberties. Already he had written a hurried memorandum to Gregory calling attention to the serious outrages being perpetrated in various parts of the country under the guise of punishing disloyal citizens and suggesting that Gregory or Wilson make a public statement "denouncing this sort of thing and calling on all loyal citizens to keep their heads and stop disorder of every sort." He now prepared a detailed memorandum for Gregory to pass on to Wilson incorporating specific comments to be used in a presidential statement. He hoped that Wilson would declare that government and state officials and volunteers were watching offenders and that "this country is being policed more thoroughly and successfully than ever before in its history." Furthermore, drawing on the results of a recent conference regarding destruction of war materials, O'Brian stated that it was now the consensus of government officials and leaders of the fire insurance business that "substantially no fire losses of this character during the past year have been caused by enemy activities within this country." It had taken over a year for the government to assemble this material which now thoroughly convinced the Justice Department that spies were not at work in industry, and from this point on, the Department's role was less equivocal in regard to foreign espionage and sabotage.

O'Brian concluded his memorandum for Wilson with a plea that Americans not besmirch their lofty motives with vile means. "This war is one for American principle and for the sanctity of long recognized standards raised by international law. Any act of any such oppression directed toward an enemy alien is an act which discredits the good name of America and its motives in this war."

But even as O'Brian sat at his desk in the Justice Department composing this realistic assessment of affairs and an idealistic statement of principles, Senator Chamberlain, in a direct affront to Gregory and Wilson, introduced the Warren bill to extend the jurisdiction of military tribunals. He scheduled hearings for April 18. "The Justice Department seems to me to confess it cannot handle the situation," he told reporters who asked him about the bill. "All I can say is that the military authorities can handle it if they are given the chance, and I think they should be."

Newspapers characterized the hearings as a probe into Justice Department activities which would equal the exposures of inefficiency in the War Department made by the same committee four months earlier. Chamberlain called to testify the chiefs of the military and naval intelligence, civilian representatives of the Military Intelligence, representatives of the Wisconsin Council of Defense and the Minnesota Commission of Public Safety, and the three directors of the American Protective League.

Until this time, the Military Intelligence had played a relatively minor role in the home front battles. During the first year of the war, however, it had expanded rapidly under the enthusiastic hand of Colonel Van Dieman and over the opposition of the Chief of Staff, General Hugh L. Scott. Originally an army surgeon, Van Dieman had received his first training in counterespionage in the Philippines, where he headed Arthur MacArthur's military intelligence bureau. In the years before World War I, Van Dieman had become the most persistent proponent of military intelligence in the United States and had been dismayed when in June, 1908, the old military intelligence section established in 1885 was incorporated into the War College Division of the General Staff. Van Dieman was convinced that without an effective military intelligence the United States was blind and in danger of ravishment by foreign powers.

Before August, 1914, Van Dieman had worried about Japan; after August 1914, he had begun to worry about the Germans, too. He had written memorandums to the Chief of the War College Division urging more be done to collect and disseminate information. He had argued, advised, pleaded. The only change he had wrought was to have officers assigned to each of the departmental headquarters within the United States to perform military information duties. By March 3, 1917, when he went to Chicago to be married, he was already on record as being alarmed at the prospect of the United States entering the war with no military intelligence organization established. A month later, when the United States did declare war on Germany, he went in person to the Chief of Staff to plead that an intelligence office be set up. The Chief of Staff said no. Van Dieman returned for a second and a third interview. The Chief of Staff curtly asked him to cease his agitating and issued strict orders that he not approach Secretary of War Baker to plead his case.

Crisis situations call for extraordinary action. Van Dieman did not disobey the orders of his commanding officer; he simply circumvented them. About the time he had been enjoined from talking to Baker, novelist Gertrude Atherton arrived in Washington, having visited the training camps at Baker's request. Her escort happened to be Van

Dieman; and by the time the afternoon tour was finished, he had convinced her of the perilousness of the situation and asked her to put his case before the Secretary of War. The next day, Van Dieman planted the same story with the chief of police of the District of Columbia, who, Van Dieman knew, breakfasted with Secretary Baker each morning.

The dual attack brought results. By April 30, Baker was on the phone instructing the president of the Army War College to have Van Dieman report to him at once. After an hour's conversation, Baker told Van Dieman that within forty-eight hours an order would be on its way to the president of the War College setting up a new intelligence section. By May 3, Van Dieman had his intelligence bureau and complete charge of it. He also had been promoted from major to lieutenant colonel.

From that time on, the Military Intelligence force had grown by means of commissioning civilians in the Army Reserve and by use of volunteer investigators. Van Dieman's agents were soon scattered about the country, working under cover among the IWW in the Northwest and among the enemy aliens in New York, Philadelphia, and Chicago. In July, 1917, Van Dieman had started a Plant Protection Section which placed undercover operatives in defense plants. By August, his men were so involved in investigating and arresting civilians that Attorney General Gregory had to complain to Baker, whereupon Baker had ordered Military Intelligence agents to report all enemy agents to the Justice Department instead of pursuing investigations and causing arrests. In contrast to his conflict with McAdoo, Gregory had settled this little difficulty by discussions with Baker and without recourse to Cabinet controversy.

Baker's order did not halt the proliferation of Van Dieman's agents, however. In fact, in August, 1917, Van Dieman was able to obtain the support of Felix Frankfurter and Walter Lippmann in urging Baker and Wilson to ask Congress for larger appropriations for Military Intelligence; and by December, 1917, Van Dieman was opening special offices in Chicago, New York, and Philadelphia.

Van Dieman's agents were soon conducting investigations of commissioned officers, civilian personnel working for the War Department, and civilians going overseas to work with the troops. Officers in the War Department who opposed tighter security controls were treated to a practical course in security. Feeling that a system of checks and guards should be extended to all offices in the War Department handling military information of potential use to the enemy, Van Dieman sent two men in plain clothes to rifle desks of confidential papers. In the morning, he called up those officers who had opposed his guard system and demanded the papers which his operatives had so easily removed. He quickly won their consent to establish stricter security control.

Van Dieman had eagerly accepted the APL's offer to conduct investigations among the civilian population in the fall of 1917, since his own agents had no right to investigate while out of uniform, and the uniform obviously put suspects on guard. When the APL directors had first arrived in Washington, Van Dieman had invited Frey to sit in at War College conferences and soon was referring cases for investigation. No opposition to the expansion of the Military Intelligence was encountered from the Justice Department, for until February even O'Brian felt that Van Dieman's force was a safer ally than the Secret Service. But then, in the midst of the February spy scare, Military Intelligence found Pablo Waberski.

Pablo Waberski was a German subject who claimed to be a Russian. When apprehended, he was allegedly working under Kurt Jancke, head of a German intelligence group in Mexico City. Two men, one a Negro, had been assigned by Jancke to accompany Waberski to the United States where, according to these two escorts, Waberski was to commit sabotage, incite rebellion among Negro troops along the Mexican border, and obtain military information. On their way to the United States, Waberski boasted to the two men that during the neutrality period he had been responsible for sabotage at Mare Island, California, and Black Tom Island in New Jersey; that he had started forest fires in the Northwest, caused explosions throughout the United States, and sabotaged ships.

When the three men crossed the border at Nogales, Arizona, on February 1, they were arrested by Military Intelligence officers, and Waberski was jailed in the nearest military guardhouse. His two companions were released. The Negro was a British Secret Service agent, the other man was an agent of the United States Military Intelligence.

Military authorities clamped the lid of secrecy on the arrest. Legally, of course, the man was not a "spy" regardless of what he said he intended to do. According to Article Eighty-two of the Articles of War, anyone found "lurking or acting as a spy" in or about "posts, fortifications, quarters, or encampments" was subject to military court-martial, and upon conviction, death. Waberski had not been in any of the places enumerated in the article. Rightfully, the Justice

Department should have had jurisdiction, but no one there even knew Waberski existed. Passage of the Warren bill could clear the way to try Waberski by court-martial, at the same time giving Military Intelligence the authority to investigate civilians accused of espionage and sedition anywhere in the United States. Hence, the Chamberlain hearings were an important testing ground: How would the administration react to such a move?

Chamberlain passed over the directors of the APL on the first day of the hearings. Their testimony would have been too much like letting a defendant plead his own cause, for the Justice Department had no other representatives present. Chamberlain went on to Norman H. White, a civilian aide who held a roving commission for the Military Intelligence in New York and was an inveterate critic of the Justice Department. White testified that the Justice Department had let spies roam at large and charged that aliens in New York were engaging in disloyal activities. From White, Chamberlain eagerly went on to the heads of the naval and military intelligence, but to his disappointment, they refused to fault the Justice Department. When prodded, they admitted their belief that military courts could act more quickly and efficiently, to be sure, but they would say no more. Chamberlain dismissed them impatiently.

Then he called his star witness, Judge John McGee, dominant personality of the Minnesota Commission of Public Safety. Fresh from an attack on Swedish and German aliens in Minnesota, an attempt to oust the Socialist mayor of Minneapolis, and opposition to farmers organizing the Non-Partisan League, McGee made Lind, the man who had suggested the Justice Department arrest the IWW, seem like a devoted constitutionalist. The entire policy of the Justice Department, he charged, had been a "ghastly failure from the beginning." What the government should have done, he thought, was to organize firing squads everywhere immediately after war was declared and work them full time. "I know of no objection or reason why there should be any further delay in organizing the squad, or why they should not, when organized, work overtime in order to make up for lost time," McGee asserted. On that cheerful, humanitarian note, Chamberlain adjourned the committee.

By the next day, April 18, the *New York Times* had turned White's 20,000 aliens into 20,000 spies and brought the American Defense Society out of retirement to urge passage of the court-martial bill.

In the Justice Department, it was O'Brian who immediately

responded to Chamberlain's challenge. Dashing off another memorandum to Gregory, O'Brian reminded him, "I have already expressed my opinion to you that such legislation is not only unconstitutional but embodies the worst possible policy." The next day Warren resigned, still insisting that the Department could not cope with the spy menace. Gregory rushed to the White House to talk to Wilson, who had just signed the Sabotage Act into law. This time a public statement was necessary.

On April 21, both Gregory and Wilson gave the press copies of letters to Congress expressing opposition to the Chamberlain bill. "I am wholly and unalterably opposed to such legislation," Wilson wrote to Overman, Chairman of the Senate Judiciary Committee. "I think it is not only unconstitutional but that in character it would put us nearly upon the level of the very people we are fighting and affecting to despise. It would be altogether inconsistent with the spirit and practice of America." In a letter to Representative William Gordon of Ohio, Gregory repudiated Warren, saying that his brief and bill were prepared without the Attorney General's consent or knowledge. Moreover, Warren was no longer in charge of matters to which the legislation related, and the general policies recommended were in fact "exactly contrary to those approved by the assistant to the Attorney General in charge of the problems involved and by the Attorney General himself. I entirely disapprove of the action taken by Mr. Warren, and it would not have been permitted if I had known it was contemplated."

On the floor of the Senate, William Borah, veteran champion of civil liberties, denounced the bill. Senator Frank Brandegee attempted to have it transferred to Overman's Judiciary Committee, where it could be killed. About this time Frey telephoned Chamberlain to ask if the APL directors would still be called to testify. Bluffing, Chamberlain said that they might be asked to return, but the following day he capitulated to the Administration and withdrew the bill. With his capitulation, the major attack of the congressional militarists came to an end.

Wilson had finally taken a stand—not against his home front volunteers but, by implication, in their behalf. His espousal of civilian investigations assured that the APL, by virtue of its Justice Department ties, would continue to be the first line of defense at home. Now that their military rivals were routed, the Justice Department set about eliminating all competition from the civilian forces still in the field. Not only that, it placed the APL completely at the disposal of the Military Intelligence by approving the establishment of a separate APL office in the War Department. The military, it seemed, would be kept from trying spies but be allowed to conduct investigations among the civilian population through the APL.

Congress now passed the Sedition Act which both O'Brian and Gregory urged should include sections allowing prosecution even for making true statements if they had a tendency to lessen the will of the people to wage war. Socialist Morris Hillquist called the bill "the nationalization of lynching." Years before, Wilson had said of the Sedition Act of 1798 that it "cut perilously near the root of freedom of speech and of the press. There was no telling where such exercises of power would stop. Their only limitations and safeguards lay in the temper and good sense of the President and the Attorney General." In 1918, the safeguards remained the same. The question was whether or not they would be sufficient to restrain the APL chiefs, who received news of Wilson's signature on the bill with great elation and hastily instructed members as to the great opportunities for prosecution under the new bill.

Meanwhile, the Military Intelligence had been too ambitious to wait quietly for Wilson to act. There was sedition to root out; it should be done even if the military could not yet try the suspects.

Volunteer operatives had been recruited indiscriminately by the Military Intelligence during the first year of the war, but only the Western Department had developed a full scale Volunteer Intelligence Corps. By April, 1918, it had a thousand "patriots" supplying western area intelligence officers with information on opponents of war. When the Military Intelligence Branch in Washington, D. C., discovered this Corps in March, the officer in San Francisco, Rolin G. Watkins, received a curt note to the effect that the organization was a "departure from regulations and disapproved." Military Intelligence officers were to utilize the APL for civilian investigations, he was reminded.

Washington had known of his Volunteer Intelligence Corps, Watkins retorted; and furthermore, he pointed out, he had an order allowing recruitment of these volunteers. Then Van Dieman received a letter from Colonel Carl Reichmann, a Military Intelligence officer, complaining about the necessity for depending upon the APL. A force of his own would enable him to develop a "sort of competition for efficiency between my force and the APL," he asserted. His men could check APL men. Perhaps, he suggested, the state councils of defense might find volunteer lawyers willing to make "an occasional investigation."

"There is a likelihood that the appointing of such agents in territories where the League is active is likely to meet with opposition from them," Van Dieman replied to Reichmann, because they felt they were entitled to government recognition and "because of the unnatural jealousy of the League in retaining and maintaining the powers and privileges which it has arrogated to itself and the prestige which it has secured." Van Dieman approved the scheme for new agents, but to keep the APL from learning of its competitors, he suggested they operate under cover as much as possible. The Western Department received no orders to disband their volunteers.

Secretly, Van Dieman began his own volunteer recruitment in the Midwest. He was inclined to avoid going to the state councils of defense. Too likely to be involved in politics, he thought. He had different men in mind: a retired brigadier general in Minnesota, a retired army officer in Nashville, Tennessee, members of the Volunteer Medical Service Corps, American Federation of Labor informants, groups of private detectives from mining and industry. An agent of the Norfolk and Western Railway Company volunteered to supply operatives. A Denver man promised to obtain the services of detectives hired by mining and industrial companies in Colorado. An agent for a railway in Virginia promised to do the same. A lawyer from Kansas City was to organize Missouri, another from Indianapolis was to organize Indiana. Three attorneys from Kansas City, Kansas, were to form the nucleus of a group for their state. And all of these would be working entirely for the military.

Van Dieman placed Reichmann in charge of volunteers in the Midwest and warned him to prepare for an increase in work. Correspondence alone had "grown by such leaps and bounds that it will be exceedingly difficult . . . for us to handle the additional work brought about by an extensive increase in the number of our agents."

But recruiting was far from over. The retired officer at Nashville asked the United States Attorney to suggest ten reliable citizens who could watch out for and report all cases of sedition or disloyal utterances. A few days later he returned to ask for eighteen more names. Van Dieman asked the American Bar Association to furnish him with the names of attorneys in five hundred cities and towns in fifteen states of the Midwest. What the Justice Department could do, the Military Intelligence could do better. Or so Military Intelligence officers thought.

Secretary Baker, who learned of developments when he returned to Washington shortly after the Chamberlain hearings, attempted to pull the military sleuths back into line. Van Dieman was ordered overseas, and Lieutenant Colonel Marlborough Churchill, a man who at first appeared more cautious in expanding military investigations, was detailed to head the Military Intelligence Division.

The attempts at restraint by Wilson, Gregory, and Baker merely drove the Military Intelligence underground. "For the present we must be careful how we handle civilians," read a June 3 bulletin from the Military Intelligence Branch to its officers. In his capacity of Judge Advocate General, Crowder gave the military hope that they might ultimately triumph over the civilians when he handed intelligence officers a "confidential opinion" that German spies operating anywhere in the United States could be tried by court-martial instead of turned over to civil courts. The issue could only be settled, he advised, by catching a spy, convicting him, and then having the Supreme Court settle the issue when the spy appealed for a writ of habeas corpus. "This means not only that we can have prompt, sure and effective trial of spies, but that evidence can be given in secret, and our operatives protected," the Military Intelligence informed its officers. Waberski, who was scheduled to be court-martialed, was to be their test case.

It was foolish for Military Intelligence officers to think that such plans for expansion could be kept secret from the APL and the Justice Department. By mid-June, O'Brian had news of their activities from the Midwest and Pacific Coast. There was only one interpretation to be placed upon the reports, O'Brian told Gregory in a memorandum, "that the Office of Military Intelligence has definitely decided to supplant the investigation services of the Department of Justice throughout the country."

Gregory was as alarmed as O'Brian. He wrote to Baker asking that the midwest volunteer plan be abandoned and that the Western Volunteer Intelligence Corps be demobilized. Baker was quick to respond favorably. "Rest assured," he wrote Gregory, "that the entire policy of the Military Intelligence Branch will be one based not only upon an understanding of the proper spheres of the two departments, but also upon a sincere desire for cooperation." Baker kept his word. The rosters of the Military Intelligence volunteers in the West were turned over to the APL, and the APL was assured it would remain the only civilian group working with the War Department.

Thus by June, 1918, the Justice Department had eliminated major competitors of the APL. All complaints by the Secret Service had been silenced, and the Treasury Department had been routed from the field. The Military Intelligence appeared to be contained for the moment. The APL could now argue that since it was conducting most of the investigations not only for the Justice Department but also for the War Department, it should receive support from the Justice Department for still greater growth. In all Gregory's public declarations—that there were no spies but the Justice Department was capable of defending the nation against them—he now stressed the work of the APL. After the laudatory article by David Lawrence appeared in early June, Bielaski even told members that their organization was an "inspiration" to the Justice Department. It was his "sincere hope," he told New York Leaguers assembled on June 10, "that when this war has been won—as it will be—that the American Protective League will continue to serve the nation."

To complete the APL monopoly, the Justice Department had only to absorb state and local investigating groups into the ranks of its federal volunteers. The states had always been major contenders for the privilege of fighting enemies on the home front. Regional planning in New England had enabled the governors there to develop committees of public safety early and uniformly throughout the states, with the result that during 1917 the APL had had no units there except in Rhode Island. Most midwestern and southern governors allowed intelligence groups to be attached to state councils of defense and to compete with the APL units. In Oklahoma and Kansas, for example, councils of defense dominated the home front war, while the Minnesota Commission of Public Safety and the Wisconsin Council of Defense exemplified their potential power. In South Carolina and other southern states, Gregory had encouraged the councils to handle disloyalty investigations early in the war. In the Far West, both state and federal authorities licensed a private statewide organization called the Minute Men to operate in the same capacity as state-controlled groups in other parts of the country. The governor of the Territory of Hawaii had turned over surveillance and counterespionage to a branch of the American Defense Society. Vigilante groups continued to share the field with the APL in the Southwest; and the California State Council of Defense, inoperative after the first few months of the war, left the field to a number of self-appointed patriotic groups. Starting in April, Gregory attempted to eliminate all remaining state and private groups and to establish the APL uniformly throughout the United States.

Absorption of state investigating units by the APL had started in New York and Illinois, where the largest units were established early in the war. In Boston, United States Attorney George W. Anderson had blocked the expansion of the APL, not on the basis of opposition to volunteer groups (although he had warned Gregory of the company spy racket), but because he had his own volunteer organization. Even when he resigned his position as United States Attorney to take a place on the Interstate Commerce Commission, it was necessary for Bielaski, Frey, and Elting to confer with him about extending the APL in Massachusetts.

On December 21, 1917, Frey had written to Briggs that plans for the Massachusetts branch were going through. "Victor had a long talk with [Anderson] yesterday afternoon. Victor and I had a long conference with Bielaski in which he assured us of his absolute backing so that neither of us have any fears of our plans going through in Boston regardless of any opposition we may encounter there." As negotiations progressed, O'Brian affirmed the Justice Department's support, writing to Hugh Bancroft, "A branch of the American Protective League seems preferable to the formation of a purely local organization because the League is conducted along certain recognized lines and it is possible for the Department to deal with it through its national officers in Washington instead of having to deal with the different local organizations." Gregory wrote to Charles F. Choate, Jr., prestigious old Back Bay lawyer who had accepted a position on the APL executive board, saying that he was "very glad indeed to learn" that the Massachusetts League had been formed because work had been "very considerably handicapped by the absence of a branch of this League." Still, it was June, 1918, before the state investigators became part of the APL.

The Massachusetts merger was a compromise, however. The League masthead there read: "Organized by the Massachusetts Public Safety Committee under the Direction of the U. S. Department of Justice, Bureau of Investigation." There remained some doubt as to whether the state or the federal government actually ran the Massachusetts APL, but it made little difference, since the government prosecuted only one defendant in that state under the Espionage Act in 1918.

Not all mergers were so innocuous, however. In the state of Washington a similar merger united the division with the Minute Men, an old, private organization that had ruthlessly suppressed the IWW during the months before it became the "Minute Men Division of the American Protective League."

At a Justice Department conference in July, 1917, it had been decided that federal troops which had become involved in labor controversies in Washington should be withdrawn as soon as other provisions could be developed for policing the state. Leaving only the War Department's Loyal Legion of Loggers and Lumbermen, most federal troops had been withdrawn in the fall of 1917. The result was that federal and state officials had recognized the Minute Men as their authorized investigators.

During late 1917 and early 1918, the Minute Men launched what the naval intelligence agent in Seattle quaintly called a "political counterirritant" to the Socialist agitation of the IWW. Men were detailed to watch the waterfront and the shipyards, and they reported federal and state offenses, alike. The mayor of Seattle encouraged them to break up all IWW meetings. Thus the Minute Men became a vigilante force working for the mayor, carrying out raids on IWW headquarters and arresting leaders on vague charges. Almost two hundred Wobblies were held for deportation by Commissioner of Immigration Henry M. White, who wrote to the Minute Men to express his appreciation for their assistance in the apprehension of the radicals and for the secrecy maintained by the Minute Men. "These are all bad men, as you know," White said.

By the end of January the Minute Men had filled the jails and appealed to Senator Wesley L. Jones for help in finding more space. There were three thousand more IWW members the Minute Men wanted to arrest. Senator Jones went to the federal government to ask if some provision could be made to lodge the expected prisoners. He went to the Council of National Defense, the Labor Department, the War Department, and the Justice Department. All refused to act.

Slowed by the lack of cell space, the Minute Men turned their attention to other activities they branded as disloyal. They planted undercover agents in all schools to report on teachers claiming draft exemption—and teaching "Hun" courses in History. German teachers and teachers of German were watched carefully. Principals even came under scrutiny. So too did professors at the University of Washington, where one professor reported his colleagues to the Minute Men. In four months Minute Men conducted over two thousand investigations in Seattle alone. By March, 1918, they had a regional monopoly. There was only one APL man in Seattle; the Minute Men had 12,000 members.

Money was no problem. United States Attorney Clay Allen had stated that it was the duty of all patriotic citizens to contribute to the Minute Men's support, and both monetary and moral support were forthcoming. Even a special assistant of the Attorney General who had complained to the Justice Department in April that the Minute Men gave vague oral reports and expected them to be the basis of investigations wrote to the Minute Men two months later that he was "deeply impressed with the fairness of the reports" they submitted; that the organization was not in politics but wanted only to bring about strict enforcement of the law, without fear or favor.

In June, after more than six months of negotiation, the APL absorbed the Minute Men, endowing one leader, Sumner J. Lombard, with the title of State Inspector for the APL. He agreed to accept the APL rules and regulations and to merge the Minute Men and APL units wherever the two existed, as in Tacoma. Investigations of radicals continued as usual, however, for between May and November they reported another one thousand arrests, over a thousand investigations of "IWW agitators," and almost a thousand investigations of pro-German radicals. Such allies the Justice Department embraced in their fear of the military.

By June of 1918 Gregory had convinced members of the executive committee of the National Council of Defense, at least one of whom, John H. Winterbotham, had been an early Chicago APL member, that the APL should supplant all the state councils' sedition investigations. Thereupon the National Council issued Bulletin 99 advising state councils of defense to undertake no new work for suppression of sedition and to turn over all investigations in progress to the Justice Department. To state officials who inquired about their role in enforcing federal disloyalty laws, O'Brian replied that they should concentrate on stamping out mob law instead. At the same time, Gregory directed the APL to expand its web to the rest of the country—to be the only home front army.

Neither the Secret Service nor the states were ever to regain the initiative in fighting sedition on the home front, not in World War I nor years later in World War II. By the summer of 1918 the American Protective League had not only vanquished or absorbed most of its major competitors, but it had begun to consider itself permanent. What the APL later called its "web" had taken real form.

This web was the answer Wilson and Gregory made to demands both for centralization and for military control. Expansion of the APL had been substituted for a central intelligence agency, for state investigation into sedition—and to contain the military. Wilson was silent on this subject in the spring of 1918, but beginning in April,

Gregory gave wide publicity in articles and speeches to the government's dependence on the APL for domestic security. In May he bestowed upon the League the official title "Auxiliary to the Justice Department" and allowed the organization to order new badges with this designation emblazoned on them. One year before, Wilson had asked Gregory if the APL should continue. Now in June, 1918, the Commander-in-Chief accepted the volunteer army as essential. Indeed, their web was his defense against critics of his own home front policy.

The Web

League members liked to refer to their organization as a web spun to entrap German spies. But not even the directors themselves were always sure just how far the web extended, who spun it, or how. In Washington, the directors could weave their own segment, visiting various federal departments, arranging for routine and special investigations of aliens, dissenters, and citizens, and passing on reports from their agents in the field. One of Frey's assistants was even able to depict on paper this network which the APL was constructing with the federal government. First, he drew two concentric circles. Then he carefully sectioned the space between the circles into small boxes. In each box he placed the title of a federal agency: State Department, War Department, Navy Department, National Council of Defense, Food and Fuel Administration, War Shipping Board, Enemy Alien Custodian. He reserved two adjacent boxes at the top of the circles for the APL and the Justice Department and then began drawing broken lines from the APL box to each federal agency. In the center of the circle where a maze of lines crisscrossed, he placed a large black dot. "The center," he scrawled at the bottom of the page, "might represent the Hun."

This diagram fairly well described the web in Washington. Although the APL was an official auxiliary of the Justice Department, it had never been allowed to actually establish its workers within the Justice Department as Frey had done in the War Department in April, 1918. The only change the directors visualized was the establishment of branch APL offices within the Justice and Navy Departments. Then the web in Washington would be complete.

On paper, the League looked neat and tidy, like a huge corporation. In reality, the organization was not nearly so well organized as it seemed, for the directors could not impose discipline on the individual city Leagues. During the early spring of 1918, overwhelmed with the task of attempting to consolidate a responsible organization, the directors appointed a number of state inspectors who checked local units to see that they followed instructions sent out from Washington. An inspector had no headquarters or office and took no part in the actual work of the League. As trouble shooter he could, if he were an effective inspector, settle disputes after they arose, but he could not help the League avoid the many private battles in which the volunteers had a tendency to engage. Only the states of Washington and Massachusetts had fully developed machinery which covered their entire states and subordinated local units to state APL headquarters, which in turn were responsible for imposing the organizational structure and regulations of the parent organization. Yet even in those states the APL continued to pursue local interests.

Recruiting reflected the problems of diffusion. Albert Briggs had originally intended that his home front army be manned by the cream of America's business and professional elite. For state inspectors, the directors had wanted "big names"; thus they went to the largest banks in the state and to the state councils of defense for recommendations, rather than elevating chiefs or members to these posts.

By the time APL recruiting for state inspectors had started in January, 1918, however, other patriotic activities had drawn most of the civic and business leaders into various forms of war work. Usually, therefore, the men who would have been the first choice of the directors could not accept APL assignments because of prior commitments. Exceptions were William C. Bobbs, president of Bobbs-Merrill Publishing Company, Ralph Smith, federal food inspector for Colorado, and William McDermid, brother-in-law of powerful New York legislator Clayton Lusk. Most state inspectors were businessmen of considerably less note, and some had their own axes to grind, like the Montana inspector who had formerly run a detective agency connected with the Pinkertons and was violently opposed to organized labor.

Eventually the directors had to accept men like Fred Voiland, State Director of the Kansas State Council of Defense, who ran a mercantile business. The directors were happy to have Voiland, as they considered him a businessman of considerable standing in the state, but correspondence revealed that he believed the APL would be "a fine handmaiden for the Council of Defense work" and planned to subordinate the APL to the state council.

Unable to find a suitable substitute, the directors were forced to go ahead with Voiland's appointment anyway. When they did, they lectured him that the two groups must be kept entirely separate and that the APL must be subordinate to Bureau of Investigation agents. "I am laying some stress upon this phase of the situation," the directors' Washington organizer, S. S. Doty, told Voiland, "because it is well at the outset to have it clear in your mind and in the minds of the Chiefs whom you will appoint, that your function and in fact that the function of this office, is a separate and distinct function of the investigation work."

In spite of these explicit instructions, two months later when the Bureau of Investigation agent in Kansas City visited Voiland, he found him conducting the APL as a side issue to the Council of Defense. Voiland blandly informed the agent that he did not know he was to keep in touch with the Department of Justice. Similar difficulties developed in Arkansas, where the state inspector for the APL directed his chiefs to get in touch with county councils of defense and cooperate closely with them.

Where there were no state inspectors—the situation in over half the states—the home office worked directly with individual chiefs, who set up their own versions of the Chicago plan, duplicating it as far as the situation allowed or their inclination dictated. Local units ranged in size from Chicago's large and elaborately organized division of thirteen thousand members to one-man affairs in small cities where the "chief" often comprised the entire organization. Local chiefs, appointed by and subject to removal by the national directors, were to have absolute control over each local branch and to be responsible for the efficiency of its work. In most cities the executive committee was eliminated because its presence tended to divide authority, and it provided an excuse for Leaguers to use powers granted by the

Application for Enrollment as a Volunteer in the

American Protective League

Organized with Approval and Operating under Direction of
United States Department of Justice, Bureau of Investigation

_____ Division

1917

A. M. BRIGGS, General Supt.
AMERICAN PROTECTIVE LEAGUE
Chicago, Illinois

Oct 23

Dear Sir:—I beg to make application for enrollment as a Volunteer in the
American Protective League and for your records in connection therewith, the following information is respectfully submitted:

1. Name in full _____

2. Residence Address 421 W. 3rd

3. City Abilene   State Kan

4. Business Phone 34   Residence Phone 615

5. Business Address Merchant - Broadway

6. City _____   State _____

7. Occupation _____

8. Age 39

9. Place of birth Abilene Kan

10. Were you ever in the service of the U. S.? No

11. If so, when, how long, and in what department of the
    service were you employed? _____

12. Are you married? Yes   Have you any objection to
    leaving the city in the interests of the work in an
    emergency? Yes

13. What foreign languages do you speak or understand? _____

14. Do you understand that you are to receive no compensation
    or expense allowances for any services rendered this organ-
    ization. Yes

15. I reserve the right to resign from this organization at any
    time, and agree to hand in my badge and commission card
    at any time upon request of the Chief.

    Signed _____

Enrolling in the volunteer home front army

133

federal government to meddle in purely local affairs, political and social. Experience proved that the directors had to be able to call any individual chief to account for the unit's activities. The temptation to corral important local men as executive committeemen remained strong in some localities, however, often providing fertile ground for conflict between chiefs and the directors, and within the local units themselves.

Recruitment of chiefs for important city units was as difficult as recruitment of state inspectors. In fact, Frey was never able to find a suitable replacement when he left the Chicago division for Washington. The directors had to replace New York chiefs several times, once because members objected that the APL should not have a chief with a German name.

In small units, the selection of responsible chiefs was even more difficult. There were always plenty who wanted the job. Not just self-interest drove these men to throw themselves so willingly into counterespionage work, although some chiefs turned their units either to local reform, to anti-labor, to nativistic, or to political causes. Nor did patriotism explain the phenomenon, although most chiefs claimed that as their motivation. As a thirty-nine-year-old New York chief whose ancestors had fought in every past American war expressed it: "There is not a man but is a better American for what the League alone made it possible to do."

Certainly, desire to participate in the great crusade, to be caught up in the vast war-making machine, to volunteer as Briggs had done on February 2, 1917, provided a great stimulus to the average man who had no particular grudge against labor or alien. But age also had much to do with the phenomenal growth of the APL. It gave those men not conscripted a way to participate. "I have plenty of time on my hands, age alone (39 years) keeping me from being in the trenches today," wrote George L. Seaton of Kansas in accepting his appointment as chief of the Atchison, Kansas, APL. "There were millions of people who felt 'The Call,' and who were unable for various reasons to go and fight," the Los Angeles chief explained, "and who would have been the most miserable people on earth if they could not have been able to get into some kind of active work." Some had worked for the Red Cross, Liberty Loan drives, or the YMCA, he concluded, "but the work of the American Protective League came nearer to satisfying that pent up feeling than anything short of going 'Over the Top.'"

Moral reform rather than "that pent up feeling" motivated the work of some chiefs. Prohibition crusaders infiltrated and controlled a number of city units. One of the jobs of the APL for the War Department was to enforce liquor control around cantonments, a task which inevitably attracted "drys" to the volunteer ranks. Raymond S. Spears, chief of the Little Falls, New York, APL was a dry as well as a newspaperman and local reform advocate. In 1918, when a bitter local option campaign began over whether or not to go dry, Spears cleared the chairman of the dry side of charges of disloyalty brought by the "wets." Another chief complained that he could obtain absolutely no cooperation from the local chief of police in his crusade against liquor. If he only had the power to arrest, wrote chief A. L. Keet from a small New York town, he could have arrested a saloon keeper—suspected of selling soldiers intoxicating liquors—and detained him for a few days on charges of disorderly conduct, merely on the grounds of the language he had used.

Whatever the motives of the chiefs, their position gave them an opportunity to intermingle federal and state jobs and to involve the APL in local affairs. The chief of the Milwaukee unit was a relative of the district attorney in Milwaukee and managed to meddle in state law enforcement. While refusing his claims to appointment as state inspector, the directors nevertheless retained this man as chief in Milwaukee. The APL chief in Atchison, Kansas, organized a company of the Kansas Home Guards and told the directors, "I believe the two positions would work well together, and enable me, as officer of the Guards, to follow out some lines of action without suspicion attaching to the League." The Clay Center, Kansas, chief was a member of the Home Guards and of a Committee of Safety, both state organizations. "It makes things rather complex," he admitted to the directors. Arrangements like these encouraged a natural tendency for individual APL units to join in investigating violations of state and municipal laws.

By far the largest involvement came with local police to whom APL units reported activities not illegal under federal laws. City ordinances forbidding "disorderly conduct" or "inciting a riot" were handy for punishing men who opposed government policies. The official APL Spy Glass encouraged this type of punishment for dissenters. The Long Beach, California, unit obtained a ninety day sentence for a man who called the President a "damned fool," and estimated it had a total of twenty-four persons tried for disturbing the peace. The Eureka chief later reported, "A great many cases dealing with IWW as well as a great many other cases were reported by members

The volunteer's oath

136

OATH OF OFFICE

Enrollment approved .... , 1917.

Chief .... Division

I, _____ do solemnly swear that I will support and defend the Constitution of the United States against all enemies, foreign and domestic; that I will bear true faith and allegiance to same; that I take this obligation freely, without any mental reservation or purpose of evasion; and I will well and faithfully discharge the duties of a Volunteer in the American Protective League; So help me God.

Signature _____

Attest:
Emma Parent
Notary Public.
Com. Expi. March 26, 1920

of the League to the local authorities who prosecuted them without the name of the League being mentioned." The sheriff's office of Los Angeles made APL units in that county veritable private police auxiliaries by deputizing members and allowing them to make arrests. The Minneapolis police department did the same.

A few chiefs became involved in local partisan politics and violated other APL tenets. Although the League oath was supposed to be attested by a notary public, the Los Angeles chief allowed clerical employees to administer it. He also collected dues, a practice strictly against the League policy, then squandered the money on two velvet rugs valued at eighty-five dollars each for the APL office. When the state inspector attempted to remove him, the chief found two federal judges, a senator, a representative, and a United States Attorney, all Democrats, who took his case to Attorney General Gregory. The Attorney General refused to intervene in this instance, consistent with his hands-off policy toward the internal affairs of the League. "I cannot and will not attempt to interfere in the internal organization of the American Protective League unless some very extraordinary condition develops," he told O'Brian. To do so would have violated his own claim that the Justice Department and the APL were now entirely separate. He was still replying to inquiries about the APL: "Its members are not officers or agents of the government in any sense, their status being purely that of private citizens volunteering to help the government." The APL directors replaced the errant chief, for all his political ties.

Bielaski had already issued a policy letter in March, 1918, reminding agents that they had nothing to do with the organization of the branches of the League, selection of members, or with internal League matters. "Any recommendations which you may wish to make for the extension of the League or persons you may think may become acceptable members or persons who are members you think should be eliminated, ought to be sent to me for presentation to the National officers of the League for such action as they may desire to take," he told one agent.

Such warnings did not have much influence on agents already inclined to be independent of their chief, though. The Bureau agent in Los Angeles helped APL members secure United States license plates for their cars and encouraged members to turn in reports directly to him rather than to their APL chief. In large cities, Bureau of Investigation superintendents who had used APL members as their own agents in the early months of the war were not inclined to disengage themselves totally from APL politics after the changes in December. Where agents themselves had been chiefs, the friendships and familiarity with APL procedures made it difficult for them to refrain from interfering.

The national directors, besides having to contend with outside interference in ordering their hierarchy, had considerable interference from within; for below the chiefs in most large units were influential businessmen who, though they could not devote their entire time to the APL, organized investigation and intelligence units within their own firms. Larger APL units were divided into two groups, active members who conducted investigations and inactive members who merely forwarded intelligence reports. But businessmen dominated both groups. And APL business tended to become their business.

Charles Daniel Frey had established the Chicago organization in the fall of 1917, and Chicago became the prototype for every other unit. The directors reproduced a chart showing how each city unit should be organized. At the top of the chart was an executive committee, below that, the chief, and below the chief, joined by straight black lines, small boxes labeled finance, administration, membership, intelligence, law, investigation, and motor service. Under the "investigation" box, black lines again linked other small boxes: Department A, comprising approximately one hundred operatives, and Department B, comprising captains, lieutenants, and operatives. Under the "intelligence" box, right in the center of the diagram, was another series of radiating lines to divisional boxes: real estate, financial, insurance, professional, industries, hotels, transportation, public utilities, general merchandise, and so on, down to small boxes for each of the spearate industries.

In Chicago, a businessman headed each of the nine intelligence divisions. A past-president of the Chicago Real Estate Board organized the Real Estate Division. An old Scottish banker who held presidencies and directorships in a dozen financial institutions organized the Financial Division. The vice-president and manager of two of the finest hotels, the Drake and the Blackstone, organized the Hotel Division. The president of the Chicago and North Western Railway formed the Transportation Division. The president of Montgomery Ward accepted the management of the General Merchandise Division. Other divisions had equally prestigious heads.

The Chicago Industries Division included packing plants, electrical industries, grain merchants, manufacturers of paints and chemicals,

Structure of the American Protective League as it looked on paper

AMERICAN PROTECTIVE LEAGUE

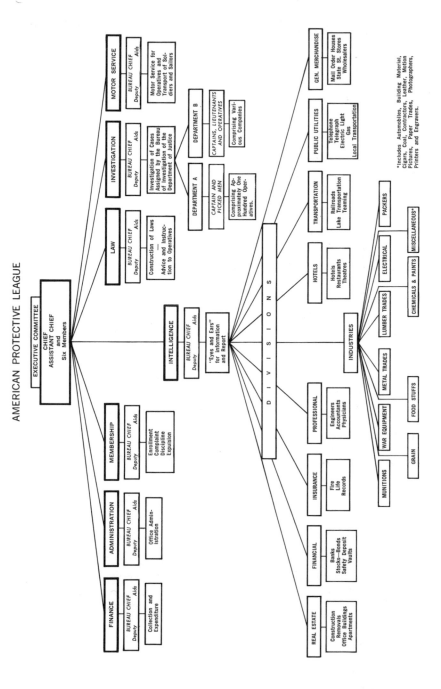

processors of groceries, and war equipment manufacturers. Such influential men as the vice-president of Armour and Company, the president of Central Electric Company, the president of Fuller-Morrison Paint Company, the chairman of the board of the largest wholesale grocery company in Chicago, and the vice-president of a mill-railway and vessel supplies company headed these branches of the League. It is difficult to see how the nominal directors of the APL could really direct these nineteen men. They were a cross-section of the ruling business elite of the Progressive Era, captains of industry or robber barons, depending on how one viewed them. But whatever their label, taking orders was not one of their characteristics.

Of the seven bureaus composing the Chicago APL hierarchy, the Investigation Bureau was by far the most powerful, for it conducted the actual investigations requested by the Justice Department. Within this section were two departments, one composed of a hundred picked operatives who probed the important cases, and a larger one, with agents organized geographically by profession and by trade, that processed such routine matters as permits for aliens to enter restricted areas. It was in this Investigation Bureau that the second level of the Chicago business and professional elite usually enlisted.

Most members of the Investigation Bureau were organized by geographical districts, each district with its head inspector, its captains, lieutenants, and squads of operatives. Each rank actually reflected the descending order of the social and economic hierarchy in Chicago, with patriotism, efficiency, and loyalty forming only the surface criteria for selection.

The captains who had control over the conduct of operatives in each district were usually of English or Scottish descent, Chicagoans by birth, educated in prep schools and major eastern colleges, and members of fraternities. They were manufacturers, lawyers, or financiers, Republicans, and members of local social clubs. Neither religion nor politics nor national origin formed any absolute criteria, however, for there were Catholics, Democrats, Irishmen, and at least one Czech immigrant enrolled as captains. They had primarily one thing in comcon: all were successful Chicago businessmen.

Lieutenants who worked under the captains were selected on the same basis: natives of Chicago, college graduates, professionals or manufacturers or financiers, and Republicans. At this level were included even more Catholics and one Jew—who obtained their positions by virtue of their efforts in lay religious organizations—and a number of Irish. Also in this group were ministers, publishers, and doctors, a number of whom had been involved in local bipartisan reform movements before the war, like the old middle class of the progressive movement.

Information on other units is not nearly so full as that on the Chicago division, but scattered references confirm that the same general pattern also prevailed in smaller units. In Washington, D.C., Bielaski proposed for membership the chief of police, the head of a paint company, the attorney for Seaboard Railroad, the president of the Washington Hotel, the president of the American National Bank and the Board of Trade, the president of the Association of Commerce, an insurance executive, a partner in a Virginia detective agency, and the chief of the Washington Home Defense League. The chief of the Asheville, North Carolina, APL unit appointed the president of the local Board of Trade, the general manager of the local Bell Telephone system, the editors of the *Asheville Citizen* and the *Asheville Times*, the city commissioner of Public Safety, who was a lawyer; the general manager of the largest industrial plant, a banker, a reporter, and a corporation lawyer. A list of the members in California units reads much the same, with the addition of two special units organized by the enterprising Cecil B. DeMille. He established a unit within the movie industry and an aerial unit for observation, no doubt because he owned one of the few planes in California. What he planned to observe from the sky no one mentioned. New York, like Hollywood, had a special actors' unit for thespians with a yen to play "I Spy."

A few units came to be dominated completely by one ethnic group. The chief and the assistant chief of the New Orleans Division and a high proportion of their members were Jewish. In San Francisco, perhaps due to the domination of Representative Julius Kahn, Jewish members were influential in the APL. So little information exists on other city units, however, that it is impossible to plot any overall ethnic pattern.

It was not the well known businessmen, however, but anonymous operatives who did most of the actual investigating. These cadres, usually composed of ten men each in the industrial units, came from the lower echelons of business. Often they were employed by the captains or lieutenants. Each operative was investigated before admission to membership; each took a loyalty oath and carried a commission card identifying him as a member of the APL. It was these men the public most often encountered, and it was at this level that motives of patriotism most often became intertwined with self-interest, intolerance, sometimes even mob violence. It was here that the APL set neighbor against neighbor.

At first the rank of operative was open to both men and women. The St. Louis APL later boasted it had a female undercover agent; the Cleveland division had a whole women's company, of which one member was a wealthy young socialite who worked in overalls in a Cleveland airplane parts factory trying to locate saboteurs. A mysterious "Mrs. B." worked for the Chicago APL. One Lutheran minister was stalked by a female Leaguer who wined and dined him, then reported his "disloyal" remarks to the Justice Department.

Male Leaguers were enthusiastic about the advantages of using American Mata Haris to track down German spies. The San Francisco chief, for one, felt his unit could obtain much more information by organizing a female division. During the December, 1917, reorganization, however, the Justice Department and the national directors decided that women should no longer be enrolled. Frey explained the reasons to a Kate Marjoribanks who had written to request a secret service badge so that she could go aboard ships to investigate. "Each one of the several hundred thousand men throughout the United States has the idea that his wife would make a wounderful lady detective," wrote Frey, "and it being impossible for us to devise or think of any argument that would still keep up his interest and retain his service and at the same time explain to him that his wife has not the talents necessary in this line, we would end in a free-for-all fight and as you see untold difficulties." In fact, there were so many inquiries from male Leaguers to enroll their wives that Frey finally composed a form letter to explain that enrollment of women would cause disorganization among the male members. He concluded: "Your wife is no doubt perfectly discreet and would render a valuable service, but if she were enrolled and the wife of the man next door refused enrollment friction would be inevitable."

Friction was inevitable anyway. The original order barring women from membership did not reach all members. In April, 1918, the San Francisco chief had to inquire what the policy was, and in July a similar inquiry came from a chief in the state of New York who thought "discreet" women should be retained to work under cover in factories. As late as July, the California state inspector explained to one chief that exceptions to the policy existed for women of "special value to the organization," simply admonishing him, "In admitting women to membership, please use the utmost care to see that their individuality complies with these requirements." Women employees in various APL units with access to confidential records were still being asked to take the APL oath and to become members.

One of Frey's personal friends, W. K. Cochrane, a New York member also unaware of the policy decision, wrote the most extensive argument in favor of using women. He sent an ecstatic letter to Frey saying he had just met several "brainy women" who were wild to belong to the APL and whom he was already using to collect information. "Throughout the country Charlie," he wrote, "thousands of women are daily visiting cafes, hotels and other public places selling Thrift Stamps. . . . They could all be American spies . . . I would have them visit all public places—all hotels, clubs, theatres and keep their eyes and ears open and report every day what they have heard. . . . Women are far more subtle than men, especially in such work as this . . . if they are attractive they have little difficulty in getting what they go after. If I had one hundred smart women on my staff, I am willing to bet that I would get a tremendous volume of first-class information." Society women, manicurists, stenographers, telephone operators, saleswomen, all should be signed up, Cochrane argued. "These women would be tickled to death to be enrolled as Secret Agents and they would work their heads off."

From this idea of a legion of female spies Cochrane made the logical leap: "I have often thought it would be a wise move on the part of the President to issue a proclamation calling on all loyal citizens of the United States, both men and women, and even boys and girls, to constitute themselves Secret Agents of the Government and report to the authorities every suspicious circumstance and disloyal remark or conversation coming to their notice."

Late in June, Frey discovered the main cause of both the confusion and the continued use of women agents: encouragement by Briggs. "Did you tell Jennings that he could enroll a lot of actresses in his Division?" he demanded of Briggs, "and is it your understanding that this is desired by Bielaski? Victor [Elting] and I have consistently told every chief throughout the country that women are not to be enrolled. If this is a point that we are not together on, let us make it the subject of a discussion while you are here, and write Jennings definite instructions."

They did get together, and Frey discovered that Briggs had indeed advocated enlisting actresses in the Theatre Division. On July 19, the three national directors issued Bulletin No. 15 to all chiefs instructing them unequivocally that "the membership of the League will be hereafter confined to male citizens of the United States of legal age . . . women shall not be eligible for membership." From that time on the excluded wives helped out as "Emergency Drivers" to chauffeur their husband-sleuths around. The membership remained exclusively male.

As with the rank and file in any hierarchy, these amateur sleuths left few records of their work or their sentiments. They enjoyed enlivening their routine jobs with the excitement of clandestine activities, yet they envied the publicity which men in the front line trenches received. As the war progressed, most of the younger operatives were drafted or they enlisted, leaving a group composed mainly of men over thirty-five years of age, men who had been born before the 1880's and reared in the atmosphere of nationalism and militarism which permeated the late nineteenth century. They accepted the American political and social system as sacrosanct; indeed, their place within it would be threatened by change. They found their security in the solidarity of the community.

Morton Grodzins has described loyalties as attachments enabling a person to organize his life so as to reduce uncertainty and anxiety. In time of crisis, such loyalties may be galvanized into a sectlike patriotism, almost religious in quality, which leads to the formation of volunteer groups. Upton Sinclair, a Socialist who supported the war but criticized the government's home front tactics, analyzed the psychology of the volunteer patriot in these same terms and created an archetype in a character called Peter Gudge.

Gudge, Sinclair explained, needed a religion, an ideal, just like everyone else. The socialist religion did not appeal to him because its followers lacked prestige and the social graces—they insisted on looking at the sordid side of life. Peter wanted a religion with clergymen in robes of white linen, churches of gold, captains of industry with power, statesmen with fame, editors with wit and learning. With a religion constructed of these elements, Peter could continue his intrigues in the name of a mighty nation rather than solely his own. He could act in the "sacred name of patriotism and the still more sacred name of democracy."

While the drive to reduce anxiety may have created a new religion which motivated some operatives, one cannot help but feel that many APL operatives were like little boys who simply wanted to wear a tin badge and play detective. In Los Angeles, for instance, the Bureau of Investigation special agent called out the APL to have them shadow General Alvaro Obregón of Mexico while he was touring the city. Ten automobiles loaded with armed Leaguers appeared at the hotel where Obregón was staying. One car was positioned at each corner of the street, while the rest cruised about slowly. Four or five operatives entered the hotel, looked about suspiciously, and stationed themselves in the corners of the lobby. On the streets, other Leaguers stopped friends who came by to say—out of the corners of their mouths, in whispers—that they were on a very important government assignment shadowing an important general from Mexico.

When the alert came from within the hotel that Obregón was about to leave, members excitedly rushed back to their cars. A Colt automatic dropped out of one man's pocket. Fortunately it did not go off. Scooping it up, the member jumped into a car which trailed Obregón to the theater. Leaguers followed the General inside and after the performance followed him to a chocolate shop. Obregón drank chocolate; Leaguers sat at the next table and drank chocolate too. Then they followed him out of the shop and back to the hotel, still whispering out of the sides of their mouths. Obregón went to bed. Leaguers waited around until 3:00 A.M., when a house detective reported that the general was fast asleep in his room. Then they all trooped home to tell of their experiences.

Occasionally, members used the APL as a cloak for questionable activities. One Boston operative used his credentials to panhandle, telling people he was the best secret service agent in the country. At least one Kansas enrollee bootlegged liquor.

Sometimes operatives were simply irresponsible. One left a dossier of loyalty reports on a Washington streetcar, an episode which caused Secretary of War Baker to complain to Attorney General Gregory. Trial boards were set up to discipline such members, and the directors voluntarily submitted records of a few cases to Gregory.

The real dangers, however, came not from the behavior of these maverick members, but from the tendency of most members to consider it their duty to discourage or punish activities which were not illegal. Especially before the passage of the Sedition Act in May of 1918, it was a common practice for operatives to visit people or call them to the APL office for a "talking to."

Sometimes members went still further. Raiding was one favorite pastime which had a great potential for violence. A local Bureau of Investigation agent could encourage the APL in this dangerous activity, as did the one in Detroit. There the agent had an APL operative accompany him on a raid where they arrested an enemy alien.

Excited townspeople took the prisoner from the two men, ducked him in the canal, and threatened worse. "This action by the mob almost resulted in a lynching similar to the Praeger lynching," Frey wrote to Briggs. Frey ordered the raiding stopped. He expelled the member responsible and told Briggs, "We are doing everything possible to clean up the situation."

Or, again, the APL could cooperate with local armed units, formed to replace the National Guard, in vigilante action aimed at making the "disloyal" recant their heresy. In Clay Center, Kansas, the APL asked two citizens accused of disloyalty to appear for a public investigation by local attorneys. Flanked by the Home Guard, with six hundred hostile citizens looking on, the two men promised to be loyal in the future. Had they not publicly recanted, vigilante action surely would have followed.

Frey acknowledged much of this sort of proselytizing for patriotism. In a later report to the War Department, he explained that where no prosecution could be instituted, members attempted "to dissuade the subject of the investigation from further words and conduct tending toward disloyalty . . . . a great number of individuals were dissuaded from further unpatriotic acts and expressions, and in many cases were actually converted to patriotic citizenship . . . [they] not only ceased to exercise an evil influence upon those about them, but by reason of their change of attitude became a positive influence for good."

APL operatives in some instances actually belonged to local vigilante groups. In Peru, Indiana, for example, many held membership in the Loyal Citizens Vigilance Committee of Miami County, a group which retained anti-Catholic overtones and which was headed by the assistant chief of the local APL division. In Napoleon, Ohio, the chief of the APL became the county president of the League of American Patriots, an organization numbering over five hundred members of whom only a select fifteen were admitted to APL membership. In Atlanta, Georgia, where the APL unit admitted only 125 leading citizens, the Citizen's Bureau of Investigation acted as an auxiliary. One member of the Citizen's Bureau, William J. Simmons, head of the then recently revived Ku Klux Klan, later claimed, "I was in touch in my wartime secret service work with federal judges, federal attorneys, and federal secret service officials and operatives. The Klan secret service reported to me." The Klan had failed miserably during its first two years of existence; the paranoid climate fostered by the war prolonged its life and gave it experience in techniques which it would use later.

Perhaps a hundred thousand APL members were actively investigating individuals around the nation, and again as many were watching neighbors and reporting "suspicious" activities. No bulletins went out from Washington headquarters warning these crusaders in the field against the more sinister activities going on. The League paper, the *Spy Glass,* began publication on June 4, 1918, with an issue primarily devoted to explaining the new Sedition Act. Tucked away on page three was a small article which betrayed the leaders' failure to recognize the dangers of vigilantism even at that late date. In fact, the article actually encouraged violence. Remarking upon the scurrilous rumors that maternity wards were necessary for returning Red Cross nurses, the editor counseled, "The limit in fines and jail sentences seems punishment too light for such cowardly attacks; social ostracism and physical violence, perhaps, should supplement the legal penalties for repeating such a yarn."

It was in this sensitive area of civil liberties that the concept of the League as the bastion of democratic values broke down. Vigilantism may not have been an official tenet, but as long as members engaged in it, as long as the League did not oppose it but instead on occasion encouraged it, the APL appeared to give federal sanction to practices inimical to the very principles the United States was supposed to be defending. Aside from Bielaski's letter of April, 1917, asking Briggs to have members protect aliens, and an occasional admonition from Elting to a chief, the APL initiated no measures to protect the alien or dissenter against mob law during its first year of existence. Since Wilson made no pronouncement either, the public had no reason to assume that the federal government was concerned. Gregory's publicity handouts dwelt on the merits of civilian control as opposed to military control; he, too, seemed indifferent to, or oblivious of, the very real assaults being made upon the liberties of individuals.

True, APL members generally preferred methods more indirect than violence to guard the public from the dangers of dissent. Some collected information on professors, pressuring trustees to discharge from their faculties persons holding unconventional views and urging administrators to cancel certain public lectures. At the University of California, several "decidedly pro-German professors" were discharged, reported one pleased Leaguer from Berkeley. In Los Angeles, an

APL'er demanded that a lecture by Professor Frank Klingberg of the University of Southern California be cancelled because he was proposing "peace" of some kind and was suspected of being pro-German. Only Klingberg's proof that his lectures were actually based on propaganda furnished by the government's Committee on Public Information cleared him of the League charges.

Members in many localities saw to it that libraries removed objectionable books from their shelves. One article in the *Spy Glass* recommended such action. Noting that the Secretary of War had banned certain pro-German books from army base libraries, the editor said, "Secretary Baker's order does not apply, of course, to public libraries. But this list is a safe guide for librarians and library trustees to follow in determining what works should be removed from general circulation and made accessible only to serious students and other folk of mature judgment."

Even when APL'ers contented themselves with investigations, the result was wholesale abuse of civil liberties and invasions of privacy. An investigation typically began with a request forwarded from APL headquarters in Washington to the city chief, who assigned the case to one of his operatives. Once the operative received this request, he had numerous investigative weapons from which to choose. Membership in the APL provided each operative with an entrée to the records of banks and other financial institutions; of real estate transactions, medical records, and, inevitably, legal records. Any material ordinarily considered confidential by private firms or corporations could be made available to operatives. Even institutions customarily regarded as repositories of confidence and trust compromised their standards. Bishop Theodore Henderson helped to spread the APL throughout the Methodist Church, with the result that Methodist ministers could often be approached for information about members of their congregations. Liaison was also established with Catholic, Jewish, and Protestant churches. The Maryland Casualty Company of Baltimore asked its agents throughout the country to join the League so that insurance information was readily available. Private detective agencies would check old records and disclose their contents. Anti-labor and nativistic groups opened their secret files to the APL.

In addition to collecting information from such sources, the APL operative could go on to the post office. Bielaski had arranged for APL personnel to be given the same kind of information supplied to Bureau of Investigation agents, so long as the local agent had asked the postmaster for the information. In practice, once the APL operative was known to be working for the Bureau, he could easily obtain such information as forwarding addresses and return addresses on incoming mail. A little jollying usually loosened the necessary data from even the most cautious postmaster.

The APL directors encouraged this practice. Director Elting, for example, suggested to chief P. A. Erlach of Mattoon, Illinois, that he secure from the postmaster in a "personal and unofficial" way, a memorandum of "postmarks, return notices, and all other data to be discovered from external examination of the mail of this woman [the suspect] including the frequency of letters from the same individual." There was no reason, Elting said, why the postmaster upon his own responsibility should not give the APL this information. Erlach had also wanted permission to intercept mail, actually open and examine it. No arrangement could be made with the post office for this practice, Elting replied. But members found ways. "Let us call the APL sometimes almost clairvoyant as to letters done by suspects," confided official League historian Emerson Hough.

Although officially the contents of mail remained inviolable to even the Justice Department, telegrams did not. The telegraph companies, Elting wrote to Colorado inspector Ralph Smith, were "loath to give information as to messages," even though the Justice Department had been able to arrange for agents of the Bureau of Investigation to secure the information they desired upon special request. Elting went to Bielaski in June to see if this privilege could be extended to APL members, but Bielaski was skeptical. Even the Military Intelligence had encountered great difficulty in securing this sort of information, he told Elting. So Leaguers had to work out their own arrangements informally with Bureau agents.

In some cities the APL found telegraph officials extremely cooperative. The Minneapolis APL reported one case where a jilted sweetheart had disclosed to the League that her former boyfriend was evading the draft. When called upon by the APL to prove the date of his birth, the young man replied that there was no authentic record of his birth—but he wired his mother to send him an affidavit placing the date one year earlier than was correct. The Minneapolis APL obtained a copy of the message, gathered additional information on his actual birthdate, and saw that he was inducted into the Army.

Telephone companies were always much more cooperative than were telegraph companies. Wiretapping was easier than copying a telegram. Although wiretapping had been a common practice among city police ever since the late nineteenth century when use of the telephone first became widespread, the federal government seems not to have engaged in such tactics before 1908. Then Attorney General Charles Bonaparte had allowed his new Bureau of Investigation to adopt the practice in immigration investigations.

Washington attorney James S. Easby-Smith had complained about wiretapping to Wilson early in 1917. Initiated during the administration of President Theodore Roosevelt, its use had "grown in infamy" under Bielaski, and Easby-Smith's own wires had been tapped without the knowledge of the telephone company, he said. Bielaski had denied that the telephone of Easby-Smith had been tapped, but he admitted that the wires of other attorneys had been.

No federal law existed at that time prohibiting wiretapping by private individuals or by federal law enforcement officers. In the few states with statutes prohibiting the practice, the Justice Department proceeded on the assumption that the laws did not apply to law enforcement officers. New York's state law provided no restraint because since the 1890's claims of the New York City police that they were exempt had gone unchallenged; and in 1918 the governor of New York had vetoed a measure which would have expressly forbidden law enforcement officers to install taps without a court order. In California, where "unauthorized" wiretapping was forbidden by state law, the Justice Department nevertheless arranged with the Pacific Telephone Company to install a telephonic device on lines so that information about labor organizers on the Pacific Coast could be obtained for Secretary of Labor Wilson. Unauthorized wiretapping, according to the Justice Department, meant only wiretapping without authorization by the Justice Department and the telephone company; it had nothing to do with a person's right to privacy.

Early in the war, the Justice Department had made confidential arrangements with the telephone companies to receive "information with respect to all matters bearing on the war." The arrangement, Bielaski wrote to the APL, "is very confidential and we confine knowledge of it, as far as possible, to our agent in charge and some responsible executive of the telephone company involved." Bielaski continued, "Inasmuch as it is a privilege which should be used very sparingly and only where matters of importance are involved and as a too frequent use of it not only lessens the likelihood of obtaining information, but leads to the possibility of embarrassment because of the increasing persons who learn about it, I suggest that your chief take up with the head of the local telephone company this matter . . . and perfect an arrangement with him whereby he can obtain information in matters of real importance, with the understanding that the information so obtained will be kept entirely confidential. Information so obtained can not be used as evidence."

Even without the understanding between the Bureau of Investigation and the telephone companies, APL men could easily gain the information they desired, for in most towns the APL had already infiltrated the local companies. A Wichita, Kansas, member explained to Briggs how his men operated in practice: "One of them is a high executive in the force of the Telephone Company whose office here controls a large part of the surrounding telephone exchanges. Through him, we will be able to place members of our organization where their ears will do considerable good."

After the government took over the telephone and telegraph lines at the end of June, there seems to have been little concern that federal law enforcement officers and their volunteers might violate the right of privacy by widespread wiretapping. Congress certainly was still concentrating on foreign espionage, for it passed a resolution asking the Justice Department what measures it had taken to combat wiretapping by German spies. The federal law passed at the end of October, making it a crime to tap telegraph or telephone lines "without authority and without the knowledge and consent of the other users," was aimed at spies, not at spy-chasers; and its application to either federal officials or their volunteers was never tested in the courts. Thus in the entire course of the war, APL operatives continued the practice with impunity.

If, in spite of all efforts, legal and extralegal, neither the government nor private companies could supply the information desired, the APL operative might stake out the suspect and watch his office or home. A favorite technique of the volunteers was to rig the quarry's apartment or office with a dictaphone. Dictaphones, along with wiretapping, had already been utilized by the Bureau of Investigation under Bielaski, in one case a dictaphone even having been placed in the office of the district attorney in San Francisco. There were no state or federal laws forbidding this newest form of electronic eavesdropping. In Arizona, where the state attempted to apply older wiretapping laws to dictaphones, the courts held that it could not be done. After this decision in May, 1918, there seemed to be no danger from judicial interference with this practice.

The APL enjoyed playing with dictaphones. In Little Rock, Arkansas, chief Durand Whipple reported excitedly to the APL in Washington that he was working with the Military Intelligence there, and that they were "on the point of 'turning up' the coterie that is at the head of the seditious work in our district." Most cases, however, turned out to be what League historian Hough later called "petticoat cases": men acting suspiciously because they were engaged in illicit love affairs, not because they were plotting espionage. Their lives were now, as Hough said, "filed away, cross-indexed, for future reference in the vast archives of the Department of Justice at Washington." Sometimes this kind of surveillance could backfire, however. One New York member, for example, forgot that he had planted a dictaphone in a woman suspect's apartment before he went in to get the evidence himself. His amorous adventures were thus recorded for his colleagues to enjoy.

Quite often an operative could depend for his information upon fellow APL members holding jobs which enabled them to eavesdrop without the aid of electronic devices. Since most branches had captains in the local gas and electric companies, the process, as one chief explained, was simple: "As members of his team are scattered through his organization in Wichita and surrounding towns, it is possible for us to gain access to any house on the grounds of checking their gas and electric service."

Sometimes, of course, the APL members simply used the old-fashioned technique of concealment. They hid in apartments and offices and attempted to overhear incriminating conversations. One Minneapolis operative, for instance, crawled into a woman's basement through the coal chute and listened to her conversations, which he then described to headquarters as seditious.

If all these techniques failed, members felt justified in resorting to outright illegal means, undeterred by ordinary moral codes. If necessary, they would find a pliant friend of the suspect and enlist his help. The New Jersey APL, to cite an example, working with the Military Intelligence, used theft in cracking one fraud case. A young private who knew the suspect was ordered to call upon his friend and, while in the friend's home, to steal the document which the APL needed for evidence. Later the courts would hold that the Fourth Amendment prohibited this type of seizure by a federal official, but the APL took credit for securing the evidence, and the Justice Department used it in obtaining a conviction.

Usually the APL members did any breaking and entering themselves. "The League has done that thousands of times and has never been detected," boasted historian Hough. The job was easiest, of course, where the building owner was a League member. It was then no problem to get a key to the suspect's office and rifle his private correspondence. The Constitution was of no help, for though the Bureau of Investigation accepted these stolen goods, its agents had not seized them; and the victims could not bring action against APL members because, obviously, it was impossible to know who did the actual stealing. Thus the right to be secure in one's house, papers, and effects against unreasonable search and seizure was subverted by the government through the use of volunteers.

Even after the war, the Supreme Court did not consider this type of activity unconstitutional. Reviewing a similar case in 1921, wherein a company detective had taken papers from a private office and turned them over to the Justice Department to use as evidence, the Court held that since no federal official had purloined the evidence, the complainant's grievance was against the individual, not the federal government, hence no constitutional point was at issue. Only Justice Brandeis spoke out in dissent. "I cannot believe," Brandeis said, "that action of a public official is necessarily lawful, because it does not violate constitutional prohibitions and because the same result might have been attained by other and proper means. At the foundation of our civil liberty lies the principle which denies to government officials an exceptional position before the law and which subjects them to the same rules of conduct that are commands to the citizen. And in the development of our liberty insistence upon procedural regularity has been a large factor. Respect for law will not be advanced by resort in its enforcement, to means which shock the common man's sense of decency and fair play."

What Brandeis said may have been true, but the Justice Department and the APL felt differently. In the pursuit of incriminating evidence, questioning of neighbors and friends of the suspect was commonplace. Here the operative sometimes posed as an automobile salesman, the representative of a credit bureau or insurance company, a salesman for Liberty Bonds, or a reporter. When looking for information on men who had not registered for the draft, the operative sought out houses displaying service flags indicating that a member of the family had gone to war. There, the operative could be sure, the occupants would tell all they knew about draft dodgers. In investigating candidates for military commissions, the operatives could establish their own tests of past loyalty and ask such questions as whether the subject or his relatives had expressed approval of the German invasion of France and Belgium or the sinking of the *Lusitania* or had opposed the entry of the United States into war. Ask whether he is susceptible to "bribery, blackmail or bad women," one APL booklet instructed members.

An even more devious method of trapping a suspect was the use of decoys or *agents provocateurs*. When the League eventually became engaged in investigating fraud in War Department contracts, members often coached selected businessmen, who then suggested certain fraudulent practices to persons already under suspicion. In August, 1918, Bielaski requested that the War Department order a particular army captain to Detroit so that the APL could trap him in a fraud involving War Department contracts. An APL operative was to pose as a truck manufacturer and lead the captain to incriminate himself. One War Department officer voiced an objection to his superior, saying that the interference of Frey and the APL was "irregular," but the suspected captain was ordered to Detroit anyway. Another War Department request for an APL investigation resulted in orders to "frame" two men suspected of shipping material to the United States in contravention of regulations of the War Priorities Board. In this case, one Leaguer who supplied information was the brother-in-law of the suspect.

No limitations were imposed by either the Bureau of Investigation or the Justice Department on methods of obtaining evidence, even though some of the evidence so obtained was inadmissible in court. The aim of the Bureau and the volunteers was to get as much evidence as possible, regardless of the means necessary. Whether or not the evidence was crucial, its very bulk might be sufficient to obtain indictments. Frey probably rationalized the whole situation as well as anyone when he explained at a fund raising dinner in Chicago that while espionage was repugnant to the American people, modern warfare, especially with Germany, demanded total espionage. To reconcile public distaste with national security, the people themselves must man the internal defenses of the country. But since not everyone could be a defender, the federal government had entrusted the APL with the duty. The state inspector for the Washington Minute Men did not even bother to describe the APL as consonant with American principles. He put the matter quite bluntly: "As a basic foundation to build upon, the thought of a reproduction in a crude way of the German espionage system was hit upon."

As the war progressed the number of APL men involved in investigative work increased. The Chicago office had assumed 75 percent of the Bureau of Investigation work there by July, 1918, a volume which necessitated hiring sixty-six stenographers and clerks and maintaining eighteen branch offices to process the more than three hundred reports received daily.

In Cleveland, the APL handled 80 percent of the Bureau of Investigation's work, a goal which the superintendent of the Bureau in New York worked toward through 1918. In New York, fifty-three clerks were needed to man the central office and six branch offices. That unit alone had processed almost twelve thousand "character and loyalty" investigations by the end of the war. Minute Men in Washington state checked out two thousand cases during the first three months of 1918. The Washington, D. C., headquarters estimated that it was handling two thousand reports daily by the summer of that year.

The Bureau of Investigation increased its force to almost fifteen hundred during the war. Such a proliferation of federal watchdogs would have been greatly opposed by state and local police during any other time, but the high volume of prosecutions that resulted seemed proof that they were needed. Meanwhile, however, the more routine investigations into character and loyalty, draft evasion, and enemy alien regulations, matters which involved operatives in the most intimate aspects of the daily life of Americans, fell more and more to the APL volunteers; and as suspicion turned more often to ordinary citizens, the enemy within became the Leaguer's neighbor.

The total number of cases investigated by the APL was never calculated, even by the directors. Frey estimated three million cases for the War Department, including investigations of draft evasion, which necessarily involved large numbers of men. If, as a number of local divisions indicated, approximately one-half of all investigations concerned draft evasion, perhaps another three million cases were undertaken for the Justice Department. Using the Chicago office cost estimate of ninety-three cents for each investigation, it would appear that several million dollars were spent by the volunteers to investigate for the Justice Department, alone.

Financing League operations varied from city to city. The Washington, D. C., headquarters received no contributions directly from members, depending upon local units which held periodic fund raising drives to furnish the three to four thousand dollars needed monthly to pay for office supplies and staff. Chicago received pledges of seventy-five thousand dollars from businessmen in November of 1917. Even this amount disappeared quickly as office expenses in this largest unit rose to seven thousand dollars a month, plus three hundred dollars a month for maintenance of each of eighteen captains' offices. None of the other units ever approached this sum, whether because of lower volume, higher efficiency, or less corruption; but the New York office had spent fifty thousand dollars by the summer of 1918 and operated on a four-thousand-dollar monthly budget. The Minute Men in the state of Washington had spent twenty thousand dollars by the summer of 1918 and had a budget of two thousand dollars a month. Even an individual businessman who only provided office space, postage, and stationery spent several hundred dollars a year. The overall cost of maintaining the APL ran into millions.

The Justice Department itself spent approximately four and one half million dollars—exclusive of personnel and other office costs—on the war work it performed. Inasmuch as Congress voted this sum reluctantly, it is difficult to imagine that the legislators would have voted another two to three million dollars for secret investigations. While the war was on, Congress was still frugal in doling out funds for home front security.

Gregory, however, never really had to test the willingness of Congress to appropriate larger sums for intelligence, since corporations and businessmen kept the APL in funds. The chief of the Central California division was able to obtain substantial sums of money in the form of monthly subscriptions for the duration of the war, donations, as he explained after the war was over, "being made by those firms mostly interested in the IWW problems." In a few cases, the APL was able to tap community fund-raising drives, such as the Detroit Patriotic Fund Committee; but usually operating costs were met by corporations. In fact, when the railroads were taken over by the federal government in December of 1917, they applied specifically for permission to continue donations to the APL.

Without the web of the APL, the federal government, including President Wilson, would have had to place more faith in the loyalty of American citizens and aliens. Allan Dulles, former director of the Central Intelligence Agency, writes in his book *The Craft of Intelligence*, "The size and power of an internal security service is generally in direct ratio to the extent of the suspicion and fear of the ruling clique." He goes on to use Russia's Okhrana as an example of response to this fear. Surely the very existence, let alone the size, of the APL must testify to this same type of fear, in this case exacerbated by fear of criticism stemming largely from political rivalries.

Wilson had been forced to turn from America's traditional reliance upon volunteer troops in the field to reliance on conscripts. Still, he seems to have been moved more by the political implications of Theodore Roosevelt's championing of volunteers than by agreements with the Chief of Staff when he damned volunteer soldiers as absolutely uncontrollable and inefficient. Similarly when Roosevelt came out later in favor of centralization of secret services—a move which might have resulted in the disbanding of the home front volunteers—Wilson decided to the contrary. Later he was forced into a posture of defending civilian volunteers against militarists. His finally allowing Gregory to turn over a portion of the APL to the War Department for use in civilian investigations was a logical outcome.

"It is true I am constantly playing a part in the formation of all the important decisions which are formed in every branch of the Government's war activities," Wilson had written to journalist David Lawrence in spring, 1918, but, he continued, "after the work is done I necessarily forget its details." Once McAdoo had given up his efforts to kill the League, Wilson forgot about the details and seldom heard about the methods used by the volunteers in stamping out dissent. He only heard about the results of the APL work from the Justice Department. And the results were impressive.

ᶜΑlien, Dissenter, Citizen

The immense web of the APL began as a response to the fear that
German spies were infesting America. In the first frightening days of
preparation for war, Attorney General Gregory had encouraged the
APL to watch for spies and saboteurs because, like most other Americans, he feared the German population might engage in violence.
For two and a half years the APL searched for spies but found none.
Even the official historian of the League, Emerson Hough, could do
no more than retell once again the old stories of German activities
during the neutrality days. Pablo Waberski was the only man ever
suspected by Gregory of being a spy, and the public never heard of
Waberski. There were no prosecutions of spies under either the Espionage Act or the Sabotage Act during World War I. Violence
erupted, but it originated with Americans, not with foreign spies.

O'Brian had suggested that Wilson make a statement regarding
mob violence against enemy aliens during the height of the spy
scare in April, 1918. Wilson, however, chose to remain silent. Reformers were distressed at his silence but did little to pressure him
into making a defense of toleration at home. If Wilson wanted to
make such an announcement earlier, political considerations must

have kept him quiet. A propitious opportunity occurred, however, late in July, after newspapers announced that the Reichstag had discussed the Praeger hanging and Germany was rumored to be sending a protest through diplomatic channels.

In his July 26 speech, Wilson did refer to mob action as both a danger and a disgrace. Every lynching, he warned, "has been a blow at the heart of ordered law and humane justice. . . . Every mob contributes to German lies about the United States what her most gifted liars cannot improve upon by the way of calumny." He called upon every man and woman to cooperate actively and watchfully "to make an end of this disgraceful evil." Let us, he said, "show our utter contempt for the things that have made this war hideous among the wars of history by showing how those who love liberty and right and justice and are willing to lay down their lives for them upon foreign fields stand ready also to illustrate to all mankind their loyalty to the things at home which they wish to see established everywhere as a blessing and protection to the peoples who have never known the privileges of liberty and self-government."

It was an eloquent plea. Even the APL thought so. On August 10, the directors of the APL followed it up with one of their own. "League members," read the *Spy Glass*, "are in a special sense, guardians of the country's internal frontier against such outbreaks as the President deplored. Concentration on alien enemy activities, on pro-German propaganda and anti-American sabotage, should not close the eyes of local Chiefs and individual members to the possibility that injustice and personal injury may thus be done to alien enemies quite innocent of doing wrong." Far from bullying alien enemies, the article went on, "the League exists to protect them, no less than to keep them in order. The League's aim, therefore—and your business— is to forestall mob action by wiping out the conditions under which loyal and peaceful citizens sometimes resort to lynch law."

Ostensibly, the deployment of APL members along the home front was for the purpose of watching enemy aliens to see that they remained loyal and that none among them turned out to be spies and saboteurs. No one knew exactly who these enemy aliens were, for many were indistinguishable from other Americans. Even the government could only estimate at approximately four million the number of people living in the United States who had been born subjects of the enemy countries.

Except with regard to Asians, Americans had been quite casual about citizenship before World War I. Eight states even allowed aliens to vote before naturalization. And, again unless they were Asians, no restrictions existed on their activities once they had been admitted to the land of the free. World War I changed all that. Many of the methods used to keep Asians under surveillance were now applied to aliens from all enemy countries, thus establishing a new pattern of life in the United States for Caucasian immigrants. They became a watched minority for the first time in American history, a situation that would not have·been possible without the ubiquitous APL.

Because the number of enemy aliens was so large, the government did not consider interning them as, for example, the French government had done. In France all enemy aliens not of military age, all women and all children, were placed in internment camps under the jurisdiction and control of the Ministry of the Interior, while all enemy aliens of military age became prisoners of war under the jurisdiction of the Minister of War. In World War II it was to be relatively simple for the American government to isolate Japanese aliens and Japanese-American citizens because their race set them apart for easy identification, and they were a small minority concentrated along the Pacific Coast. In World War I, no group among the enemy aliens could be so readily singled out for vindictive treatment, and therefore all enemy aliens became subject to harassment and to the changeableness of an experimental control system. If one includes the treatment of the Japanese in World War II in a comparison with World War I treatment of enemy aliens, the policy of Wilson seems mild next to that of Roosevelt. If, however, one compares the policy only with regard to European enemy aliens, then the record of Attorney General Francis Biddle in World War II seems far more restrained and efficient than that of Attorney General Gregory.

Prosecution of enemy aliens under war statutes would have been one means of deciding who among the four million deserved punishment for their activities. The APL diligently collected evidence for such prosecutions and fully expected to help secure many convictions. In instructions on handling espionage cases, the APL reminded members that enemy aliens were "without the guarantees accorded American citizens," and advised that nationality could be depended upon to have an influence on the loyalty of aliens to the United States, although even the APL admitted that many enemy aliens wished only to obey the laws and avoid personal connection with the war.

Only 150 enemy aliens were convicted under all the war statutes, however, and it soon became evident that juries would not indiscriminately convict under the treason statute, however diligently the Justice Department tried to obtain such convictions. Thus all of the 150 convicted, most of them under the Espionage Act, received prison terms of ten years or less.

The *Philadelphia Tageblatt* case serves as well as any to illustrate the difficulty encountered by the APL and the Justice Department in silencing enemy aliens who opposed the government's policies. The editor of the *Tageblatt*, Louis Werner, was a naturalized citizen, but his associate, Martin Darkow, was not. Articles in the *Tageblatt* had, according to the Justice Department, glorified Germany's strength and success, discouraged enlistments, attacked the sincerity of the United States, and in general encouraged opposition to the war. In the fall of 1917, the APL and Bureau of Investigation special agents raided the newspaper office and seized files, books, and papers. Warrants were issued for the arrest of Darkow, Werner, and three other associates. All five were charged with treason.

APL members helped assemble evidence. They secured proof of the defendants' signatures from APL bankers. They investigated jury members and did everything possible to ensure conviction. But in March, 1918, the court held that mere published words did not constitute treason, whereupon the Justice Department brought a second charge under the Espionage Act, this time securing Darkow's conviction, along with the four other men.

Such a process was obviously cumbersome and uncertain for the APL and the Justice Department; they preferred internment. With the help of the APL, the Administration placed 6,300 enemy aliens in concentration camps during World War I. In 1917 arrests were made openly by the Justice Department and the Labor Department, the latter arresting 1,800 officers and crew members of German merchant ships as soon as Congress voted for war. By 1918 the Labor Department had taken into custody 700 more enemy aliens who were housed with the others in the Mountain Park Hotel at Hot Springs, North Carolina. In June, 1918, they were all transferred into the custody of the War Department and taken to Fort Oglethorpe and Fort McPherson, camps where the enemy aliens arrested by the Justice Department were already housed.

Although approximately 4,000 enemy aliens were arrested by the Justice Department itself, only 63 of these arrests took place in April, 1917, when one would think the danger from enemy aliens was greatest. At that time the Justice Department wished to use the Alien Enemies Act of 1798 with discretion. "The Department desires to follow a conservative course in matters of this kind and to detain only those alien enemies who seem dangerous to the safety of the United States or who deliberately violate the regulations prescribed in the Proclamation of the President," Charles Warren had explained to R. E. Byrd, United States Attorney at Roanoke, Virginia.

But within a month the Justice Department had arrested as many more enemy aliens, and by the end of October almost 900 had been interned. By that time, Bielaski already had lists of Austro-Hungarians whom special agents considered a "menace" and who were to be arrested as soon as the United States declared war on the Austro-Hungarian Empire.

In Gregory's *Annual Report* for 1917, statistics on internments were published, but after that time the Justice Department refused to publicize its figures. "The thought that hostile activities of enemy aliens would be kept down by the fear [of] silent and mysterious governmental activity" caused this policy, Alfred Bettman of the Justice Department explained to congressmen in 1919. "The less the German agents knew about the Government's activities relating to enemy aliens, the more they would fear those activities, and thereby the hostile activities would tend to be reduced." Publicity as to the actual number of internments and the reasons for internments, said Bettman, could have caused a public clamor and forced the government into wholesale internment as in France and England. Not only would this have resulted in disrupting industry, but the government would have had to assume the burden and expense of needlessly large internment camps. It would have complicated the situation without doing any real good.

Only once did the Justice Department consider interning all enemy aliens. In July, 1918, as German submarines prowled off the Atlantic Coast, Gregory asked United States attorneys and marshals to report on possible places for detention of large numbers of enemy aliens if it should be necessary through "attack, or anarchist outbreak," but Allied victories made such drastic action unnecessary. As many as 3,000 enemy aliens may have been arrested in 1918, however, thus reflecting the concern of the Justice Department and the pressure upon them to intern more and more potential German spies.

How many of the men interned were actually dangerous to national security? Senator Knute Nelson asked that question of Bettman during the 1919 hearings. "Have you interned anyone who was not shown to be, or strongly suspected of being, a member of the German spy system or propaganda branch?" the Senator asked. Were men interned for having a "decided German accent?" Nelson asked sarcastically.

Bettman replied, "You are the only man who thought we interned too many, that is refreshing. The usual complaint against us is that we haven't interned enough." He did not answer Nelson's question.

Nelson may have been close to the truth, for all types of enemy aliens were swept into camps during 1918, amidst great confusion as to exactly why they were considered dangerous. The Dr. Muck internment case illustrates how anti-German hysteria during March of 1918 led to a change of standards on internment. Dr. Karl Muck, conductor of the Boston Symphony Orchestra, had been born in Hesse but claimed he had acquired Swiss citizenship when his father became a Swiss citizen in 1867. The Swiss Legation supported his claim. The Justice Department had investigated Muck early in the war. Finding nothing to incriminate him as a German agent or as having performed any act prejudicial to the national interest, Justice left him to his conducting. The Department did, however, consider him German by birth and sympathy, as did audiences, who in the fall of 1917 began to harass him during performances. After a concert in Providence, Rhode Island, one of John Rathom's employees became abusive, and Maryland's ex-governor threatened a riot would occur if the orchestra were allowed to perform in Baltimore. Late in November a second investigation again cleared him. As opposition and threats continued, however, backers of the Boston Symphony finally cancelled concerts scheduled in the Midwest. Then suddenly, on March 25, 1918, a little more than a month before Muck was to end his engagement, the Justice Department arrested and interned him as a dangerous enemy alien.

The process under which enemy aliens were arrested and interned differed from the process applied to other aliens and citizens. Enemy aliens could be arrested summarily on presidential warrants issued by the Justice Department rather than by a court, judge, or justice of the peace. In an emergency, Bureau of Investigation agents could even arrest them without a presidential warrant and telegraph the facts to the Justice Department, which would then issue the warrant. This did not mean that enemy aliens could be held illegally, although Bielaski had trouble convincing special agents and Leaguers of this. As late as January, 1918, special agents were arresting enemy aliens without notifying the Justice Department so that warrants could be sent. "In the absence of a local ordinance authorizing arrests for twenty-four or forty-eight hours on suspicion, the detention of an alien enemy is illegal unless a presidential warrant, or one charging a crime, is issued for his arrest," Bielaski had to warn his agents.

As long as the enemy alien was arrested legally, the courts upheld the practice. An alien might argue that he was not a citizen of an enemy country and thus possibly obtain release through *habeas corpus* proceedings, but the courts refused to extend this privilege to men who admitted they were enemy aliens. When an avowed Austro-Hungarian applied for a writ of *habeas corpus,* for example, the court quickly decided it had no right to intervene. Nor did anyone question the use of the APL, its investigating methods, or the process of internment.

Once arrested, the enemy alien faced two possible futures. Arrest did not inevitably mean incarceration for the duration of the war. About two thirds of those arrested were paroled and asked to report periodically to local APL offices. APL units in cities with high alien populations established Enemy Alien Bureaus which had as their sole function the investigation of enemy aliens and surveillance of all released men. The Cincinnati APL, for example, set up a parole system under which Germans released from Fort Oglethorpe reported once a week. In Chattanooga, the APL—to safeguard the interest of the government, it claimed—even had wives of internees report weekly. Many APL men urged more arrests and larger concentration camps, but the total camp population at any one time probably did not number more than three or four thousand. In April, 1918, 2,000 were held; by the end of the war only 2,500. Actually, the small number of men permanently interned gave the APL one important reason for existence—one which Gregory certainly considered important—since it seemed to prove that surveillance was very effective.

Once prisoners were interned at Fort McPherson, at Fort Oglethorpe, or at Fort Douglas, the APL did not cease to influence their lives. Physically, these men now came under the control of the War Department, but they often left property behind.

When A. Mitchell Palmer was appointed Alien Property Custodian in the fall of 1917, his job was to acquire records of property in the United States owned by German citizens or citizens of Germany's allies. In cases where he felt such ownership was dangerous, he could require that the property and money be turned over to him for the duration of the war. His control did not extend to enemy aliens, and it did not provide for confiscation of property.

Under Palmer's aggressive policies, however, the office soon became a weapon to wipe out permanently all enemy-controlled business in the United States, a goal which he pursued relentlessly, ruthlessly, and successfully. At the end of 1917, Palmer had one room and one clerk; by February, 1919, his staff of 550 occupied an entire building.

On February 5, 1918, Wilson had added to Palmer's powers by declaring that all interned enemy aliens in the United States were to come under the term "enemy" in the Trading with the Enemy Act. The APL *Spy Glass* announced happily, "The effect of this is to subject all property of such aliens within the United States to sequestration by the Alien Property Custodian."

Palmer already had his own investigating bureau, but as the opportumities for taking over more property increased, he began to solicit volunteer assistance in locating such property. Then he managed to have Wilson sign into law an executive proclamation classifying as enemies "all persons, citizens of enemy countries, who have assisted in the dissemination of German propaganda or in plotting or intriguing against the United States or the Government of any of the Allied nations."

O'Brian had previously objected to just such a proposal, and when he discovered the proclamation, he reminded Gregory that it was a serious matter to give Palmer and his subordinates "the power to seize property of individuals whom *they* think have been engaged in enemy propaganda," a power which would infringe on Justice Department powers. Gregory immediately asked Palmer to suspend enforcement of the provision until they could confer. The dispute went to Wilson, who agreed that it was up to the Justice Department, not the Alien Property Custodian, to screen enemy aliens and determine which ones were dangerous. But apparently the price of Palmer's compliance was utilization of the APL in searching out German-held assets.

By August, 1918, when the APL began to assist in locating enemy property, Palmer had already taken over more than $500,000,000 worth. "Fine as this record has been," the *Spy Glass* editorialized, "Mr. Palmer is not content with the progress made. He has appealed to the APL, therefore, to aid him in discovering, particularly in the small communities, such enemy owned concerns as are not yet in his hands."

Members eagerly went to work. They checked the files of banks, real estate agencies, and insurance companies, forwarding their information to Palmer. At the end of Palmer's first year as Alien Property Custodian, the *Spy Glass* reported proudly that the value of property confiscated totaled over $700,000,000, compared to a mere $14,-000,000 in American assets taken over by Germans in Germany, evidence not of German lenience toward American capitalists, but of the "invasion of Boche business" into the United States. Of this sum, more than $2,500,000 worth of property had been taken from interned enemy aliens alone. In June, 1918, Palmer had received full discretion to sell this property, and when the German textile and chemical plants went on the block later in the year, the *Spy Glass* editor gloated that they would be sold to "100% Americans," and referred to the sales as "the naturalization of Boche industries."

Those enemy aliens who escaped prosecution, arrest, internment, and confiscation of property still were subject to other investigations by the APL because of regulations established by the Justice Department limiting their movement within the country. By the end of the war, these regulations had been extended to all male and female German aliens over fourteen years of age. They were required to register as enemy aliens, to obtain permits to enter restricted zones or to travel, and were barred from Washington, D. C. Every enemy alien was investigated by the APL before a registration card was issued. Over two hundred thousand were more carefully screened before being permitted to enter restricted zones. And a large number of aliens were also carefully checked before being granted passports to leave the country.

In addition, the APL investigated all aliens working in defense plants, even if the plants were not within the restricted areas. Then their plant protection duties enabled members to watch such workers constantly and report any opposition to the war, even to request discharges. The Pittsburgh, Cleveland, and Dayton branches of the APL were particularly zealous, but everywhere the enemy alien was a potential suspect. At the Woodbury Bag Loading Plant in Philadelphia, more than one thousand investigations were made of men with German names, whether citizens or aliens. More than a hundred Austrians and Hungarians were discharged, and two hundred cases were remanded to the Justice Department for action.

Over sixty thousand special investigations of enemy aliens were conducted under Justice Department instructions. In addition, though, thousands of unreported investigations were undertaken by free-lance APL members. Free-wheeling activities of the volunteers during the first year of the war often embarrassed the Justice Department. In January, 1918, Bielaski had to reprimand his special agents and APL volunteers for having enemy aliens discharged from defense plants without so much as asking his permission, this at the very time Bielaski was working with the Labor Department to keep the number of alien discharges at a minimum and to find new employment for those already discharged for security reasons. The presence of unemployed men on the streets of large cities, idle and discontent, gave rise to a great many spy stories woven around their activities, but not until the spy scare of April, 1918, did the Justice Department realize that less rigorous control over enemy aliens might be a better policy. Then it began to channel APL energy away from investigations to surveillance.

In April, O'Brian appointed special assistants in Massachusetts, Ohio, Indiana, California, and Illinois, states with high alien populations where the United States attorneys seemed unable to take on alien supervision in addition to their regular duties. The Justice Department's special assistants were charged with handling only enemy alien work. By July the new system was in operation, and O'Brian was asking for a "quiet investigation" by the APL and the Bureau of Investigation in places like Cincinnati to determine how regulations governing enemy aliens could be reformed and made less onerous. This change in policy received no publicity, but surveillance became more general. Many enemy aliens were now admitted to areas formerly off limits, but, like convicts on parole, they were required to report weekly to the local APL offices.

Gregory continually urged the APL to organize in plants which employed enemy aliens. As late as August, 1918, he asked Bielaski to see that the APL placed agents in the Wright-Martin airplane factory in New Brunswick, New Jersey. He opposed neither the development of a separate Bureau of Plant Protection Section in the Shipping Bureau nor a Military Intelligence Plant Protection Section which eventually operated in over five thousand plants in cooperation with the APL. But surveillance of enemy aliens in defense plants remained primarily the job of the APL.

Regulations, internments, confiscation of property—the eternal vigilance of the APL plus outrages by American mobs—led many Germans in America who had previously thought United States citizenship unnecessary to demand that they be allowed to attest their patriotism and gain the protection of the law by becoming naturalized. Congress agreed that this step should be encouraged and on May 9, 1918, amended the naturalization laws, allowing the courts to admit certain classes of enemy aliens to citizenship. Within the next few months, seventy-five thousand enemy aliens filed applications for citizenship. A new job resulted for the APL: investigating these applicants. Operatives conducted about four hundred investigations in Seattle, eight hundred in St. Louis, almost four thousand in Chicago, and thousands in other cities. Upon the evidence furnished, the

Bureau of Naturalization either endorsed or opposed naturalization proceedings; and into the ranks of citizens passed those enemy aliens who had left no record of opposition to the war for the APL to discover.

For a few German-Americans the naturalization process was reversed. Until 1912, naturalization had been considered permanent, but in that year a Montana man, a citizen for sixteen years, had his citizenship cancelled on a charge that he had obtained it fraudulently by not being "of good moral character." In 1917 Senator W. H. King of Utah had proposed that anyone naturalized within the previous twenty years who acted disloyally should have his naturalization papers revoked and be declared an enemy alien, but the idea did not take root in the Justice Department until April, 1918.

Late in April, Sterling Edmunds, the assistant APL chief in St. Louis, sent director Elting a letter maintaining that enemy regulations should be stiffened and recommending that a statute be passed permitting cancellation of naturalization upon proof of sympathy with the enemy. Such a statute had been under consideration, O'Brian told Elting when the suggestion was passed on to him. Where there was proof that the original forswearing of allegiance to the enemy country was false, the department was already willing to proceed in court for cancellation. "When you have a clear and strong case of this kind, the Department suggests that you submit the facts to it," O'Brian told Elting.

It did not take long for the Justice Department to find a test case, once it had decided to push denaturalization. Soon after O'Brian's request to Elting, the courts heard the case of German-American Frederick W. Wursterbarth, who had been a naturalized citizen for thirty-six years but had refused to subscribe to the Red Cross or the YMCA fund drives because, according to reports of the canvassers, he said he did not want to injure Germany and did not want the United States to win the war. The Justice Department brought suit in New Jersey, arguing that Wursterbarth had obtained his certificate through fraud because he had not renounced his allegiance. Wursterbarth did not refute the testimony, and his certificate was cancelled on May 13, 1918. Nine days later, a Seattle man who had been in the United States for twenty years and a citizen for six years had his certificate cancelled on grounds of fraud and was interned for the duration of the war. The following month, a German-born farmer living near Emporia, Kansas, who had fed wheat to his livestock in defiance of food regulations and made "disloyal" remarks to a county food administrator, was denaturalized. The court said he had not acted in good faith when swearing allegiance to the United States.

Encouraged by these court decisions, the APL directors announced the results of several recent cases and instructed members to intensify their search for information on suspect naturalized aliens, promising that such denaturalized persons could be subject to internment and confiscation of property. The Chicago division secured at least one cancellation and internment in August, and the APL would undoubtedly have chalked up many more denaturalizations had the war continued.

Denaturalization could have been a more cruel weapon had the Justice Department been able to employ it as extensively as was done during the 1920's and in World War II. But such action remained sporadic compared to World War II, when the Justice Department engaged in a relentless drive at the beginning of the war and had 2,500 cases under investigation by the end of the first year. Instead, the Justice Department relied upon the Espionage Act as an instrument to punish naturalized and native-born citizen alike for their alleged disloyalty to the government.

Of two thousand indictments obtained by the Justice Department under the Espionage Act, none involved persons actually accused of being spies. Most were aimed at people who opposed the war or criticized the Wilsonian methods and goals in waging it. These prosecutions became the chief weapon leveled by the federal government against dissenters, who gradually replaced spies and aliens as the major enemy at home. For the APL, the existence of dissent seemed to cast doubt on the validity of the Leaguers' own patriotism by calling into question fundamental policies of the Administration. Anyone at odds with the League view of national policy must of necessity be dangerous. Thus the most vindictive attacks were reserved for those Americans so unpatriotic as to oppose the war policies of the government.

The goal of the Justice Department in applying the Espionage Act was explained to Frey by Alfred Bettman, the Harvard law professor who administered it under O'Brian. Bettman said the aim was to interpret the law "so as to make of it an effective weapon against dangerous propaganda, that is, against propaganda whose effect would be to seriously reduce the participation of the American people in the active prosecution of the war and thereby retard the raising of the Army and the production and transportation of the necessary munitions of war, as well as to reduce the war morale of the civilian population, which reduction would sooner or later be reflected in the morale of the Army itself." The problem was to determine what was "dangerous propaganda."

Bettman admitted to Frey that it had been difficult to prove enemy instigation or support of specific propaganda, that the source of most propaganda was "colorably or genuinely" social, political, or religious convictions, such as being opposed to all war; or belief that war was "brought about and is fundamentally being fought for financial interests rather than for liberty and democracy"; or that the war was opposed to the dictates of Christianity. The problem was, as Bettman said "to effectively suppress propaganda" obstructive of the war "without an undue suppression of that freedom of conscience, freedom of speech, freedom of press, and freedom of discussion, which constitutes the essence of democracy." The Justice Department had realized, Bettman said, that the government "could not win the war if we were to destroy our fundamental democracy at home," that free discussion of causes and aims of the war would benefit the Administration, and that there was danger of the Administration's being "led into the use of its great powers to suppress criticism of itself." Statutes relating to foreign enemies should not be used for "suppression of the free discussion and fighting out of purely domestic, social, and political issues."

Dissatisfaction with scrupulous application of the Espionage Act, Bettman explained, came principally from people "who desire a more autocratic and less democratic interpretation of the law," and from those who wanted to punish individual expressions of disloyalty which were not part of deliberately organized propaganda. At first, according to Bettman, the Justice Department had felt that individual expressions of dissent should be handled under local breach-of-peace ordinances, and hence the APL had been called in to attend to these individual cases. But as time went on the Justice Department became convinced that these isolated expressions of "disloyalty" were a "serious menace" and so advocated that the Espionage Act be amended to cope with these utterances. During the first few months the resulting sedition amendment had been used with great caution. It was more important, Bettman concluded, to use constructive measures to evoke loyalty and to activate latent and potential loyalty and to avoid repelling people who might through unjust suspicion and unwarranted persecution "join the forces which are aggressively fighting this war."

According to the Justice Department, then, its policy was lenient. Gregory had warned his subordinates in May to administer the sedition amendment "with discretion" and not to use it to suppress honest, legitimate criticism of the Administration or discussion of government policies. Nor was it to serve as a weapon in personal feuds. "Just where to draw the line has already caused many sleepless nights at Washington," the *Spy Glass* told Leaguers, "and the Department of Justice examines carefully every case of this sort before it permits local district attorneys to begin prosecution." The APL saw to it that the United States attorneys had plenty of cases to submit.

The APL directed the attention of members to one technique of gathering information used by the St. Louis division. There APL members supplied Liberty Loan canvassers with report forms which they had only to fill out and return to the APL. Violators of the Espionage Act, these cards counseled, could be "any person who shall wilfully make or convey false reports, or say or do anything with intent to obstruct the sale of United States Bonds, or by word or act oppose the cause of the United States." Such cards could bring in many "reports of pro-German conduct which otherwise might go unrecorded and unpunished," said the *Spy Glass*. "It not only is an ever-present reminder to the salesman to look out for anti-American sentiments, but more important still, it makes reporting them easy."

The search for activities construed as disloyal came to absorb a great part of Leaguers' energies during the summer of 1918. To facilitate this search, the Washington APL allowed local units to publicize their presence in communities, to announce the name of their chief, and to enlist the aid of the public in reporting "enemy activities, disloyalties and evasions of the war statutes." City units posted bulletins in street cars, store windows, bowling alleys, on factory bulletin boards, in elevators, and in smoking rooms, requesting citizens to report their suspicions to the local APL office. Posters put up by the Buffalo, New York, APL were recommended by the directors as a suitable pattern. They read, "Report the man or woman who spreads pessimistic stories; divulges or seeks confidential information; cries for peace or belittles our efforts to win the war. . . . Use your eyes and ears and report these people to the American Protective League. . . ." Frey later reported to the War Department, "Much important information resulted from this practice."

Not everyone agreed with Frey, of course. "From all accounts," ran a notice in the *New York American Liberal* of July 18, 1918, "the vast system of espionage that has been called into being is flooding the Department of Justice officials, bureaus, offices of public prosecutors and blotters of police stations with such masses of spite work and tittle-tattle that the difficulty is already being experienced in sifting the wheat of useful information from the chaff of pure malice."

Nor did all jobs end successfully for the APL. Amos Pinchot, a progressive reformer, complained to Wilson in May, 1918, that United States Marshal McCarthy, in discussing the trial of Max Eastman for statements made in his radical newspaper *The Masses,* said that "evidence didn't matter in such cases; that now juries convict anybody who is indicted."

But McCarthy was exaggerating. Actually only half of the two thousand prosecutions begun against dissenters under the Espionage Act resulted in convictions. This 50 percent score reinforced the suspicion among dissenters that the Justice Department merely wanted to harass and silence opponents of war rather than to obtain convictions. Even more disconcerting to them was the evidence that no uniform criteria existed for initiating prosecutions. In Massachusetts, where George Anderson had been United States Attorney during the first months of the war, there were few prosecutions and only one conviction under the Espionage Act, despite considerable criticism of war in that state. In other states, the slightest negative comment might be picked up by the APL and reported to the United States Attorney, who was then pressured by the APL, sometimes through local police officials or influential members of the community, to institute action. When occasionally attorneys demurred, the APL went so far as to obtain affidavits charging them with neglect of duty.

Much of the evidence collected by the APL was hearsay, malicious and slanderous; but grand juries seldom refused to return indictments if the Justice Department demanded them. Socialists soon discovered how the system worked.

The Socialist party members were no outcast group like the IWW, the first target of the APL attack. The IWW was bound together only by a vague platform of anarchism, and had the IWW engaged in violence, it could easily have been controlled through local laws. The Socialists were far more dangerous political opponents of the Administration because they had a positive platform and a perfectly legal, democratic plan of action. Moreover, in 1918 Socialists had reached their greatest power in United States history. They were respectable middle-class and working-class American citizens who wanted reform.

The war had split the Socialists into two groups, those who believed the war to be a moral issue and thus supported it as a democratic venture, and those who believed the war to be an economic issue and thus opposed it as a capitalistic adventure. The APL had their own classification for the Socialists: those supporting the war were "true Socialists" and those opposing the war were "foreign sympathizers." According to the APL even the "true Socialists" might be influenced by the enemy to dissent. Thus, the goal of the APL came to be removal of all dissident Socialists from public office and public view and their imprisonment along with the IWW. The IWW had interfered with industrial mobilization; the Socialists were interfering with the mobilization of manpower. The two seemed equally dangerous to the League. Ohio was the stronghold of the Socialist party, so the Cleveland APL played a leading role in eliminating the Socialists—as the Chicago division had in eliminating the IWW.

Preliminary skirmishes between Socialists and the APL in Cleveland occurred early in the war. APL members boasted that they were responsible for the dismissal of two Socialist members of the City Council and that they had collected the evidence which resulted in the sentencing of a Socialist member of the Cleveland School Board to ten years imprisonment under the Espionage Act. By the time Eugene V. Debs toured Ohio in June, 1918, the APL was ready for him!

Debs had planned to deliver a major antiwar speech in Canton, Ohio, on Sunday, June 16. Picked APL operatives came all the way from Cleveland to reinforce the small Canton unit. Some members circulated through the audience while others sat on the stage taking careful shorthand notes. After Debs had finished his speech and was duly arrested on a charge of violating the Espionage Act, the APL members deposited several transcripts with the Justice Department to be used at the trial. During the trial, members showed up to finish what they regarded as their job. They searched people admitted to the courtroom and generally stood guard over the proceedings. After Debs had been convicted and placed behind bars, the Canton and Cleveland divisions even disputed over credit for the victory.

Socialists and the IWW were not the only radicals to criticize the war, however, and although the APL considered these organizations their prime targets, other groups also came under fire. Religious radicals, particularly the Jehovah's Witnesses, then known as Russellites, attracted the attention of the volunteers.

The APL investigation of the Russellites began when a distressed Polish woman reported to the Chicago APL that her husband was involved in a strange new religious movement which preached non-resistance. The south-side division of the Chicago APL arranged a raid during one of the sect's services and had the entire congregation arrested. Then an APL captain confiscated copies of Joseph Rutherford's book *The Finished Mystery* and other pamphlets which he considered seditious. These he passed along to the Justice Department. This evidence resulted in the conviction of Rutherford, head of the International Bible Students' Association which had published the book, and seven other Russellites. Rutherford received a sentence of twenty years for conspiracy to cause insubordination, mutiny, disloyalty, refusal of duty in the military and naval forces, and conspiracy to obstruct recruiting and enlistment. Sentences of the seven other Russellites totaled eighty years.

The *Spy Glass* reported with approbation on June 28, 1918, that the sentences were particularly heavy because the Russellites were carrying on sedition under a mask of religion. These religious radicals spent the remainder of the war in Fort Leavenworth, and not until eleven months later did a federal judge reverse their conviction on the grounds that they had not had a fair trial.

Irish radicals were another group singled out for special attention by the APL. Most famous of the Irish radicals snared in the web was Jeremiah O'Leary, leading exponent of Irish nationalism in the United States. O'Leary had first gained national prominence for his insistence that President Wilson take a stand on Irish independence, a demand which Wilson fiercely denounced. When O'Leary's crusade for Home Rule in Ireland did not slacken in 1917, the State Department released German documents implicating him in German sabotage plots. The Post Office Department barred his newspaper, *The Bull,* from the mails. In November, 1917, the Justice Department indicted him under the Espionage Act for conspiracy to cause insubordination in the Army and Navy. O'Leary jumped bail while under indictment and disappeared. The Justice Department promptly indicted his brother and a friend, also on conspiracy charges.

By this time Gregory, himself a man of Irish descent who had sympathized with Irish Home Rule at the beginning of the war, had become particularly hostile to Irish nationalists. He was convinced that they were "slackers" who had not fought alongside the Scots, Welsh, and English, but waited for Home Rule as a reward for their dubious patriotism. Many Irish-Americans, he now believed, loved Ireland more than the United States and "in their hearts" wanted Germany to win the war because it would benefit Ireland. O'Leary was a prime example of this Irish "disloyalty." The Justice Department sent the APL out to get him.

APL operatives spread a net, stopped hundreds of people on the streets of New York, searched the home of the Irish patriot, and questioned his family. Finally, one Leaguer trailed O'Leary's friend Albert Lyons and, with an agent of the Bureau of Investigation, obtained information as to the fugitive's whereabouts. O'Leary was arrested at a ranch in Sara, Washington. Rushed secretly back to New York, he was arraigned before Judge Learned Hand. During the trial, O'Leary charged that APL members had removed private papers from his home, threatened aliens of his acquaintance with deportation if they would not implicate O'Leary in a German plot—and then packed the jury panel. If his charges were true, then the APL did not do a thorough job, for the jury could not decide on conviction. O'Leary triumphed over what he called "the Wilson-Gregory gag law."

Dissenters quickly learned that the APL was often called in to check jury members for "loyalty" so that the United States attorneys knew whom to challenge and eliminate. Only about two hundred of the two thousand trials under the Espionage Act were heard by juries; in the remainder, judges decided the issue. But regardless of whether judge or jury finally ruled on the evidence assembled by the APL, the number of prosecutions continued to increase during the summer of 1918. Both volunteers and agents of the Bureau of Investigation looked upon the increasing number of prosecutions as evidence of their effectiveness in protecting the armies in France. The main complaint of the APL was that the Justice Department did not institute enough prosecutions or take seriously enough the evidence the League collected.

Prosecutions accomplished two things: they stopped criticism of war measures by radicals and they quieted criticism of the Justice Department by conservatives and militarists. But the prosecutions also had two by-products: they snuffed out the legitimate criticism Wilson needed to formulate policies which could hold the support of liberal elements at home, and they dangerously undermined the prestige of the courts as defenders of civil liberties. Opponents of reform had warned before the war that reformers, by strengthening the central government, would create an instrument for oppression. Now, ironically, because reformers were not prepared to repudiate the men they had brought to power, they were helping to turn the federal government into that very force for oppression during a regime that was nominally liberal. Like the policy of the Justice Department toward aliens, the Administration policy toward dissenters received little criticism except from those who thought it too lenient.

The APL had begun its investigative function with enemy aliens. It had then turned to dissenters. With the passage of the Sabotage

Act, effective April 20, 1918, the League moved into the affairs of ordinary citizens, pressuring the Justice Department to apply the Act to someone.

Since no German saboteurs were available, the APL submitted data on manufacturers who they alleged had made deliveries of defective military raincoats for the sake of greater profit. In August, twenty indictments were returned by a federal grand jury in New York against the "raincoat conspirators." One defendant was sentenced to two years in prison, another to seven. In a second case, two Ohio men were convicted on the testimony of an undercover agent that he had been asked to tamper with a lathe used by a nonunion man, this as part of a struggle to gain support for a closed shop. Such were the applications of the Sabotage Act.

But the APL did not depend upon congressional legislation such as the Sabotage Act for authority to intervene in the affairs of non-dissenting citizens. In April, 1917, the Civil Service Commission had recommended to President Wilson that the public interest be safeguarded by excluding from the government any persons whose loyalty was in reasonable doubt. Wilson had then issued a confidential executive order authorizing the heads of departments and agencies to remove any employee believed to be "inimical to the public welfare by reason of his conduct, sympathies, or utterances, or because of other reasons growing out of the war." At first the War Department felt no need to protect itself against its employees, but once the Military Intelligence had the APL available to conduct investigations, each prospective War Department employee was screened. Although no formal machinery was set up for reviewing or appealing these cases, about eight hundred persons were debarred from future civil service examinations during the war for reasons classified as "disloyalty."

Civil service was only the beginning. An even larger number of investigations were conducted by the APL into the lives of persons applying for overseas duty with such service organizations as the Red Cross, the YMCA, and the Knights of Columbus. This was another "first" in security investigations. Since all of these individuals could come under military jurisdiction once they reached France, the War Department insisted that they be cleared for "character and loyalty" to ensure that they would not cause the War Department any embarrassment by their activities.

With Bielaski's approval, the APL began Red Cross clearances early in January of 1918. APL operatives were asked to decide for themselves whether an individual should be allowed to go overseas, turning over their recommendations directly to Red Cross officials. Most Red Cross personnel shrank from cloak and dagger methods, preferring candor. In New York, for example, one representative told a rejected candidate what the APL operative had reported and even supplied the informant's name. Despite vigorous protests from the APL, Red Cross officials continued to reveal the contents of reports to applicants. One applicant for dishwasher retaliated by accusing an APL operative of demanding $100 for approval. Not surprisingly, the APL defended its own man and proclaimed him "absolutely above reproach"; but as Red Cross officials continued to show the reports, some APL men were even threatened with lawsuits by rejected candidates.

The Red Cross continually tried to free itself of these investigations. Failing that, it asked that APL members be assigned directly to Red Cross offices so that assignments did not have to go through the War Department. Instead, the APL directors ordered chiefs not to accept direct requests at all, nor to mention investigations to the Red Cross, but to report confidentially to the War Department, which in turn was to inform the Red Cross of all decisions. When this routine had been perfected, it was extended to the YMCA and to other service groups. By the end of the war thousands of these character and loyalty investigations had been processed by the APL.

The APL conducted thirty thousand, an estimated 90 percent, of all individual "character and loyalty" investigations requested by the War Department. "The League had its faults of course," Captain B. Woodruff said in summing up their work, "but the quality of its reports were high, on an average, and when one considers its operatives were unpaid, and for the most part untrained in the work of loyalty, the League did remarkably well and deserves much credit and thanks. The principal faults we encountered were lack of speed and indefiniteness of its reports."

Indefiniteness was hardly a surprising feature, considering the casualness of the methods used. Provided with a subject's name, the APL member was instructed to wire immediately yes, no, or doubtful. To arrive at one of these conclusions, the operative could use any technique he felt appropriate. He might simply ring up a friend in a neighboring town to ask if the individual under investigation were "loyal." Yet once the APL member had made his decision, it was accepted by the War Department, however vague the explanation of just how that decision had been made and upon what evidence it rested.

In all fairness to them, APL members did not as a rule welcome these orders to investigate citizens. They had joined the APL to hunt spies, at the very least to investigate enemy aliens or "disloyalists"; and this type of routine investigation held little charm for them, despite the fact that their reports might determine the future of a person's career. "No member of the American Protective League is deeply interested in making character and loyalty reports upon citizens," the APL directors admitted to the Red Cross. Delays about which the War Department often complained were caused by this lack of enthusiasm. Had the directors not kept the rank and file interested by hinting that a real spy might still be discovered during a routine investigation, many members would have quit.

Once the APL had implemented the policy of requiring character and loyalty investigations, it was easy for the federal government to adopt the practice of routinely checking all citizens who wished to leave the country. Before World War I, the United States required no passports at all for American citizens, although in practice many obtained them to use as identification in European countries. In November, 1917, the United States announced for the first time a policy of rigid control over entrance of persons from abroad to prevent enemy agents from coming in. Foreigners were required to furnish complete histories to the State Department, and returning Americans were compelled to have their passports validated by American consular agents abroad. To make controls more rigid, Gregory approved a passport bill which was introduced into the House on February 26, 1918.

The bill was still stalled in a House Committee when O'Brian wrote to Gregory on April 19 urging passage to prevent information from being taken to Mexico where, according to military intelligence reports, a new wireless was being constructed. "Every precaution must be taken to close the border effectively against the transmission of information which could be used by these wireless towers when completed," O'Brian wrote in a "very confidential" memorandum to Gregory. In turn, Gregory passed the memorandum to Wilson, and with Administration support, Congress passed the bill on May 22.

The APL, which had already been investigating passport applications of enemy aliens, was now called upon to investigate all aliens who wished to leave the country. On May 28 Bielaski wrote to the Bureau of Investigation superintendent in New York that passports were being obtained under false names by German agents, necessitating the investigation of all applicants. This job was also turned over to APL investigators. They were to check with the local police, election boards, immigration service, local draft boards, real estate offices, and federal agencies to obtain the necessary information. When interviewing people with a poor command of English, the APL advised its operatives to say only that the applicant being investigated was waiting to catch a boat and could not leave before complete information was obtained. Only more educated persons were to be told that the investigation was being done by the Justice Department. The volunteers were to act in a "semi-judicial capacity" on these cases, with their "conscience as their guide." Between March and June eight hundred passport investigations were made in New York alone. By fall, the investigations had been extended to cover all American citizens who wished to leave the country for any reason. Freedom of Americans to travel at will had become a permanent casualty of the war.

No one complained, so it is difficult to know how many American citizens were refused passports on the basis of APL reports. Not until after the armistice did people begin to question this loss of freedom of movement. Lincoln Steffens, despite his friendship with George Creel, Colonel House, and others in the inner circle of Wilson's intimates, believed with good reason that his request for a passport would not be granted. "Many influential men have been turned down: Taft, President Eliot [of Harvard] . . . and many more. And the bureaucracy is so mighty now that it can block even Wilson himself," he wrote in November. (Senator Sherman of Illinois accused the Administration of refusing passports to Gifford Pinchot and to Oswald Garrison Villard, editor of the dissident *Nation*. Villard had not actually applied, however, and when he did, the State Department promptly granted his request.) No one seems to have known that the APL was conducting these investigations. Hence what criticism did arise was directed at the State Department rather than at the Department of Justice.

Long before the first protests were raised against passport restrictions, another precedent had been permanently shattered. Traditionally, congressmen had played a major role in obtaining commissions and promotions in the Army, but in World War I for the first time the War Department attempted to break this tradition by insisting that officers be investigated for "security." Screening did not begin until February, 1918, when the Military Intelligence asked the APL directors to investigate eighteen applicants for commissions in the Signal Corps. Within a few months, operatives were conducting investigations of all commission applicants—including those for chaplaincies. According to the *Spy Glass,* the APL had the "responsibility of guaranteeing the loyalty of thousands whose devotion to the country must be quite beyond question."

By October, 1918, the APL was checking civilian records of all men inducted into the service for evidence of statements or acts considered "disloyal or seditious," forwarding the information to the Military Intelligence. Requests for furloughs to visit sick relatives were also sent to the League, which checked to see whether relatives were really sick.

As long as the APL could keep their volunteers investigating citizens, the War Department was able to reduce its dependence upon congressmen for information about personnel. At least one Democrat, C. F. Lea of California, protested to Wilson that "underground methods of appointment and promotion prevail," that the bureaucracy was "prostituting" the departments by not considering congressional advice, and that the practice was "an unjustifiable insult to every member of Congress," as well as to Americans who "love bureaucracy little less than autocracy." Lea warned Wilson that "the attitude of the administration toward Congress is leading to dissension, bitterness and defeat for both administration and the Democratic Party." Thus did the APL help lay the groundwork for the bitter executive-congressional battle which would come up when Wilson wanted to establish a League of Nations.

As extensive as were the APL's character and loyalty probes, its biggest job for the War Department was far different: the APL was entrusted with the unlikely task of enforcing vice and liquor regulations in areas around army camps and naval bases. Until World War I, the War Department had shown no concern about the soldierly pastimes involving liquor and prostitutes, pastimes as traditional among American servicemen as among all other armies. During the intervention in Mexico in 1916, in fact, border towns had supplied saloons and bordellos to meet the demand. But Secretary of War Baker could prove, moral considerations aside, that great loss in efficiency resulted from venereal disease and from the alcohol poisoning which often resulted from the consumption of cheap liquor. Raymond B. Fosdick, in charge of training camp activities, testified before the House Committee on Military Affairs that troops called down to the Mexican border to help chase Villa had been decimated by venereal disease. In San Antonio, the rate had been 288 per thousand. Despite the employment of prophylaxis, one regiment alone had developed nineteen cases in two months. Now in this later war, it was known that 30 percent of the enlisted men in the services of two of America's new allies were incapacitated by venereal disease. The War Department had therefore recommended that provisions be made in the Selective Service Act to give the military authority to protect soldiers from the dangers of diseased women and alcohol.

Senator Wesley Jones of Washington introduced the measure. The climate was right for passage, since reformers had already pushed through federal legislation like the Mann Act, and many states had enacted laws aimed at the total suppression of prostitution. These measures to protect servicemen met with unanimous support. Without debate or roll call, the Jones measure was adopted and became Section Thirteen of the Selective Service Act.

Along with legislation against prostitution came regulation of liquor. Nineteen states had already established prohibition; Congress had made Washington, D.C., a dry city, and there was growing support for an amendment which would establish prohibition nationally. The Selective Service Act, through Section Twelve, prohibited the selling of intoxicating liquor to men in uniform anywhere and to servicemen out of uniform near cantonments. Only the question of who would enforce these prohibitions remained.

Local police had long been parties to vice and liquor payoffs. As a result, bills already passed by states and by Congress were indifferently enforced, except in a few isolated cases where reformers were able to infiltrate the offices of district attorneys. Bielaski had enforced the Mann Act vigorously, but local opposition remained strong. During the early months of the war there was little effort to enforce the new provisions of the bill at old established camps, but as the conscriptees arrived at the cantonments in September, 1917, the War Department began to consider methods of enforcement. At first the British system of appointing a women's protective committee was tried. Women officers patroled camp areas for prostitutes and "flappers," rounding them up and taking them home to their mothers. It was soon evident that a force of sixty-five women could do little to enforce the law at hundreds of camps. Something else was needed.

The efforts of the female patrol had been augmented by APL members who had been drafted and who continued their sleuthing in the cantonments. Conflict between the Army and the League had quickly developed when APL'ers began to report officers and men, however. After resentful officers in Alabama complained, all APL men were ordered to discontinue investigations once they had entered the Army. As Frey explained, "A man cannot belong to the Army and belong to any other organization where he is subject to orders or any outside influence." Many APL men were subsequently enrolled by the Military

Intelligence, and APL headquarters regularly forwarded the names of men entering the service. But the APL had to stay outside cantonments.

In December, 1917, the Supreme Court upheld the Idaho prohibition law, and Congress adopted the prohibition amendment. Now there seemed every reason for the federal government to move to enforce the laws against liquor more strictly, and the War Department asked the Justice Department to do so. The Justice Department assigned one Bureau of Investigation agent to each cantonment to work with the army intelligence officer. The APL was asked to establish units in the town nearest any military post and to cooperate fully.

Early in January, 1918, Briggs went south to set up units near the 174 cantonments. He was delighted with the new assignment. At a time when lack of work was causing dissension and bickering among members, he felt this job would appeal to them. "You know that old story about idle hands," he wrote to Frey.

New Orleans, with its notorious twenty-eight block red-light district, was the first target for Briggs's new organizing efforts. "Give me all the dope you possible can regarding the New Orleans situation," he wrote to Frey. "While I am in the South this time I want to clean this situation up so that I won't have to go back there."

Briggs arrived early in March. A federal judge appointed the chief of the APL division in New Orleans to the post of United States Commissioner. In this capacity the chief devoted his entire time to cases involving violations of the liquor and vice laws. By the end of the war, he had heard over five thousand cases.

In the belief that fair ends justified foul means, APL men donned army uniforms and boarded trains to mingle with departing troops, although this meant violating the law against impersonating military men. If they unearthed hidden sources of illegal spirits, they felt their mission was accomplished. They recruited ministers to help search for violators. They recommended that United States marshals who did not enforce the five-mile limit around cantonments be dismissed. In some areas, APL men themselves became implicated in bootlegging, but in New Orleans they led the crusade. Secretary of the Navy Daniels sent Colonel Charles B. Hatch, in charge of the Military Police in Philadelphia, to New Orleans to see if a branch of that organization was needed there. Hatch reported no, as long as the APL was on the job.

Briggs called in reporters to tell them of his crusade. The APL, he said, was giving its entire strength in an attempt "to settle the question of commercialized vice in America." A volunteer organization of "hard-headed businessmen," wrote one reporter, had taken the problem of vice in hand and planned to stamp it out. Not all members were that enthusiastic, however. One dubbed Briggs "the emancipator of folks no longer able to enjoy the exhilaration of vicing commercially" and wrote to him, "Alas, poor Yorick! I grieve that I can't go along with you, but youth cares not for old age." No matter. Briggs had plenty of middle-aged members to follow his banner.

Briggs's enthusiasm carried him far along the road toward advocacy of total federal control. He asked Frey to check with the Justice Department to see if conviction of saloonkeepers for selling liquor to soldiers and sailors in uniform could not be followed by revocation of their licenses. Frey had to reply, "Mr. Bielaski states that he has gone over this matter thoroughly, and that it cannot be done."

Briggs was more successful in having the laws against prostitution extended. On returning from New Orleans, he and the other directors of the APL met with Fosdick and Bielaski to work out enforcement of Section Thirteen. Authority for the plan formulated was "a bit weak," Fosdick admitted, but crusader Briggs was immensely pleased.

As approved by Gregory, this plan called for medical examinations by local or state health authorities of all women reported to be diseased. If local laws were inadequate or local health authorities lax, the United States attorneys were to bring the suspected woman to trial as soon as possible. If conviction followed, a brief delay of sentence should be requested to allow time for a medical examination. If the woman was found to be diseased, the judge would commit her to an institution having facilities for treatment. The legal basis for this action was the principle that the state had a right to restrain the liberty of persons with contagious or infectious diseases. Enforcement of the new plan was turned over to the APL, with the Surgeon General of the Army promising his full support.

With a note from Elting acclaiming the plan as a "great advance," APL chiefs received copies of orders from the Attorney General setting forth the method devised for detention and compulsory cure of the arrested women. League chiefs were to cooperate with mayors, police officials, and health commissioners to work out coordination and to press for passage of necessary local ordinances. APL involvement in local affairs was in this instance actively encouraged; and through the League, the federal government was to become responsible for enforcing state and local laws.

Briggs rushed back south for another inspection tour. He reported that the new plan for subduing prostitution in Little Rock, Arkansas, had practically cleaned up vice there. Already a clinic had been opened and twenty-five women confined. "Naturally," he reported to Frey, "the news that women are being so confined until cured has spread throughout the district with the results that we anticipated that they would not stay in any section where they were liable to be picked up at any time and subjected to treatment." Everyone seemed enthusiastic about the plan. Of the 28,000 men at Camp Pike only 140 were under treatment, new cases being reported at a rate of only .051 percent per thousand. If not vice, at least the disease problem was being conquered.

In New Orleans and in Duval County, Florida, the League became so interested in extending health reform to moral reform that they laid plans for "Amproleague Farms" for the rehabilitation of prostitutes after they had been forcibly cured. Instead of serving prison terms after the cure, girls were to be paroled to these farms, where they would be taught socially acceptable self-supporting occupations. Through the efforts of the APL, the percentage of United States service men incapacitated by venereal disease dropped to between 3 and 4 percent as compared to 30 percent among the other Allied forces. So successful were League efforts that in August, 1918, vice zones were enlarged to ten miles around any post or station with a complement of 250 men or more. Entire cities now lay within the jurisdiction of the APL, which had become, in effect, a federal vice squad.

The League became a federal prohibition squad at the same time, and bootleggers were no better able to defend themselves than were prostitutes. A determined APL often had to fight local courts and police in its efforts to stem the flow of liquor into cantonment areas. The battle was especially fierce in Arkansas, where a court decision had lifted the absolute ban on importation of liquor into the state, granting permission to bring in for personal use as much as one person could carry. This "lets the bars down to a considerable extent," Briggs reported unhappily to APL headquarters. Liquor, some of a quality "closely approaching poison" according to Briggs, was brought in from Louisiana and Missouri and disposed of through jitney drivers. Several enlisted men and one officer at Camp Pike had been turned temporarily insane through drinking it. To solve the problem, the APL was allowed to search automobiles coming into town and those entering camp limits, as well as to aid in making arrests. Soon the League was helping the authorities plan raids and round up bootleggers and bootlegged liquor besides participating in campaigns to close saloons. They were doing a thorough job.

The federal government did not stretch the law as far in regard to prohibition as it did toward red-light abatement. Dry zones were established for only one-half mile around installations of 250 men. Only where local or state law prohibited the sale of liquor was the distance extended to five miles. Nonetheless, every soldier in uniform and every saloon was watched by the APL.

Vice raids and bootleg liquor hunting continued throughout the war. Thus Leaguers touched directly the lives of large numbers of private citizens. Their influence helped to mobilize public support for federal prohibition through constitutional amendment. Again there were few complaints from reformers. Like the harassment of aliens and dissenters and the probes which could effectively exclude civilians from employment and deprive military personnel from advancement, the APL's control over the sex and drinking customs of Americans was scarcely questioned.

Federal sanction of these investigations allowed the APL to probe deep into the lives of millions of American citizens. The last step, one that brought the APL into the life of almost every citizen, was its assignment to collect domestic intelligence for the War Department. Beginning in January of 1918, APL members collected information on all rumors current in their communities which they considered to be harmful to the interest of the United States in the prosecution of the war. For six months this information was forwarded to the War Department in a rather desultory manner. Then in June the Military Intelligence was reorganized and a new Military Morale Sub-section established, charged with the duty of "psychological stimulation of troops." The root of most soldierly dissatisfaction, decided G. B. Perkins, the new officer in charge, came from the contents of civilian letters to soldiers. He went to the APL for help.

At first it was not clear how the APL could be utilized to boost military morale, but Perkins asked the directors to have members report on all propaganda "tending to dishearten the civil population," to discourage "indiscreet talk about troop movements and other confidential military matters," and to urge relatives and friends to write the boys in service "encouraging letters full of only the cheerful home news."

By the end of July the new chief of the Military Intelligence Division, Marlborough Churchill, had developed a more concrete plan. Churchill explained to the directors that the Military Intelligence was "required to make a weekly report of conditions within the United

States of morale, the trend of public opinion, enemy activities and the like." This report was prepared on Monday of each week and was, according to Churchill, "one of the elements taken into consideration in the adoption and execution of civil and military policies." His plan was to have the APL sample public opinion and report periodically, either every six months or soon after "the happening of some event of national or international importance" likely to affect the country's morale. He enclosed a questionnaire with suggested topics and asked the APL to be "on the watch for any and all changes, and report them at the earliest possible moment." He was interested in every group in American society and suggested that members work closely with newspaper reporters as a means of keeping current with each group.

At the same time, Churchill instructed each of his own intelligence officers to contact APL state inspectors to obtain information on what he considered to be "dangerous" propaganda. The Chicago intelligence officer dispatched requests to APL state inspectors in fourteen states in the Midwest.

Not all state inspectors were eager to add this new task to their list of jobs for the federal government. The state inspector for Wisconsin returned his questionnaire stating that he had so much other war work that he could not take charge of the matter. The Chicago intelligence officer contacted the Chicago APL chief, who in turn complained to APL headquarters that this inspector was "not giving as much attention to League matters as he should." But state inspectors in Colorado, Ohio, Nebraska, Minnesota, Iowa, and Illinois dutifully began to comply.

A sampling of early reports reveals the detailed information the APL was requested to submit and what they reported. The Mason City, Iowa, branch replied that there was very little disaffection in their town, no enemy alien activities or propaganda. Otero County, Colorado, reported that women there were extremely loyal and optimistic, the laboring classes generally loyal, the businessmen and farmers satisfied, and that there was no progress of bolshevism, socialism, no IWW, no anarchism, but possibly some enemy activity and espionage among Non-Partisan League members. Pueblo, Colorado, reported no disloyalty among Negroes, Catholics, Lutherans, or Jews, but reported that railroad workers were "covertly disloyal."

The Cincinnati chief reported at length on Negro unrest there but then concluded, "Disaffection among Negroes, where found, can be traced to a very definite cause or grievance. If press utterances are guarded and they are made to feel that they are going to be dealt with fairly, such feeling will cease to exist. The country does not realize to what extent ignorance, the sheer inability to read and write, has made many Negroes appear to be slackers." He added that white laborers were hostile to Negroes, although Negroes were appealing to the white workers for friendship and a chance to earn a living and believed their support for the war would inevitably bring greater freedom. There were no organizations spreading propaganda and no sabotage, the chief concluded, but the masses needed education on war aims.

In North Platte, Nebraska, on the other hand, the APL chief found "all Germans disaffected at heart," and at Blue Earth County, Minnesota, the chief found noticeable disaffection among Germans and Austrians. The McLeod County, Minnesota, chief described German Lutherans as "generally disloyal." He believed that propaganda circulated by the Non-Partisan League would justify prompt prosecution of its members. From Prowers County, Colorado, came a protest that the federal government was adhering "too closely to the regular legal procedure in dealing with cases of questionable loyalty" and the suggestion that "a more expeditious and less formal procedure" should be adopted. The state inspector for Minnesota suggested that foreigners be kept from colonizing in large cities. Instead, all municipalities should emulate those villages which had run out foreigners and kept their communities truly American. City dwellers who shared that view, of course, accounted in large measure for the urban growth of the Ku Klux Klan.

By August there were few actions or attitudes of American people which were not duly noted by the APL and referred either to the Justice Department or to the War Department. Escape from the web of the APL was no longer possible. Neither Secretary of War Baker nor Attorney General Gregory questioned the necessity of continuing this surveillance of the entire populace. Nor did Wilson. Nor did the public, except for those people caught in that web. The first instance of public controversy over the APL arose not from its investigations of enemy aliens or of dissenters or even of average American citizens: the outcry only came when the League attempted to locate an estimated 300,000 slackers who had evaded the draft. And it came just at the moment when President Wilson was ready—for the first time—to express publicly his appreciation to the volunteers.

Slacker Raiding

So far Crowder had been lucky enough to be spared public criticism of the draft. The War Department halted mobilization in December, 1917, not because of the draft system itself or resistance to it, but because of lack of food, equipment, and medical care for the average conscriptee. In the congressional investigation and public indignation which followed disclosure of these shortages, the methods of obtaining men were still not challenged. The fact that young men did not want to go to war—and that many were being subjected to all types of cruel and illegal treatment because they did not want to go—attracted little attention, except among radicals. Everyone else accepted the proposition that the heterogeneous American public should be forced into Crowder's vast soldier-making machine.

After the confusion of the first draft call, however, Crowder did attempt to reform his deferment and delinquency policy. Each registrant who had not been called for a physical or who had not responded for mobilization was now reclassified. Men who had been previously classed as delinquents for not appearing to be examined were given a chance to fill out a questionnaire and to file claims for deferment. These deferment claims were to be investigated by the

APL before men were called up for the physical. Any man who did not return the questionnaire was then declared a delinquent—or slacker, in popular terms—whether or not he had previously been classified as a deserter. In addition, state quotas, which had previously included all alien and citizen males, now were established on the basis of numbers available for service after deferments had been granted. Investigation of deferments and the location of delinquents now became critical in the determination of how many men had to be called in the various states.

On Crowder's orders, large numbers of men who had been labeled deserters were restored to delinquent status. Only by express order of state adjutant generals could men now be classified as deserters. When the questionnaires were completed in January of 1918, however, the number of deserters was still estimated to be 50,000 and the number of delinquents over 300,000. So Crowder declared spring open season for hunting down men who did not comply with the new rules.

In the past, the APL had confined its draft-evader activities to investigating specific individuals and to sporadic roundups of suspected delinquents. But now there was to be a concentrated effort to locate delinquents and deserters. The League promised the government that members would not claim the fifty-dollar bounty offered by the War Department if they were given a monopoly on slacker hunting. The entire membership would be available to assist draft boards in locating young men who did not want to go to war. In return, however, the APL wanted the power to arrest.

At first, Crowder considered contacting the adjutant generals and recommending that APL members be deputized by local mayors. Such an action would have turned the APL into an agency similar to that used by the War Department during the Civil War, with the difference that Leaguers were civilians, while the agents of the Provost Marshal General during the Civil War had been military. Crowder even had a telegram prepared for the adjutant general of Illinois recommending the deputization of APL members. Then, for some reason, he began to have qualms. The telegram was pencilled "not sent," and Crowder conferred with the Justice Department.

Gregory was in the difficult position of having to make a decision as to the actual authority of Leaguers. If they were to be given responsibility for locating delinquents, he wanted the volunteers to remain under his control, but he did not want to invest them with federal authority to arrest. Even agents of the Bureau of Investigation had received from Congress no statutory right to arrest: their authority came from Gregory as Attorney General. But endowing volunteers with the same authority would certainly have provoked questions from congressmen. As R. L. Deal, legal advisor to Gregory, told the APL directors, the matter was a "somewhat complicated question."

Legally, there was no way out of the dilemma. Under common law APL operatives, like other citizens, had a right to arrest a person committing a felony or breach of the peace. A slacker was doing neither. According to Crowder, civilians could also arrest deserters on the order of a military officer. Most slackers were not deserters, however, so common law was not enough. If APL members were to catch draft dodgers, they had to have authority to arrest.

Eager to have the Justice Department work out some way to hedge the constitutional difficulties, Bielaski promised APL director Frey that the Department would give the APL "all possible authority in the matter." However, it was Gregory who finally formulated the official compromise on the legal issues in a letter to Briggs. Members assigned to each of the 4,700 local draft boards were "to locate and cause to present themselves to the boards or to the proper representatives of the Justice Department, any man who had failed to complete his questionnaire, had not reported for his physical, or who had not responded to his call to duty." Gregory was careful to protect himself. He said that should a member of the League, after locating a delinquent, "find it impracticable to induce him to present himself to the proper authority and an arrest be necessary, he should take the matter up immediately with the proper State or Federal officer in order that the arrest may be effected in accordance with the law."

This left open the whole question of how an APL man could "induce" a young man who did not want to go to war to report to his draft board voluntarily. Officially, the APL simply ordered members to do what Gregory had ordered them to do, "to locate and cause" the men to present themselves to the proper authorities. This left the word "cause" open to interpretation, as Gregory apparently wished it to be. But Crowder and Bielaski were less vague. Crowder announced that the APL was cooperating in "apprehending delinquents and deserters." And Bielaski, realizing that the APL might run into trouble unless the public was reassured that they were acting upon federal authority, told his special agents, "In instances where [Leaguers'] authority may be questioned you will explain they are acting at the request of the Provost Marshal General." The APL sent each chief a copy of Crowder's orders.

Apparently Gregory and Crowder considered the euphemisms "cause" and "apprehend" sufficient authority for their volunteers. Neither had actually used the word "arrest," but both knew exactly what they were doing when they approved these circulars; much consideration had gone into the wording of each. They consciously left it to the APL and other subordinates to interpret the words.

And the subordinates began to interpret. The Military Intelligence officer in Chicago assumed that the APL had received "a government status." Many members assumed they were being asked to make arrests for the government without any legal authority. The Minneapolis division solved the problem by having the city police deputize each member.

As far as the local draft boards were concerned, they no longer had any choice: they were to use the APL to locate delinquents. During the summer of 1918, though, many boards attempted to resist this further federalization of the draft by continuing to organize their own investigating groups.

In Bakersfield, California, for instance, politicians formed what they called a "Safety Committee" of one hundred to which the exemption board turned over all draft delinquency cases. The APL was convinced that H. A. Jastro, the political boss of Kern County, was behind the move and appealed to APL headquarters in Washington for support. "Cannot order be secured Attorney General to exemption board instructing them to operate solely with League?" California APL inspector White wired the directors. Two days later a wire from Crowder to the adjutant general of California called his attention to the Bakersfield "Safety Committee," said it was opposing the APL, and directed: "Please call attention to Boards that the Department of Justice and the American Protective League which is auxiliary to the Department of Justice are the only investigating bodies to be recognized by Boards." The Bakersfield draft board heard from the adjutant general immediately. "I thank you for your prompt action through the Provost Marshal General," White wrote to the APL directors four days later.

The Minneapolis APL seems to have inaugurated the practice of citywide slacker raids which most League units soon adopted. On March 26, 1918, they staged the first major raid. From eleven o'clock that night until two o'clock in the morning, 120 League operatives spread a dragnet through hotels in a lower class lodging district. They took one hundred men to a temporary detention place and had twenty-one of these locked up in the county jail as slackers. Meanwhile, they asked soldiers to surround the show lot of the Ringling Circus while they combed tents and wagons. Delighted with the results, the APL planned a second raid ten days later, this time with twice as many operatives and an escort of seven hundred national guardsmen. They visited saloons, cafes, pool rooms, and dance halls, picking up over a thousand men. Questioning went on through the night, and two hundred men were served Sunday breakfast in jail. Twenty-seven were locked up as slackers. So successful was this second haul that the Minneapolis APL instituted nightly patrols of two or three members who raided each night from seven-thirty until eleven-thirty.

The Justice Department, which had used the raiding process extensively with radicals, saw no reason that the same method should not now be used to find the thousands of slackers who lounged about the home front. The fact that Minneapolis men had acquired legitimate powers to arrest, unlike most other APL units, made no difference to Justice Department officials. Those few men who challenged the authority of the APL found its members defended in court by United States attorneys. When in April APL chief Robert E. Ferguson of the Lansing, Michigan, division was sued for five thousand dollars' damages by a slacker he had taken before the local draft board, John Lord O'Brian wrote to the United States Attorney in Detroit, "You are instructed officially to appear and defend Mr. Ferguson in this action." Thereafter Bureau of Investigation agents began to order APL men to "take" or "hold" men. The agents were never admonished that this was the same as ordering an illegal arrest.

As far as the APL was concerned, it could follow no other course. One chief warned his men that anyone charged with the duty of enforcing the Selective Service Act and failing to perform his duty would himself be guilty of a misdemeanor and subject to a penalty of up to one year imprisonment. "Having subscribed to the oath of the American Protective League, you come under the provisions of this act and you *must* comply with the instructions sent you or lay yourself open for prosecution under this section," he told his men.

Despite the extralegal powers exercised by the APL, Crowder found the number of men available for the draft dwindling rapidly by summer of 1918. Local boards had indulged their exemption powers so freely that nearly one half of the men originally called had been exempted from service, most on the basis of having dependent relatives. Of almost ten million men originally registered, three million had been called. But by the time exemptions had cut into that number and over 700,000 had been judged physically unfit, the total certified was only a little over 76,000. New men were being called rapidly, but convincing them that they should respond was another matter. So the hunt for slackers flourished during the summer in much the same way that the hunt for spies had flourished in spring.

Vast and ambitious measures were proposed to Crowder to locate the 350,000 deserters and delinquents still at large. Some military officers thought that Class I registrants, using their own classification cards as badges, should be used in the hunt. Others suggested that lists of delinquents be published in newspapers and that the boards of education distribute copies of them to teachers to be read to children along with admonitions to have the young males in their families report. One plan was to flash notices on screens of moving picture theaters between films; another, for proprietors of hotels and rooming houses to ask for classification cards before renting rooms and to report any suspicious men. Secretary McAdoo, who had been put in charge of the railroads when the government took over their management in December of 1917, proposed that no train tickets be sold without checking the prospective purchasers' draft status. But the favorite stratagem was the raid as conducted by the APL.

During the summer of 1918 the League embarked upon slacker raiding in earnest. The Cleveland unit began to stage periodic raids in Luna Park and Euclid Beach, large amusement parks. Thirty-six thousand men had been stopped, the division reported later. In St. Paul the APL worked with special agents of the Bureau of Investigation and two battalions of Home Guards in rounding up a horde of fifteen hundred men and taking them all to the local armory. Detroit, Davenport, Dayton, Philadelphia, St. Louis, Louisville, Galveston, San Francisco—each had at least one raid and usually a summer series. In Birmingham, Alabama, the APL planned a giant county-wide raid to locate some fifteen hundred men listed as delinquents and deserters. In every case the procedure was to stop everyone of draft age and "hold" him until his draft status could be ascertained. By the end of June the raids had netted twenty thousand slackers for Provost Marshal General Crowder's manpower barrel. Assuming that at most 20 percent of the men actually "held" and taken to detention centers were classified as slackers, this means that about one hundred thousand men had already been arrested by the APL up to July 1.

In the furor over collecting slackers, not only was the previous no-arrest policy reversed by the new "holding" plan, but the Justice Department also relaxed its opposition to its subordinates' collecting the bounty. On April 15, 1918, Gregory announced that federal officials could be "reimbursed for necessary and reasonable expense"—coincidentally, up to fifty dollars—for apprehending each deserter, and APL members were allowed to collect the bounty so long as they turned it over to APL units and did not pocket it themselves. Frenzied competition ensued during the spring and early summer. Southern sheriffs spent their time rounding up slackers in the back country. City police kept a close eye on young men roaming the streets. A generous Treasury Department held that police officials could receive the reward for merely delivering slackers to the nearest army camp; it was not necessary that they even do the actual apprehending.

Soon the whole business of locating deserters became a nasty, bounty hunting practice. The *New York Tribune* reported on July 9 that $30,000 had been paid out at Fort Jay the previous Saturday for the apprehension of six hundred delinquents. The article estimated that two thousand slackers were being apprehended a month at a cost to the government of $100,000. That didn't bother the editors, however, one of whom spoofed, "The bounty will not be paid on the ears, scalp or other parts of the untied animal; the policeman must bring him to the station house all in one piece and still breathing."

Nasty as was the bounty hunting itself, the treatment of suspected slackers taken to the station house was even worse. Whether arrested legally by officers of the law or "taken" illegally by civilians, suspects were held indefinitely while telegrams were sent to local draft boards to confirm their status. Sometimes weeks passed before the draft boards replied and the suspects were released. Some special agents, a bit squeamish about holding men without warrants, filed complaints for violation of the Selective Service Act while the investigations were pending. Usually, however, the men were simply held upon no legal authority. Even when they were found to be real delinquents, no one was sure what to do with them, for the draft regulations were not precise on this question. Were they to be prosecuted or merely packed off to the nearest camp? It all depended on the APL, the draft board, and the special agents.

There was little chance that the system would be abandoned, however, for on June 25 General Pershing notified the War Department that he would need three times as many men as he was now receiving, and a second registration for the draft to be held on June 5 was expected to produce very few new twenty-one-year-olds. As much as the actual men apprehended, the War Department wanted public pressure on draftees; this the slacker raids encouraged.

Meanwhile, once the spring spy scare had passed, Republican critics, led by Theodore Roosevelt and Leonard Wood, switched their attention to the draft. They demanded extension of the draft to raise a larger Army, and when Secretary Baker balked at this, they began to use their differences as a campaign issue. By June Republican Senator Albert B. Fall of New Mexico had stalled the army appropriation bill by offering an amendment to extend the age group subject to the draft to include all men between twenty and forty. Only a promise from Baker on June 26 that he would submit a new draft bill within ninety days could shake an unamended appropriation bill out of the Senate.

Yielding to the Republican clamor for more ruthless enforcement of conscription, the Justice Department asked for a major slacker raid in Chicago. The purpose of the raid was to instill respect for the Administration's conscription machinery and to quiet criticism, as well as to corral reluctant males.

In the early hours of July 11, the Chicago APL launched a major offensive. Like everything else the Chicago division planned, it was big, and it was well organized. Members met at League headquarters, where some remained while two other groups dispersed to the Federal Building and to the city's main police station. At each of the rendezvous points, members, joined by police and navy men, formed squads of four or five men and took up posts at various locations throughout the city, stopping young men on the street and asking them to show their draft cards. Men who could not produce the proper identification were marched off to APL headquarters, the Federal Building, or to jail. Raiders searched ball parks, movie houses, cabarets, parks, and beaches. They met incoming trains, stopped motorists, inspected picnics. They visited homes and shops. When they found a suspect, they loaded him into a car, wagon, bus, or streetcar and sent him to join the growing hordes of accused slackers. Night came. Those still unable at a late hour to prove their innocence were jammed into Bureau of Investigation rooms, courts, jails, and vacant public offices. The Municipal Pier became an internment camp where over a thousand men passed the sultry night under police and naval guard.

For three days the attack continued. At the end of the third day, the chief of the Chicago APL estimated that 10,000 APL members had interrogated 150,000 men. Over 40,000 of these had needed their draft status changed, and 16,000 had been arrested on suspicion of being slackers, of whom 1,200 men had been found to be evaders and 265 deserters.

The Chicago APL reported no complaints about their attacks. The *Chicago Tribune* even congratulated the volunteers for their tact and good sense in accomplishing a difficult task with "a minimum of friction and a maximum of thoroughness." In fact, there were few complaints about any of the summer raids, for the war front absorbed the attention of most citizens, and they were reluctant to criticize the war effort at home. Chief dissatisfaction came from some APL divisions which protested that the League was being changed from a secret investigatory agency into a type of police auxiliary. The state inspector of Arkansas wired APL headquarters, "Our work is mainly investigation and confidential reports. I think if our identity is revealed our efficiency would be lessened."

To the complaints of the Arkansas state inspector, APL headquarters replied that slacker raiding would secure "the good will of the best citizens of the community" and that "the Federal Government has frequently expressed itself as feeling that the services rendered the Country by the League in this respect is one of its best efforts." By the end of August, pressure from central headquarters in Washington had raised the total of slackers apprehended by the APL from 20,000 to 30,000. Only one large city remained untouched by the raiders— New York, known as the slacker's paradise.

Early in August, Crowder received alarming news: available military manpower would be gone by October 1. This news prompted Crowder to request an even more drastically revised draft bill than the Republican critics had demanded in June. The War Department asked that the enlarged age group be not twenty to forty, as Senator Fall had suggested, but eighteen to forty-five. In addition to this proposal, Crowder scheduled a third registration for August 24 to pick up any twenty-one-year-olds missed in the first two registrations. Then he asked Attorney General Gregory for help in a concentrated effort to locate more slackers immediately. The Justice Department responded by ordering the APL raiders to strike New York.

There had been no large scale slacker raids in New York because that APL division had other problems. The number of competent men in the New York unit was small in the beginning, and from the very first there were members who wished to use it for political purposes. The first chief, a lawyer appointed by Briggs, had resigned after one month with the excuse that he could not spare the time from his law practice. The second chief, a special agent named Richmond Levering who had been recommended by Bureau of Investigation Superintendent William Offley, made many plans but executed none of them. Half of the members he recruited considered the League some sort of honorary patriotic group and wanted no part in actual investigations. The other half, composed of former policemen and self-interested men, assumed authority and used it illegally. Former policemen had resorted to strong-arm tactics, as a later chief put it, "such little things as breaking in doors in people's apartments and things of that character." By October of 1917, the Washington office of the Bureau of Investigation was conducting an investigation of Levering, as a result of which Bielaski recommended that Levering be asked to resign. An operating committee was then set up with Paul Reinhardt, a competent executive and organizer, as chairman. But Levering, who still had a following in the APL and support from Superintendent Offley, stirred up opposition to Reinhardt on the basis that he had a German name and was therefore suspect. Other men within the unit agitated for recognition as official investigators and for the power to arrest. Without that power, they felt that the Justice Department might disavow their work at any time. As one member expressed it to Briggs, they were "on the tip end of a branch of a tree and could be shaken off at any moment the Department desired."

After almost a year of conflict, with pressure on him to remove Reinhardt and with no likely man available as a replacement, Briggs had finally given up his organizing efforts in New York and turned over the tangled affairs of the division to Frey and Elting. "I certainly have had my troubles in that darn old town and I feel as though I have just recovered from the smallpox in turning it over to you and Victor," Briggs wrote to Frey.

But Briggs's troubles with New York were not yet over. For almost four months Frey and Elting struggled with the New Yorkers. They brought in a new chief, tried to interest friends in joining, and appealed to Bielaski for stronger backing. Reinhardt and Levering were shipped out of New York with army commissions. Offley was transferred to Washington. By April, the new Bureau of Investigation superintendent, Charles DeWoody, was writing to Briggs that the organization had "accomplished wonders" in New York and that it would soon be carrying one-half of the load of federal investigation work there. Despite DeWoody's enthusiasm, however, the division was still drawing criticism from various civilians and from federal agents. Some questioned their authority, some questioned their methods, some questioned their standards of admittance, and some questioned their right to exist as an auxiliary to the Justice Department.

Then in May, a new crisis developed. General T. Coleman DuPont tried to form the New York League into a Republican club for the 1920 campaign. Elting and Frey moved quickly to block the plans of several captains to turn one meeting, called ostensibly for organizing purposes, into a fund-raising benefit for the party. One captain had to be asked to resign. No sooner was that danger averted than another member was arrested on charges of extortion. By the end of May, even Frey was discouraged. The New York division needed to recruit more members, but, he confided to Edmund Rushmore, the latest chief there, most of the applicants appeared to be "about 100% rotten" and only wanted to play detective. He warned Rushmore that publicity for their recruiting efforts would only increase their difficulties.

By the summer of 1918 the New York division was so overworked with the routine investigations for the Justice Department that it had hardly concerned itself with draft problems. Although the members, like those in other cities, had received instructions to work with local draft boards, New York draft officials had hired their own investigators, issued them badges, administered oaths, and sent them out on the trail of slackers.

Early in May sporadic canvassing organized by local boards in New York City had begun. A law student, after having been drafted and then rejected for physical disabilities, had volunteered to look for healthy men refusing to serve their country. The young man, Arthur Rosenfeld, had eventually been put on the payroll as a clerk, but he actually spent his full time investigating. A badge received from the chairman of the local board served as his authorization. In May, single-handedly, he rounded up eighty-five slackers. Early in June he organized another raid with three army men and an APL member. During that raid two men bearing APL commission cards stepped out of the crowd and joined the party. The police congratulated the raiding party as they brought in the first batch of forty-one men to the 26th Precinct station before going out for more.

While rounding up the second batch of men at a cigar store at 50th Street and Broadway, Rosenfeld and his assistants ran into United States Marshal Thomas McCarthy. McCarthy had always opposed federal use of volunteers and had backed the attempt of the Secret Service to establish a central intelligence agency. He promptly took Rosenfeld's badge away and released all the prisoners. The Marshal told reporters that neither he nor the APL men had a right to wear badges nor to take draft slackers into custody, and that the Justice Department should be notified whenever a raid was to be made. One League captain, complaining of McCarthy's action to the New York chief, summed up: "It is obvious that we are supposed by headquarters to have the right to take these men into custody. If we have no right to make arrests under special instructions of this kind, and no right to wear badges, orders of this kind are likely to bring us into extreme difficulties." Nothing could have been more prophetic.

The ill omen of the June controversy deterred neither the Bureau of Investigation nor the directors of the APL. Bielaski looked upon the raids as a means of impressing Congress, the War Department, and the general public with the work that the Bureau had done in enforcing the Selective Service Act. The APL directors looked upon them as a means of both putting an end to criticism leveled at them and proving the League indispensable to the Justice Department.

On August 15 Bielaski instructed Superintendent DeWoody to institute a raid in New York. He cautioned Frey in Washington that details should first be worked out thoroughly and submitted for his final approval and that of the Provost Marshal.

Although Briggs had been unable to solve the earlier problems of organization in New York, Frey wired him to begin plans for the New York raid, entrusting him with the preliminaries. Briggs assumed command, spending the last two weeks of August in New York working out the plan of attack. He installed himself in DeWoody's office to facilitate cooperation with the Bureau of Investigation. Frey joined him for three days to review the methods worked out in the large Chicago raid the previous month. DeWoody, Briggs, and Frey discussed the proposed raids with the draft director, Martin Conboy. Frey sensed no impending problems and returned to Washington to handle coordination there. Briggs, who now seemed to have the New York situation well in hand, remained in charge.

In Washington, Bielaski offered his complete support for the coming raid. Any accusations that Leaguers were impersonating federal officers, Frey wrote to Rushmore, would be taken up with Gregory by Bielaski. This "should be very encouraging to you and ought to convince you that the Attorney General and Mr. Bielaski are back of the American Protective League to the limit," Frey assured him.

Originally Frey and Briggs chose to schedule the raid five days after the third registration. But these dates, August 29, 30, and 31, the draft board considered too soon after the registration of the twenty-one-year-olds; new classification cards would not yet be issued. More-over, draft officials would be busy enough with registration and classification; they did not want a raid at that time. Members of the New Jersey APL supported the draft board, even protesting to Secretary of War Baker and Attorney General Gregory that the raid should be cancelled.

Protests brought only postponement. Baker and Gregory ordered the raids shifted to a later date but left the choice to the New York Bureau of Investigation. This time Briggs and DeWoody took no chance of running into opposition by premature discussion with the draft boards. They scheduled the raids for September 3, 4, and 5, and proceeded with their plans without discussing them with the director of the draft.

On August 29 the blueprints were complete. The raids were to start on Tuesday, September 3. This gave the organizers six days to work out coordination with city and state officials—but the last three days were Saturday, Sunday, and Labor Day. This left only three working days, Wednesday through Friday. Coordination began.

With the help of DeWoody, Briggs arranged to use the Sixty-ninth Regiment armory in New York City and the Twenty-third Regiment armory in Brooklyn as central detention points. Seventy-five APL men and twenty special agents of the Bureau of Investigation were assigned to the New York armory, fifty APL and ten special agents to the Brooklyn armory. Two APL operatives were to be detailed to each of the 189 local draft boards and two to each police station. In the Bronx, the courthouse was to be used as headquarters, and in Newark another armory was to serve as a detention area. Admiral Usher of the Brooklyn Navy Yard promised to supply a thousand sailors for the raids, and commanders at camps and forts near the city offered to send several thousand soldiers. The raid began to assume the dimensions of a major campaign.

Neither Gregory nor Baker was too concerned about the proposed New York raid, however. As soon as Congress had passed the new draft bill late in August, Baker left secretly on another trip to the battle front. Gregory expected to start his vacation. President Wilson was planning a campaign tour through the West. In all three important offices, subordinates were to be left in command.

On Thursday, Briggs finally notified draft director Martin Conboy that the raid was planned for Tuesday, the day after Labor Day, and that the APL would be detailed to each local draft board. Conboy immediately objected, saying it would be impossible to make the necessary preparations. Finally at Briggs's insistence he agreed that the local boards would participate and do the best they could.

By Friday Briggs was convinced that his small army of soldiers and sailors would be insufficient to guard the thousands of slackers. He decided he must have three regiments of national guardsmen as well as federal forces. But getting national guardsmen was a complicated affair. When DeWoody called the colonel in command of one armory regiment, the officer insisted he could act only on orders from the adjutant general of the state. At noon DeWoody phoned the New York adjutant general to ask for the three regiments. The adjutant general in turn claimed that only the governor could call out the Guard, and that the governor must have a request from the War Department. DeWoody impatiently replied that time was too short for formalities of that kind; he would have the Provost Marshal General's office call the adjutant general. Briggs called Frey in Washington to ask him to make the request.

Frey immediately contacted Bielaski and asked him to arrange with the War Department for the use of the troops. Friday noon was a bad time to be calling generals, but Bielaski tried.

The only person Bielaski could locate in the office of Provost Marshal General Crowder was the chief of the Delinquency Division, a young captain named Breckenridge Jones. Bielaski asked that Adjutant General Sherrill of New York be requested to furnish some national guardsmen for the proposed raid. Jones said he would see that General Sherrill was called. The problem seemed solved. Then Bielaski hastily wrote a telegram for the Attorney General's signature asking Governor Seymour Whitman of New York to cooperate with the Justice Department on the raids. This dispatched, he called Frey, who wired Briggs that Bielaski had talked to the Provost Marshal General, who in turn had talked with the adjutant general in New York, and that Bielaski was doing everything possible to get the services of the National Guard for three days.

Bielaski had not talked to Crowder, however, and Crowder had not talked to the adjutant general. In fact, Crowder later maintained he did not know anything about plans to use any soldiers and sailors on the raiding parties. Captain Jones did not talk to Crowder either. In view of the laudatory press comments concerning previous raids under the auspices of the Justice Department, Jones assumed that neither the Administration nor the Provost Marshal General's office had any objection to them—that the New York raid was simply routine.

Young Jones's call interrupted General Sherrill at lunch. Sherrill replied impatiently that he could act only with the authority of the Militia Bureau of the War Department, and that any request would have to be in writing.

Jones went back to his desk, wrote an order requesting the guardsmen, and took it to the executive in charge of the Militia Bureau for his signature. At the same time, Jones requested permission to go to New York himself to observe the raiding methods. The officer refused flatly either to sign the order or to send Jones to New York. He had more respect for the anger of Crowder than did the young captain. Besides, he told the impatient Jones, the Militia Bureau had no jurisdiction over New York's state troops.

Jones should have called Bielaski; instead he telephoned Draft Director Conboy in New York, telling him that Sherrill did not seem eager to cooperate and that the Militia Bureau would not act. By this time on Friday afternoon, the War Department offices were rapidly being abandoned. Jones decided to drop the whole matter.

Meanwhile, in New York, Briggs carried on. He informed Conboy that the raids would begin on Tuesday and that as men were picked up, the APL would be calling local boards to check on the draft status of all suspected delinquents. As far as DeWoody was concerned, the armory examinations by APL men would be considered final, and delinquents would be sent immediately to camp. The acting representative of the adjutant general's office, however, sided with the local boards, who insisted on being the primary examining agents. He suggested that the draft boards be stationed at tables placed along the walls in the armory. Here board members could immediately issue either changes of classification or induction orders, depending on eligibility for service of the men brought in. Briggs and DeWoody finally agreed, telling the draft director that the time for the raids was set for 9:00 A.M. Draft officials began to alert those board members whom they could reach to be in the armories on Tuesday morning.

On Labor Day, newspapers devoted space to the fact that the APL had been active in slacker raiding, and a press release issued by Crowder to the *Philadelphia Public Ledger* boasted that one raid in Ohio, manned by APL and policemen, had resulted in a thousand arrests. Registrants must carry their credentials or be liable to arrest, the statement warned. After debate, Congress had passed a revised draft bill, and Crowder had already issued a proclamation calling for the registration on September 12 of men within the extended age limits. He assumed slacker raiding would encourage a large turnout.

Continuing their preparations, Briggs and DeWoody held a series of briefing sessions for APL men who were to participate in the New York raids. What DeWoody actually said at these meetings is unclear. Bielaski later maintained that DeWoody told the men not to make any arrests. Edmund Rushmore, the New York APL chief, insisted later that this was "absolutely untrue," that he had attended each session, and that the men were told—and printed circulars signed by DeWoody instructed them—to "hold and bring" the men: that this implied the men could arrest. It is not likely that at this stage De-Woody worried too much about the niceties. Rather, he accepted the policy of the War Department, that the APL was to assist in "apprehending" delinquents and "holding" suspects. That is what the APL did during the New York raid: they apprehended and held.

In contrast to this disregard for technicalities, the Newark, New Jersey, APL proceeded without the necessity of such orders. The 125 APL captains of the Newark force met with the Newark police in the federal courtroom where, as the state inspector said, "the law was laid down." Members were warned that there was to be "no rough stuff," no "cossacking," nothing but "firm politeness." The police arranged to have an officer and two unarmed Home Guards with each APL team. Army officers were to be present only as observers, staying in the officers' quarters in the Newark armory; and all soldiers were to remain within the armory as guards. Policemen were to make all arrests. An auxiliary motor corps made up of wives of League members was to be on hand to taxi men home to get registration cards or because they had been cleared. There was no confusion in Newark.

But in New York, confusion simply increased. On Monday night DeWoody made one more attempt to use the National Guard. This time he called Colonel Praeger, commander of the Twenty-third Regiment, requesting that he call up his men. Praeger called Adjutant General Sherrill, who again replied that Governor Whitman would have to be contacted. DeWoody hung up the phone in disgust.

The next morning, Tuesday, September 3, 1918, with the matter of arrests still unclarified and the use of the military still undecided, the plan for the New York slacker raid was put into effect. Draft officials had been told that the net would be out at 9:00 A.M. At almost the last minute DeWoody and Briggs advanced the starting hour to 7:00 A.M. They did not notify the draft boards. Impatient as the time drew near, the zealous raiders advanced the hour once again, to 6:30 A.M., at which time soldiers and APL men blockaded all exits and entrances to the New York subway. The great raid was on.

For those early morning commuters who had read the *New York*

Times, the slacker raid came as no surprise. The paper announced in the morning that a raid would begin that day, with Leaguers, agents of the Bureau of Investigation, and military personnel participating. Had a commuter read the *New York Tribune,* he would also have known that he could be required to show his draft classification card sometime during the next three days.

Most young men probably thought the raid would cause them no inconvenience. As they reached into their pockets to produce draft cards, however, some realized they had forgotten them. Some had neglected to apply for new cards when the old ones, printed on cheap paper, had disintegrated. Others had forgotten to have their classification changed when they married or changed jobs. But the APL agents were cordial, even friendly, as they told the young men to come along to the armories to prove to their draft boards that they had complied with the regulations. Men who had their cards smugly passed onto the streets and went to work.

Suspected draft delinquents good-naturedly lined up and marched off to the armories. They expected only a slight delay. Once at the armories, they could call wives or other relatives to bring down forgotten cards, or they could get new classification cards from the draft boards. No one seemed to object to the inconvenience, a small thing compared to the sacrifices of the boys in the front lines. No one wanted to appear unpatriotic.

Streams of men began to converge on the armories. At the gates, the raiding squads turned over their quarries to the waiting military guards and APL men and returned to the subways.

Once inside the armories, the captives realized that something was wrong. Instead of finding their draft boards lined up around the walls as the APL men had said they would be, the men found only more APL men and soldiers. They were told they must wait; the draft board representatives would arrive at 9:00 A.M. The lucky ones lined up at the telephones and reached relatives who could bring down their cards. Those who needed clearance from the draft boards had to wait.

More men arrived. The armories became crowded as the raiding squads deposited their prey. When the draft board members arrived on schedule, they had trouble pushing through the crowds to their designated positions. The men, some of whom had already waited over two hours, were beginning to get restless. There seemed to be no priority for those who had arrived earliest. More suspects arrived.

DeWoody and Briggs began to worry about the jam. If the men weren't released by noon, their captors would have to provide soldiers to take them out for lunch. But all the soldiers were already occupied on raiding squads or patrolling streets near the armories. DeWoody rushed over to the apartments of Governor Whitman at the St. Regis Hotel and personally requested the services of the National Guard. Only if his commanding general approved, the governor replied. Only if the city police could not handle the situation, General Dyer advised the governor when he called to ask. So DeWoody climbed back into his car, picked up General Dyer, and together they rushed over to confer with Police Commissioner Enright. At the police commissioner's office they received a placid reply: no reason why the police could not handle the situation. It seemed like a plot to DeWoody as he rushed back to the Sixty-ninth Regiment armory muttering that the state had refused to assist the federal government.

At the armory, DeWoody prepared a news release accusing the adjutant general of refusing to help the Justice Department. As he was about to hand his manifesto to newsmen, Martin Conboy appeared. He calmed the superintendent and convinced him that such a release would only aggravate a bad situation. DeWoody thereupon turned back to the problem of bringing order to the overflowing armories.

It was now almost noon, and anxious relatives had begun to besiege the Sixty-ninth Regiment armory to obtain the release of their imprisoned men. The crowd outside threatened to surge through the gates and join the milling crowd within. At two o'clock two companies of the Provost Guard from Fort Niagara, which were stationed at barracks in Mulberry Bend Park, had to be called to disperse the crowds outside the fortress. The gates clanged shut, and the troops threw a cordon around the armory.

Inside, good humor was giving way to anger. Some men, too ignorant or inarticulate to explain their status to the APL, though in the clear, had been marched to the armories by impatient interrogators. Others whose special classifications were unfamiliar to the APL were caught in the net unnecessarily. One defense plant worker who had been standing in line for hours discovered that a slip of paper thrust into his hands without explanation two hours earlier had been meant to discharge him. As the men began to question the validity of their imprisonment, military guards tightened their control.

By afternoon word had reached Washington of the confusion in New York. Gregory had planned to start a short vacation Tuesday morning and was not in his office at the Justice Department. Only the day before, ironically enough, he had discussed the work of the APL with Wilson, who had endorsed the work of the organization and asked Gregory to express his appreciation and his pledge of support. A signed letter to that effect lay on Gregory's desk when the first ominous rumble arrived from New York.

John Lord O'Brian, whom Gregory had left in command, received the first call. He immediately telephoned DeWoody, ordering him to see that no men were detained over night. Then he called Gregory back to Washington.

In New York, raiding continued into the evening. By 9:00 P.M., APL units were combing places of amusement and theaters, sifting men and looking for slackers. One raiding party of twenty-five seamen and a petty officer stopped a performance by soldiers from Camp Upton of "Yip, Yip, Yapyank" and ordered all men in the audience between the ages of twenty-one and thirty-one to stand up and show a registration card. During the ensuing hubbub, the commanding officer of the soldier-actors persuaded the sailors to defer their search until after the performance. Then all exits were blocked and a number of playgoers who could not produce cards were marched off under military guard.

By this time DeWoody was attempting to comply with O'Brian's orders to empty the armories. But he was reluctant to give up the men whom APL stalwarts believed guilty of draft evasion. His Bureau agents took almost three hundred men down to The Tombs, the New York city jail. The warden accepted this first group without commitment papers, but when the agents brought a second group, he refused to admit more. Undaunted, the agents hustled nearly a thousand men up to neighboring Camp Dix. The rest of the suspects were released, and by morning the armories were entirely cleared.

Newsmen attempting to find out exactly what had happened received a variety of answers. One paper reported 20,000 men detained, another 40,000. One APL inspector was quoted as saying that over 50 percent of the men detained were slackers. DeWoody was said to be "extremely pleased" with the way the roundup had gone and satisfied that more slackers had been found than expected: at least 5 percent of all the men seized. (That 95 percent were subjected to outrageous treatment unjustifiably seems not to have disturbed him.) Federal Marshal McCarthy, on the other hand, insisted that most of the men committed to The Tombs were from out of town, that the APL simply had not received an answer from draft boards as to the men's status. Before either the public or the Justice Department could determine exactly what had happened, 7:00 A.M. Wednesday arrived, and the second day of raiding began.

Leaguers started the second day with considerably less enthusiasm. DeWoody had warned them to be more careful in bringing men to the armories and to make sure that only those within the draft age who had no proper identification were detained. Still, raiding parties continued to operate throughout the day and into the evening. Belmont Park and a number of hotels were raided. Automobiles manned by wives of Leaguers and trucks manned by sailors steadily conveyed suspects to the Sixty-ninth Regiment armory. Naval Reserve officers filtered through cabarets, restaurants, lunchrooms, and cigar stores. Off Times Square, soldiers and sailors armed with rifles and bayonets patrolled cross streets to see that no dodgers escaped the net.

That same evening at the Atlantic Avenue subway station in Brooklyn, there was a near riot when Justice Department agents, assisted by soldiers, sailors, and APL operatives, stopped every man of apparent draft age coming out of the terminal and demanded his credentials. Five hundred were sent to the armory for further examination after a preliminary interrogation at the subway station. In another part of town a man reeled out of a saloon, flashed a card purporting to show that he was a member of the military police, and was immediately put to work by a raiding party. He began by cornering grey-haired men and marching them down to the armory. Some APL men had on their old "Secret Service" badges, which they had been instructed not to use, and one of them was heard to say, "I am a Secret Service man." By the end of the second day, another four to five thousand suspects had been arrested by these methods and taken to armories.

On that same Wednesday, congressmen returning from the long holiday weekend, alert for possible issues in the coming elections, discovered the slacker raids. Only the day before the raids began, Republican Senator Lawrence Sherman of Illinois, in a burst of Labor Day oratory, had assailed Wilson for undermining civil liberties, offering no specific accusations but generally damning what he termed socialistic tendencies in the Administration and voicing his fear that the government would not return to normal after the war because Wilson intended to maintain a centralized autocratic government. Hostile anti-Administration Senator William Calder, at home in Brooklyn during the first day's raiding, cornered Gregory as he was returning to Washington on Wednesday morning and angrily demanded to know who was responsible for the wholesale arrests. Gregory admitted that he did not know but said he would find out.

Thursday morning the Senate was the arena for an all-out Republican attack on the Administration. Senator Calder announced that he had seen military personnel involved in the raids and that officers he had questioned said they were under the authority of the Justice Department. Senator George Chamberlain of Oregon, as critical now of the Justice Department as he had been during the unsuccessful fight to place spies under military jurisdiction, quoted from the *New York World* to the effect that APL operatives used in the raid had no warrants for arrest or official standing. Hiram Johnson produced a letter from a friend in New York estimating that fifty thousand men had been rounded up and that those sent away as slackers were simply "not intelligent enough" to make themselves understood. Along with the letter, he produced a copy of DeWoody's instructions which clearly stated that the raid was being staged at the direction of the Attorney General, with the approval of the Provost Marshal; yet both denied prior knowledge of the event. Senator Henry Cabot Lodge declared the country should know who was responsible, and Utah Senator Reed Smoot asked for a resolution calling on Chamberlain's Committee on Military Affairs to ascertain just that.

The threat of an investigation by Chamberlain brought North Carolinian Lee Overman, stalwart friend of the Justice Department and Chairman of the Judiciary Committee, to the defense of the Administration. He announced that Bielaski had told him he would take full responsibility for the arrests. Arkansas Senator William Kirby, champion of the War Department during earlier Republican attacks, and progressive Republican Miles Poindexter added their support to Overman. Together they managed to have the vote on Smoot's resolution held over until Friday in hopes that they could have the investigation switched to Overman's committee, which could quietly bury it. When word of the Senate battle reached Wilson, he called Gregory into conference.

In Washington the raids began to take on the aspects of a major political controversy; in New York the raiders continued their work. On Thursday APL men arrested another group of twenty-five men at a New York restaurant. At noon one squad of APL men and sailors placed guards at the entrance to the Equitable Building, demanding identification from all men attempting to leave. Newspapermen who crowded DeWoody's office noted the frequency of calls from the

Justice Department and asked the superintendent if the senators were "making a goat out of him." He retorted that no one could. Furthermore, he flung out, "The Justice Department is not a damned bit on the defensive."

Yet the carelessness of his volunteers was already evident as slacker suspects were questioned more carefully. Most of the men committed to The Tombs the day before were freed. Camp Dix officials complained that none of the so-called slackers turned over to them had papers from their draft boards ordering induction, although legally every recruit was to carry such papers. Indeed, some of the men still carried registration cards showing that they were exempt.

By Thursday afternoon DeWoody was worried. "It is silly to assume that I would ever have undertaken such work without the authority of my superiors in office," he snapped at reporters. One of DeWoody's special agents told another reporter that Gregory's orders to APL men to aid the Justice Department in the raids were sufficient to make them "recognized police officers."

United States Attorney Henry Ward Beers had a different story. He stated categorically that the arrest of suspects by APL members was "without authority." Marshal McCarthy, who was at the Sixty-ninth Regiment armory observing the chaos, remarked sarcastically to the press: "The system is perfect. I congratulate Mr. Briggs and Mr. DeWoody for their splendid work." A pro-Wilson paper, the *New York World* nonetheless ran an editorial under the heading "Amateur Prussianism in New York," demanding an investigation and comparing the raid to "the kind of treatment that the Prussian commanders impose upon the helpless inhabitants of a conquered province," all done "under pretext of inspiring public respect for military conscription." It concluded that "the arrest of any number of slackers could not excuse this rape of the law—this wanton ravishing of the very spirit of American institutions."

Wilson did not wait for the senators to pass their resolution on Friday launching an investigation of the Justice Department. He seized the political offensive. After conferring with Gregory, he sent him a formal letter requesting an investigation. "May I not ask that you let me know at your early convenience exactly what action the representatives of the Department of Justice was in New York, and the circumstances of that action, in making arrests of persons charged with being slackers," he wrote. "The arrests have aroused so much interest and are likely to give rise to so much misunderstanding that I would be very much obliged to you if you would let me know all the facts and circumstances." The President decided to cancel his proposed trip to the West.

Gregory gave a copy of Wilson's letter to the press with an announcement that an investigation was in progress. At 8:00 P.M. Thursday DeWoody officially called the raiding off. By then John Lord O'Brian, head of the War Emergency Division of the Justice Department, was on a train heading for New York to investigate the circumstances surrounding the raids.

More than any other man in the Justice Department, John Lord O'Brian was concerned with civil liberties. Brought into the Department by Gregory in October, 1917, one of his first tasks had been to interview Frey and Elting and to decide whether or not the APL should be given official status. Although favorably impressed by the two dapper Chicagoans, he had advised Gregory to keep the APL as a purely voluntary association and to disassociate it from the Bureau of Investigation as much as possible. O'Brian continually wrote letters during the next months instructing the public and government officials as to the unofficial character of the APL. Yet he had been in on the February deliberations about granting the League authority, and there is no evidence that he opposed the original decision of the Provost Marshal General and the Attorney General to use the Leaguers as slacker raiders. He was much more opposed to their use as secret investigators and spy catchers.

At the time that the decision was made in February to use the APL in locating slackers, O'Brian was still consolidating his own power within the department. Until the April conflict with the military over extension of jurisdiction, his Emergency Division had played a minor role. With the exit of Charles Warren during the dispute, he rapidly became chief advisor to Gregory and to President Wilson on matters involving civil liberties. Although the advice he gave Wilson in April (that a public statement be made denouncing mob violence) was not followed until the end of July, he had successfully persuaded the Attorney General to take a more positive stand on the issue.

O'Brian's being a Republican, his reputation as a progressive interested in civil liberties, and his determined containment of the military made him an excellent choice as investigator of the slacker raids. When he arrived in New York he announced the investigation would seek to determine whether the raids constituted interference with the personal liberty of citizens. Furthermore, he declared that the APL, although recognized by the Attorney General, was a "private concern." His investigation, O'Brian told reporters, would include the question of whether persons conducting the raids exceeded their instructions, whether there was any abuse of power, whether there was any undue hardship imposed, and what methods were employed in carrying out orders.

Wilson and Gregory had been able to undercut Republican criticism by showing an immediate interest in civil liberties. But there were other more serious complaints against the APL arising in non-political quarters. Congressional criticism, engaged in by some senators who really were not much concerned about civil liberties, had given courage to men who were. Their comments about the APL had raised again the issue not only of the legality of the activities of the APL, but of the necessity for its work and the basic wisdom of using volunteers.

Civilians outside the government had at last begun to criticize the APL, and the raid brought more complaints. From New York, a newspaperman who had spoken out earlier against APL tactics lodged a second protest. "It is a source of uneasiness to many persons . . . that a semi-official body of this character should be permitted to carry a brief for the Morgan banking interest in Wall Street in its attempted persecution of innocent men," he wrote after the raids. A New York attorney who had criticized the APL in August also dashed off a letter to Gregory. "I respectfully suggest that the association styled the American Protective League is conducting its affairs in a manner inconsistent with propriety, and Americanism; and it deserves your official scrutiny," wrote the attorney. "I know that we are living in extraordinary times, calling for unusual methods, but I do not believe it is the policy of our Government to put weapons of oppression in the hands of private organizations."

Others were now demanding that President Wilson as well as Attorney General Gregory give proper attention to the activities of the APL. Journalist Frank I. Cobb, a liberal supporter of Wilson's Administration, had called the raids "a shameful spectacle which I would not have believed could happen outside a conquered province under Prussian military control" and recommended an investigation. Nevin Sayre of the National Civil Liberties Bureau, precursor of the American Civil Liberties Union, visited Wilson soon after the raids to complain about the Administration's general disregard of civil liberties. *The Nation* of September 14, under the heading "Civil Liberty Dead," blasted the Administration for allowing arrests to be made by "irresponsible agents of a volunteer self-appointed protective (!) league."

If Wilson were to retain his leadership of "the world of liberalism," the article warned, he would have to examine what was being done to make democracy unsafe in America.

It was a crucial moment for the Wilson Administration. Conservatives were shouting that the military should be given greater jurisdiction in matters governing war investigations, aliens, and draft problems, while liberals were insisting that the Administration abolish the APL and adopt a more lenient policy toward opponents of the war. On the Justice Department's report might hinge not only the future of the American Protective League, but also future support by liberals of Wilson's war policies. American intervention in Siberia was already under attack. Now the President's home front policies were in question as well.

O'Brian was in New York for only two days. Having taken no staff with him, he had to depend on APL officials and Bureau agents in that city for his information. They assured him that conditions had not been nearly so bad as those in Newark. Once O'Brian had accepted this proposition, the apologists proceeded to show him that conditions in Newark had really not been bad at all, that the newspapers and politicians had exaggerated: no sailors had taken part in the Newark raids; there was no evidence of maltreatment or assault; few men arrested had credentials on their persons which would have prevented arrests; and police had made all arrests. Soldiers and Leaguers in New York had made illegal arrests, it was true. However DeWoody showed O'Brian figures that convinced him that the raids had located large numbers of delinquents. O'Brian returned to Washington certain that the dragnet method was effective and convinced that the Justice Department needed the continued aid of the APL in locating these men for the draft. As the state inspector for New Jersey later observed, "It was a whitewash for the APL as a whole, but a nice tribute to our superb outfit."

Based on the results of O'Brian's hurried and superficial investigation, Gregory drew up a reply to Wilson. Citing the results in Newark, Gregory insisted that the raids were justified by the number of former delinquents inducted into the Army. He assumed full responsibility for the dragnet, declaring it the most effective method of dealing with the problem. He upheld the use of soldiers, sailors, and APL men generally. The only aspect of the raids which he admitted was unlawful and ill-advised was the use of volunteers and military men by special agents of the Bureau of Investigation in making arrests. This had been done, he insisted, solely on the authority of the Bureau of

Investigation, without consultation with himself or any law officer of the Justice Department.

Gregory's opinion was a carefully worded brief in defense of his department. He acknowledged no official authority or status for the APL, only acceptance by the Justice Department of their voluntary assistance. "Contrary to my express instructions," he wrote to Wilson, "instructions which I have repeated over and over again, and contrary to law, certain members of the investigating force of this Department, without consultation with me or with any law officer of the Department, used soldiers and sailors and certain members of the American Protective League, I am satisfied, in making arrests." Besides being unlawful, Gregory admitted that the use of military forces and the APL in making arrests had been "ill-judged," for they were not trained or experienced enough "to exercise the discretion required in the circumstances." He maintained that no persons were known to have been assaulted or maltreated. Just the same, he cited Newark, not New York, as an example of proper raiding methods.

When Wilson released Gergory's letter to the press on September 12, his action was accepted by the public as presidential approval of the whole raiding process. He timed the release to appear in the papers on the day of the fourth draft registration. Since over two hundred thousand APL members participated that day in registering thirteen million men, the statement could hardly have been interpreted as a disavowal of the volunteer policy. When the Justice Department announced the following day that they would use Leaguers in launching a nationwide effort to locate men who had not registered, Wilson's decision to allow the APL to continue was confirmed. The Philadelphia office of the Bureau of Investigation warned in a press release that the past raids were only a preliminary to the "real raids" coming up.

Whatever the public impact of Wilson's press release, Gregory's statement caused consternation among New York APL members. Boards, banks, and post office officials, now convinced that Leaguers had no official status, refused to give out information needed in their investigations. Lawyers counselled members not to engage in further raiding, for they might be sued for false arrest. Morale was low. Resignations began to pour in.

When Gregory referred to the APL simply as a volunteer patriotic organization which assisted the Bureau of Investigation, it seemed to members that the League had been relegated to the purely private status of many other volunteer patriotic groups. Publicly stripped of its assumed authority, the New York APL struck back by halting all investigations. The chief, Edmund Rushmore, demanded a statement from Gregory acknowledging that the APL was an official auxiliary of the Justice Department. If they had no authority, they would accept no duties. Gregory called this mutiny; although he did want to divest the APL of all their assumed powers, he did not want to dispense with their help.

"I indignantly and emphatically deny that we are on strike. The League has been so discredited that it cannot work," Rushmore wired Briggs. Then in a long telephone conference on September 16, Bielaski, Rushmore, Briggs, and a New York APL inspector clashed over this APL "strike." It was almost midnight and tempers were short. Rushmore argued that his men would be subject to bodily injury and lawsuits if Gregory did not issue a statement restoring their official status. Bielaski retorted that members had no power to arrest but that they were not justified in halting investigations. He was angry. "You know the Attorney General's real position with the League just as well as he knows it himself," he snapped.

"The only tools we had to work with was [sic] the assumed authority from the Department of Justice, and now people say this had been taken away from us," retorted the New York inspector. Bielaski maintained that orders to "hold and bring" men carried the fundamental idea that members had no authority to arrest. But, the inspector replied, the APL assumed the Justice Department would clear up the matter with the public. "We are ready to fight this thing out to the last publicity," he insisted defiantly. "OK," Bielaski shot back, "good bye!" Then he hung up in anger.

If Bielaski's orders to "hold and bring" really meant that members had no authority to arrest, then there should be some evidence that he instructed his own agents on this subject before the raids. There is none. That it was still a common practice for Bureau of Investigation agents to tell civilians to "hold" individuals is evident by the fact that on September 18 such an order was given to draft board members by an agent in Los Angeles.

It is difficult to believe that Gregory, who had approved the earlier bulletin asking APL members to assist in "causing" delinquents to present themselves to the draft board, really believed there was a legal distinction between "hold" and "arrest." Both O'Brian and Gregory were good lawyers, well trained in constitutional law. They knew arrest meant not only formal arrest by an officer but any restraint of an individual's freedom to be at large, and that "to hold" a person was to restrain his freedom to be at large. Yet they approved of the vague wording which legal clerks in the Justice Department had formulated. And they did it, evidently, to escape the constitutional problem presented by the lack of legal authority for their subordinates. As the *New York Times* commented editorially, Leaguers, soldiers, and sailors could hardly have understood the "technical distinction laid down by the Attorney General."

Perhaps Gregory thought that Bielaski had instructed his subordinates in the "technical distinction." But regardless of what Gregory thought, Bielaski for the first time instructed his agents and volunteers on this matter *after* the raids and the ensuing complaints on the part of the APL concerning the confusion. Not until September 19 did Bielaski dispatch a policy letter to his special agents telling them what he should have told them eight months sooner: the APL had no authority to arrest slackers, and "apprehension" and "detention" amounted to arrest. Special agents of the Bureau, he informed them, were regarded by the Justice Department as police officials who could arrest, despite the lack of statutory authority. Members of the APL, on the other hand, could only request that persons go "entirely voluntarily" to their draft boards. They could not "hold" persons or take any further action except to find a police official. Gregory sent a letter to the APL coldly reminding them to keep within the law.

Despite his reluctance to give public support to the New York division, Gregory continued to use the APL on slacker raids, even increasing the size of the drives. When the registration of September 12, 1918, had been tabulated and the government found that more men had registered than expected, the raids went right on. Late in September, Gregory asked the Washington State APL to cooperate in a three day roundup of slackers. The campaign was launched simultaneously in all cities, towns, and industrial settlements of the state. Each raiding party had a federal or local police official to make the actual arrests, however. The APL paper, the *Spy Glass*, announced after the Washington raid that conditions were still grave enough to make further drives necessary.

According to the Justice Department, nothing had changed: Leaguers had always been only volunteers, and the legal and constitutional limits of the volunteers had now been clearly defined. But Gregory could not so easily shrug off responsibility, for he made no effort to withdraw the other privileges he had granted the APL nor to terminate its semiofficial status as a Justice Department auxiliary. His letter, though it insisted that the APL demonstrate its determination to stay within the law and correct the isolated cases of violations

Confidential

The SPY GLASS

A Bulletin of News and Better Methods
issued by The American Protective League

Vol. I	WASHINGTON, D. C., November 22, 1918	No. 12

"Carry On!" Attorney General Gregory Urges

Office of the Attorney General
Washington, D. C.

November 21, 1918.

National Directors,
    American Protective League,
        Washington, D. C.

Gentlemen:

I feel it my duty at the present juncture to call upon the officers and members of the American Protective League throughout the country to carry on steadfastly for the present their most effective aid and co-operation with the Department of Justice.

The sudden termination of hostilities has reacted strongly upon the public, and there is everywhere evident a desire on the part of patriotic citizens, heretofore intent upon winning the war, to withdraw immediately from war work. Such a course, if generally followed, would involve serious consequences.

Your organization has performed a great task, both in active and passive service. The number of investigations participated in by you, many of which have resulted in the uncovering of serious enemy activities and disloyalties and the apprehension and prosecution of the individuals concerned, the large number of draft evaders detected, and your many other activities, have been an important factor in winning the war. A service of equal value has been the passive but powerful influence exerted by your organization upon alien enemies and disloyal persons. The knowledge upon their part that everywhere about them were the eyes and ears of a great organization auxiliary to the Government raised a fear in their hearts as to the consequences of hostile action, and became a powerful deterrent of enemy and disloyal activity.

These services cannot yet be dispensed with. Illegal activities harmful to the public morale during the discussion of peace terms must be watched for and reported. Violations of the war statutes, all of which are still in force, must be prosecuted. Pending investigations must be continued and others instituted.

I sincerely trust that, in view of these grave considerations, your members will be aroused to the need of carrying on your work for the immediate future with the fullest degree of efficiency. I earnestly ask your continued aid and co-operation.

Respectfully,

T. W. GREGORY,
Attorney General.

The Spy Glass, official bulletin of the American Protective League of rules, was hardly the type of letter that the New York members could use to regain their status as government investigators. When Rushmore read it to several of his men, they agreed that to publish it would only weaken their position. In fact, they were convinced that the whole *denouement* of the slacker raids was connected with politics.

Certainly it was true that Wilson was particularly concerned with the political effect of APL activity at a time so close to the elections. One story sent to New Mexico newspapers late in September by the Administration hinted that criticism of the slacker raids was purely partisan, noting that "official Washington" had interpreted Senator Fall's charges as evidence that he had "broken loose again." Fall was "one of the several Republicans assailing the Administration, despite the fact that the raids rounded up many hundreds of dodgers in New York City and elsewhere," according to the article.

The old problem for the APL, how to persuade delinquents to accompany them "entirely voluntarily," was now exacerbated. Even after Bielaski's order to agents regarding arrests, some of them continued their practice of asking civilians to "hold" delinquents. APL members also still received orders from military officials to arrest deserters. Finally, late in September, Bielaski called DeWoody to Washington. The Justice Department denied that the purpose was to reprimand him for his part in the slacker raids but admitted that the raids would be discussed.

A former APL chief and special agent in New York took up the cause of the APL in a letter to Gregory on September 30. "Make sure that none of your division superintendents ask the League to do anything which is illegal," he cautioned. What bothered the New York members most, he wrote, was the fact that the Justice Department seemed perfectly willing to continue to use their services freely but would not give the division "frank, generous support." The New York members waited in vain for another letter from Gregory giving them that support. It never came.

By the end of the war, APL raids had netted forty thousand delinquents for the War Department. Of the three million investigations made for the government by the League, the directors estimated that at least two million had involved the Selective Service system.

Even though no legal cases resulted from the New York raids, the courts would later be called upon to decide that civilians like the APL had no right to "hold" a person and that their attempt to do so was an infringement of the due process clause of the Constitution. In 1922, the Circuit Court of Appeals for Northern California reviewed the decision of a trial court in awarding damages to an individual "held" by a draft board member on the instructions of an agent of the Bureau of Investigation. The United States Attorney in San Francisco defended the draft board member in court, explaining to the Attorney General, "We have urged and have fully believed that the Regulations so authorize such an arrest," thus indicating that the Justice Department still persisted in its old policy. But the court disagreed, finding no authorization in the Selective Service Act and holding that war did not automatically suspend due process of law. Consequently, arrest without a warrant was still unconstitutional except in cases where public security required it, and public security required it only in the case of a felony or breach of peace committed in the presence of an officer. The Court of Appeals upheld the decision of the lower court, citing the Civil War decision of *Ex parte Milligan*, which held that a person had the right to be at liberty until arrested in accordance with the law.

But in 1918, once the slacker raids were over and the Administration's defense had been made, New Yorkers forgot the whole episode. On September 27 President Wilson arrived with great fanfare to open the fourth Liberty Loan drive. He received an enthusiastic welcome.

The Danger Line

"We have just passed through a trying situation, growing out of the New York drive, which has affected the League in every part of the country, and I am not so sure that there are not to be many more trying situations in the future, and that it is entirely too much responsibility for the small body of men who are now directing the affairs of the League to assume," Frey wrote wearily to Briggs on September 25. As he wrote, complaints from all over the United States about the activities of APL agents were arriving in his office.

State inspectors reported a variety of discipline problems to the national directors. One complained that a former chief who had been dismissed for alleged violations of the Espionage Act was attempting to force his way back into the League. Another reported that a man already in difficulty for misappropriating funds wished to become a member. The state inspector for California had to extricate the chief of the San Francisco branch from an unsavory tangle involving an illicit love affair, anti-Semitism, and political intrigue. As the mess was about to reach the front pages of the San Francisco newspapers, an influential Jewish member of the APL Executive Committee with important Chamber of Commerce affiliations hushed up the matter.

The North Carolina state inspector reported that a member was ranging through the back country as a self-styled marshal, dressed in an old Texas Ranger uniform, carrying a high powered Winchester and an automatic "resembling a cannon." He was rounding up deserters and pocketing the fifty-dollar bounty. "I anticipate serious trouble if he continues to operate without authority with the kind of people that he is apprehending in the mountains of this state," wrote the worried inspector to APL headquarters.

Chiefs added other complaints. One member, said the New York City chief, was a "plain, simple nut," and an embezzler besides. "We don't want to be bothered with such a man," he warned. In New York, the raids had dissatisfied and disheartened the members. The division was 50 percent less efficient than before, wrote one officer, and complaints, both from within and from outside, were now the rule rather than the exception.

Frey did not need to depend upon letters to realize the problem. He was worried about the shaky organizational structure which the slacker raids had revealed. Lack of communication, lack of control, and too much independence at the local level marked APL operations everywhere, and he was convinced that Briggs was the source of many of the discipline problems. While he and Elting worked for centralization and uniformity, Briggs roamed about, substituting a system of personal loyalty for institutional discipline.

The danger of this feudalism became most evident in the Chicago League. In large APL units like Chicago and New York, inspectors had been appointed to supervise investigations. Gradually, as investigations had expanded, these inspectors had become feudal barons, each encouraging personal loyalty to himself while considering himself subject to no authority. As Frey explained, "They have interfered with other Bureaus and officials of the League and have either because of overzealousness or because of their assumption of power have [sic] almost refused to get in line and perform their duties according to the rules and regulations of the original Chicago organization and those set forth in the Handbook issued by the National Headquarters."

Citizens were being brought to the APL office, an illegal practice which O'Brian, Frey, and Elting had continually fought. The Investigation Division in Chicago consisted of 6,000 members, approximately half of the members for the entire city organization. Their investigations into labor affairs had brought in donations from businessmen. They now wanted to gain control of the entire division, pick a new chief, and depose the other regional officials. Frey, to halt this struggle, had carefully chosen a new chief and state inspector; and to let members know that it was the state inspector who was in control, had asked him to announce the choice of the new city chief. The city inspectors were unhappy and went to Briggs.

Briggs, instead of insisting on strict enforcement of national policies, adherence to the decisions of the national directors, and the subordination of city inspectors to the state inspector, promised to appoint an advisory committee. This device had been tried before and discarded as leading to irresponsibility because chiefs under advisory committees had tended to take orders from the committee instead of from the national directors.

Frey and Elting immediately disavowed Briggs's action, and Frey rushed off to Chicago to untangle the mess a second time. Briggs must abide by the decisions which the three national directors had made, Frey and Elting agreed. As for Chicago, he warned, "There are serious trouble makers who must be removed."

If reform did not come from within the APL, there was now more often someone outside the organization to report backsliders. A Military Intelligence officer in Bordeaux, France, found an APL badge on a member of one of the war relief societies and insisted that members be instructed not to take their badges overseas for use there. APL credentials were turning up in the hands of extortionists and forgers. Some units were still using letterhead stationary with "Secret Service Division" printed on it. After all these months, some members still flashed "Secret Service" badges.

Sometimes, however just the cause, members were overzealous. In Lansing, Michigan, for example, the division had a restaurant man locked up for refusing to serve an East Indian in United States uniform. Only after they had him in jail did they appeal to the Adjutant General for advice as to what federal or military laws the man could be prosecuted under. The Judge Advocate General advised the Adjutant General that no law required the owner to serve colored persons in uniform. In another case, the War Department reported that the New Orleans chief had tried to prohibit all horse racing in the city and had freely used APL records for other reform projects. One of his antagonists was suing for slander.

Various federal agencies reported strange activities by APL members. The State Department informed Gregory that some members were writing directly to American consuls in foreign countries asking for information. One, for example, requested a list of all motorcycle dealers in the capital of Norway. George Creel, head of the Committee on Public Information, protested to Bielaski that the APL was investigating his friends. Military Intelligence officers complained that the APL was "overzealous" in investigations of conditions at American University in Washington, D.C.

More serious complaints reached the Justice Department concerning the treatment of alien laborers and Socialists. A marshal in Milwaukee found that members of the APL were telling enemy aliens that if they changed jobs they would be interned. From the Socialist party in Cleveland came a complaint that the APL had invaded their meetings under the pretense of hunting for slackers and had used coarse language and rough tactics. At a Socialist picnic, agents of the Bureau of Investigation and APL men had conducted a raid, rounded up all the men, and asked each, "Are you a Socialist?" Cleveland Socialists also charged APL members with pulling a Negro speaker from a stand and hauling him and most of his audience off to the local jail. "The Socialists of Cuyahoga County are law abiding citizens, and the only violations of law, occurring at the present time, are instigated by the so-called representatives of the Federal Government," their allegation concluded.

Another United States marshal claimed APL members were insubordinate. One local APL official, reported Marshal S. W. Randolph to Gregory, "insisted that this office take its direction in many instances from the League when to do so, would violate instructions from the Department."

In some cities, of course, both APL men and Bureau of Investigation agents operated within the law. In others, however, it was Bureau special agents who led the volunteers astray. Agents not only instructed civilians to make illegal arrests, as they had done in New York, but they themselves caused suspected draft delinquents to be locked up and then forgot about them. During the summer of 1918, agents instituted prosecutions under war statutes without consulting the United States attorneys, continued to stage raids, to arrest without warrants, and to harass radical laborites and Socialists under the pretext of safeguarding security.

Like the national directors of the APL, Bielaski continued to dispatch orders to his agents. He warned them away from politicians. He told them to secure approval for prosecutions from the United States attorneys. He insisted that they obtain arrest warrants. He reminded them to check the jails daily to be sure that they had not forgotten anyone. He pointed out that the Socialist party was a political party whose creeds were not unlawful, and that the constitutional guarantee of the right of assembly applied equally to them. "It is especially important that during these war times the Department of Justice and all of its officers and agents shall take particular care that their conduct shall be at all times in accordance with the law," he said.

But the illegal acts continued. Sometimes they were not reported to Bielaski. Sometimes he had no effective way of investigating his investigators. Sometimes he did not insist strenuously enough that agents be subordinate to the United States attorneys, nor did he instruct them in sufficient detail as to the rights of individuals and the scope of their own activities. The Bureau of Investigation had strayed so far from its primary function, the investigation of violations of federal law, that it was difficult now to draw the line. Bielaski had few guidelines for his own operatives. Little wonder that the APL volunteers who worked with the operatives had a tendency to wander off into illegal activities.

Marshals and United States attorneys were generally more circumspect regarding the law, but not always. Traditionally, attorneys were appointed on recommendation of congressmen; consequently they sometimes felt more obligated to their sponsors than to the Justice Department. The Department had long functioned in a decentralized manner that gave to these political appointees almost complete independence in their states. Before the war, the Attorney General had even encouraged these men to apply federal policies to local conditions in ways consistent with local customs.

This policy of near-autonomy continued into the war period. United States attorneys often submitted to local pressures and brought an excessive number of prosecutions under the Espionage Act, utilizing information from APL investigations which was merely hearsay, malicious or slanderous. By fall, 1918, the number of prosecutions was rising rapidly, especially in the West, where the federal government had become deeply involved in labor-capital disputes. "The situation in the Attorney General's office seems almost hopeless," United States Tariff Commissioner William Kent wrote to Wilson in October. "The policy of endorsing local prosecutors and backing them up whatever their course, is bound to produce intolerable injustice with terrible results, unless guarded against and corrected."

Kent's complaints brought an order from Wilson to Gregory that he "put some very pointed questions" to his subordinates in the North-west, concluding, "We are in danger of playing into the hands of some violently and maliciously partisan Republicans."

Activities more dangerous than partisan politics were occurring in the Northwest, however. Prosecutions were only a part of the story. APL members were breaking away from the Justice Department to work with the Military Intelligence Division, especially where troops had been called in for strike duty. Leaguers encouraged Military Intelligence officers to engage in illegal activities, and the officers in turn encouraged the APL to do likewise. The spring offensive of the Military Intelligence had not ended; it had only entered a new phase.

Secretary of War Baker had promised to restrain his intelligence officers when Gregory had complained to him in June of their inter-ference in sedition cases. But Baker could never convince his sub-ordinates that this was a proper course. Dissatisfaction with the actions of the Justice Department continued. Officers were impatient with the handling of alien internments. They felt the Department was too lenient in demanding proof of some overt act on the part of suspects before moving to intern. Operatives were also impatient with the Department of Labor because immigration officials refused to use deportation as a counterespionage measure. "This leaves only the slow and orderly process of criminal prosecution before juries with the necessity of proof beyond reasonable doubt," lamented one officer.

During July, the impatience of Military Intelligence officers with the Justice Department grew. Symbolic of this impatience was their elation when a farce called "Why Worry" opened on July 29, 1918, in Washington, D.C. The hero was a Military Intelligence officer who, after being chased through three acts as a German spy, appeared in the last scene to foil the Bureau of Investigation agent, arrest the real spy, and marry the heroine. An MID bulletin reviewed the pro-duction with satisfaction.

But the Military Intelligence Division had other things to be satis-fied about as well. At the end of July, General Crowder issued a twenty-six page opinion defining the crime of treason and authorizing the "detention" of all persons engaged in the destruction of life or property, or the delay or obstruction of the war effort. Treason was defined so broadly that all strikes or agitation for them appeared trea-sonable. Any persons detained for treason were to be turned over to the civil authorities, but the regulations governing investigation and arrest amounted to martial law, despite the fact that military courts had no jurisdiction.

Meanwhile, the Army had held a secret court-martial of Pablo Waberski, the alleged spy. On August 25, he was condemned to death. The case was to be appealed to Wilson rather than to the courts. The Military Intelligence had reason to hope that if the situation seemed critical enough at the time Wilson considered the appeal, the military's claim to jurisdiction over spies might be recognized.

A few days after Waberski's conviction, Secretary of War Baker left for a second tour of the war front. With their civilian chief out of the way, the Military Intelligence officers who wished to do so could indulge their desire to play detective on the home front. They received no restraining orders from their superior officer. In fact, Brigadier General Marlborough Churchill reorganized the MID in August, creating a special Negative Branch under Colonel K. C. Masteller and assigning to it the investigation of graft and fraud affecting military contracts, as well as enemy activity, disloyalty, and sedition.

Meanwhile, the MID encouraged the APL to continue its reports on all propaganda. Felix Frankfurter and the War Labor Policies Board had complained that the APL seemed to be solicitous for sensitivities of employers only, not of employees, and under Frankfurter's supervision a new questionnaire was worked out. When the APL sent out this new form in early October, it carried the instructions, "You are to exercise the utmost care not to disturb or alienate labor leaders or workmen. It is imperative that the viewpoint of employees should be taken into account and respected as much as the viewpoint of employers. It is in no sense the purpose of the questionnaire to raise any questions whatsoever as between capital and labor.... Similarly you are to exercise the utmost care not to stir up animosity among various groups of foreign-born Americans or among the various religious bodies. In every instance the presumption must be that all the groups and bodies are loyal to American war aims; disloyalty is the exception not the rule."

Such objectivity hardly seemed possible when, at the same time, Military Intelligence officers were asking Leaguers to pry into the affairs of labor radicals more actively than before. In the South, a governor was investigated for his "radical" leanings. In the Northwest, all sheriffs received requests to provide the Military Intelligence officer at Portland, Oregon, with lists of IWW members under arrest and to report on labor conditions in their counties. In Spokane, where fear of military courts had driven the IWW underground, Military Intelligence officers infiltrated secret meetings or encouraged the APL to do so. From Spokane came an order to the Military Intelligence officer at Butte, Montana, that IWW agitators be taken "hostage," and that agitation which might lead to serious general strikes among miners be "snuffed out."

The Military Intelligence agent at Butte contacted the local APL chief, James H. Rowe. Rowe was one of the Anaconda Copper Company employees taken into the League by Briggs early in the war. On June 22, 1917, he had been sworn in as a deputy sheriff of Silver Bow County. Then he had become chairman of the local draft board and had agitated openly for more convictions for sedition. When Lieutenant Will P. Garmer of the Military Intelligence arrived in Butte in April, 1918, to establish a branch there, United States Attorney Burton K. Wheeler was out of town. Rowe and other local men, dissatisfied with Wheeler's cautious policies, took Garmer aside and voiced their suspicions that Wheeler was, if not disloyal, at least playing party politics. The Bureau of Investigation agent was not to be trusted either, nor federal Judge Bourquim, who had held in January that the treason statute could not be applied to mere utterances.

The following month, Garmer vigorously opposed the reappointment of Wheeler. He had the Military Intelligence officer for the western states telephone complaints directly to the MID. Patriotism, the officer said, was being abandoned to political expediency. Obstructors of the war program were making progress easier for the German Army in France. The Justice Department should appoint someone who could clean up the situation. Churchill went to O'Brian with the complaints.

Even O'Brian had been disappointed with Judge Bourquim's decision, but he believed that Wheeler was doing his job properly. He told Churchill just that.

The officers were unhappy. Next, they hinted at graft among Bureau of Investigation agents and asked for more Military Intelligence agents to watch the Justice Department agents. Churchill encouraged this; he thought that the Military Intelligence was less affected by local politics and that the people would have confidence in the government if more of these agents were sent. When the reinforcements arrived, they caucused with Rowe and his APL volunteers. Then things began to happen.

On August 23, the Military Intelligence officers and APL men arrested over twenty IWW, had them jailed, and seized their records. No charges were lodged against the IWW, but their membership rolls were taken to the MID office in Butte. From these records, names of Spokane members were obtained, and arrests followed in

Spokane. By September, the Bureau of Investigation agent was complaining to Bielaski that the Military Intelligence was stirring up labor unrest with its illegal activities. The miners in Butte called a strike for September 13.

The strike began quietly. Then the APL and Military Intelligence went into action. On the evening of September 13 they met to plan a raid on the printing plant of the striking Metal Mine Workers Union. A young West Pointer, Major Omar Bradley, had just arrived with his Fourteenth Infantry, and they asked him to join the raiding party. He went along.

The raid proceeded in the usual manner. Men were seized, their papers confiscated. They were taken to military intelligence head-quarters and interrogated. Then they were jailed without charges. The next day Justice Department representatives called in young Major Bradley and told him the raid had been illegal and Military Intelligence had no authority to do any of the things it had done. Bradley admitted that he had known nothing beforehand of the raid but acknowledged that the Military Intelligence had been in charge of the party, a fact which everyone else involved was now denying. A few days later Bradley and his Fourteenth Infantry were ordered out of Butte, but a company of guardsmen were ordered in. Illegal arrests continued.

By this time the county jails were filled with men. Rowe was insistent that the raids continue. "Damn the law: we want results," he was quoted as saying.

The local Bureau of Investigation agent soon realized that all the arrests were being made under the guise of slacker roundups. More-over, another systematic, large-scale raid was being planned. He warned the Justice Department that such a wholesale roundup might touch off violence.

Crowder intervened. He ordered the Montana governor, the adjutant general, and Rowe not to proceed. The governor was on the side of the APL, however, and argued that the plan should go forward. Crowder went to O'Brian with this bit of news. O'Brian replied, "It is the view of the Department further, that under any and all circumstances it is opposed to military participation with the civil authorities on the work of arresting slackers in a general roundup." But by this time Rowe was running the show. He would not be stopped.

Among IWW members arrested falsely had been a man named Napora. Judge Bourquim issued a writ of *habeas corpus* for Napora, and the sheriff's office of Silver Bow County was notified to bring the prisoner before the judge so that he could inquire into the legality of the arrest. But Rowe did not recognize the authority of the federal courts; he went down to the jail to get the prisoner himself.

"I wish to talk with Napora and will bring him back when I'm through," he told the deputy sheriff. The deputy sheriff, knowing that Napora was one of the men being held for the local draft board and that Rowe was its chairman, turned the prisoner over. Rowe marched off with the terrified Wobbly. The deputy sheriff waited.

When Rowe did not return, the deputy sheriff became alarmed. Frank Little, an IWW member, had been lynched the year before. The same could have happened to Napora. When Rowe reappeared in town without Napora, the deputy sheriff confronted him and demanded the prisoner. Napora had gone to Camp Lewis, Rowe replied coolly, continuing. "If there is any responsibility I'll shoulder it, if there is any fine to pay, I'll pay it." The deputy sheriff was enraged. It was kidnapping, he said; Rowe was "not a good citizen," and it was a mean trick to play on a fellow officer. As for Napora, he remained at Camp Lewis. As for Rowe, he was still a deputy sheriff and a fellow officer. No charges were brought.

Yet despite all these antics, many of which were known to Attorney General Gregory, the APL remained in his good graces. In June, 1918, the Council of National Defense had cautioned its state councils "not to build up an organization for the suppression of sedition or to undertake secret service investigations without first securing the approval of the local representatives of the United States Department of Justice." In early October, however, Gregory took the matter a step further. Having lent his prestige to the APL fund-raising campaign, he ordered the state councils of defense out of the security field again, insisting that the APL replace them. Units established by state councils were to be disbanded or merged with the APL.

On October 9, the National Council of Defense reminded state councils of the previous orders and asked them to meet with state APL officials to help select members and establish new units where none existed. In Oklahoma, Maine, New Hampshire, and South Dakota, the state councils subsequently withdrew from counterespionage. In states where councils were in the process of forming counterespionage divisions, plans were halted. Sometimes members of the local councils of defense became APL members. But in all cases, the APL became the sole civilian investigative body assisting federal operatives.

Had federal government agents, not the APL, been delegated to take over investigation from the states, this new order could have been an important landmark in the defense of civil liberties. There is no doubt that the state councils of defense had strayed far from sedition in their investigations and that it was essential that they be banished from loyalty investigations. O'Brian was much opposed to the continuance of these councils of defense and later characterized them as having seriously interfered with civil rights. Of three thousand complaints received by one federal official in a midwestern state from its council of defense, said O'Brian, less than one hundred had been worthy of serious attention.

O'Brian also felt that state statutes providing punishment for certain acts in opposition to war measures were an embarrassment to the Justice Department and a danger to the public. In fact, he maintained that a Minnesota bill against sedition increased discontent and that the "most serious cases of alleged interference with civil liberty were reported from that state." A historian for the Minnesota Commission of Public Safety later maintained that the state had little room for action because of the wide powers of the federal government; and except for informing the federal government of disloyalty and encouraging the federal government to act, the state could do little regarding opposition to the war.

The truth was that the activity of the states did interfere with the federal government and was a real danger to civil liberties. The important question, however, was whether in strengthening the APL the federal government was really extending federal power, or whether it was only expanding a private group of investigators against whom the Bill of Rights could provide no defense.

In 1920, when the Supreme Court reviewed a conviction under the Minnesota statute, a majority of the court felt that states were intimately concerned in the outcome of the war and that state measures were appropriate adjuncts to the federal war powers. Only Chief Justice White and Justice Brandeis dissented from this view to argue that federal legislation left no room for state action, that Congress had preempted the field once it passed the Espionage Act of 1917.

Gregory was the first Attorney General ever to assert federal supremacy over the states in sedition investigations. This supremacy the Supreme Court would affirm in 1954 in the *Pennsylvania* v. *Nelson* case. By then federal supremacy in the internal security field was accompanied by an extension of constitutional safeguards for the individual against the federal government. But in World War I the citizen was defenseless against the APL volunteers on whom Gregory relied to implement his assertion.

Their monopoly meant that the APL could offer its expanded services to the War Department, thus becoming involved even more intimately with the activities of the Military Intelligence. On October 19, 1918, the Negative Branch of the MID urged the APL to extend its operations throughout the United States, and two days later, S. S. Doty, the man in charge of organizing new branches, told Frey, "With the exception of North and South Dakota, I think you may report to the War Department that all of the territory about which they inquire will be in a fair state of organization within the next three weeks."

From the standpoint of the Justice Department, of course, it was a question of either utilizing the volunteers or allowing the states and Military Intelligence complete control over the domestic defenses. The Department certainly had neither the manpower nor the money to do the job itself. But once the decision had been made to back the APL, O'Brian determined to reform its practices, along with those of the Justice Department, its federal attorneys, and the Bureau of Investigation.

Slowly O'Brian began to take command of the home front war. He insisted on stricter accountability of all subordinates and a narrowing of their jurisdiction. He took over direction of all the IWW prosecutions still not completed. Although he could do nothing to stop the prosecutions of these radicals as a group, he saw to it that members of the Non-Partisan League, a radical farmers' organization of the Northwest, were prosecuted only for individual violations of the Espionage Act and not, by virtue of their membership, for conspiracy. To insure that he be kept completely informed of all related matters, O'Brian even instructed the mail department that all correspondence concerning either war legislation or criminal prosecutions must go through his office before being passed on to subordinates in Washington.

Then O'Brian turned his attention to discipline within the ranks. By the end of October he had convinced Gregory that a thorough revamping of the organization was necessary in order properly to defend individual civil liberties. Together they ordered all United States attorneys to submit cases under the Espionage Act to Washington for review before proceeding, and once these began to come in, large numbers of pending cases were ordered dropped because of insufficient evidence. Many requests for new prosecutions were opposed. O'Brian refused to subject the National Civil Liberties Bureau to such harassment, for example.

Meanwhile, Gregory tried to instill in his officials a proper regard for the departmental chain of command. United States attorneys were the highest officials in the field, and agents of the Bureau of Investigation must consult with them. In important matters, particularly cases involving interpretation of statutes and applications for search or arrest warrants, the attorneys were to exercise final authority. Bielaski instructed his agents not to initiate prosecutions under the Espionage Act or other war statutes until they had received clearance from the attorney for their district.

United States attorneys were also to investigate complaints regarding APL activities which had previously gone unnoticed. Referring to the Cleveland episode in which Leaguers had questioned Socialists about their party membership, O'Brian warned of the impropriety of "a person representing the Government officially or in any auxiliary capacity, to do or to say anything which gives color to the claim that discrimination is practiced against the members of one particular political party."

Although these policies were eighteen months late and should have been enunciated at the outbreak of the war, at least they revealed that the Justice Department could reform itself from within and introduce policies of bureaucratic restraint even during a time of national crisis. With his own house in order, O'Brian then urged Gregory to challenge the claims of the Miltary Intelligence.

When Baker returned from Europe, at Gregory's behest he ordered an investigation of the false arrests in the Northwest, sending a special investigator to Butte. The investigator, Colonel Thomas J. Lewis, concluded that the military had made no arrests; they had merely made seventy-three "detentions." There had been no time to secure formal warrants or to comply with all legal technicalities, he said. Baker sent the report on to Gregory with the comment, "Clearly the War Department ought not to permit the military to do anything which cannot be properly backed up by the civil process . . . I shall be happy to cooperate as you may suggest."

By this time the Military Intelligence Division was fighting what seemed to be its own war against the War Department. Churchill had gone so far as to argue, "It is not disparaging the problems of our military forces abroad to emphasize the fact that they are threatened more seriously and numerously here at home than in France." Moreover, other defenders of the MID were quick to assure Baker that criticism of the military in Butte was coming from elements in sympathy with the IWW, not the "responsible and reliable" element in the community.

But Gregory was persistent. The evidence convinced him that the Butte strike had actually been provoked by undercover agents of the Military Intelligence, working with Anaconda detectives, and that the soldiers at the scene had been encouraged by the Military Intelligence to violate the rights of citizens.

Contrary to Colonel Lewis, there was no difference between "detention" and "arrest," Gregory asserted. Unless a man was in the process of committing a crime, a warrant had to precede the arrest; it was still an arrest when the man was "held or detained" without his consent. "Raids must not be made without duly issued search warrants." He went on to reiterate that an officer must not substitute his judgment for that of the United States Attorney. Baker should instruct his commanding generals and the Military Intelligence that they must turn information over to federal and local officials who had responsibility for law enforcement. Moreover, O'Brian insisted that undercover agents enlisted by the Military Intelligence from within companies be prosecuted: cases were being brought for conspiracy against the government, not against the copper companies, and these agents had been parties to the crimes.

A few days later, the Waberski case came before President Wilson for a decision, and Gregory made a strong plea that the accused man not be executed. To allow the execution, he reminded Wilson, would be to acknowledge the claim of the military to jurisdiction over spies. Before the outcome was determined, O'Brian and Gregory turned their attention to the APL.

Under O'Brian's prodding, Frey and Elting reevaluated their organizational structure. They had to admit that the original plan had proved weak at every level. At the top, the practice of having Briggs coordinate city and state operations had resulted in abuses of power and confusion in lines of communication because of his lack of interest in enforcing discipline. State inspectors lacked the power to command because they had no staff of their own and took no part in the actual processing of investigations. Within each unit existed the problem of keeping the investigation divisions subordinate to the unit chief. As the investigative duties of each unit had increased, these divisions had expanded, and decentralization seemed to be the invariable consequence. A very grave concomitant danger lay in the tendency of individual groups to succumb to local municipal pressures. If these units were to take orders from the local authorities rather than from the federal government, then the League would be useless to the Justice Department; it would continue to be a frightful instigator of injustice and vigilantism. The APL directors in Washington held responsibility for controlling the investigative activities of branches, a power too potentially destructive ever to have been given to volunteers. The time for rescinding that power was past; the problem at hand now was how to control it.

The solution conceived by Frey and Elting, however belatedly, was to attempt to place all city units under the strict supervision of state inspectors. Not only would these men act as watchdogs, but their offices would also serve as clearinghouses for all state investigations. When agents of the Bureau of Investigation assigned tasks to local units, they would advise the state inspector. Similarly, every case transmitted from national headquarters would go through the state inspector to local chiefs. Local chiefs would furnish their own state inspectors with copies of all communications involving other local chiefs or state inspectors. National headquarters would receive a copy of every case report, whether assigned from Washington or through Bureau agents. Although complicated, this new routine meant that Frey and Elting had to deal with only forty-eight inspectors rather than hundreds of individual chiefs.

More sophisticated office procedures were also adopted in Washington. Frey and Elting moved their headquarters to a larger building and reorganized the staff, dividing responsibility more systematically and adding more clerks to the overburdened office force. A system approaching modern office security was reached with the hiring of armed guards, who saw to it that each employee signed in and out.

Even more important than bureaucratic reform was the decision of the directors and O'Brian to limit the scope of investigations conducted by the APL. O'Brian had already forbidden the APL and Bureau special agents to investigate persons simply because of membership in unpopular political groups like the Socialist party or the Non-Partisan League. He also had objected strenuously to agents' investigating actions not classified as crimes under federal law. O'Brian's standards now prevailed: Gregory refused to allow the Chicago office of the Bureau of Investigation and the APL to conduct a special investigation for the Labor Department. The Attorney General told Secretary of Labor W. B. Wilson that he opposed the investigation because he believed it "absolutely essential that we shall not become involved in any labor questions or controversies between capital and labor, or different branches of capital or labor, except where the violation of Federal laws is involved."

O'Brian next convinced Gregory that the APL should not be

allowed to participate in enforcing statutes like the Corrupt Practices Act passed by Congress in mid-October, which did not relate to the war. The APL was no longer to range freely into all investigations which the Bureau of Investigation was called upon to handle. In 1864, Lincoln and the Union party had been quite willing to transform the Union League from a group ferreting out disloyalty to a political club blocking Lincoln's political opponents. The APL was not to be allowed to follow the same route. "In view of the danger of involving members of local divisions in political controversies and so dividing organizations locally upon partisan lines," the national directors instructed the state inspectors, they had agreed with the Justice Department that it would be "unwise" to have the APL take part in enforcement of the act.

The League directors accepted these new limitations and attempted to impress them upon the rank and file. In a long article titled "Where the Danger Line in League Activity Lies," the directors warned members not to consider themselves guardians of public morals or executors of the dictates of the public conscience; their job was concerned only with violations of war statutes. They were not to become involved in crusades against gambling, vice, or local "bad men." They were not law-and-order committees for local police, but a purely federal force.

By November, 1918, the web of volunteers covered most of the United States. Almost every state now had its own inspector, while each large city and most small towns had units. Rural areas, too, were patrolled by APL members. In eighteen months the United States had fielded a corps of sleuths larger than any country had done in all history. And they called it the American way.

Word of this volunteer army had spread beyond the borders of the United States, and at least two other countries, Canada and Australia, had sent government representatives to study APL methods, with a view to their possible adoption. The British War Office was also considering sending a man to Washington to study the uniquely American organization in November of 1918. Then rumors of peace began to circulate.

Keep the
Home Fires Burning

For almost a month President Wilson had been discussing a negotiated peace with representatives of the German and Austrian governments. In Austria the two-century-old Hapsburg monarchy was a shambles. The Czechs had issued a Declaration of Independence, the Italians had launched an irredentist offensive, the Yugoslavs and Poles were setting up independent governments. The German Navy had revolted at Kiel, to be followed by revolts at Lübeck, Hamburg, Cuxhaven, and Bremen. Politically, too, Germany was disintegrating. On November 7, Kurt Eisner proclaimed a Republic of Bavaria. The next day the King of Bavaria and the Duke of Brunswick abdicated. On November 9, the Kaiser fled to Holland. The way was now open for an armistice based on Wilsonian principles. In his effort to enact those principles into practice, Wilson turned back to the domestic scene for support. He found very little.

As Americans went to the polls to choose House and Senate members, they were just recovering from an influenza epidemic which had killed 400,000 to 500,000 people between the ages of 20 and 40, far more than the nation lost in all the battles of the World War. There was much opposition to what Wilson had called a "just peace";

many wanted retribution. The Republicans made great gains in the states and in Congress.

Reform had come too late to convince many liberals, let alone radicals, that the Justice Department was not really an agent of suppression which was making democracy meaningless at home under the pretense of carrying it abroad to reform the world. "All the radical or liberal friends of your anti-imperialist war policy were either silenced or intimidated," George Creel wrote to Wilson in an election postmortem. "The Department of Justice and the Post-Office were allowed to silence or intimidate them." Others offered their reasons for substantial Democratic losses at the polls: no soldier vote; lack of party leadership in the House and Senate; the opposition of the pro-German vote, of whiskey and beer interests, and of those taxed most heavily to support the war.

Gregory believed Wilson himself to be the principal cause. Republicans and Independents had worked to further the President's policies, supporting him in partisan conflicts and working under his leadership; but their reward had been Wilson's partisan appeal of October 25 for a Democratic majority in Congress.

The President needed the support of those people who had opposed United States entrance into the war and of those who had opposed the suppression of dissent at home if he was to establish a moderate peace. But most of those groups now considered Wilson their enemy. German-Americans feared that talk of moderation would only be labeled "sedition." Bitter experience had taught many other elements of the population to keep their opinions to themselves. One Military Intelligence officer had presciently posed the question in August: "Is it possible that by taking too violently and indiscriminatingly an anti-German attitude we may not be doing our part to support the future diplomatic policy of the President, who has shown several signs of wishing to take advantage of opportunities to separate the German people from their present Government?"

Nevertheless, the Administration refused to relent in its battle on the home front, even when the prospect of Germany's defeat became a reality. The APL continued its hunt for signs of sedition, and Bielaski urged members to continue their vigilance. As late as November 4 he sent a hurried letter to the League stating that the government still needed help in protecting the Army and the property of the United States from espionage.

The national directors sent copies of Bielaski's letter to all chiefs. Recent military victories, they wrote, would undoubtedly cut down the response to the appeal for funds launched a few days earlier among bankers. Publication of Bielaski's letter would "safeguard your own financial support, will maintain the morale of your organization and will have a favorable effect upon all with whom you come in contact." Frey suggested to reporter David Lawrence that he interview Gregory about the APL and try to elicit a statement that it would be continued. The desired statement appeared on November 9 in the *Washington Star.* The same day Gregory opposed a pardon for civil libertarian Roger Baldwin, jailed for opposition to the draft, whom Gregory described to Wilson as one of a "dangerous class of persons."

Leaguers didn't need much encouragement from Gregory. They were eager to remain on duty. The United States Attorney in the state of Washington invited the APL Minute Men to assist him in enforcing all federal laws and to work on immigration and naturalization investigations. So much for O'Brian's directive confining APL activities to war-related probes. In New Orleans Briggs announced that the APL would help rehabilitate returning soldiers. In Chicago 16,000 members reported to police captains throughout the city on Armistice Day to help preserve order among jubilant celebrants. Their future as government investigators seemed assured. From Washington Frey wired Briggs, "Situation charged many possibilities. Impossible transmit information by wire."

Had the Great War ended in total victory for the Allies, the League might have been demobilized immediately. But cessation of hostilities did not mean the beginning of peace. It meant only the beginning of an armistice period—scheduled to be in effect for only thirty-six days—which was to last in the United States until July 1, 1921, nearly three years.

In November of 1918, though, no one knew how prolonged this respite would be. War might be resumed on December 17, the day on which the armistice agreement was scheduled to terminate. Even if it did not, war statutes were still in force, and the federal government intended to see that they were not violated with impunity. Selective Service regulations dealing with vice and liquor remained in effect, slackers were still to be hunted, alien regulations continued in force, and espionage still had to be guarded against. On November 13, Bielaski sent a special message to the chief of the New Orleans division reassuring him that the League would continue.

Wilson's decision to attend the Peace Conference at Versailles, announced on November 18, seemed to indicate to many American liberals that Wilson was ready to abandon domestic reform for international reconstruction. While the armistice had marked the beginning of a great debate over reconstruction at home and abroad, it was evident that Wilson would have little time to devote to domestic plans for the future.

Without Wilson's leadership, the departments drifted. Some became preoccupied with fears of radical revolution at home and looked to the APL for help. The Labor Department wanted the League to continue investigations of alien applicants for citizenship so that opponents of war and radicals could be barred. A new bill passed by Congress on October 16 allowed the Labor Department to deport aliens who advocated anarchism, syndicalism, or violent revolution. The Commissioner General of Immigration wanted a search for these aliens. The War Department wanted information on Bolshevik propaganda, which Military Intelligence officers feared might lead to revolution. The Justice Department told the APL directors it was relying on the League to assist in keeping down any Bolshevik movement which might be attempted. By November 21 Gregory, Churchill, Crowder, Bielaski, and numerous local representatives of federal agencies had appealed to Leaguers to be on the lookout for radicals. The directors advised branches they would play a large part in reconstruction; they were to await orders.

Then on November 22, Gregory released for publication in the government's *Official Bulletin,* a statement commending the APL for its wartime work. "Uncovering serious enemy activities and disloyalties and the apprehension and prosecution of the individuals concerned, the large number of draft evaders detected and your many other activities have been an important factor in winning the war," Gregory said. "A service of equal value has been the passive but powerful influence exerted by your organization upon alien enemies and disloyal persons." He called upon the APL for continued vigilance.

Strangely enough, only one outside criticism of Gregory's November 22 call for the APL to remain on guard has survived in Justice Department files. From New York an Irishman named Shielen Mahon excitedly wrote to Gregory that the League was composed mostly of Republicans who had thrown hundreds of Democrats into jail and converted many Irish to Republicans. "No wonder the people voted the Republican ticket, I can hardly blame them," he mourned. Gregory pencilled "No answer" across the top and filed the letter away. If liberals considered the continuance of the League a threat, their complaints did not reach the Justice Department. Either, like

Wilson, they were more concerned with international peace than with domestic civil liberties, or the specter of Bolshevism had quieted them.

Liberals were disquieted, however, by Wilson's lack of reform plans and Gregory's willingness to continue harsh attacks on dissenters. Wilson had asked Gregory for his opinion regarding a general amnesty for everyone convicted under war statutes. Such a move would have restored much of Wilson's liberal support at home and transformed reformers' reluctant cooperation in wartime suppression into leadership in peacetime reconstruction. But Gregory was opposed to a general amnesty, and Wilson indicated to reformers that his ideas about reconstruction differed from theirs. Brandeis, talking to Felix Frankfurter a few days later, found him "well crushed by the President's expressions on reconstruction." The pre-war reforms were not to be resumed.

Those League divisions especially interested in fighting radicalism were elated with Gregory's pronouncement that they should continue their work. The Los Angeles branch issued a formal statement: "The Bolshevik spirit in this country has been held in check to a large extent by fear of the wrath of our patriotic citizens," chief O. P. Adams announced. "The League will have much to do in reporting on this element of society during reconstruction."

To effect this reconstruction of radicals, the Los Angeles chief revitalized his force by adding a Consulting Committee made up of fifteen of the city's most conservative Republicans, all selected by the majordomo of Los Angeles politics, O. J. Brandt. These men promised to lend their financial and moral support to a most ambitious scheme of postwar activities which included assembling a master index of all persons of "undesirable character" in the area. These files would then be made available to the army and navy intelligence and the Justice Department and to the Los Angeles police department and the sheriff's office as well.

What the Los Angeles chief really had in mind, the distressed and disillusioned California state inspector informed the national directors, was the use of the League by local political interests to shoo politicians into office. He advised the directors to forestall plans to build local units on the remnants of the League by keeping secret any mustering-out plans until a general order could be issued. "If they want something to play with let them build it up in their own way and to their own liking," the inspector wrote. Backers of the League had been patriotic during the war, he felt, but were not above using the League for their own interests afterward. "We have all fought to maintain the League as a nonpolitical proposition," he finished firmly, "and I for one, will not stand for its debasement into a near political machine after its war service is ended." He urged the directors to disband the League as soon as possible.

Slowly it became clear to the directors that unless the APL was disbanded immediately, its local units would become self-perpetuating. Within the APL a majority of members vigorously endorsed dissolution. Like the state inspector for Colorado who expressed his desire to be mustered out quickly, the best divisions had no interest in embarking on campaigns which were not directed against a foreign enemy. They had no desire to save the Justice Department money in peacetime. The most responsible members had donated their full time to the League while allowing opportunities for wartime profits to pass, and these members wanted to return to their businesses and professions to recoup some of their losses. The intensity with which the home front war had been fought had exhausted their emotional resources, as well. Only a small proportion of the rank and file desired to continue their crusades into 1919.

The directors began to damp plans for future activities. "Frankly, we do not believe that there is any place in American life for a volunteer espionage system," Briggs wrote to the Los Angeles chief on December 5. He suggested that the League wind up affairs with a bang and so remain a "great tradition of how Americans met a great national emergency."

Elting gave no hint of demobilization plans in an interview with the *Philadelphia Inquirer* on December 9. An organization of the size and strength of the APL should not be casually dismembered, he told the reporter; but, he continued, it was formed for war work, and organized citizen espionage in peacetime would be contrary to the spirit of American institutions. He gave no indication of when the League would end. In fact, he listed two tasks which had yet to be completed: investigation of applicants for naturalization and investigation of organizations advocating the overthrow of, or change in, the government by unlawful means. Also, he felt that propaganda regarded as detrimental to the public welfare and tending to foster violations of law should be discovered and counteracted, and that unfinished war work should be completed. "The activities of the League must continue for a considerable time to come," he concluded. The December 14 issue of the *Spy Glass* likewise gave no intimation that the League would disband.

Antagonism among the trio heading the League insured that it would not long continue, however. Frey was already spending much of his time in Chicago, while Elting was determined to maintain control of the Washington office until it closed. Briggs, irked at being nudged out of the command position by Elting, informed Emerson Hough, the member who had volunteered to write the official League history, that his own important role in organizing the League should be emphasized. When Frey discovered this, he wrote to Elting, "I feel that because of the great effort we have put forth we are both entitled to a square deal, and for my part I am going to insist upon having it." The bond forged by patriotism was dissolving.

Wilson sailed for Europe on December 4, leaving the APL still intact. The War Department had ordered their Military Intelligence officers to withdraw from all investigations of disloyalty and enemy activities among the civilian population, and the Army had withdrawn troops from restricted areas. The Secretary of the Navy had withdrawn guards from waterfronts and ships. Work on war contracts halted throughout the country. Yet Justice Department prosecutions went on, and all over the country the APL remained on patrol.

Although Wilson had ordered Burleson to discontinue wartime censorship on November 27, the Postmaster General went on refusing to deliver radical publications. Two days after Wilson left for France, the *Official Bulletin* carried a presidential proclamation listing 324 individuals, groups, and classes of individuals to be considered enemies of the country. The home front war seemed far from over.

One immediate effect of military cutbacks was to give additional impetus to retention of the APL, for the Military Intelligence directed its officers to turn over unfinished civilian cases to the League. Although the War Department told the APL it should discontinue commission and passport cases on military personnel, the volunteers were to continue propaganda reports until June. Attorney General Gregory went on vacation the first two weeks in December, and while he was gone, the League went right on with its investigations.

Meanwhile, League divisions engaged in a variety of projects. The Cleveland division helped the Red Cross mail Christmas packages to the front, where men awaiting peace remained poised for war. The Philadelphia division switched its attention from slacker raids to vice raids and roundups of bootleggers. The state inspector in New Jersey urged the Justice Department to institute additional prosecutions of persons his unit considered guilty of disloyalty during the war. The Washington state inspector laid plans for a fund-raising drive, looking toward renewed activity. Other units were drawing up reports on their war work for the national directors. Seven thousand members were putting in orders for new badges which the directors had placed on sale for three dollars apiece to help liquidate the debts of the Washington office.

As usual, the Chicago division was the most ambitious in its plans. Insubordination had never been completely quelled in Chicago, and it took little coaxing from the local Military Intelligence officer and the officials of the Labor Department to send the Leaguers off on new crusades.

Radicalism emerged quickly after the armistice. Believing that the wartime suppression had ended, Socialists staged a gigantic rally at the Chicago Coliseum on November 17. Representative Victor Berger, a Socialist party member whom Congress had refused to seat and who was under indictment for violation of the Espionage Act, was the main speaker. APL members were alarmed. Berger, they reported, had suggested that a Socialist soviet republic was a possibility in the United States. The Socialist party convention had adopted resolutions backing German attempts to establish working-class governments on the Russian model, had demanded American troops be withdrawn from Europe, and had denounced political repression engaged in by the government under the pretense of war necessity. The *Spy Glass* printed a properly indignant rejoinder: "Signing of the armistice has unmuzzled forces in the United States which have made little progress since America entered the war . . . the socialists of Chicago embraced the Bolsheviki doctrine in a body."

That was the opinion of the majority of Chicago APL members, at least. Following the Coliseum meeting, the Socialists had scheduled a parade to bring their message to public attention. The APL brought pressure on the police department to refuse a permit. To the Socialists' request, the chief of police replied, "There are 12,000 APL men in this village who are opposed to this sort of thing, and my men don't want to get in wrong with any 12,000 APL men." The Socialists cancelled their parade.

It bothered APL men that some aliens with radical ideas might be admitted to citizenship and acquire political influence. The chief naturalization officer had pigeonholed thirty-five hundred petitions from Chicago aliens during the war. Now he asked the APL to help indoctrinate applicants. Chief R. A. Gunn arranged for a telegram embodying this request to arrive while he was addressing a group of six hundred League members. For ten minutes the chief ex-

pounded on the great opportunity for APL men to act as "big brothers" in the Americanization of aliens applying for citizenship. Members roared their approval.

Chief Gunn already suspected that Gregory intended to disband the
APL, despite the call to remain on guard. Working for the Labor
Department in peacetime seemed better than getting out of the detective business completely. He therefore explored the possibility of the
Chicago unit's working directly for the Labor Department in the
cause of Americanization. Since Chicagoans had originated the APL,
he proposed that the Chicago division become a model for postwar
activity. The Labor Department sent a special assistant to work out a
new program. Meanwhile Chicago members continued to hunt slackers
and to applaud the imprisonment of enemy aliens and men who had
opposed the war. All looked with satisfaction upon the decision of the
Justice Department to proceed with the trial of Victor Berger.

By December 5, the Labor Department had worked out a proposal for the Chicago APL. "This work will primarily deal with
those who come into citizenship by naturalization," the Commissioner
of Naturalization began. "However, it will as definitely though probably indirectly, deal with and embrace the citizenry of the country."
The League was to investigate qualifications of candidates who applied for citizenship and assume responsibility for "arousing in the
minds of the candidates for citizenship and the foreign-born permanent residents of the community a regard and desire for what has
been termed the 'priceless heritage' of American citizenship." The
members' job was to "bring the message of America" to foreigners.
They should urge aliens to declare their intention to become citizens.
"When a foreigner has taken this step he has become one of us," the
Commissioner philosophized. "Until he performs this act he cannot be
said to be wholly one of us." Members were also asked to work
against prejudice by attempting to substitute the words "friend, neighbor, and brother" for "wop, gink, hunky, and dago." The APL would
be joining other groups in this work for an effort "toward the great
objective, winning the foreigner to a regard for the institutions of
America by big brother relation."

The Military Intelligence had in mind a future with the APL also.
The officer in charge at Chicago was Briggs's former assistant, Thomas
Crockett. He hated to see the League die.

On November 20 all Military Intelligence officers were notified
that since an emergency no longer existed, they should undertake
no new cases among the civilian population except those connected

with plant protection or graft and fraud in War Department contracts. All unfinished loyalty and enemy alien investigations were to be turned over to the Justice Department.

They were notified, but not all responded. The Military Intelligence officer in Indiana immediately turned over his pro-German investigations to the Bureau of Investigation agent. But from Chicago, Crockett wrote to say that he had heard about the order but had not received a copy. Did the orders apply to him, he asked.

Crockett's inquiry landed in the Military Intelligence Division simultaneously with word from the Justice Department that the Chicago officer had not complied with the new ruling and a demand that he do so. Crockett received a curt telegram informing him of the message from the Justice Department and an order: "Report if true and reasons for non-compliance of instructions." On December 4 the reasons for the reluctance of some Military Intelligence officers to withdraw from civilian investigations became a topic of the weekly interdepartmental intelligence conference in O'Brian's office.

Other Military Intelligence agents also objected to their orders. They did not want to close up shop. According to APL reports from Texas, the IWW was ready to launch a new campaign. "Everything tends to the point of active organization just as soon as the government relaxes censorship and other methods employed in keeping the organization in check," wrote an officer from Houston. In Bisbee, Arizona, where APL members had infiltrated the IWW and were working as undercover agents for the Military Intelligence, they balked at giving up their inside leads on IWW activities. Other officers argued that their files would be incomplete if they now turned investigations over to the Justice Department. Couldn't they at least have copies of the completed reports, one officer asked. The MID representative proposed to the group meeting in O'Brian's office that investigations of radicals continue.

All the men present were concerned about the Bolsheviks and believed that none of the laws already enacted could be used to eradicate this menace. They decided to recommend a bill which would permit deportation and exclusion of all "undesirable persons or persons inimical to the peace and welfare of the United States." If Congress did pass such a bill, argued the Military Intelligence, it would be unwise to discontinue investigations of dangerous radicals. Two days later an MID representative called Crockett long distance and on December 7 confirmed by letter a new decision: "It is our policy to continue undercover work with radical organizations."

Crockett urged the APL to send in reports of any radical activities they could find. He contacted state inspectors and asked for reports on suspect organizations, on the number and character of meetings, on the sources and amount of income, on the actions taken by the APL and the Justice Department. Stay on the alert and report radicals was the word received by the APL in Illinois, Indiana, Iowa, Kansas, Kentucky, Michigan, Minnesota, Missouri, Nebraska, North Dakota, Ohio, West Virginia, and Wisconsin.

To those APL inspectors who did not reply to Crockett's first request, he sent special queries. To Arthur Nichols, Missouri state inspector, he wrote, "This office is greatly interested in the continuation of the American Protective League, and requests information as to your policy with regard to the future." By the time Gregory returned to Washington to make a decision concerning the continuation of the APL, the League was already firmly established in its postwar role.

Gregory returned to Washington on December 13. One of the first things he did was to ask Wilson to remove all restrictions on enemy aliens, effective on Christmas Day. Except for requiring clearance to enter or leave the country, enemy aliens were to regain the right to move about at will. It would have been useless to retain the restrictions, of course, after the withdrawal of army and navy guards from areas formerly off limits. These areas no longer held anything of value to the enemy. "Everywhere there is manifested a desire to return as quickly as possible to normal conditions of business," Gregory wrote to Wilson, "and I feel this Department ought not to run the risk of adhering to a legalistic interpretation of a condition of war while all of the country is earnestly seeking to readjust itself to peace conditions."

This did not mean, however, that Gregory was ready yet to halt his punishment of wartime slackers. Five days later he sent out a circular to United States attorneys announcing special arrangements with the Provost Marshal General to obtain records from local boards to prosecute men who had dodged the draft. Offenders were no longer to be inducted into the military; they were to be prosecuted under the Selective Service Act. The Attorney General's aggressive stance may have been prompted by the generals, who thought all slackers should be arrested, brought to camps, court-martialed, and punished. The Cabinet might have agreed but for the ten million dollars such a policy of retribution would have cost. Instead, Gregory promised to see that every son of a rich man who was sent out of the country to escape the draft would be punished.

Not only punishment of slackers, but also punishment of violators of the Espionage Act, was to continue. The trial of Victor Berger proceeded according to schedule. Two indictments for treason were brought in New York. A Socialist was arrested in Brooklyn. In Sacramento the trial of forty-seven members of the IWW had opened on December 7.

In spite of the continued war on the home front, the desire to be demobilized was strong among Gregory's subordinates. Bielaski tendered his resignation as of Decemebr 21, 1918, and on December 17, the day that the Germans signed a second armistice, he announced his decision to his special agents. He directed Bureau of Investigation superintendents to reduce the number of special agents to the prewar level. And he agreed with Gregory and O'Brian that the APL should be officially disbanded; civilian patriotic organizations were not to be used in peacetime for volunteer espionage. If superintendents needed help, they could contact volunteers as individuals rather than as a group.

O'Brian proposed that all APL reports be deposited with United States attorneys so that they could not be utilized to satisfy personal grudges or for political manipulation. To ensure compliance with the plan, he insisted that each APL division obtain a receipt from the local United States Attorney upon deposit, and then forward the receipt to Washington.

Elting agreed to stay on at the APL office to liquidate the League. O'Brian's War Emergency Bureau would continue to function as long as necessary to oversee dissolution of the APL, to review wartime prosecutions, and to recommend reduction of sentences. Then O'Brian, too, planned to resign. Gregory decided to withhold his resignation until after Christmas. None of the men in the Justice Department had any political ambitions. They only wanted to leave the Department as they had found it. Gregory ordered the demobilization of the APL.

On December 21, the *Spy Glass* printed the Attorney General's decision to disband the League and issued instructions for finishing up work. The directors' list of reasons for disbanding included such practical considerations as lack of work, resignations of members, and financial difficulties. More important, they told members that conditions of peace essentially altered their status. During the war, members had acted under "color of Governmental authority," and "the warrant for their inquiry into the interests and activities of their fellow citizens was the existence of the national emergency." With the country at peace, there was no place for organized citizen espionage. So far as the APL was concerned, the directors admitted, "many of its members would quite naturally turn themselves to combating those radical movements which they consider hostile to the best interests of their country." Some of these radical doctrines violated no law. Others involved disputes between labor and capital. "It would be inevitable that through individual activities local divisions would find themselves in the position of combating that which they might consider political heresy or industrial menace, but which would nevertheless be lawful agitation which the Department of Justice could not well oppose," concluded the directors.

As individuals, members could exercise a stabilizing influence in times of agitation or unrest and remain a powerful force in opposition to dangerous movements and tendencies wherever they might arise. This was to be their future role.

Soon after the directors announced their decision, Bielaski went to Chicago to tell the APL division personally that the Justice Department would no longer need their services after the first of January. He also instructed the federal sleuths to reduce their local force from fifty to twenty-five men immediately and to return to the pre-war total of fifteen special agents by January.

After Bielaski's visit, intransigent members rallied around Crockett. Radicalism was a grave concern; they offered to work for him after their organization disbanded on January 1.

Crockett hurriedly wired Washington for permission to enlist a number of the APL volunteers to act as undercover agents for the MID. "Services have been tendered and assistance is thought to be indispensable," he wired. While he waited for a reply, he commiserated with the Chicago Leaguers for being laid off.

Feelings among members were quite bitter, a Leaguer named Ratcliff told Crockett. The impression among the Chicago men was that they had received a severe slap in return for their efforts. One member, Ratcliff said, had spoken for all in saying that "ever since the League had been in existence, it had been scratching the back of some Government official in order to placate it and this in spite of the fact that the services of the League had been purely voluntary, and that it had paid its own expenses."

A meeting of the entire Chicago membership was planned for the evening of December 30, not just to wind up wartime League affairs as the Justice Department had requested, but also to sound out members on continuing as an independent peacetime organization.

Crockett recommended that Colonel John M. Dunn, Acting Director of the MID, send a telegram to the Chicago League on that occasion. "The moral effect would be very great for future cooperation of the League with this office."

To keep Leaguers interested in the radicals, Crockett asked them to continue sending in reports. Indiana, Ohio, Michigan, Illinois, and Kentucky were areas that Crockett considered particularly in danger from subversion. State inspectors there received requests to send information to him on "Socialist-bolshevik agitators."

The League was not to go out of existence on January 1 as Crockett thought. MID officers in Washington soon discovered that. Leaguers were only to discontinue receiving requests from the Justice Department on that date. League offices would stay open until February 1, 1919, to finish up the rest of their investigations. Colonel Dunn therefore responded to Crockett's request by suggesting that Crockett specify the kinds of undercover work he wished assigned to the APL and submit the names of operatives selected before approval could be given to adopt the child being abandoned by Justice. "A question of policy is involved which may require some further consideration," Dunn said.

Conferences had already taken place in the MID regarding peacetime operations. During the last two weeks in December there had been talks among General Staff officers as well, and a decision had been reached to cut back the Military Intelligence to a staff of 103 officers. At the time this seemed a drastic enough cutback to the several hundred officers on duty. The General Staff also decided on a complete reorganization of the MID to consolidate duties. A separate intelligence force had been developed in Europe under Colonel Ralph Van Dieman. Now the domestic and foreign forces were to be joined in Washington. The primary peacetime functions of the MID were to be disseminating information to the press, maintaining military morale, and decoding.

Looking back on the immediate post-armistice period, director of the MID Marlborough Churchill would write: "After the armistice, the investigation of disloyalty and enemy activity stopped, and we expected to see all investigational work on the part of the MID gradually disappear." It did not stop, nor did all Military Intelligence officers want it to. The web of sedition seemed endless.

Hope for postwar APL activities had been stirred by Crockett's encouragement to midwestern League units. The *Cleveland Plain Dealer* carried an editorial on December 24 denouncing lawlessness and announcing that the APL had placed its services at the disposal of the police. An editorial in the *Cleveland Press* advised, "Chief, call out the APL," and advocated a system whereby every hotel and rooming house would have to report each arriving guest to the police, who would then have the APL investigate persons of "doubtful" connection.

Late in December APL members in Cleveland began to accompany police on their nightly rounds. Members openly objected to disbanding and made plans to perpetuate their division. Their chief was already busy running down Bolsheviks and wanted to continue his probes. The chief of the Cincinnati division also promised to send Crockett information regularly on the Bolshevik situation. To encourage postwar cooperation, Crockett sent condolences for the coming demise of the APL to Ohio state inspector Clifford Shinkle: "It is with considerable regret that we received notice of the dissolution of the American Protective League."

Unwittingly, Elting helped the League's revival along. He believed that a congressional resolution expressing appreciation for the services of the League would convince the members that the League was through. He talked to Congressman Mann, Republican leader slated to be the next Speaker, who advised him to have a Democrat on the Judiciary Committee introduce the resolution.

Late in December Representative Warren Gard of Ohio offered a Joint Resolution in the House "extending the thanks of Congress to all members of the American Protective League for services rendered the Government during the War." On January 4, Elting talked to Senator Overman, Acting Chairman of the Senate Judiciary Committee, who cautioned him that while the League was highly regarded and widely acknowledged to have rendered great service and was indeed entitled to the thanks of Congress, it seemed highly unlikely that such a resolution would carry. So, notwithstanding the fact that it had never been put to a vote, Elting had copies of Representative Gard's resolution sent to APL members as evidence of congressional gratitude for their services. This gesture served to increase the clamor for continuation.

Now other units were fighting to reverse the Attorney General's death sentence. In Philadelphia on December 31, the homes of the superintendent of police, a judge, and the president of the Chamber of Commerce were bombed. The APL was called out to look for Bolshevik anarchists. Editorials appealed to members not to disband.

Elting believed that publicity was needed to acquaint divisions with the Justice Department order to disband. Late in December he had the *Washington Post* carry a small item on the dissolution, and he attempted to have the Associated Press send out a second notice. On January 9 the government's *Official Bulletin* printed a copy of the dissolution orders, on the same day that Bielaski, testifying before the Committee of the Judiciary on wartime German activities, summed up his view of the APL.

Throughout the war, the Justice Department had successfully avoided any investigation by Congress. In fall, 1918, Alien Property Custodian A. Mitchell Palmer had urged the Senate to investigate German brewers whom he was trying to drive out of business, but in September Gregory had detailed William R. Benham to work with the Senate committee in an attempt to keep the committee from prying into the records of his department. When congressmen persisted in their probe, he designated Bielaski to testify as to the government's wartime policies at home.

Bielaski told Senators that the German-Americans were "to a very high degree, loyal to this country, and that the alien Germans here were exceptionally well behaved." Why then did the Department license the APL, a senator asked. Bielaski explained that the Justice Department had anticipated "great disorders" and "trouble of all kinds" which did not develop, that apprehension had been the result of activities of the "official German representatives" before the country went to war. These men, he said, had been agents of the German government, not resident aliens. Because of this fear, the APL had been asked to help. "We prepared for eventualities that did not materialize," Bielaski told them honestly.

A Major Humes, one of the Military Intelligence officers present at the committee hearings, attempted to get Bielaski to credit the watchful presence of the APL for the fact that the German-Americans had been loyal to the American government. Was not their loyalty due to effective organization and constant surveillance of the different agencies rather than a change in heart, he asked. Bielaski admitted that to some extent this might be true, but that such an interpretation could not apply to most of the enemy alien population. Major Humes persisted: "But a very small percentage of the German sympathizers, as they existed prior to our entrance into the war, could have caused untold trouble if it had not been for the psychological effect of the constant vigilance of these departments and the fear that they had of action on the part of the Government?" Bielaski still refused to endorse the eternal vigilance theory. He replied: "Other things contributed to the same thing . . . German operation is essentially one of organization. Their organization in this country, which had been developed through the period of our neutrality, was entirely broken up, or at least to a tremendously large percentage, by the arrests made at the outbreak of the war and by the surveillance which was maintained over those who were not arrested."

Bielaski did give due praise to the APL, admitting that members had done effective work in enforcing the Selective Service Act. But the implication was clear: the APL had not been necessary to ferret out spies. To soften this confession, he hastily added, "I do not mean by my testimony to say that the American Protective League, because it did not have active service to perform, did not do a wonderful work, because it did." He explained that the major contribution of the 300,000 to 350,000 members of the APL, besides helping to enforce the draft, had been to maintain a feeling of security throughout the country by investigating every instance where people talked in an "unseemly manner." According to the chief spy catcher, the APL had been no more than a security patrol to see that people did not exercise their right of free speech during the war. It had, of course, been much more. But his statement was an admission that past APL activities had nothing to do with espionage.

A few days later Ralph M. Easly, head of the American Civic Federation, who had joined forces with Samuel Gompers, head of the AFL and leader of the conservative labor forces in the United States, wrote to Gregory to solicit the help of the APL. Easly and Gompers considered the growing bolshevism in America "no light matter" and wanted the help of the APL in countering the movement. "They certainly have a number of good people who are as keen to fight this Bolshevist game as we are," he concluded.

Prime opponents of dissolution of the APL were Military Intelligence officers who wanted to continue investigations of radical groups. They kept stressing the danger of subversion. From Seattle came a warning that if Bolsheviks—even now beginning to infiltrate the American Federation of Labor—were allowed to carry out their campaign, the United States would be under their control within two years. Citizens were demanding that uniformed men raid meetings of these radicals. According to the same reporting agent, the situation was equally critical in Butte, where Bolsheviks were gaining control of the entire city. A law was needed to prevent the printing and disseminating of radical literature.

Crockett gave his superiors the impression that conditions were as bad in the Midwest as they were reported in the Northwest. In Gary, Indiana, he told Churchill unequivocally, a strike was being instigated by Wobblies and Bolshevists; businessmen had told him so. Newspapers were notified of the menace. The local chief of police was encouraged to investigate people accused of being radicals.

Crockett asked his agents and APL volunteers to study race riots in Omaha for evidence of similar radical instigation. He ordered all officers to submit weekly letters covering activities in their communities and the surrounding country within fifty to a hundred miles. They were to keep him fully apprised not only of radical activities, but also of the "labor situation, conscientious objectors, draft board evasions, imposters, various forms of propaganda." He began sending regular orders to the APL demanding investigations of articles appearing in newspapers. William Bobbs, state inspector for Indiana, was told to place Socialists and Bolsheviks "under close surveillance . . . the result of . . . further investigation be forwarded to [Crockett's] office."

During the second week of January a group of APL Chicago members who wanted to continue work for Crockett voted to reorganize to help the MID in peacetime. Crockett sent the good news on to Washington.

Military Intelligence officers in the Southwest began to probe the radical menace. Labor Department officials in Arizona were investigated as radicals and reported. In Texas, APL men did the same. Requests from local Military Intelligence officers for complete lists of names and addresses of APL members began to reach League headquarters in Washington. The Justice Department apparently complained to the War Department, for on January 24, 1919, the MID reversed its policy of December. All intelligence officers were ordered to abandon investigations of civilians and to stay on military reservations. One loophole was left by Churchill, however: they were still permitted to receive information from individuals not officially connected with the Military Intelligence. This made the cooperation of the APL seem ever more desirable.

As efforts toward revitalizing the League gained momentum, the directors increased pressure to disband. On January 25 they issued another long directive to members listing reasons for dissolution, reasons thoroughly familiar by now: not enough work, no authority, no request by government agencies for continued work, wartime statutes expiring, and vanishing popular support for peacetime surveillance. During the war, League activity had been hailed as patriotic and efficient; in peacetime it would be condemned as prying curiosity and usurpation. There was danger in any secret organization's accepting from local or state governments any powers which might be directed to personal, economic, or political ends. Already, the directors disclosed, some League members had, with public approval, been used as strikebreakers during the war. But local Leagues must not be used in capital-labor conflicts now that no real public interest was involved. The League had been a national organization, working under national laws for national defense; but if divisions continued, their standing would descend to that of local, extra-legal police reserves. Stating that 99 percent of the units had already dissolved, the directors closed by insisting that the reluctant units accept an honorable discharge and the country's thanks for their notable services.

What was a closed issue for the directors continued to be debated by the Chicago division. On the same day that the directors issued final orders to disperse, the entire Chicago division assembled to decide whether they would obey or continue independently. Their discussion was typical of the debate within other dissident units.

The Chicago meeting opened with one member offering a resolution that no organization of any kind be created to take the place of or perpetuate the League for any purpose, and that neither the name "American Protective League" nor any similar name be adopted by any organization. Attorney Warren Everett immediately objected. He argued that certain people should be disfranchised because they had spread radical propaganda and did not value their citizenship; and that the League should be perpetuated as a check upon Socialists and Bolsheviks who cared nothing for law and order. According to Everett, the issue was settled anyway, for a charter in the name of the American Protective League had already been obtained from the state of Illinois, and no one could take the new charter away.

As other members disputed the lawyer's authority, the debate revealed a deep schism within the organization. One group wished to continue their crusade against radicals, maintaining that members must combat the "evil influences working in the country by looking into the actions of those opposing the present form of government or governmental authority." Members should spread propaganda for good government and encourage passage of laws which would "restrain those people who talk too much on this proposition of personal liberty." A more moderate group felt that their first duty was to respect governmental authority and to support it by disbanding as directed. They objected that the other members had no authority to incorporate the League in Illinois. They also held that citizens should report suspected enemies of the government to the Justice Department, which could handle the matter—that there was no need for a private organization whose members had no real authority to investigate anyone. A member named Barnes, summing up this view, asserted, "Investigation means that you must go into a man's business, into his life, into his neighborhood, into his home, into every angle of this thing, and you have no authority to go into these things, and you cannot as American citizens assume that authority." Authority, he said, had been given temporarily by the Justice Department, but now the Attorney General had taken that authority away.

Other members added arguments to those of Barnes's. The League consisted of "espionage on neighbors and seeing that certain people were not elected to certain political offices," one noted. Another reminded members that the directors were absolutely opposed to the continuation of the APL and the use of its name. Finally one speaker concluded, "Are we going on to save America by flaunting the recognized authorities in the face? I don't see how we can do it and be American citizens."

Gradually the moderates won a majority to their view, and the vote to disband carried. Yet one more matter remained to be settled: disposition of the APL records. Some members objected to turning their files over to the marshal and the Justice Department in Chicago because politicians might have access to them. APL chief Gunn maintained that organized labor was running the city and that the president of the American Federation of Labor in Chicago could obtain any information he wished from the Bureau of Investigation. "I can tell you on the authority of the ex-Division Superintendent of this city," he maintained, "that he has been forced by his superiors to show the files to that man containing the names of our operators." Gunn moved that all files, proceedings, and records of membership be burned. A lone dissenter protested that the records belonged to the Department of Justice and that the League had no right to burn them. He was ignored; the motion carried.

Thus the Chicago division ended as it had existed, in a posture of compromise between subordination and insubordination to the Justice Department. Its members had never wholeheartedly acknowledged the jurisdiction of the Justice Department, though they had been happy to claim the Department as their authority to pry into neighbors' affairs. For most members, however, the issue was now closed. They stored away their new gold badges, which the directors had distributed just before demobilization with the admonition that

American Protective League

CHICAGO DIVISION

Organized with Approval and Operating under Direction of United States Department of Justice Bureau of Investigation

KNOW ALL MEN BY THESE PRESENTS THAT

Chief Charles A. Frey

HAS LOYALLY AND FAITHFULLY SERVED THE AMERICAN PROTECTIVE LEAGUE IN THE EXECUTION OF THE VARIOUS DUTIES ASSIGNED TO IT BY THE GOVERNMENT OF THE UNITED STATES OF AMERICA IN THE PROSECUTION AND WINNING OF THE WORLD WAR AND IN TOKEN OF APPRECIATION OF A WORK WELL DONE IS NOW ENTITLED TO

HONORABLE DISCHARGE

FROM THE SERVICE OF THE LEAGUE AND THE SAME IS HEREBY GRANTED WITH ALL THE RIGHTS AND BENEFITS THAT ARE NOW OR MAY HEREAFTER BE CONFERRED UPON SUCH MEMBERS

GIVEN UNDER OUR HAND AND SEAL THIS THIRTY FIRST DAY OF JANUARY 1919

CHIEF BUREAU MEMBERSHIP

ASSISTANT CHIEF

CHIEF

Honorable discharge from the American Protective League

they were not to be used but could be kept as "souvenirs of their service in the great war." They framed their certificates of honorable discharge. They became private citizens once more.

To forestall a similar discussion in the New York division, the Justice Department took an active part in planning an elaborate dinner which would lend finality to the dissolution. Hundreds of American Protective League members met at the Hotel Astor for the final muster-out on the last day of January. Gregory, pleading illness, sent along a letter of thanks for the work of the League and left the speech-making to O'Brian and Bielaski. In the keynote address, O'Brian told Leaguers they had "performed no small part in protecting the rear of the armies that fought, and making the soil of your country safe from the machinations of enemies and the treachery of the disloyal."

With satisfaction the veterans downed their *Gâteau de Victoire* and *café noir* and filed out of the banquet to the strains of "Keep the Home Fires Burning."

The Veterans

It took exactly two hours for the first APL phoenix to rise from the ashes. In Minneapolis, members reconstituted themselves as a law enforcement league, a "Committee of Thirteen," to continue their activities. "We felt that the reconstruction period problems were just as serious as those of the war days, and Minneapolis for some time had been planning to organize a law enforcement league similar to the work carried out in other cities," the chairman of the Committee of Thirteen explained. It was, he said, the right "psychological moment" to launch the project; like the wartime APL, the committee members were vested with "special police authority." Minneapolis, in other words, was to have its own peacetime vigilante group formed of "100% of the old membership" of the APL.

Cincinnati was not far behind Minneapolis. APL veterans there reorganized under their wartime chief, John L. Richey, and with the encouragement of the Military Intelligence took up the campaign against bolshevism with great élan. In Cleveland the APL was already reorganizing as the Loyal American League to collect information for city, state, and federal government, and to protect the country against "treason, lawlessness and disorder." The Loyal American

League stationery bore the title: "successor to the American Protective League." The movement to form new groups spread. Former members of the Investigating Bureau of the Chicago APL held a meeting early in April and decided to offer their service to the Military Intelligence officer there.

Senators helped the revival along. On February 7, Senator Wesley Jones of Washington introduced a memorial from the Tacoma APL demanding that all aliens be given only provisional citizenship and be subjected to stricter regulations. Many aliens, the memorial read, were only "half American in real sentiment"; APL investigations had shown, according to the document, that at least 90 percent of all persons found to be disloyal, disobedient to law, destroyers of property, and seditious were of foreign birth. All aliens should be required to register, they should be carefully investigated before being granted citizenship papers, and citizenship should be forfeited for "sufficient cause." Immigration and naturalization laws should be made retroactive; a peacetime sedition act would be of help too. "We are gravely apprehensive of after-war conditions, when Europe shall settle down to orderly government and its Bolsheviki seek the freedom of America to carry on its propaganda of tyranny and destruction, and we therefore, pray your earnest, prompt, and conscientious consideration of these momentous problems, always having in mind that you are representing the American people, for whose benefit and protection its laws should be primarily made."

Back in Seattle the Minute Men went right on with their investigations. On January 18, 1919, an operative submitted a report objecting to the adoption by the school board of the textbook *Outlines of European History* by Charles A. Beard and James Harvey Robinson. Several times since 1916 the book had been proposed, and each time a member of the school board had seriously objected to it. Defenders of the text said it had already been rewritten to eliminate the most objectionable feature—a too tender regard for German culture in the Middle Ages. Opponents objected that the book should not be used because the authors had been disloyal. As proof of disloyalty they cited the fact that Robinson had contributed to an IWW defense fund in Chicago and that Beard had been named by the Justice Department as one of the sixty-five educators in the country who had proven themselves "un-American."

There were other controversies to attract the attention of the Seattle APL. On January 21, 1919, seventeen unions of the Seattle Metal Trades Council went on strike. Within two weeks the strike had turned into a general strike. The strike was peaceful, but when a young radical named Harvey O'Connor wrote a pamphlet titled "Russia Did It," in which he urged workers to take over the management of the shipyards, the APL went into action. On February 2 an APL operative arrested two men who attempted to distribute the pamphlet on the street. Strike leaders disavowed the pamphlet, but APL veterans claimed the strike would lead to a takeover of property. The United States Attorney in Seattle agreed. He wired the Justice Department: "Intention of strike is revolution led by extreme element openly advocating overthrow of Government."

Rumors of dynamitings, shootings, and violence spread. The wealthy fled to Portland. Immigration officials hustled fifty-four aliens arrested earlier by the Seattle APL onto a train and sent this "Red Special" toward Ellis Island amid extra security precautions. Captain J. C. Fisher issued instructions that the previous prohibition against radical investigations by military personnel should be ignored, and facts should be gathered to determine whether troops should be called in. At the same time, another Military Intelligence officer in Seattle, Captain F. W. Wilson, received a seemingly contradictory order from Washington, D.C.: "Everyone in your office keep absolutely out of strike situation."

On February 6, Secretary Baker authorized the commanding general in Seattle to order in federal troops. With their appearance, the mayor was able to crush the strike within a few days. Before he could, however, the Military Intelligence had been reactivated throughout the Northwest. Officers who had been in the process of closing their offices decided the Seattle MID should be maintained so that agents could "cover" the strike. The United States Attorney told officers that he believed the situation betokened rebellion and he needed their help in collecting evidence for conspiracy charges against the strikers.

On February 11, the same day that the strikers returned to work, an intelligence officer attended a regular monthly meeting of the International Brotherhood of Bookbinders, and a few days later he attended a meeting of the Union of Russian Workingmen. When he reported his visitations to the MID, the acting directors of the MID promptly ordered him out of undercover work and reiterated MID policy: it was perfectly all right for a civilian to volunteer information and to attend meetings, but the military intelligence must not use volunteers as regular agents for their offices to conduct espionage on behalf of the MID. The officer was unhappy about his orders. This was a "revolutionary-strike emergency," he replied. He had only been gathering evidence necessary to put down rebellion. Moreover, he was convinced that bolshevism was spreading in Montana, as well. Reluctantly, he agreed to discontinue his radical investigations and rely informally upon the volunteers. By February 26 the new pattern had been established in the Northwest.

Meanwhile, in Washington, D. C., a political debate was going on which would decide the future relation of APL veterans to the Justice Department. In January Gregory had told Wilson of his intention to resign, recommending as his successor George Carrol Todd, a New York Democrat, a good lawyer without political pretentions who had started at the bottom of the ladder in the Justice Department and worked his way up to Assistant Attorney General. Todd had handled a wartime investigation of the aircraft industry efficiently and had an interest in peacetime reform like enforcement of the Sherman Anti-Trust Act, which he and Gregory had both advocated before the war. On January 11, while Wilson was still in Europe attending the Peace Conference and before a decision had been made as to Gregory's successor, the Attorney General announced his resignation to reporters.

Gregory felt he had left a good record behind. "I take considerable pride in the administration of the Department of Justice during some five years I was in charge of it," he was to write to a friend later in defending his work. As for summing up his principles, he claimed at the end of the war that his department had proceeded on the theory that the "constitutional rights of free speech, free assembly, and petition exist in war time as in peace time, and that the right of discussion of government policy and the right of political agitation are most fundamental rights in a democracy." No person had been convicted for *"mere expression of opinion,"* Gregory insisted to Wilson.

It looked a bit different from outside the Justice Department, however. An anonymous author writing for the *Harvard Law Review* noted that there seemed to be little room for adverse discussion of the war and argued that opinions could not properly be penalized, inasmuch as the causes of the war could not be proven. *The Nation*, without openly criticizing Gregory, cited figures to show that the Justice Department had disregarded civil liberties. Quoting from Gregory's *Annual Report* for 1918, the editor pointed to "An Impressive Record": 988 prosecutions under the Espionage Act and 11,809 under the Selective Service Act. An editorial in the *Public* rationalized Gregory's record by commenting that the position of Attorney General was one of "responsibility without power." Gregory's subordinates had been responsible to politicians because their appointments had to be confirmed by the Senate, this editor concluded, and thus during the war "Mr. Gregory's office spent fully as much time trying to stop prosecutions initiated by its local representatives as it did directing prosecutions."

If Gregory was truly concerned about the rights of individuals, he was not active enough in defending those rights. Almost always he seemed willing to compromise. The APL, of course, offers the prime example. Gregory could not produce one spy to prove that eternal vigilance in counterespionage was more important than eternal vigilance in defense of civil liberties. Radicals were aware that while thousands of men and women had gone to jail for their dissent from the war policies of the Administration, not a single spy had been caught. The silent war between the Justice Department and the War Department over Pablo Waberski was a well-kept secret, nor was the public ever to hear the conclusion of the tug-of-war over this one alleged spy. Waberski died in prison, and with him died the Administration's concern about German espionage. Gregory's successor would have to find another pretext if he wanted to continue the home front war.

Wilson wanted to appoint as Gregory's successor A. Mitchell Palmer, whose September, 1918, accusation that German brewers were disloyal had stirred the Senate to launch an investigation. The publicity attendant upon his campaign against the brewers had brought him national prominence as a fighter of the Hun.

At the same time that Palmer began his push to have German brewers investigated, he was manipulating the term "enemy" to enlarge the scope of his office. At first, only the property of interned aliens or property of residents in Germany could be taken over by the Alien Property Custodian. Under Palmer's enlarged term, "enemy" was interpreted to mean the wives of enemy agents or men in enemy territory, those doing business within enemy territory, and persons who were prisoners of war or interned by an ally. In February, 1919, Palmer even wanted to declare members of the Indian National Party enemies so that he could confiscate property of East Indians convicted for revolutionary activities during the neutrality period. This latter scheme O'Brian absolutely opposed. Palmer, however, went right on with his other plans.

By the fall of 1918, Palmer had developed his own flourishing Bureau of Investigation under Francis P. Garvan and was soliciting information on new classifications to be included in the term "enemy."

At the end of November, he urged the APL to continue their search and promised "Americanization of German-owned industries in the United States will go right on until the Hun grip on our essential industries is completely broken. Industrial disarmament must come along with military disarmament." In January, 1919, Palmer announced that the property protections embodied in the Fifth Amendment did not operate against the exercise of war power, and he began to expound the theory that war claims against Germany should be paid by confiscation of property owned by German aliens. "Germany and the United States are still at war," he insisted.

As it became clear that Palmer meant to continue his crusade against aliens into the postwar period and rumors began to circulate that six million dollars' worth of confiscated property was being sold to "friends" at reduced rates, Gregory protested to Wilson against Palmer's appointment as Attorney General. Wilson hesitated. The appointment of Palmer, Wilson wrote from Europe to his secretary, Joseph Tumulty, "is much against Gregory's judgment and this disturbs me."

It didn't disturb Tumulty. "Frankly, our party here is greatly dispirited and needs stimulation," he cabled Wilson. The selection of Todd, he pointed out, would have no political value; and someone in the Justice Department had told him that Todd was not "broad-visioned or sympathetic with . . . Democratic purposes." Moreover, Todd had originally come from the South, and there was talk that Wilson already had too many southerners in the Cabinet. Palmer, on the other hand, was "young, militant, progressive and fearless. . . . Stands well with country, Congress, appeals to young voter; effective on stump." Wilson's attitude toward the future of the party would be measured by this appointment, Tumulty assured him. "This office great power politically. We should not trust it to any one who is not heart and soul with us." A loyal party man, Tumulty neglected to consider the potential power the Attorney General held affecting the civil liberties of everyone in America. Wilson didn't think of that either. It was announced that Palmer would become Attorney General on March 1, 1919.

February was spent by APL director Elting finishing up the affairs of the League, attempting to liquidate a five thousand dollar deficit for operating expenses, and closing the Washington office. Bielaski's resignation had taken effect on February 10. William Elby Allen, a graduate of the University of Texas who had been a United States Attorney and special assistant to O'Brian, took over as Acting Chief of the Bureau of Investigation. Allen and O'Brian stayed on in the Justice Department after Palmer became Attorney General.

As soon as Palmer settled into his office, APL veterans came around looking for Justice Department permission to reorganize. Edward Yates, an attorney in Pittsfield, Illinois, inquired about the "propriety" of former APL members' perfecting a social organization—complete with badges—pledged to constant vigilance. O'Brian immediately replied for the Department, "Both Attorney General Gregory and the writer have been opposed to the continuance in any form of any private organization which should exercise, or appear to be exercising, semi-official functions in espionage after February 1, 1919, and the wearing of any badge, such as you mention, would be equally objectionable."

The Yates letter was followed by others from around the country. It soon became evident to O'Brian that his intended coup de grace had been seized upon by the APL as days of grace; the idea of the League was very much alive. Moreover, the most antiradical members were regrouping to fight the Red menace. Some moderate voices were heard to protest, however. The Cincinnati City Club passed a resolution condemning former APL chief Richey for his postwar activities. An attorney who shared Richey's views resigned from the club, claiming he could prove bolshevism existed in Cincinnati and was being promoted by pro-Germans and by so-called Americans who were afraid to let patriotism interfere with money-making or political success. He praised the APL. The *Cincinnati Enquirer* gave the whole controversy considerable publicity on March 28.

O'Brian was insistent that the APL not be revived. On April 3, 1919, Attorney General Palmer announced that Justice Department officials had been instructed to have no official dealings with any private investigating organizations. Information which was germane to the work of the Department was to be welcomed, but private investigators would not be recognized or used by the Justice Department in peacetime. Local papers printed the news under such headlines as "War Time Detectives not Recognized Now" and "Palmer Rejects Aid of Private Detectives." Cincinnati APL veterans saw their crusade against Bolsheviks being threatened. Said one, "The message which Mr. Palmer sent out and which appeared in newspapers in the United States was received with great glee by the Socialists, IWW and Bolshevists. In one meeting here the newspaper article was read and brought forth tremendous cheers and applause."

Palmer's announcement also drew indignant complaints from APL veterans in Minneapolis. They interpreted the article not only as a present threat but as proof that their services had not been appreciated by the government during the war. "We did not pose as war time detectives or anything of that kind," wrote the former Minneapolis chief; "the proposition was put up to us that it was a patriotic duty and work where we could be of some help to the government." Perhaps Palmer had not been properly quoted, this chief concluded hopefully, asking for a letter of clarification. Palmer didn't reply.

The Cincinnati Loyal American League sent their chief, Arch C. Klumph, to talk personally to Palmer. O'Brian waylaid the veteran and told him that the Attorney General had no desire to "affront, humiliate or discredit in any way the citizens who, at great personal sacrifice, had aided the Department during the war," but that the Loyal American League must not use the name of the APL on its letterhead, as to do so would imply that the new group was affiliated with the Justice Department.

Klumph became indignant. "We feel that we should be commended and encouraged by the Department of Justice and any other Department of the Government, and also by every loyal American citizen, but we want no legal recognition," he wrote home. He could not comprehend why the Justice Department had not encouraged their activities, which involved attending meetings of "disloyalists," taking notes of everything said and done there, then turning over these notes "to those whom we feel should be interested." Why would this interfere with Bureau of Investigation agents, he asked. He claimed that a prominent Cleveland banker, who was also a government official, had assured him that businessmen would provide a fund of not less than $100,000 to sustain the antiradical crusade. (If this boast was true, then Klumph's reluctance to destroy five thousand sheets of stationery with "successor to the American Protective League" printed across the top is difficult to understand. His suggestion to his assistant that perhaps they could just draw a red line through the title or stamp across the top "not affiliated with the United States government" indicates, rather, that he first needed official recognition in order to obtain money for postwar probes.)

But O'Brian remained unmoved. "The officers of the League apparently understand the general attitude of the Department and we trust that they will conform to that attitude," he replied to Klumph. As to the letterhead, he would not say what form it should take, only what form it should not take. To the assistant secretary of the Cleveland Chamber of Commerce, with whom the new League planned to cooperate, O'Brian explained, "The American Protective League had at least a semi-official relationship to this Department, was treated as an auxiliary of this Department and operated under the general supervision of this Department. This official or semi-official status was well known to the public. The use of another organization of any such expression as 'successor to the American Protective League' might give the impression that the new organization has succeeded to the official or semi-official status of the American Protective League. Such an impression would be misleading and harmful and should be avoided." The present policy, he reiterated, was to avoid "official relationship to unofficial espionage organizations."

Because of his policy against recalling the volunteers to service, Palmer had by now gained a more favorable reputation among radicals than Gregory had enjoyed. Albert DeSilver visited the new Attorney General in April on behalf of the National Civil Liberties Bureau and found him most reasonable in his attitude.

On April 23 the *Cleveland News* reported that Palmer had asked the APL not to watch radical meetings and not to submit reports to the Justice Department. APL veterans were resourceful, however. The Chicago branch passed a resolution expressing its "appreciation and confidence" in the work of Chicago Military Intelligence officer Major Crockett and sent it on to Marlborough Churchill, head of the MID. Churchill was more cordial than O'Brian and replied, "We assure you that if your Bureau is continued as you anticipate that the further assistance of its members will always be welcome and Major Crockett will be able to inform you as to the matters in which we are still interested and wherein you may be of assistance in the manner *prescribed* by our instructions." To Crockett, Churchill gave his authorization to receive any information the APL wanted to furnish and to tell former APL chief Gunn what kind of matters MID wanted investigated. The War Department began to look much more promising as an APL ally than did the Justice Department.

Word of encouragement from the War Department spread. Another splinter group of the Chicago APL calling itself "District No. 8," under the command of I. D. Berg, volunteered its services to Crockett. "We are ready and willing to serve the Government with proper credentials, at all times, and as Commanding Officer, I am tendering this organization to you for any work which may arise in the future or I will be glad to confer with you if there is any work at the present time that you would like to have us undertake," Berg wrote. Crockett only thanked him for the offer. But communications were established.

Not only veterans looking for new jobs, but requests to use the old APL records, began to disturb the Justice Department and the War Department in the spring of 1919. Many divisions, like the Chicago League, had burned their records or kept them for their own private uses. But public officials and politicians were asking to see records turned over to the Justice Department.

The president of the Louisiana State Board of Health, Oscar Dowling, was one of the men who tried to gain access to APL files after the war. In September, 1918, he had been so incautious as to use APL reports as the basis for a statement that a local sanitarium should be closed because its head physician was a drug addict. The physician had sued Dowling for slander, and Dowling had gone to the War Department to ask if he could use APL records to substantiate his charge. The Judge Advocate General had advised Secretary of War Baker that APL reports should not be opened for private purposes and that under law they could not be produced in court in response to a subpoena. Baker himself had written to Dowling at the end of November refusing access to draft files, telling him this was part of a uniform policy, and concluding, "I think that a little reflection will convince you not only of the wisdom of this course, but that any other course could not in fairness and justice be followed." A little reflection did not convince Dowling. He visited generals and wrote letters. Baker remained adamant. Early in March, 1919, Provost Marshal Crowder wrote one last letter declining the information. War Department files remained closed.

Governor James M. Cox of Ohio went directly to the Justice Department with his request for APL files. He wanted to use these as the basis of a postwar probe into alleged pro-Germanism in the Cincinnati schools. O'Brian refused. He stated that these files contained not only authentic information but "an infinitely greater amount of misinformation, some of it based on malevolent motives." Traditionally, he said, the Bureau of Investigation had used its records only for prosecutions, and he advised Palmer that it would be "popular doctrine as well as sound policy" to adhere strictly to this rule and to announce that adherence publicly. Palmer agreed with O'Brian. He wrote to Cox, "It is our opinion that information of this character could not be used without danger of doing serious wrong to individuals who were probably innocent and none of it could be used in any way without great danger of having the attitude of this Department misconstrued and possibly discredited."

Meanwhile, congressmen were also looking for material for their postwar campaigns. After Bielaski had testified in January, the myth of the danger from German brewers was pretty well laid to rest. Instead of returning to its regular work, however, the Senate Subcommittee of the Judiciary decided that it might profitably extend its hearings to Bolsheviks. It filled page after page of the transcript with documents detailing the activities of radicals and Russian ex-patriots who were sympathetic to the cause of the Russian revolution. The probe went on through the spring but without encouragement from the Justice Department.

Gregory, who had gone to Paris as an unofficial observer of the Peace Conference, returned to preach domestic peace. While in Paris, he had discussed the Communist threat with Colonel House, and he told the North Carolina Bar Association on his return that the Bolsheviks were "in no sense a real menace to our government." They would doubtless attempt to do and would do "many outrageous things," he observed, "but they were not sufficiently numerous to do more than commit individual crimes. . . ." Gregory still defended the wartime use of APL volunteers, however, on the grounds that their surveillance had enabled him to avoid interning great numbers of aliens in response to demands by "fanatics." "*The price paid was eternal vigilance,*" he concluded.

As congressmen, governors, the Military Intelligence, and APL veterans rushed about in search of postwar crusades, O'Brian tried to finish up his war work. He wanted to return to his law practice in Buffalo, but he felt that a review of the prosecutions and internments by the Justice Department was more important. On February 5, 1919, Gregory and Secretary of Labor Wilson had urged Congress to grant them the power to deport interned and imprisoned aliens believed to be dangerous. However, O'Brian had told a law officer of the Bureau of Immigration, "We do not want that law to apply to persons who really ought now to be no longer interned." So he spent the early months of 1919 releasing all the men who had been interned for reasons "quite sufficient when the war was on" but whom he considered no menace to the peace. All but the one hundred and fifty aliens convicted for violations of wartime statutes and five hundred German seamen who refused repatriation had been released by April.

A second task O'Brian set himself was to review each prosecution under the Espionage Act, a review he claimed was without precedent. On his recommendation, President Wilson issued three pardons and 102 commutations. "The work," O'Brian wrote to Attorney General Palmer when he had finished on April 30, "I think, is regarded by the general public as a creditable job," and he had a "distinct regret" that he had not been able to review the IWW cases at Chicago, Sacramento, and Wichita, which had not been under the jurisdiction of his division. Not reviewing the IWW cases would put the Justice Department "in the attitude of deliberately failing to review convictions under the Espionage Act simply because the defendants were members of the IWW," an attitude at variance with the declaration that the Justice Department had prosecuted men only on the basis of personal guilt and not because of political or economic opinions. "Aside from the Debs and Stokes cases, these IWW convictions are the favorite illustration of alleged excessive and unwarranted sentences, and I still think it would have been wiser to have subjected them to the same treatment as the rest of the espionage cases," O'Brian concluded.

In April, 1919, it appeared that the only recourse of convicted men and women would be to executive clemency, for the Supreme Court continued to display an unwillingness to reverse decisions of the lower courts which had upheld the Executive in its decisions. In March the Debs case on which the APL had worked so long had come up for review, along with other wartime prosecutions under the Espionage Act of 1917. Oliver Wendell Holmes had approved the convictions. "I greatly regretted having to write [the decisions]," he admitted to his friend Harold Laski, "and (between ourselves) that the Government pressed them to a hearing." But he concluded, "On the only questions before us I could not doubt about the law," even though the federal judges had "got hysterical about the war." He hoped Wilson would do more pardoning. (Later, Zechariah Chaffee, while exonerating Holmes for his Debs decision, said, "We cannot rely on the Supreme Court as a safeguard against the excesses of war legislation." Trial judges and prosecutors are the main defenses, Chaffee concluded.)

O'Brian believed that the defense of civil liberties rested with the Justice Department, not with the courts at any level. He summed up his reflections in a Senate document published in the spring of 1919. "There is no other department of the Government whose activities during the war have more nearly affected the life and habits of the citizen," he wrote, "none has been so fully responsible for the protection of the constitutional and civil rights of the citizen." In reviewing the nation's wartime experience, he scoffed at the suggestion that the Central Powers had 200,000 spies in the United States. All the alleged spies had turned out to be men engaging in harmless activities. But he concluded that "this country had unquestionably a more efficient and better organized secret service than any other nation in the world."

This, of course, was the very place where O'Brian's vaunted defense of civil liberties broke down. He was unwilling to admit that he saw anything wrong with such a network of citizen counterespionage during wartime. Bielaski estimated that the total number of men—APL, state and local officials—engaged in defending the home front had been 700,000. And O'Brian applauded this policy of internal defense. The Justice Department had adhered to four principles, O'Brian said: no repression of political agitation unless directly affecting the state; enforcement of constitutional guarantees to life and property; opposition to arbitrary interference by military and naval authorities with the lives and habits of individual citizens; and protection of the innocent as well as punishment of the guilty. That these principles had been violated, O'Brian admitted; but he insisted that the violations, including the APL slacker raids in New York, were the acts of subordinates.

O'Brian did not say that the policy of using volunteers had been wrong. "No other nation came through the struggle with so little disorder and with so little interference with the civil liberty of the individual," he maintained. His only opposition to citizen espionage was in times of peace. "Organized espionage on a large scale is at variance with our theories of government," O'Brian concluded in a second article.

O'Brian's defense of the Justice Department ignored most of the difficulties with the APL and did not mention the wide reach of its activities. But O'Brian did enunciate principles for the safeguarding of civil liberties by the Department, the first time such a thing had been done. He attempted in the spring of 1919 to lay the foundation for greater attention to civil liberties in peacetime. He disbanded the War Emergency Division and recommended that Palmer oppose a new peacetime anti-sedition act. He saw to it that the APL was disbanded and not revived, and that the Bureau of Investigation was cut down to its pre-war size. The number of persons employed in the Justice Department as a whole steadily decreased from January to March 15, 1919. Overtures from the Immigration Bureau to the Bureau of Investigation to work in deporting IWW and anarchists received little encouragement from Palmer while O'Brian was still around. When O'Brian left the Justice Department on April 30, it seemed certain that the Justice Department would not return to its wartime policy of using APL volunteers.

War Plans White

John Lord O'Brian's influence on Justice Department policy and practice ended at precisely the time the Red scare began to gain momentum. On April 29, 1919, a servant of Senator Thomas R. Hardwick of Georgia had her hands blown off by a bomb packaged and addressed to the Senator. The following day a clerk in the Post Office discovered thirty-six similar packages addressed to Attorney General Palmer, Postmaster General Burleson, Secretary of Labor Wilson, and other government officials. Assuming radicals to have been responsible, soldiers, sailors, and APL veterans raided Socialist newspapers and broke up Socialist parades on May Day. In Cleveland the radical press accused the Loyal American League of starting the riot which left one person dead and forty injured. Loyal American League supporters retorted that the patriots had only been defending the Stars and Stripes.

Newspaper headlines described the bomb plots as Communist and anarchist inspired, thus bringing more demands that Palmer revive the APL to run down Bolsheviks. "It has struck me," wrote a veteran from St. Louis, "from what I read in the papers in connection with these bomb fiends, Bolsheviki, IWW's and other fiends, who do not seem to want to conform to our government or any other organized government or respect our glorious 'Stars and Stripes,' that it might not be a bad, in fact might be a splendid idea to revive the 'American Protective League' to assist and help in running down these opponents of our government and institutions, and individuals who seem to prefer some kind of a rag, red or black, in place of 'Old Glory.' ' "

Although in May Palmer had new indictments brought against a group of IWW's who had been imprisoned in Kansas since December, 1917, he still offered no encouragement to the APL. But some congressmen were less willing to spurn the veterans. On May 19 Representative Warren Gard of Ohio once more introduced a joint resolution "extending the thanks of Congress to all members of the American Protective League for services rendered the Government during the war." Prospects for a peacetime call to arms brightened.

Later that same month, more encouragement came in the form of thousands of copies of *The Web*, Emerson Hough's hastily assembled official history of the League. Many former divisions undertook distribution of the volumes and secured wide publicity for the organization.

Emerson Hough, official League historian, was an Iowan who had tried teaching school, practicing law, and writing for magazines before discovering the art of writing western novels which revolved around the physical conflict of man and man, against a backdrop of anti-intellectualism and suspicion of civilization. He had first joined the Chicago APL and was working in the Washington headquarters when the war ended. From brief summary reports submitted by about a hundred divisions, from letters of chiefs and interviews with the national directors, Hough concocted what the dust jacket of the book claimed to be "a revelation in patriotism." It was, more accurately, a revelation in nativism.

Instead of putting a period to League history, Hough urged members to renew the battle against the Hun by reshaping the whole concept of citizenship in America. Selective immigration, deportation of un-Americans, and denaturalization of "disloyal" citizens and anarchists comprised his basic program. Corollaries included proposed laws to deport interned aliens and aliens who failed to become citizens within a prescribed time. The study of German was to be eliminated from the schools; alien labor was to be barred and German goods boycotted.

Hough warned that bolshevism was blocking the peace parliaments of Europe and could come to America through the IWW, Socialists, or

The
Web

by

Emerson
Hough

A Revelation of Patriotism

The Story of
The American Protective League

How 250,000 American Business Men
Became Detectives to Help Win the War

Jacket design of *The Web*, official history of the
American Protective League, by Emerson Hough

the Non-Partisan League. He ended his long exhortation on the future duties of ex-members with a nativistic quotation from *The Passing of the American* by Monroe Joyce: "The curse these immigrants bring upon themselves is plainly to be seen, for it is immediate. They form a body incompatible with the healthy growth of this country.... They take the work and the bread out of the hands and mouths of native Americans, and the question of their means of living must soon become one of the most pressing and social problems of the day."

What had begun as a detective story ended as a rallying cry. "It is time for another oath, sworn indeed for the protection of America," Hough declaimed.

Conveniently, at the same time that veterans in the midwestern states received copies of *The Web*, they also received invitations from the Military Intelligence officer in Chicago. On May 28 Major Crockett addressed letters to all former state inspectors in his department asking again for information on radical activities. To secure this information, he assured the veterans, they need only talk to former APL associates and friends and collect information from local newspapers.

Up to this point, Palmer had maintained a scrupulously correct position regarding the APL veterans and their records. Even after O'Brian left the Justice Department, Palmer made few moves to translate his earlier militant pose against Germans into action against radicals. He said he was reorganizing the department, and in May he asked William Flynn, the flamboyant former head of the Treasury Department's Secret Service, to become the new chief of the Bureau of Investigation.

Then on the evening of June 2, someone tossed a bomb at the door of Palmer's home. The explosion so frightened Palmer that it restored his use of the Quaker "thee and thou," according to Franklin D. Roosevelt, who rushed over to offer assistance. But Palmer soon abandoned any Quaker pacifism. He was ready to fight. He asked Congress for an appropriation of half a million dollars "to build up an investigative force which will successfully cope with the criminal class in this country."

"Criminal class," it soon became evident, meant political radicals. Under attack as fomenters of violence, Communists and Socialists fought back by denouncing government wartime activities as ruthless. The Platform and Program of the Communist Labor Party accused the Justice Department of having licensed "anti-labor strike-breaking groups of employers—such as the National Security League, the

American Defense Society, the Knights of Liberty, the crushing of labor organization and all class activities of the workers, similar to that of the Black Hundreds in Russia." With the boasts of *The Web* at hand, the Socialist *New York Call* announced that the Justice Department had in fact commissioned the APL for anti-radical purposes, not for counterespionage.

A *Washington Post* editorial replied to the Socialists the following day by calling on the APL to help protect society against bombings. Chicago APL veteran I. D. Berg sent another offer to the local Military Intelligence office, putting his fifty-five operatives and officers at the MID's command. All of these men held honorable discharges from the League, Berg said. Meanwhile, Professor B. M. Brigman of the University of Louisville, anxiously wrote to Palmer, "In view of the past week's occurrences would it not be wise to recall the services of the American Protective League to assist your Department in ferreting out this new menace that threatens the Peace and Security of our country?"

Palmer didn't respond to the Kentucky professor's suggestion, but in Chicago, Crockett's assistant, John Campbell, contacted Berg at once, telling him of his "great pleasure" at receiving the offer and asking that a volunteer with a car report for duty each day for the next week or ten days to cover radical meetings.

The former state inspector for Nebraska, F. M. Pond, warned Crockett that the only way to combat the growing radicalism in the country was to call the APL back into existence and to clothe it with the official sanction of the federal government. Crockett sent the suggestion on to Churchill in Washington. Briggs had already received a Military Intelligence badge from Crockett. When he lost it on a train in early June, Crockett urged the Washington MID to help recover it. Everything possible was done to encourage the assistance of the old veterans. Churchill followed Palmer's path to Congress. He, too, wanted half a million dollars to continue his investigations.

Meanwhile, in Minneapolis the Committee of Thirteen was busily engaged in investigations. Still using the old APL letterhead proclaiming government status, the former chief was investigating for the Immigration Commissioner and the Naturalization Board, sending the information to the Justice Department. Over a hundred naturalization cases had been handled, but he was anxious to press for more. "If we are going to avoid trouble in the future similar to that which threatens us now from Red Radicals, this sort of work must be thoroughly done, so that we may be sure that these applicants, at the time the acid test was applied, were at heart real Americans," explained Charles D. Davis to Representative Walter H. Newton. To fill spare moments, the Minneapolis League veterans continued their vice work and investigations of army and navy veterans who, under a new Minnesota state law, were eligible for a bonus if they had been "loyal." The Committee's job was to prevent conscientious objectors from securing their fifteen dollar bonus.

Volunteers were also back in the field working for various states. In May the New York Senate's Judiciary Committee created a special committee under Senator Clayton D. Lusk to look into the role of New York radicals in the Russian Revolution. There was potential political profit in hunting Reds now, and Lusk organized his own secret service force to gather information. On June 12, 1919, it staged the first of its series of Red raids. Through his brother-in-law, William McDermid, former APL state inspector of New Jersey, Lusk was able to contact APL veterans. On June 21, forty of them joined the New York police and the state constabulary in raiding the Rand School of Social Science, the Socialist party, and the New York headquarters of the IWW.

Congress gave Palmer the half million dollars he had requested. On July 1, William Flynn became the new chief of the Bureau of Investigation, and Francis Patrick Garvan, in charge of intelligence for the Alien Property Custodian during Palmer's tenure, became his assistant. They found a young man named J. Edgar Hoover already in the Bureau and ready to fight radicals. This trio mobilized the Justice Department for battle against the Bolsheviks. By August 1, a new Anti-Radical Division had been created, with Hoover as its head.

Garvan had worked out a system with the Labor Department whereby Hoover's division would be notified of alien radicals who might deserve deportation. The Justice Department began to plan a giant drive to locate all radical aliens. On August 12, notice went out to all Bureau of Investigation agents to collect information on radicals from private individuals and companies, local, state, and military authorities. APL veterans dug out old reports, searched their memories for incriminating evidence, and offered their suggestions as to who might be a "Red."

Before the radical investigations were well under way, the Justice Department had already begun to change its attitude toward the APL veterans. In response to Republican pressure, Wilson had inaugurated a crusade against the high cost of living in early August. Palmer had recalled wartime federal food administrators and ordered Bureau of

Investigation probes into violations of wartime food laws still in effect. APL veterans volunteered to join the fight. From Pennsylvania came an offer to President Wilson from a former APL chief to help combat the "octopus human beings" who were keeping the cost of living high. An Assistant Attorney General expressed his appreciation for the veteran's offer and referred him to the federal food administrator for Pennsylvania. The United States Attorney in Kansas City accepted a similar offer of help in enforcing fuel conservation from APL veterans still operating under their old name.

But neither Wilson nor Palmer was willing to impose absolute control over prices. Consequently the investigations and prosecutions of food hoarders during the fall of 1919 did little to halt rising costs or to stem criticism of the Administration. Wilson gave only slight attention to the growing distress of workers caught in the vise of low wages and rising living costs. He continued to be preoccupied with foreign policy. On September 4, 1919, he left on a speaking tour to the West, the one cancelled a year earlier because of congressional criticism of the September slacker raids. He now went to the people to preach the necessity for ratification of the peace treaty. The speeches were eloquent in behalf of the League of Nations, but unfortunately, they ignored the conditions at home which would make it impossible to obtain support for such an international venture.

While repeatedly warning of the danger of revolution at home and abroad, Wilson failed to take domestic affairs into account. In the absence of effective price controls, the only solution for laborers was to strike for higher wages. No sooner had Wilson left Washington than the Boston police, unable to gain an increase in their minimum yearly wage of $1,100, walked out. State guardsmen were called up. Volunteer police were recruited. Massachusetts Governor Calvin Coolidge made himself a national hero with his retort to Samuel Gompers that there was "no right to strike against the public safety by anybody, anywhere, anytime." But the strikes continued.

Federal troops were alerted for strike duty; the Military Intelligence blossomed, having received $400,000 from Congress. By September 18 the counterespionage system in the Northeast had been reestablished in case federal troops would have to be sent to Boston. As MID agents sent in rumors and reports of threatened strikes from other areas, they received permission to reopen wartime offices and to enlist APL and other volunteers in undercover work. By the end of September, all large cities had resurgent Military Intelligence units.

Mobilization against the Bolshevik conspiracy in the United States began to replace the fervor of the late war. Americans were girding to defend their communities against radicals. So far, APL veterans had reorganized only locally; now they attempted to reorganize on a national basis. The former state inspector for Washington wrote to Frey (on old Minute Man stationery advertising its affiliation with the Justice Department) to announce that he was drafting a new national constitution for APL veterans. "The necessity is here, and it should, in the interest of American institutions and citizenship, be a going institution at the present time instead of just being talked of as we are," inspector W. A. Blackwood wrote. Such an organization, he continued, would give the government a friend in every community. He asked Frey and Elting to become officers in the new league.

Frey was noncommittal. He told Blackwood that such an organization would no doubt be very "successful" and asked for information concerning the new group, but he refused to commit himself to joining its hierarchy.

Meanwhile, Wilson consumed his energy in speeches. He spoke at Billings, Montana, on September 11: "We need peace more than we ever needed it before." At Helena, Montana, the same day he said, "The world is not fit to live in, my fellow-citizens, if any great government is in a position to do what the German Government did—secretly plot a war and begin it with the whole strength of its people, without so much as consulting its own people." He spoke at San Francisco on September 17: ". . . those Americans who are opposing this plan of the League of Nations offer no substitute"; and again at San Francisco the following day: "My fellow citizens, I believe in Divine Providence. If I did not, I would go crazy." And at Pueblo, Colorado, a week later: "There is one thing that the American people always rise to and extend their hand to, and that is the truth of justice and of liberty and of peace. We have accepted that truth and we are going to be led by it, and it is going to lead us, and through us the world, out into pastures of quietness and peace such as the world never dreamed of before." Those words ended the last public speech of the tour. That night he collapsed. He was rushed back to Washington, where a week later he suffered a stroke.

The Commander-in-Chief was out of the battle, but the home front war went on. Crockett and his assistant John B. Campbell stepped up their search for radical influence behind working-class restlessness. Crockett doubted, for example, that race riots in Elaine, Arkansas, and

Fort Omaha, Nebraska, could have sprung spontaneously from racial injustice. He preferred to look instead for radical fomenters. When intelligence reports from those cities were negative, he turned impatiently to the steel strike in Gary, Indiana, placing his agents and the volunteers at the disposal of the mayor.

In late September thousands of steelworkers had walked out in protest over low wages and long hours. It was the first steel strike since the ill-fated Homestead Strike in 1892, which had led to so much violence. The steel company claimed that radicals had caused the current strike, that they were being backed by anarchists, "Bolshevists," and IWW activists attempting to gain control of the American Federation of Labor. A Senate investigation hurriedly called to look into the strike agreed that "behind this strike there is massed a considerable element of IWW's, anarchists, revolutionists, and Russian soviets, and that some radical men not in harmony with the conservative elements of the American Federation of Labor are attempting to use the strike as a means of elevating themselves to power within the ranks of organized labor."

The Senate committee's solution was to recommend a law to deal with anarchists, revolutionists, and the IWW. Secretary of War Baker, meanwhile, took a remarkable step: upon the request of state legislatures, or of governors when the legislatures were not in session, army commanders were authorized to furnish troops without consulting the War Department. The old decentralization so conducive to violations of civil liberties during the war was setting in once again. A little over a year later, the Judge Advocate General would recommend revocation of the order, as it was "probably illegal"; but for a year the federal government worked for the states—and thereby for private industry—in putting down strikes.

Since December of 1918, Mayor W. F. Hodges of Gary had been concerned about radicalism in his city. Crockett had urged him to employ an undercover agent to work among the radicals and had kept his own agents and volunteers reporting on labor activities in Gary. The first few days of the steel strike passed quietly, but businessmen were edgy, and Crockett was, too. Company spies, MID operatives, and Bureau of Investigation agents began to infiltrate the ranks of strikers. As they did, dissension among the strikers grew. The more radical strikers—some of them actually agents—gained control. By October 3, Military Intelligence officers reported increasing tension and violence. Crockett reported that radicals were inciting Negroes against strike pickets and strikers against Negroes who returned to work. He expected race riots. The APL, reorganized as the American Patriotic League, sent Crockett scare reports. Its members secretly collected maps and laid out routes for the Army between Fort Sheridan, north of Chicago, and the steel city.

On October 4, violence came. Militiamen called into East Chicago, Indiana, and Gary could not quell the outbreaks. Open warfare occurred when strikers attempted to force their way into the United States Steel Corporation plant. Governor James P. Goodrich asked for federal troops, and on October 6 General Leonard Wood marched into Gary with fifteen thousand men.

Wood called a conference of city and county officials, Military Intelligence officers, and the Bureau of Investigation agent, then placed the city under what he called "modified martial law." His announced intention was to go after the radicals. Raids started immediately.

Former Chicago APL chief Robert Gunn came down to help organize volunteer assistance. American Patriotic League members and members of the Gary Citizens Committee, composed mostly of superintendents and foremen of the Gary steel mills and anyone else interested in being a vigilante, each received a list of alleged "Reds." Known members of the Socialist party were automatically included.

Raids were staged each morning between 12:30 and 5:00 A.M. Sleeping families were roused while locks were opened, bureaus ransacked. Anyone protesting was informed that the city was under martial law. Suspected radicals were hailed before a Military Intelligence officer to be questioned; some were jailed. The raids became nightly affairs, to the satisfaction of the mayor who, until the Military Intelligence intervened, had been unable to get the federal government to help him rid the city of Bolshevists.

On October 9, after raiding had gone on for three days, a Lieutenant Van Buren arrived in Gary as the representative of the Army Chief of Staff. With him he brought a stenographer, some more agents, several filing clerks—and files collected during the war. He commandeered an office, opened his files, and prepared to do business.

Van Buren found that the sheriff had sworn in volunteer deputies and had a little intelligence operation all his own. The police department, too, had sworn in volunteer policemen for the same purpose. That was all right, but it was confusing. Van Buren determined to act as a clearinghouse for all these little groups. He suggested they send their reports over to him so that he could compile a master card index on all radicals.

The following day, labor officials complained to Secretary of Labor

W. B. Wilson that Justice Department and Military Intelligence operatives were cooperating with steel company officials and detectives in their employ to intimidate workers and coerce them into returning to work, threatening aliens with deportation unless they returned. Wilson went to Palmer and Baker. The Bureau of Investigation disclaimed responsibility: its agents had ordered no arrests. APL veterans and other antiradical hunters had worked with the military, the Bureau said. Baker went to Churchill.

Meanwhile, in Gary, the Military Intelligence and the APL went on with their work. Alleged radicals rounded up on October 11 and 15 were taken to Lieutenant Van Buren for interrogation. According to the press, books, pamphlets advocating a "dictatorship of the workers," papers revealing a bomb plot, and a large cross painted red were among the objects confiscated.

After each raid, samples of radical literature went into Crockett's file; then reports went on to Washington, with predictions of radical revolution.

In response to Baker's inquiries, Churchill defended the actions of his subordinates in the Military Intelligence, insisting that operatives worked only in zones occupied by troops. He did order a quick investigation of his own, however, John Campbell replying for Crockett that MID men were not intimidating strikers, only interrogating suspected radicals; former APL chief Gunn was assisting as a civilian agent.

Churchill himself was fully convinced that Bolsheviks constituted a serious threat. On October 27, he recommended to General William G. Haan, Director of the War Plans Division of the War Department, that a program be developed and officers trained for handling "radical rebel groups" attempting to overthrow the government. In the meantime, where Military Intelligence officers were not available, recruiting officers were to be assigned to confidential investigations within the military and for liaison with APL veterans. An "Intelligence Reserve" was to be set up in the Quartermaster Corps.

By this time O'Brian's dictum regarding APL records was being totally disregarded. In August Senator Knute Nelson had appealed to Palmer for APL files for the Minneapolis Committee of Thirteen. At that time he received a polite "no." By October, however, when Representative Walter Newton of Minnesota requested access to the same records, he was told that state officials could obtain information in Washington APL files through regular channels. The Justice Department was no longer discouraging members from forming new units, nor was it holding sacrosanct the unreliable APL files.

It was in October, too, that Frey made his first anti-Red speech before the American Legion. Early in 1919 the American Legion had been formed in Paris by a group of soldiers who wanted to "preserve the history and incidents of our participation in war." As soon as the veterans returned to the home front, however, the anti-radical movement metamorphosed this modest historical goal into a crusade against un-Americanism. By the time the organization had adopted its official name in March, 1919, its constitution had been revised to dedicate the association not only to war history, but to defending the Constitution, maintaining law and order, fostering 100 percent Americanism, inculcating a sense of individual obligation to community, state and nation, combating autocracy, making right the master of might, transmitting the principles of justice, freedom, and democracy to posterity, and promoting peace and goodwill on earth.

Their first move toward promoting peace and goodwill was to demand that conscientious objectors not be pardoned for their refusal to fight. Then they turned their attention to the Bolsheviks.

As veterans of the home front, APL members were not eligible for membership in the American Legion, but they could offer their moral support and recommendations. However, by virtue of the army commission he had received in the early days of the APL, Frey could also speak as a military man. Addressing the Legion at Evanston, Illinois, he claimed that the Military Intelligence had cleaned up a nationwide German spy network at the beginning of the war. He knew what was necessary to stop postwar seditious propaganda, he told the Legionnaires. First, the Justice Department should be supported and enlarged. Then, stronger peacetime laws should be passed to deal with "agitators, radicals, bolshevists and undesirable aliens." As far as aliens were concerned, they should all be registered, as was required in France. They should be forced to become citizens if they wished to stay, but before becoming citizens, they should be obliged to read, write, and speak the English language. At this point in his speech Frey was interrupted by loud applause. Then he added, "And while I am on that point, we do not want any foreign publications."

Point four was an exhortation to all veterans to join the American Legion. "You returned soldiers have got the biggest fight on your hands you ever had. And you need a strong and unified organization to carry it on." He concluded, as a local newspaper put it, with a "thrilling appeal to the American Legion to get back of a movement to prevent the further spread of German and red propaganda in peace times," an appeal that brought cheers from the Legionnaires.

By November Palmer had stood idle long enough. The Communist party now boasted 75,000 dues-paying members and a million sympathizers. Congressmen were criticizing the Justice Department for inaction. No one in the Labor Department any longer counseled forebearance. Flynn and Hoover were anxious to fight radicals, and Palmer let them. Hoover recalled APL veterans, recruited local police, enlisted new volunteers, and planned attacks for New York, Chicago, Detroit, Philadelphia, St. Louis, Newark, New Haven, Hartford, and other cities. Raids on the offices of all foreign-born Communists inaugurated Palmer's spectacular postwar campaign against radicals that earned him his lasting reputation, eclipsing his earlier moderate stance. The New York Senate's Lusk Committee reacted to the new climate by rounding up two thousand radicals in seventy-one raids. Everyone was doing it.

Former APL members left out of the action complained to Palmer. The *New York Evening Telegram,* in an editorial under the banner "Our Silent Army," asked, "Why not revive the American Protective League to help deal with the Bolshevist situation here which Congress, the government generally, admits not only the existence but the menace of?"

In fact, chiefs were already being recalled to duty by the Military Intelligence for surveillance of radicals. Shortly after the November raids, Briggs sent the complete list of APL chiefs and their addresses to the MID in Washington. There the names and addresses were carefully copied, and on December 2 Colonel Coxe, head of the Negative Division, forwarded them, classified geographically, to intelligence officers throughout the country. Each chief was to be asked either to act as a correspondent for his community or to recommend a reliable person for the job. "It should be made perfectly clear that no attempt is being made by the military authorities to reorganize the American Protective League or to create an organization to conduct investigations of any kind," said Coxe. Members were only to report, not to conduct investigations or act as military agents.

Within the next few days letters went out to former chiefs asking their cooperation in supplying information. They were to furnish maps and strategic information to be used for troop movements. They were to report on radicals and Bolshevik agents. And they were asked to report on loyal organizations which might be counted upon to combat un-American activities and aid in preserving law and order in case the Army needed assistance. They were to keep their activities secret; for, as one intelligence officer said, radical agitators were disposed to misconstrue and criticize the collection of information by military authorities, however legitimate and proper it might be.

The response was gratifying. Long lists of names came back of APL veterans willing to serve once more. The Minneapolis chief wrote to Crockett that his boys were "fully equipped and ready for business," all members having been deputized by the Minneapolis police. The Missouri chief replied that the American Legion was taking care of the local situation, and that on twenty-four hours' notice complete maps and strategic information of any trouble spots could be furnished to the military. By December 15, just eight days after the request, replies had been received from nearly five hundred former APL members. All were enthusiastic and ready to serve. On December 30 Crockett dispatched Circular 65, asking for information on specific radical groups. One hundred and sixteen reports had already been received, he told the veterans, evidence that their desire to render patriotic service had survived the cessation of hostilities.

In December, 1919, the Supreme Court had a chance to encourage the Bolshevik hunt when it reviewed the Abrams case affecting Russian expatriates who had been convicted under the revised Espionage Act of 1918 for opposing American intervention in the Russian Revolution. A majority of the Court upheld the conviction. This time Justice Holmes spoke out strongly in defense of the right to dissent. "We should be eternally vigilant against attempts to check the expression of opinions that we loathe and believe to be fraught with death, unless they so imminently threaten immediate interference with the lawful and pressing purpose of the law that an immediate check is required to save the country." But only Brandeis supported Holmes's contention. The Justice Department was not deflected from the view that unpopular ideas posed a greater threat than did officially sanctioned subversion of civil liberties by 100 percent Americans.

A new raid was to be launched on an even grander scale than the raid of November. Picked APL veterans were to receive temporary, short-term commissions as special agents of the Bureau of Investigation. For example, the New Jersey state inspector and twenty of his men received three-day commissions. Undercover agents, in a massive strategy of entrapment, were to call meetings of the Communist party for January 2.

This time J. Edgar Hoover's troops were deployed among thirty-three cities. In Boston alone, the men temporarily enlisted numbered between three and five hundred. It was a "governmental mob," editorialized the *New Republic,* organized by Palmer in a "colossal conspiracy against constitutional rights."

The raids were the best guarantee that the Communist party would survive. The party was trimmed of its fair-weather fellow travelers and left with a hard core of sixteen thousand members whose persecution was to give them a cause célèbre for decades. But the raids also galvanized liberal opinion into something of a common front for the first time since the United States went to war. Technically, of course, the country was at war. Still, the armistice was in effect, and a group of prominent liberal lawyers who had backed the war machine now opposed the use of harsh wartime measures to stamp out radical dissent.

As far as the veteran Leaguers were concerned, Palmer's January raids led them into the arms of the waiting military. Chiefs from all over the United States were volunteering for intelligence duty. Forty-three former chiefs from California and eighteen from Idaho volunteered in January, along with the California state inspector who had fought so hard in December of 1918 to disband the League.

The Bureau of Investigation and the Military Intelligence Division were now in a position to terrorize not only radicals, but those liberals who protested, as well. J. Edgar Hoover asked Marlborough Churchill to check his records for evidence that critics of Attorney General Palmer were affiliated with the radicals or had assisted the IWW in any way during the war. Card indexes were compared, new files set up. Defenders of dissent became more suspect than dissenters themselves. Few men had the courage to speak out against the white terror.

Gregory was strangely silent. Bielaski was, too. The most charitable view is that, having vacated their posts, they were loathe to criticize the methods of their successors. But O'Brian and George Anderson objected when the New York Legislature attempted to unseat Socialist assemblymen. "This discussion has been entirely irrelevant," O'Brian told the New York State Bar Association. "The only thing here involved is the ancient and well-established Anglo-Saxon principle of fair play." Obviously, even the principle was not so well established. George Anderson went on to liken the new terror to the war hysteria over German spies. "I doubt the 'Red' menace having more basis in fact than the pro-German peril ... many of the same persons and newspapers that for two years were faking pro-German plots are now promoting 'The Red Terror.'" The *Survey*, a magazine for social workers, placed O'Brian and Anderson in their gallery of "Keepers of the Faith." The Senate's Lusk Committee in turn denounced The *Survey* as having the support of "revolutionary groups." The five Socialist members of the legislature were expelled.

Even senators who tried to find out what was going on within the Justice Department were rebuffed by Palmer. Senator Morris Sheppard of Texas wrote to ask if it was true that, as a speaker had recently claimed, the federal government had thirty thousand spies in the field. He also inquired how many spies it had during the war.

"It has long been the practice of the Department to hold as confidential, information concerning the number and identity of its agents," Palmer replied curtly. Certainly not thirty thousand, Palmer went on, for the Justice Department had used the APL, which was disbanded immediately upon the signing of the armistice.

By the spring of 1920, the home front war had degenerated into guerilla warfare, waged by the federal government and its former volunteer allies. In the violence of the strikes, the government's forces had been manipulated into an anti-labor stance, dissent had been labeled Communist subversion and rebellion, and the old reform movement had been torn to shreds in the tug-of-war between labor and capital. Wilson had been ill for six months and was unable to act. He could only cling to his vision of world order.

Wilson's Attorney General meanwhile joined his anti-radical crusade to a political program, beginning early in February 1920, to ready his department for the political role he wished it to play in the coming Democratic presidential nominating convention. Denunciation of Reds had now replaced denunciation of Germans as his rallying cry. He puffed and blew on the dying embers of the Bolshevik conspiracy, hoping to light his own path to the presidency.

But even men within the Military Intelligence were beginning to have qualms about pursuing the phantoms of conspiracy any longer. One of these, Gardner Harding, asked Churchill to scrutinize the activities of his agents more carefully to see that hunting radicals and liberals did not become their main preoccupation. If investigations into the civilian population were to continue, he asserted, they should include capital as well as labor. He noted that the Chicago office particularly was the source of reports bitterly biased against labor. Should not the Military Intelligence be discouraged from peacetime spying and confine its activities purely to collecting strategic information, he queried. Should not the Justice Department, even with its political orientation, be the chief peacetime collector of domestic intelligence?

Others in the Division countered that the Justice Department's job was prosecution, while the Army had to be prepared for domestic rebellion. Any question of how Churchill felt was settled by an article appearing in April, 1920, in the *Journal of the United States Artillery*. The use of troops in disturbed areas had made the continued investigational activities of the MID necessary, he said. "We had to stay in the field, but it was necessary to remember that our government is based on the principle that military authority in time of peace is subordinate to civil authority." Then he described the peacetime situation as he saw it: "Theoretically, the civilian investigational agencies, the Department of Justice and the Secret Service of the Treasury, should find out everything there is to know and should tell us. Practically, they at present work under almost insuperable difficulties which tend to complicate the situation and make almost impossible the normal relation between civil and military authority."

Was the Military Intelligence with its APL watchdogs to remain in the field permanently, then? Apparently Churchill thought so, for the Gary incidents of September, 1919, were repeated in the Butte, Montana, strike of May, 1920. As usual, on that occasion Military Intelligence and their volunteers demanded that the government impose martial law, convinced as they were that strikers were radicals and revolutionaries who should be stamped out so that order could be restored. The Military Intelligence agents then bred the very disorder that allowed the vigilantes to pose as guardians of the peace. Politicians who wanted the federal government to suppress strikes so that they could maintain the support of capital without completely alienating labor found the system convenient.

Fear within the War Department that the radical danger was "not a transitory affair," but likely to be present "as a permanent feature to be reckoned with," culminated in "War Plans White." The effect of intelligence on military strategy was never more evident than in this plan concocted to deal with an expected uprising of labor and radicals.

Then in May, 1920, Congress attempted to declare the war at an end. The country was now ready for peace. Suddenly even the white terror had ended. Although a shattered Wilson sat amid the wreckage of reform and of party and called Debs a "traitor to his country," the war was over at home as well as abroad.

Palmer adopted a go-slow policy toward prohibition enforcement between January and the 1920 Democratic Convention. He continued to prosecute men for wartime activities in an effort to regain his popularity, but he lost his enthusiasm for that cause, too, after being defeated at San Francisco in his bid for the Democratic nomination.

The Radical Division of the Justice Department remained intact, and surveillance of a few groups like the National Civil Liberties Bureau continued. But when Palmer left office in 1921, the crusades of the Justice Department were over.

Technically, the war had not ended but a few people questioned the activities of the APL volunteers and charged the government with the responsibility. A New Orleans woman whose husband had been run down and killed by the driver of an APL car bearing federal license plates took her complaint to the War Department. The Adjutant General labeled the accident a result of "military operations" and shooed the woman to her congressman for redress. Senator Joseph E. Ransdell of Louisiana took up her cause, inquiring of Secretary of War Baker as to the extent of moral responsibility assumed by the government for acts of the League. In response to Baker's inquiries, Charles Weinberger, former APL chief for New Orleans, explained that the license plates on the APL cars were among the "special privileges" given to him as an APL chief. The Adjutant General scrawled across Weinberger's reply: "By whom!" But the War Department admitted no responsibility. Secretary Baker wrote Senator Ransdell at the end of April, 1921, "The War Department was in no way responsible for the fact that the automobile concerned in the accident in question was operated under a United States license plate. Mr. Weinberger, representative of the American Protective League in New Orleans, was responsible solely to the Department of Justice and did not act under the authority or control of the War Department." The Justice Department had, of course, already disavowed all responsibility for League activities. The case was quietly closed.

The Republicans who came into office in April, 1921, showed no interest in encouraging the volunteers. At first, the new Secretary of War, John W. Weeks, announced a drive to round up unpunished draft evaders and deserters. Chicago APL member A. H. Schroth offered to check into wartime activities of certain Democrats, something he claimed he had been prevented from doing under the Wilson Administration. But in July Congress finally declared the war ended and the Secretary of War lapsed into peacetime repose.

Republican Attorney General Harry M. Daugherty was more interested in California oil than in crusades. During 1924, most of the remaining wartime indictments against radicals were dismissed, and the Justice Department was allowed to wallow in corruption. The new Bureau of Investigation chief, William J. Burns, asked for money to fight radicals and sometimes used his own private detective agency for their surveillance, but without the support of the Attorney General he was unable to mount any major offensive against them.

In 1924, Harlan Stone replaced Daugherty and promptly instructed the Bureau of Investigation to confine its investigations to violations of the law. Agents were to discontinue many of their questionable investigative tactics, including wiretapping. Burns resigned and Hoover, who became the new chief, promised to abide by Stone's dictates. By 1925 there were only three hundred agents working for the Bureau of Investigation, and the number was declining. Hoover had convinced even the American Civil Liberties Union, successor to the National Civil Liberties Bureau, that he had been an unwilling participant in the Palmer raids. The ACLU became a staunch defender of the Bureau of Investigation.

As late as 1924 Military Intelligence officers were being instructed to maintain friendly relations with former APL members as well as other counterradical groups who might be called upon in time of trouble. Counterespionage investigations had been discontinued, but questionnaires were being sent out to collect information on domestic affairs. A few men in the Military Intelligence realized that the MID's roving activities among the civilian population had given them an "evil reputation" that they must live down by scrupulously avoiding civilian investigations in the future. One book on Military Intelligence, published in 1924, alarmed some officers because it told how the secret service of the general staff had operated far beyond military limits. But 1924 marked the end of anti-radical activity for both the War Department and the Justice Department.

The War Department under Secretary of War Dwight F. Davis, lapsed into virtual inactivity. Disarmament talks were being held. Military Intelligence men came to the conclusion that there would be no more war. APL files, along with wartime investigation reports, were placed in dead storage; many other documents were destroyed. Training of Military Intelligence officers practically ceased. In 1929, Secretary of State Henry Stimson even closed down the army decoding section. "Gentlemen," he said, "do not read other people's mail."

Word of the old APL veterans still reached the Justice Department occasionally. APL badges, meant to be souvenirs, were carried around by vets. In Boise, Idaho, police arrested a man for some violation of a local ordinance, and the state district attorney notified the Attorney General that the prisoner had in his possession a badge identifying him as an investigator for the Justice Department. As late as 1927 a League veteran, L. O. Rice of Warren, Ohio, wrote to the Justice Department, "I never received any discharge so must still be in the service, this I hope is so, for this City needs a clean up and I would like to do my bit, liquor, gambling, and houses of prostitution are in full force. Will you please inform me if I am still in the service, and if the above does not come under your Department that I may be transferred to the proper department."

Most former APL members still interested in sleuthing turned to private organizations rather than to the federal government. William Simmons, mastermind of the KKK, planned to make his group into a super-spy system, a private organization to "clean up America" and to turn over information to the Justice Department to help enforce the law. His idea, he said later, came from the Atlanta APL. He had been a member of an APL auxiliary in Atlanta called the Citizen's Bureau of Investigation, and the secrecy of the APL had given him the idea that the KKK should also be secret.

If the Klan was not always able to recruit APL veterans, it was able to adopt its techniques. Vigilante activities by the Klan in the South and Southwest, especially between 1920 and 1922, before the organization went into politics, were preceded by secret investigations. Each local Klan had a Nighthawk whose sole function was to probe the backgrounds of prospective members and to ferret out community wrongdoers. Klans in Texas had elaborate spy systems, surveillance squads, and regular reports on suspects. Phones were tapped, telegraph messages intercepted, and spies stationed in post offices. A new, sinister dimension had been added to the older vigilante tradition of the KKK. War hysteria and the APL example had opened new vistas to groups specializing in suppression of minorities.

It is not possible to determine how many APL members became KKK members during its flourishing from 1920 to 1924. In New Orleans, where the APL had been dominated by Jewish members and a sprinkling of Catholics, former members would have lined up against the Klan. But in the smaller backwoods areas where native white Protestant Anglo-Saxons had dominated the League, the Klan became in a way a perpetuation of the League.

Many of the same projects which had attracted men to the APL attracted some of them to the Klan. In the Southwest the KKK continued the moral crusades begun by the APL against bootleggers and prostitutes. The Atlanta Klan had already joined in APL hunts for slackers, bootleggers, and prostitutes; with war over they dedicated themselves anew to "cleaning up" communities by protecting morals, the very activity that the national directors had fought to keep APL members out of during the last year of the war. Hundreds of thousands of Americans joined these Klan crusades, not primarily to attack the Negro, the Jew, or the Catholic, but to chastise the errant white Protestant who swerved from the principles of chastity and sobriety. Otherwise, the Klan could never have survived outside the South.

In much of the country, the Klan took these crusades into politics in 1923. After failing in its attempt to have McAdoo nominated for the presidency in 1924, the Klan became primarily a pressure group preaching against "Rum and Romanism." It had practically died before its last campaign of bigotry against Catholic presidential candidate Al Smith. Then dissension and lack of interest in fraternal organizations liquidated the KKK almost everywhere but in the South.

One more organization appealed to APL veterans for members: the Civil Legion. In 1926, Frank Comerford, Chicago lawyer and opponent-of-corruption-turned-Bolshevik-hunter, devoted himself to the cause of professional patriotism by organizing a Civil Legion, planned as the civilian counterpart of the American Legion. Comerford sought out old APL members, levied dues of five to fifty dollars, and drafted a bill for Congress providing for incorporation similar to that of the American Legion, its program—national preparedness. But it soon languished.

The real epilogue to the League came with the bogus medal episode of 1923. More than anything else, it revealed a significant change in the general attitude toward "100 percent Americanism." In the popular mind, patriotism had become a cloak for scoundrels, and superpatriotism was now a joke, as the three veteran national directors were to learn.

On May 8, 1923, at an impressive ceremony at Chicago's Blackstone Hotel, Charles Daniel Frey and A. M. Briggs received medals from the French government for their part in winning the war. Perhaps Elting's keen perception enabled him to sense something off-key about this gracious gesture; his wife's illness kept him from attending, he said.

A month later newsmen, discovering that the whole affair had been engineered by a gassed doughboy who wanted to feel important, turned the incident into an *opéra bouffe*. The *Chicago American* spoofed the consternation of the French Consul, M. Barthelemy: "What to say to these so grand Chicagoans when they learned that M. Boisumeau [the doughboy] had no more business conferring medals than he, M. Barthelemy, had conferring decorations to an Eskimo in the name of Tut of Egypt."

When the French government decided to replace the bogus medals with authentic ones, editors were enraged. "Why," queried one, "is the 'honor' of the French government so sensitive when no money is involved and so imperious when Uncle Sam tries to collect his long overdue billions? Luckily, there is no sign that Secretary Mellon is willing to accept any French decorations." A generation which insisted that debtors always pay their bills could hardly understand the pride with which Frey always regarded the document which he received from the French Minister of Foreign Affairs. It read simply, "Charles Daniel Frey, an American, Advertising Agent. For distinguished and devoted services rendered to the French cause."

Legacy of the League

The existence of the League depended originally upon the assumption that Germany was conspiring to subvert the American government by clandestine means and upon the belief that the best way to meet this menace was by a volunteer counterconspiracy organized by the federal government.

Like almost everyone else, Wilson accepted the conspiracy thesis. Like almost everyone else, he seemed to think only a spy could catch a spy. Thus he allowed the counterconspiracy to flourish. Once organized, the counterconspirators could, predictably, develop a vested interest in their own perpetuation, and continuing to publicize the threat of subversion proved a surefire method. The Justice Department, in warding off criticism from other departments, chose to emphasize its vigilance; it felt under no obligation to demolish the conspiracy theory. And so it was that the United States, in fighting for democracy, came more and more to resemble Germany in its methods.

At first, it was difficult for progressive historians schooled in the conspiracy theory to see the home front war in terms different than the Wilson Administration had used to describe it. Men like Charles Beard tended to look at politics as a conspiratorial process in which "real" historical processes were masked by abstractions. But at first such historians applied the conspiracy theory only to Germany. As Beard said in October, 1918, when appealing for subscribers to the fourth Liberty Loan, the Germans had been engaged in a "forty years conspiracy against the democratic nations of the earth." He sounded much as Wilson had in his speech asking Congress for a declaration of war.

Few historians questioned Beard's theory then. Jeremiah O'Leary condemned the APL for its illegal activities in his bitter political memoirs written in 1919, but reformers at first accepted the same rationalization as Hough for the necessity of the League. Florence Finch Kelly, a novelist turned booster of the Wilson Administration, proclaimed the APL a "unique development of the situation and in spirit and methods thoroughly characteristic of the American people." The League, she said, had been "born out of a realization of the danger the country faced, overrun as it was with enemy agents directed by some of the most skillful intriguers and spy captains that a nation specializing in spying and intrigue had been able to train, and out of the loyal wish to serve." She estimated that from 200,000 to 300,000 German agents and their volunteers were in the United States during the war. Thus a comparable number of American operatives was not only legitimate but necessary.

But disillusionment among reform historians came swiftly. When suppression of dissent continued, when radicals continued to be harassed, arrested, and prosecuted, when to label someone a Bolshevik was to discredit him as effectively as had a pro-German label a few months before, the progressive historians became a bit more skeptical about applying the conspiracy theory even to Germany. Carl Becker, who had supported the war, expressed this feeling in the summer of 1920. The war, he wrote, was "the most futile, the most desolating and repulsive exhibition of human power and cruelty without compensating advantage that has ever been on earth," the result of "thousands of years of what men like to speak of as 'political, economic, intellectual and moral Progress.'" "The death knell of American liberalism was sounded the minute its false leader put it into the war," commented the editor of *The Nation*. As intellectual Harold Stearns shrewdly remarked in *Liberalism in America,* Wilson had silenced his critics by putting them in the government. "There was one period," Stearns wrote, "when in self-protection one had to pretend one was on some mysterious mission in order to avoid the suspicion of one's friends that one was in the secret service."

Within a few years the pendulum had swung completely. It became popular to accept the thesis that Americans had been "taken in," had been "gulled" by seductive lies and deceptions. War at home and abroad had been a hoax. Historians who rejected the tenets of this revisionism risked being classed as allies of the proponents of 100 percent patriotism.

Reform historians felt more comfortable once the conspiracy theory had been reestablished as an explanation for American history. The onetime pro-war historian Harry Elmer Barnes headed the march toward revisionism in the United States with the argument that pro-Allied sympathies of the Wilson Administration had led the country into war. Others attributed the cause of America's entrance to economics, to propaganda, or to inept statesmanship.

Applied to the home front war, the conspiracy theory meant that the men in charge of the Justice Department had been reactionaries who had subverted liberalism during the war. Disillusioned radicals applied the theory boldly. Soon after the war, Socialist Upton Sinclair had written in *The Brass Check*, "The spy-system which the government developed for the war has been turned against the radicals." According to Louis Adamic, a close student of radicalism in America, former federal detectives had gone into industrial espionage and helped to stir up hysteria after the war. Literary radical John Dos Passos wrote in *1919*, "At the Harvard Club they're all in the Intelligence Service making the world safe for the Morgan-Baker-Stillman combination of banks." Reform historians took up the same theme.

Almost a decade of peace passed, however, before Charles Beard published his version of the conspiracy theory. In *The Rise of American Civilization* he wrote a searing indictment of the Justice Department. "Judging by its official reports," Beard said, "the main business of the Department was not the apprehension of the people who gave aid and comfort to the Central Powers with which the country was at war but rather the supervision of American citizens suspected of radical opinions about the perfection and perpetuity of the capitalist system of economy at home." According to "authentic" evidence, he continued, "tools" were planted among organizations of "humble working people, supposed to have dangerous tendencies, and were instructed to incite them to unlawful acts; meeting places . . . were raided without proper warrant, property was destroyed, papers seized, innocent bystanders beaten, and persons guilty of no offense at all rushed off to jail, subjected to police torture, held without bail, and released without recourse."

Beard went on, "To the official army of the grand inquest was added a still greater force of more than two hundred thousand private citizens enrolled by the Department of Justice in the work of watching neighbors. To these volunteers no test of intelligence or efficiency was applied; any person, man or woman, willing to play the role of informer was admitted to the fellowship. So in offices, factories, mines, mills, churches, homes, schools, restaurants, trains, ships, ferries, and stores, government watchers could be found listening to conversations, insinuating and suggesting, noting prattle and tattle, and reporting 'findings' to Washington to be filed in huge dossiers of 'information'—recalling the fateful days of 1692 in Salem."

From all this activity, Beard finished, not a single first-class German spy or revolutionary workingman was caught and convicted of an overt act to give direct aid or comfort to the enemy. The only result was that the conservatives had been given an opportunity to blacken the character of persons whose opinions they feared and hated. Beard had not mentioned the APL by name, but his "private citizens" became a part of the general story of wartime suppression.

Except for some historians who remained loyal to Wilson during the 1920's, few quarreled with Beard's interpretation. Now even politicians like Oscar W. Underwood condemned the Wilson War Administration for its wartime spy system. The "so-called intelligence bureaus," he said in his memoirs, had accomplished but little on this side of the Atlantic Ocean, "except to prejudice the minds of the people against the German Empire and its people."

While reformers and intellectuals condemned the whole principle of counterespionage during World War I, some APL veterans held to their convictions through the 1920's and into the Depression era, when fear of subversion began to revive. One such veteran wrote to the Justice Department from Wichita Falls in 1932 to say, "I cannot help but beleive that the present time would be a good time to reorganize that League as with all the unrest and propogander that is being circulated I beleive thay would get results" [sic].

But faith in the basic loyalty of most Americans had become firmly enough rooted during the years of peace to offset the few demands that civilian volunteer counterespionage be revived. As the United States approached the brink of another world war, civil libertarians pointed to the APL as a mistake which should not be repeated. Carl Swisher termed APL members "untrained and undisciplined" and predicted that J. Edgar Hoover, by then Director of the Federal Bureau of Investigation, would probably "not be content to use the undisciplined and uncoordinated services of an American Protective League which engaged in witch hunting during the war."

There was evidence to support this prediction. For years Hoover had been replying to inquiries about the APL that it had never been a part of the Justice Department and that he would supply no information on it. One Florida Leaguer who lost his badge, which he had been carrying around for years as a "pocket piece," wrote to ask Hoover where he might have a duplicate made. Hoover gave his usual reply, and the old vet complained to Attorney General Homer Cummings that the Director had "showed as much interest and appreciation as tho I was a communist." In view of the work the APL had done for the Justice Department, he went on, work which it had gladly accepted, Hoover's lack of attention made him "sore as a pup." Cummings didn't reply.

Swisher was right about Hoover. When the United States did enter World War II, APL vets were ready to defend the home front once more. Cecil B. DeMille and others offered their services, only to be rejected abruptly by Hoover. John Lord O'Brian, who returned to Washington to advise the Roosevelt Administration on internal security measures at the beginning of the war, endorsed Hoover's views and supplied enough information about his difficulties with the APL in World War I to quickly convince Attorney General Francis Biddle and President Roosevelt that they must rely on Hoover's professional agents for counterespionage. When a former New Jersey APL state inspector stopped in to chat with Hoover during the war, Hoover openly condemned the APL. According to the director of the FBI, counterespionage was the proper province of a small group of highly trained and organized professionals rather than a diversion for volunteers.

In the climate of preparation for another war, criticism of the government's actions during World War I diminished. As for the Military Intelligence, the public assumed that it had operated mainly in Europe. Many historians concluded that the Justice Department had done a good job on the home front. A debate between liberal historians George Mowry and Max Lerner ended in essential agreement that vigilante action had come from local groups and that the federal government was a force for restraint. Even greater excesses might have occurred, they concluded, if the government had not acted to defend civil liberties. H. J. Tobin charged lapses to "overenthusiasm" for the war. "Public opinion," he said, had been responsible for suppressing dissent impatiently and sometimes violently. The federal government and its officials were exonerated, and the APL condemned.

Civil liberties for most Americans—if they were not of Japanese origin—were well defended during World War II, and even the Japanese found strong defenders east of the Rocky Mountains. Partly, this defense resulted from the pro-war stance of most radicals, including Communists. It derived partly from influential newspapers and individuals defending dissent because of the World War I experience and partly from knowledge of vicious suppression of civil liberties in Germany and the resolution of the government and the American people to uphold these freedoms at home. Mainly, though, civil liberties survived intact in World War II because the Justice Department did not have to compete with the states or with other federal departments in its hunt for subversives and because it did not encourage volunteer spy-catching. Thus the impulse to stamp out dissent and abridge civil liberties was kept under control.

On the whole, conscientious objectors were wisely and sympathetically handled, and loyalty and security investigations were carefully controlled. Nevertheless, denaturalization proceedings were processed hastily enough by the Justice Department to cause consternation among civil libertarians, and the suppression of newspapers and publications by refusal of mailing privileges was a major concern. But despite talk of spies and the investigation of twenty thousand suspected cases of sabotage, few people were prosecuted as Nazi sympathizers under the new sedition legislation passed in 1940, the Smith Act.

Then, as American civil libertarians were congratulating themselves on the home front record in World War II, postwar skirmishes began to break out between dissenters and subversion-hunters. Some said Truman's Loyalty Program started the new battle in March, 1947, by encouraging the ferreting out of those suspected of "sympathetic association" with subversive groups. Some saw the cause in the attempt of Congress to reassert its leadership through a stepped-up program of subversive-activities investigations. Certainly, it started long before that day in February, 1950, when Senator Joseph McCarthy waved a little list and said it contained the names of 205 Communists working in the State Department. Most likely it started in 1946 when rivalry broke out again between the federal investigative groups.

Interservice rivalry should have been eliminated by the establishment in 1947 of the Central Intelligence Agency, which was given the responsibility of advising the President directly on foreign intelligence.

But the CIA did not displace the old intelligence groups; it simply became an independent super-spy agency. The FBI was permanently withdrawn from foreign intelligence, but it was not required to report its domestic intelligence to the CIA. The CIA, in turn, was to stay out of domestic intelligence.

There seemed to be a clear-cut division between intelligence at home and abroad, but in reality the CIA merely became a new capstone for the old intelligence pyramid. Existing agencies kept their interest in subversives, and each built up its own force of backbenchers who could be depended upon for support when appropriations were needed from Congress or when interference from other groups threatened its jurisdiction. Tips were given out when necessary, interest feigned where helpful, articles published to stir up interest in what each team was doing in the spy hunt. It began to look very much like World War I all over again.

Soon the activity of the federal government and the publicity of its spy hunt began to entice ultraconservatives into action. Fear of leaving the field to right-wingers pushed reformers—now labeled liberals—into an anti-subversive stance. Most liberals were not really convinced of the internal menace from Communism, but they were convinced of the internal menace from reactionaries. Many feared Communism abroad; most felt that tighter restrictions upon Americans at home could be a symbolic act of faith in an election year.

The arrest of the Rosenbergs as Russian spies seemed proof, to the fearful and to those who despaired of America's ability to survive criticism, that disloyalty could come from the least expected persons. To the sedition legislation of 1940 was added the Internal Security Act of 1950—sponsored by liberals—which gave heart to those who felt civil liberty to be less important than conformity. All over the country civilians volunteered to ferret out subversives for the Bureau of Investigation.

Suppression of dissent gained in popularity. The Justice Department and Hoover might have helped restrain the growing hysteria, but, as in World War I, encouragement rather than restraint came from Washington. Despite Hoover's earlier condemnation of the APL, he did not hesitate to exhort the public to help the FBI by reporting neighborhood subversives. All the patriots who had languished during World War II mobilized during the Korean War. A new horde of voluntary counterspies was unleashed on the American people. They were not organized as an auxiliary of the Justice Department, but Hoover's request for aid encouraged them to form private intelligence units wherever they wished and to stalk whomever they feared. Organizations like the Veterans of Foreign Wars undertook to investigate neighbors and to assemble card files on all persons suspected of disloyalty. These groups were soon joined by military men and exploited by politicians. The game of "I spy" once again became a national pastime.

As the Communist scare spread, radicals attacked the FBI, seizing upon World War I activities as evidence for alarm. Max Lowenthal concluded that the Bureau should never have been allowed to chase spies at all during World War I, that Secret Service agents were much better trained for the work, and that other intelligence groups had done most of the real work anyway. He used the slacker raids as an example of the infringement of civil liberties by Bureau of Investigation agents.

On the other hand, O'Brian, still alive and still concerned with civil liberties, defended not only the Bureau but its use of the APL. During the war, he maintained, APL men had "sometimes performed detective service high in quality and results," and they had accomplished good results in patrolling and protecting munition plants and harbor fronts and running down draft dodgers. He urged that someone write the real story of the home front in World War I.

J. Edgar Hoover didn't agree with O'Brian. When radicals attacked the FBI, he attempted publicly to disassociate his organization from the APL. Leaguers had been little more than vigilantes, author Don Whitehead implied in his history of the FBI for which Hoover wrote an approving foreword.

Rediscovery of the APL in the 1950's deflected criticism of the FBI, for liberal historians saw centralized, controlled intelligence as the only protection against irresponsible anti-subversive activities on the part of local officials and volunteer sedition hunters. The APL came to be regarded as a unique group, symbolic of the wrong way for the government to use private citizens to suppress dissent. But no one at that time knew enough about the APL to go from criticism of the consequences to analysis of the reasons for using the volunteers. More careful attention to the interplay of national, state, and local organizations devoted to uncovering subversion might have provided some clues.

Meanwhile, the search for the enemy within continued. Private patriotic groups pledged to defending the home front from subversion were far from dead in the early 1960's. McCarthy may have been gone, but his supporters were still active. Best known of the national security groups—aside from the security committees of the Daughters of the American Revolution and the American Legion—was the Chicago-based American Security Council. The ASC announced that the country was already engaged in World War III, a war it defined as one which Russia was waging by subversion and one which the federal government could not fight alone. "Business concerns, private citizens and private groups must fill this gap in our defenses," warned one of its brochures. Lamenting the fact that federal intelligence agencies' files were confidential, the ASC developed its own subversive files. Its published aim was "to gather and disseminate facts concerning the International Communist Conspiracy."

Into these massive files of the ASC went all sorts of material. According to Tristram Coffin, commentator on American militarism, the nucleus for the collection was supplied by a right-wing newspaper called the *American Vigilante*, a former congressman, and private investigators. Former FBI men cooperated, sometimes informally, sometimes by filling executive positions.

Based on these files came publications for ASC members—newspapers, colleges, foundations, banks, defense industries. According to the ASC, thirteen hundred companies joined in 1960. Texas and California had in that year respectively 134 and 144 companies as dues-paying members. For thirty to ninety dollars a year, depending on the size of the company, members received publications like the *ASC Newsletter*, which provided "internal security information and a behind-the-scenes view of what the Communist Party, USA, is really up to," and the *ASC Washington Report*, edited by Admiral Chester Ward, which reported on "national and international developments affecting the nation's security." For an additional fee, special reports were furnished on individuals for personnel screening programs.

The ASC not only provided intelligence on "the Communist Conspiracy," but it also provided speakers to alert high school students and other groups to the Red menace. During 1960, it distributed to member companies over one hundred copies of the movie "Operation Abolition" which, it said, showed "the Communist-Party-organized student riots against the House Committee on Un-American Activities in May, 1960." Former FBI agent W. C. Skousen, author of *The Naked Communist*—in a seventh edition with teacher's manual by 1961—took charge of high school and college speaking tours, while Admiral Ward was the star of the Speaker's Bureau, often telling audiences, as he did in Pittsburgh, that negotiations with Russia on disarmament were "appeasement." An old friend of Joseph McCarthy, General Albert C.

Wedemeyer, and former Chairman of the Joint Chiefs of Staff Admiral Arthur W. Radford shared speaking tours of duty with Admiral Ward.

Wedemeyer also rode the California Christian Anti-Communist Crusade circuit. Not as businesslike or as military-minded as the ASC, the CACC preached an evangelistic attack on the "Communist Conspiracy," sweeping into its ranks scores of religious fundamentalists who learned only that Communism was the personification of evil and their chief enemy in life. Like the ASC, the CACC operated on the premise that "Both governmental and nongovernmental action is necessary." Its self-appointed purpose was to establish schools to instruct citizens in the "deceitful techniques and objectives of Communism." Fred Schwarz, its president, announced that "the enemy is the world Communist conspiracy with its godless philosophy and its program of human enslavement." For a time he appeared at "national security" seminars sponsored by the Defense Department.

Finally the activities of the CACC became so notorious that California Attorney General Stanley Mosk, in February, 1962, told a television audience that the Crusade was "not a school but a promotion," and went on to call the movement "Patriotism for Profit," its leaders "entrepreneurs of indignation" and "apostles of despair."

Besides national organizations like the ASC and state groups like the CACC, the Communist scare spawned new local anti-subversive intelligence agencies like the San Diego Research Library. Colonel Ralph Van Dieman, former head of the Military Intelligence, retired from the Army in 1928 and settled in San Diego. Still believing counterespionage to be a primary defense against subversion, he set up his own private files on suspected subversives in a small room off his bedroom and set about warning civic groups of the dangers of Communism. As one admirer later boasted, "It was a rare Red whose appearance in this area was not duly noted."

With the beginning of the Korean War, Van Dieman's enterprise received a boost when the FBI urged volunteer informants into action, and the adjutant general of California established miniature intelligence units throughout the state within the Defense and Security Corps. Two years later the Defense and Security Corps became the California National Guard, and its Counter Intelligence Corps took over the investigatory work.

When Van Dieman died in 1952, three National Guard officers formed the San Diego Research Library to continue his work on the subversive files. They employed a secretary and received permission from the adjutant general to move the records to the National Guard armory. In December, 1961, the Counter Intelligence Corps of the National Guard Reserve was inactivated, and its San Diego files were merged with those of the San Diego Research Library and left under private control.

To these files law-enforcement agencies and private individuals contributed information on the Civil Rights Congress, Fair Play for Cuba, the American Civil Liberties Union, labor organizations, and also on anti-subversive organizations like the John Birch Society. There were files on individuals as well as organizations. Like the APL files, they included odds and ends of gossip and rumor about the personal lives and political activities of members of the community. Retired National Guard Major General George Fisher told a *San Diego Union* reporter that the library had 250,000 file cards on anti-subversive activities investigations.

At least three governors—Earl Warren, Goodwin Knight and Pat Brown—used the files. They asked for and received information on persons before appointing them to state jobs. The National Guard ran security checks before admitting prospective members. The state's Department of Civil Service and the County of San Diego consulted the files; they were opened to the sheriff's office as well as to the FBI.

According to State Senator Hugo Fisher, they were also opened to individuals. In the 1958 election, Fisher ran against Republican incumbent Fred H. Kraft, and Kraft claimed to have obtained documents from the San Diego Research Library files which showed Fisher to be an associate of Communists, to have debated the question of whether the FBI was jeopardizing the rights of citizens, and to be a member of the ACLU.

Fisher won the election in an upset victory, but he and others in San Diego complained to Adjutant General Roderick Hill, apparently believing that the files would be used again in the 1962 election. Hill later announced that the files were "a hazard and liability."

On February 13, 1962, Hill went to the National Guard armory in San Diego, ordered the removal of the files, and sent them to the state capital, Sacramento. Two days later the *San Diego Union* ran banner headlines: STATE SEIZES SAN DIEGO FILE ON SUBVERSIVES. George Fisher, representing the San Diego Research Library, claimed that the files were private, not state files, despite the fact that they had been stored in the armory. He threatened a lawsuit to obtain their return.

After months of denunciation, debate in the California legislature, criminations and recriminations, court cases and judicial decisions, a suit against Governor Brown, Adjutant General Hill, and other California officials, the whole issue became mired in the politics of the 1962 election. At the end of July, the issue was removed from the campaign by returning the files to the San Diego Research Library. They were returned virtually intact, according to the triumphant sedition-hunters.

As long as the cold war continued, the war on the home front would go on. Soon the Vietnam War replaced the Korean War as the focus for conflict at home and abroad. As dissent over his Vietnam policy increased, President Lyndon B. Johnson called upon his war front general, William C. Westmoreland, to defend that policy on the home front. The general accepted his orders and tried.

The enemy, said Westmoreland at an Associated Press luncheon in New York on April 24, 1967, "sees every protest as evidence of crumbling morale and diminishing resolve" and believes "that he can win politically that which he cannot accomplish militarily." American troops, he asserted, "are dismayed, and so am I, by recent unpatriotic acts here at home. . . ."

What the general meant by "unpatriotic acts" he did not specify, and he carefully omitted the phrase from a subsequent speech before Congress. But the import of his remarks was unmistakable. Whether or not he was accusing all dissenters of being "unpatriotic," his message was clear. The military and home fronts were inextricably linked; questioning of aims and methods at home affected the spirit of the men at the front.

To this message dissenters replied with one of the most vigorous defenses of dissent ever made in the United States in wartime. Westmoreland's appearance here, editorialized *Life* magazine, "has crystallized the thinking of many Americans on the whole matter of dissent." *The Nation* bluntly called his visit a "propaganda mission," his speech "propaganda bludgeoning." United Nations Ambassador Arthur Goldberg, Senators George McGovern of South Dakota, J. W. Fulbright of Arkansas, Mark Hatfield of Oregon, Robert Kennedy of New York, Ernest Gruening of Alaska, Frank Church of Idaho, Charles Percy of Illinois all spoke up in defense of dissent. Alongside the congressmen, intellectuals hastened to defend the proposition that loyalty and patriotism could sometimes best be expressed in criticism, and that a dialogue over policy alternatives was absolutely necessary.

If supporters of dissent believed the battle to be over, they were too optimistic. Escalation of war bred escalation of protest, and protest made the Administration long to extinguish it, or at least contain it.

In October, 1967, thirty-five thousand peace protesters gathered to demonstrate at the Pentagon. One month later, Lieutenant Colonel George Creel, Assistant Chief of the Army's public information office at the Pentagon, admitted that the Army had "infiltrated" the demonstration. "We would have been remiss if we had not," he explained. "We were trying to protect against the burning and looting of the Pentagon." He did not explain why helmeted troops and federal marshals massed around the Pentagon were not sufficient to prevent burning and looting, why military "infiltrators" had to be employed among the civilian population. Or were they volunteers?

Before the public knew of the infiltrators Lt. General Lewis B. Hershey, head of the draft, had undertaken to use his office to limit civilian dissent. Three days after the demonstration, he issued an order to draft boards to forward to Washington the names of any persons who destroyed or threw away draft cards. The following day, even more determined to punish draft opponents, he ordered that anyone who refused to carry his registration card or who interfered with the induction process was to lose his deferment.

To carry out these orders, the local boards had to know who was destroying, throwing away, not carrying, or interfering. The implications were obvious: talebearers would do their share. In Tulsa, Oklahoma, a board reclassified a deferred University of Oklahoma student as 1-A, apparently on the grounds that he was active in the Students for a Democratic Society, a group actively opposing the United States policy in Vietnam. Senator Philip A. Hart of Michigan warned fellow senators that boards were reclassifying students for belonging to organizations board members did not like. "At the risk of sounding dramatic," he said, "I think a reasonable question might be: can the Republic endure a policy that allows federal officials to decide what political organizations are in the national interest and permits them to induct the membership of any group that doesn't pass the test?"

Senator Hart might well ask. He might also have asked just how the information would be obtained for draft boards and who would obtain it.

Perhaps students on campus who supported the United States policy might volunteer their services to draft boards as they had in the past to the FBI. In 1964, for example, one freshman at Duke University had watched with growing concern the circulation on campus of anti-war literature. "According to the manner in which I was brought up," he later said, "these flyers and handouts seemed less than patriotic and so I gathered several and mailed them to the FBI headquarters in Washington." A special agent contacted the worried freshman soon after and asked him about the material, where it had been posted, and which students on campus were in the University Liberal Action Committee. The student told him what he knew. In the spring of 1966, before the Vietnam protest march in Washington, another FBI agent contacted the student to ask him what he knew about student participants. By this time the student was a junior; he replied that he knew nothing. A year later, the student told a reporter for the *Duke Chronicle* of his activities, and the student newspaper denounced informers as "destructive to the University's atmosphere of free inquiry, investigation, and expression."

But not only FBI agents are involved with student organizations these days. As opposition to draft and desertion from the Army increases, additional inducement is present for involvement of the military in civilian affairs. As more and more Military Intelligence agents are being recruited to trail servicemen suspected of anti-war feelings, they will inevitably become involved with the "peace agitators" to whom the dissident soldiers go for counsel. With the Students for a Democratic Society encouraging chapters to aid soldiers "in opposition and disruption inside the armed services," it seems impossible to keep the military out of investigation of civilian dissent.

Evidence of that involvement has already appeared. When the left-wing Youth Against War and Fascism opened a base for organizing dissenting soldiers at Fort Sill, Oklahoma, newspapers announced the fact, and an angry crowd of several hundred citizens surrounded the organization's motel base and demanded they leave. The organizers refused, whereupon they were arrested and charged with trespassing. Out on bail, they then organized University of Oklahoma students to protest courts-martial of dissenting soldiers.

Police cars trailed the participants by land and helicopters by air. Their cars were stopped at a roadblock at Fort Sill, and the organizers were again arrested and charged with trespassing on government property. The post commander appeared to testify that they were a serious danger to military discipline. A jury took twelve minutes to find them guilty. The federal judge sentenced them to six months in jail and fined each five hundred dollars because "acts of lowering the morale of the troops at Fort Sill are a serious matter."

As for the angry crowds, they were now often composed of laborers making common cause with the lower echelons of business, who still vented their fear and insecurity by opposing change and engaging in vigilantism, in contrast to World War I, when laborers were the hunted.

These clashes between dissenters, angry crowds, federal officials, and the military symbolize anew the confrontation between a President and opponents of his policy. They remind us that over fifty years ago, when President Wilson faced the problem of internal dissent, he and his home front generals threw up massive defenses to crush that dissent. In the interim, American intellectuals have tended to feel that to expose and condemn suppression of dissent is enough. Following in the Beardian tradition of muckraking progressivism, they have often assumed that verbal attacks would lead to reform.

Obviously, attacks are not enough. Looking back at the example of World War I, it is evident that Americans need to devote considerable more attention to the theory and process of internal security than they have in the past. Selective Service must again be subjected to scrutiny, not just in its theory, but also in its implementation. In the attempt to avoid military domination of the draft system, civilian draft boards have enjoyed great latitude in making decisions, free of restraint and public criticism. However, the forced retirement of sixty-five California board members at the end of 1967, under new regulations limiting draft board service to persons under seventy-five years of age, spotlighted the decrepitude of the system, as well as many of the men implementing it at the local level. One retiree was quoted as lamenting the degeneration of young men and their objection to going to war. "But what can you expect," he told reporters, "the way kids are living now—using dope, growing their hair long, running around." He was eighty-seven years of age.

Just as the draft has not changed much, so the tactics of local police in dealing with anti-war demonstrators sometimes resemble those of World War I. Police may not yet be using auxiliaries like the APL, but during the December 4, 1967, peace demonstration in New York City large numbers of plainclothesmen were deployed to assist the police. They wore brightly colored plastic lapel buttons for identification, but they carried no badges and displayed no numbers to make them accountable in the event of complaints of misconduct. Aryeh Neier, the Executive Director of the New York ACLU, complained that although he personally witnessed several cases of rough handling no complaints could be filed without identification.

And the results of the 1967 police tactics began to look much like the results of World War I raiding tactics. During the New York demonstration, one hundred protesters were arrested, interrogated, and photographed. Then they were released without charges by the police who termed the incident an "honest mistake."

As the war in Asia makes increasing drains on the economy and curtails essential programs at home, disaffected minorities, seeing their hopes for a share in the nation's wealth dashed, question commitment to an American society made entirely in the image of the majority. One Midwest sheriff proposed recruiting, arming, and training a thousand men, to be deputized in the event of riot. A former military policeman, holding no public office, announced the establishment of a "security force" of one hundred armed men. And so the self-appointed guardians volunteer once more, but this time in a tenser atmosphere, with a greater willingness to employ deadly tactics.

In addition to scrutinizing the activities of the draft administrators and the local police and the new vigilantes, Americans must now face the issue of military intelligence in domestic matters for the first time since World War I. As long as there is a growing military force, there will be a burgeoning intelligence function associated with it, and the line between civilian and military authority must be clearly demarcated. Rivalry beween intelligence agencies might once more result in suppression of dissent by civilian agencies determined to retain control.

Increasingly the role of the President in internal security demands reexamination. To defend order when the old order is being questioned is not enough. Wilson's education of the public against mob violence did not include instructing the public in respect for civil liberties. He said no word in defense of dissent. As with an individual, so with a people: freedom must come from within; it must be an internal truth. It cannot be imposed from without. The price of freedom may indeed be eternal vigilance, but that vigilance must be in defense of civil liberties, not in their suppression. Americans must reject the legacy of the League if they ever hope to establish in fact the ideal of freedom to which they have for so long given lip service without real commitment.

Appendix

Until the 1950's, all records of the federal government for World War I were closed to researchers. Carl Wittke wrote to the War Department and the Justice Department in 1923 and 1924 to ask for information on the government policy toward German-Americans and received the reply that these records were not open to researchers. At that time, the archives of defeated Germany were already opened for the scrutiny of scholars, and selected documents of the Czarist government had been published by the Communists. The records of the victors, however, were still tightly closed. The new concern with internal security during the 1950's coincided with the release by the federal government of many of the World War I records. Curious historians began to drift into Washington in search of the government's past.

Documents which showed the APL had recruited many men who were violent nativists looked particularly ominous to historians convinced that current nativism lay behind the resurgent anti-radicalism and fear of foreign subversion. Soon John Blum was castigating Leaguers in the *Midwest Journal* as "hysterical amateur detectives." John Higham, in *Strangers in the Land,* reported that the APL had silenced German Lutheran ministers, threatened German aliens who tried to change jobs, and reorganized after the war to carry on against Bolsheviks. Historians still didn't know much about the APL, but they were learning.

Robert Murray in his *Red Scare* delivered an even broader indictment against the APL. According to him, the "government-sponsored" APL, along with other groups, "converted thousands of otherwise reasonable and sane Americans into super-patriots and self-styled spy-chasers by spreading rabid propaganda which maximized the dangers of wartime sabotage and sedition. Supposedly these agencies represented the nation's first line of defense against wartime subversive activity. But by the close of the war they actually had become the repository of elements which were much more interested in strengthening a sympathy for economic and political conservatism than in underwriting healthy patriotism. Under the guidance of their leaders, these organizations often used 'Americanism' merely to blacken the reputation and character of persons and groups whose opinions they hated and feared." Murray was concerned primarily with the effect of spy-catchers on the postwar Red scare, however. He said little about their wartime activities.

The first historian to use the APL records was Harold Hyman, who came looking for material on loyalty tests in American history. After studying the records, Hyman decided that there was no reason for the League's existence after mid-1917, when the spy threat disintegrated, and that Attorney General Thomas Watt Gregory should have abolished it after President Wilson's June inquiry. "At its best, the APL was merely a useful adjunct to responsible authorities," he concluded, "But at its worst . . . the League was a force for outrageous vigilantism blessed with the seal and sanction of the federal government." He placed the blame squarely on the federal government, not on public opinion or on the group itself.

Hyman's short chapter on the APL enticed scholars into greater interest in the policies of the Justice Department during World War I. Donald Johnson ran across the trails of the APL as he analyzed the treatment of the National Civil Liberties Bureau by the Justice Department. Traditionally, A. Mitchell Palmer had received most of the criticism from historians, while Gregory was seldom mentioned. Now, Johnson argued that Wilson was anxious to appoint a progressive when he appointed Palmer and that a "short-lived trend toward leniency" set in when Gregory left the Justice Department. Harry

Scheiber, another historian then at work on the Wilson Administration, objected.

True, Scheiber said, Gregory had requested legislation abridging traditional liberties, assisted in directing vicious attacks against the IWW, and condoned wartime imprisonment of many American left-wing leaders guilty only of condemning war as a capitalist fight. But he went on to echo O'Brian that subordinates often committed acts in disobedience to explicit orders, such as in the slacker raids. He cited Gregory's public campaign against mob violence, his warnings to United States attorneys to avoid unjustified prosecutions, and his decision to review all cases before allowing prosecutions. Gregory, he reminded Johnson, had successfully opposed trials by courts-martial. The trend toward leniency began not with Palmer, but with the armistice and the policies of Gregory and O'Brian, said Scheiber. On denunciation of the APL, however, Johnson and Scheiber were in complete agreement.

Scheiber pronounced the record of the APL "deplorable" and in a larger study of civil liberties said of members: "Often exceeding or ignoring orders, these amateur detectives indulged in illegal arrests and searches, impersonation of federal officers, and irresponsible propaganda activities. By the time of the Armistice it had become obvious that the League was a stronghold of reactionary elements. A source of embarrassment to the Administration, the organization lost its official status shortly thereafter." If Gregory had only followed Wilson's advice in June 1917, Scheiber concluded, "many injustices might have been avoided." The next logical question to ask was why Wilson didn't insist.

As early as 1947, O. A. Hilton had commented that Wilson's action on civil liberties remained an enigma because, although he took no aggressive position on civil rights, he was not stampeded by unreasonable demands of patriots. But by the end of the 1950's, the tag "enigma" was no longer a satisfactory one. Richard P. Longaker took a long look at *The Presidency and Individual Liberties* and attempted to substitute a more concrete analysis of Wilson's actions.

Longaker rejected the "enigma" tag. Because Wilson had anticipated the impact of modern war on liberty and did little to counteract it—in some cases encouraged intolerance—Longaker felt Wilson must be criticized. He could not forgive Wilson for the "ritual patriotism" enforced by the Chief Executive's agents, even though Wilson did oppose military trials. Wilson, Longaker concluded, could have used his appointment and removal powers to transform "administrative slashing" into "controlled prosecution" related to winning the war. "In his rush to make the world safe for democracy Wilson gave little attention to the domestic substance of that democracy which he was waging war to preserve," said Longaker.

As for the APL, Longaker considered its founding "a low point in government personnel policy" and compared the amateurism of the APL with present amateurism in investigation. Yet he ended by defending the present FBI as having an "impressively clean record—contrary to the liberal myth."

It remained for John P. Roche, in *The Quest for the Dream,* to take the theme of condemnation of the APL to its logical culmination. To him the APL appeared a "government sponsored lynch mob."

But the APL was much more. For Wilson, the APL was a conscious compromise between states' rights and federal intervention in matters of subversion, a tool by which he enforced war statutes without direct federal coercion or martial law. Neither Wilson nor Gregory ever revealed publicly the extent to which the federal government utilized this tool to accomplish war mobilization at home. Nor did they reveal publicly the widespread discontent with that war mobilization. Determined to keep the military in a subordinate role, Wilson yet failed to develop a substitute federal civilian police force or to consolidate or expand federal investigating agencies. Restraint in official expansion of federal forces led to lack of restraint in unofficial expansion.

In World War I there were few guidelines in setting the bounds between internal security for the government and defense of individual rights. Reformers compromised on invasions of civil liberties, believing that the confusion of the first months of war would lead to more tolerance. Instead, intolerance bred more intolerance and compromise led to more compromise. What came out of this pyramid of compromises was not only suppression but the birth of a new concern for the defense of civil liberties against the federal government. Historians have reflected these concerns. Some have concentrated on damning the use of volunteers and some on damning the Bureau of Investigation. Others have pointed to the necessity of restraint and regard for civil liberties on the part of the Justice Department, while a few have given the ultimate responsibility for civil liberties to the President. All, however, have accepted the principle that the job of hunting subversives belongs to the federal government, not to the states; to trained government officials, not to volunteers. What they have overlooked is the extent to which pressure from the military and militarists pushed the Justice Department into hasty decisions and unconstitutional practices.

Wilson's greatest contribution to the development of federal security policies was his opposition to military trials. His major failure was in not building on this basic principle a policy of opposition to the interference of the Military Intelligence in internal security affairs, and in not insisting that every man who acted for the government was responsible to it and that the government was in turn responsible for his activities.

To say, as Wilson did, that civilian courts shall have control is, of course, not enough. The President is responsible not only for a coherent internal security policy, but also for seeing to it that the home front war fought by his subordinates does not degenerate into guerilla warfare, ranging dissenter against conformist, pacifist against militarist, and radical against conservative.

Notes on Sources

References to specific documents, books, government periodicals, newspapers, and pamphlets relating to the American Protective League and to the internal security policies of the Wilson Administration will be found in the following notes. The main printed source for the APL is Emerson Hough's official history, *The Web* (Chicago: Reilly and Lee, 1919), which furnished authentic but selective information on the League, together with anti-German, anti-foreign, and anti-radical tirades by Hough. It is especially valuable for the early history of the League and of state units for which no documentary sources have been found. The only other printed source on the League is the brief but critical chapter by Harold M. Hyman in *To Try Men's Souls: Loyalty Tests in American History* (Berkeley and Los Angeles: University of California Press, 1959). It was he who suggested that the APL deserved a full history and who helped me through the first stages of this work at the University of California, Los Angeles.

In many ways the Frey Papers, made available to me by Charles Daniel Frey, Jr., and now in the Special Collections, The University Library, University of California, Los Angeles, are the most important source on the APL, not only for letters, pamphlets, and bulletins on the APL, but also for information on its relation to the Bureau of Investigation and the Military Intelligence Division.

The National Archives are, of course, the most extensive, richest depository of material on the home front during World War I. Unfortunately, the APL Records there (RG 65) are incomplete. When the FBI turned them over to the Archives in the 1950's, archivists selected the files of New York, North Carolina, Arkansas, California, and Kansas as representative and destroyed the rest. Thus, part of the record of the APL is permanently lost. Also, in the early 1960's the FBI ordered the archivists to remove all material which related to the Bureau of Investigation from APL and Justice Department files. Every letter, every memorandum, every document which had originated in the Bureau of Investigation (or had been signed by A. Bruce Bielaski) was closed to researchers. Consequently, my references to the Bureau of Investigation are either from other manuscript sources or from the works of historians who had a chance to look at the records before they were withdrawn from public scrutiny.

The General Records of the Department of Justice (RG 60) contain correspondence relating to the APL and to specific policies of the Justice Department. The Abraham Glasser Files, started in the late 1930's as a study of military involvement in labor disputes, are essential for an understanding of the interplay of Military Intelligence officers, agents of the Bureau of Investigation, and Leaguers.

Many of the Military Intelligence Division Records (RG 165) are now open to researchers and contain vast quantities of information on all aspects of the home front war. The Provost Marshal General's Bureau Records (RG 110) have hardly been tapped by scholars as yet and are especially interesting for the background of the New York slacker raids and the relationship of the APL to local draft boards. Scattered references to the APL are in the General Records of the Adjutant General's Office (RG 94), the Agricultural Department (RG 4), the Naval Intelligence Records (RG 45), Immigration and Naturalization Service Records (RG 84), Labor Department Records (RG 174), Conciliation Service Records (RG 280), and State Department Records (RG 59). The Bureau of Investigation Records were entirely closed to me, as were the Secret Service Records. The Naval Intelligence Records are open but difficult to use; many of the Labor Department Records are still closed, as are most of the records relating to intelligence activities of the State Department.

In the Manuscripts Division of the Library of Congress, the Woodrow Wilson Papers and the William G. McAdoo Papers contain the arguments about the APL and the Secret Service. The Newton D. Baker Papers are useful for the early period of the war and the Joseph P. Tumulty Papers for Palmer's selection as Attorney General. Gregory burned most of his papers before his death, and therefore the collection is meager. Copies of some of his speeches and letters were kindly furnished to me by his sister, Cornelia G. Hartman of Baytown, Texas, and are now in the Frey Papers. The Charles Warren Papers had not yet been deposited when I completed my research in Washington, but they should shed additional light on Justice Department policies during the first year of the war. It is to be hoped that John Lord O'Brian will also deposit his papers to fill out the story of the War Emergency Division.

The University of Washington, Seattle, Washington, has a group of APL Papers relating to the Minute Men. Additional references to the Minute Men are in the Thomas Burke Papers and Wesley Jones Papers there. The New Jersey State Library has some questionnaires on the APL which provide an occasional insight into the cooperation of local volunteer investigating units and mayors.

A personal interview with John Lord O'Brian in 1961 furnished some clues to his policies and attitudes, as did correspondence with William McDermid of New York City, former APL State Inspector for New Jersey. A memorandum written by Ralph Van Dieman in 1949, a few years before his death, and made available to me by General George W. Fisher of San Diego, California, reveals his role in reestablishing the military intelligence in May, 1917.

Sources

Introduction

Page 9. *Hindenburg and Ludendorff:* Ernest K. May, *The World War and American Isolation, 1914–1917* (Cambridge: Harvard University Press, 1956), 414.

Page 10. *East Indians:* Although the term has in the past been more commonly used to refer to inhabitants of present-day Indonesia, distinguishing them from residents of the West Indies and the continents of the Western Hemisphere, it is used throughout this book to refer to natives of the Asian subcontinent and their descendants.

Pages 9–10. *Treason and espionage:* U.S., *Statutes at Large,* XXXX, Part 1, 1650 for Wilson's proclamation on treason; U.S., *Statutes at Large,* XXXVI, 1084–1085 for 1911 law; the best discussion of the Articles of War is in Charles Warren, "Spies and the Power of Congress to Subject Certain Classes of Civilians to Trial by Military Tribunal," *American Law Review,* LIII (March-April 1919), 195–228; his article on treason "What is Giving Aid and Comfort to the Enemy?" *Yale Law Journal,* XXVII (January 1918), 327–347, is also helpful. Both present his interpretation of the law, however.

Page 10. *McAdoo and Gregory:* Arthur S. Link, *Woodrow Wilson: The Struggle for Neutrality, 1914–1915* (Princeton: Princeton University Press, 1960), 557–558; E. David Cronon (ed.), *The Cabinet Diaries of Josephus Daniels, 1913–1921* (Lincoln: University of Nebraska Press, 1963), 97.

Page 11. *"Poison of disloyalty": Congressional Record,* 64th Congress, 1st Session, 99 (December 7, 1915).

Pages 12–13. *Bureau of Investigation:* Homer Stillé Cummings and Carl McFarland, *Federal Justice: Chapters in the History of Justice and the Federal Executive* (New York: Macmillan, 1937), 426–427; Don Whitehead, *The F.B.I. Story* (New York: Random House, 1956), 14, 18–28; U.S., *Statutes at Large,* XXXV, Part 1, 328 for 1908 prohibition; James A. Blair to P. Hurley, September 8, 1918, File 190470, NA, RG 60, for 1893 law.

Pages 12–13. *Albert Papers:* W. H. Houghton, "The Albert Portfolio," *World's Work,* LVII (August 17, 1929), 117; Robert Lansing, *War Memoirs* (New York: Bobbs-Merrill, 1935), 77; John P. Jones and Paul M. Hollister, *The German Secret Service in America, 1914–1918* (Boston: Small, Maynard, 1918), 165–168; *New York Times,* August 20, 1915, 7:6; Walter S. Bowen and Harry E. Neal, *The United States Secret Service* (Philadelphia and New York: Chilton, 1960), devoted an entire chapter to investigations of Germans during the neutrality period.

Page 14. *"Intrigues":* Arthur S. Link, *Wilson: Confusion and Crisis, 1915–1916* (Princeton: University of Princeton Press, 1964), 56; *New York Times,* November 20, 1915, 1:4, December 9, 1915, 1:8, December 11, 1915, 4:6.

Page 14. *Matters not covered by federal law:* U.S., *Statutes at Large,* XXXIX, 311.

Pages 15–16. *Gregory:* Belle and Fala LaFollette, *Robert M. LaFollette* (2 vols.; New York: Macmillan, 1953), II, 937, made on the occasion of Gregory's resignation in January 1919. For Gregory and progressives see Joan M. Jensen, "Annette Abbott Adams, Politician," *Pacific Historical Review,* XXXV (May 1966), 185–201; Alpheus T. Mason, *Brandeis: A Free Man's Life* (New York: Viking, 1946), 405, 467, 496, 499; personal characteristics described by John Lord O'Brian in interview, June 20, 1961, and in Raymond B. Fosdick to the author, April 23, 1961, and William G. McAdoo, *Crowded Years: The Reminiscences of William G. McAdoo* (Boston: Houghton Mifflin, 1931), 184. Gregory discussed his own political attitudes in letters to C. J. Joiner, January 1, 1916, and E. M. House, June 10, 1920, Gregory Papers, LC, Box 2. See also Arthur S. Link, *Wilson: The Road to the White House* (Princeton: University of Princeton Press, 1947), 333–334.

Page 16. *Bielaski:* "German Plotters Fear Him," *Literary Digest,* LV (September 29, 1917), 61–62.

The Volunteers

Page 17. *Briggs's offer:* Emerson Hough, *The Web* (Chicago: Reilly and Lee, 1919), 483–485.

Pages 18–19. *The Union League:* E. Bently Hamilton, "The Union League: Its Origins and Achievements in the Civil War," The Illinois State Historical Society, *Transactions* (1921), 110–115; George M. Fredrickson, *The Inner Civil War: Northern Intellectuals and the Crisis of the Union* (New York: Harper and Row, 1965), 131–132.

Page 19. *Eternal vigilance:* "The Chicago Conspiracy," *Atlantic Monthly,* XVI (July 1865), 108–120.

Pages 19–20. *Bielaski's use of volunteers:* "German Plotters Fear Him," 61–62.

Page 20. *Spy bill:* Roosevelt to Lodge, February 25, 1917, and Lodge to

Roosevelt, February 27, 1917, Theodore Roosevelt and Henry Cabot Lodge, *Selections from the Correspondence of Theodore Roosevelt and Henry Cabot Lodge* (2 vols.; New York and London: Scribner's, 1925), II, 496–497; Gregory to McAdoo, February 26, 1917, File 9-4-90, NA, RG 60; *New York Times*, November 22, 1916, 2:3; Attorney General, *Annual Report* (Washington 1917), 56; Franklin H. Martin, *Digest of the Proceedings of the Council of National Defense During the World War* (Washington, 1934), 111.

Page 21. *East Indians: New York Times*, March 7, 1917, 1:1 and March 13, 1917, 2:5; Warren to Polk, March 16, 1917, File 9-10-3, NA, NG 60.

Page 21. *"Wire immediately"*: Hough, *Web*, 484.

Page 22. *Conditions in Washington:* Gregory to Senator Thomas S. Martin, April 4, 1917, File 190470, NA, RG 60.

Page 22. *Briggs's third proposal:* Hough, *Web*, 485.

Page 23. *Bielaski wire: ibid.*

Pages 23–24. *Cabinet meeting of March 20:* Cronon, *Cabinet Diaries*, 117–118; Anne W. Lane and Louise H. Wall (eds.), *The Letters of Franklin K. Lane: Personal and Political* (Boston: Houghton Mifflin, 1922), 292; Private memoranda, Papers of Robert Lansing, quoted in Daniel M. Smith, *American Intervention, 1917: Sentiment, Self-Interest or Ideals* (Boston: Houghton Mifflin, 1966), 184–189. The April 2 prediction of intolerance attributed to Wilson by Frank Cobb has been seriously questioned by Jerold S. Auerbach in "Woodrow Wilson's 'Prediction' to Frank Cobb: Words Historians Should Doubt Ever Got Spoken," *The Journal of American History*, LIV (December, 1967), 608–617. Auerbach argues (among other things) that because of Wilson's anti-libertarian posture the statement seems "less than plausible." I agree.

Page 24. *"No arrests"*: Hough, *Web*, 486.

Pages 24–25. *"A volunteer committee"*: Bielaski to Special Agents, March 22, 1917, Charles Daniel Frey Papers, University of California at Los Angeles; Briggs to Clabaugh, March 22, 1917, quoted in Hough, *Web*, 486.

Page 25. *Recruiting:* U.S., Congress, Senate, Committee on Military Affairs, *Hearings, Extending Jurisdiction of Military Tribunals*, 65th Cong., 2d Sess., 1918, 5, 21–22.

Pages 25–26. *Organization:* Form letter dated March 27, 1917, and other undated form letters and Bureau of Intelligence Bulletin No. 1, Chicago Division, Frey Papers, UCLA.

Page 26. *Operatives:* Basford to Briggs, April 18, 1917, and E. D. Farrow to Briggs, May 25, 1917, California File, NA, RG 65.

Page 27. *Troop movements:* Thomas H. Barry to Governor of Michigan, March 26, 1917, Newton D. Baker Papers, Library of Congress, Box 1: William Preston, Jr., *Aliens and Dissenters* (Cambridge: Harvard, 1963), 105; John D. Pershing, *My Experiences in the World War* (2 vols.; New York: Stokes, 1931), I, 12–13; Irene H. Mix, *Connecticut Activities in Wars: A Summary* (Washington 1932), 58–59; Elliott M. Rudwick, *Race*

Riot at East St. Louis, July 2, 1917 (Cleveland, Ohio: World, 1966), 18.

Pages 27–28. *Milwaukee:* Memorandum of General King, Baker Papers, LC, Box 1.

Page 28. *California:* Edgar Eugene Robinson and Paul Edwards (eds.), *The Memoirs of Ray Lyman Wilbur* (Stanford: Stanford University Press, 1960), 237, 240; Donald Hayne (ed.), *The Autobiography of Cecil B. DeMille* (Englewood Cliffs: Prentice-Hall, 1959), 184; "History of the Cabrillo Rifles, 1917–1918," San Diego Public Library, California Room.

Pages 28–29. *"Bunk about ... preparedness":* Chester Rowell to Ray Lyman Wilbur, April 21, 1917, Rowell Papers and Hiram Johnson to Charles H. Rowell, April 5, 1917, Johnson Papers, Bancroft Library, University of California, Berkeley.

Page 29. *"Dangerous leaders":* Warren to Attorney General, March 30, 1917, File 9-4-94, NA, RG 60; Daniel R. Beaver, *Newton D. Baker and the American War effort, 1917–1919* (Lincoln: University of Nebraska Press, 1966), 24.

Page 29. *Cabinet approval:* The date of the Cabinet meeting at which Gregory discussed the volunteer groups has never been definitely established. Approval is mentioned by Charles Frey in notes for speech of November 21, 1917, Frey Papers, UCLA.

Page 29. *"Miasma":* Cronon, *Cabinet Diaries,* 125; Gregory to Davis, March 31, 1917, File 190470, NA, RG 60.

Page 30. *"Serious blot":* Bielaski to Briggs, April 2, 1917, Frey Papers, UCLA.

Page 31. *The fruit of autocracy:* Wilson, *Public Papers,* V, 12–14.

Page 31. *Six thousand units:* Briggs to Walter B. Cherry, March 31, 1917, New York File, NA, RG 65.

Into the Lists of Honor

Page 33. *Ford motor plant:* Reports in File 186233, NA, RG 60.

Page 33. *"Howling for protection":* Barry to Baker, May 17, 1917, Baker Papers, LC, Box 1.

Pages 33–34. *St. Louis:* Barry to Gregory, May 6, 1917, *ibid.*

Page 34. *Alternatives:* Various letters in Glasser File, Box 9, NA, RG 60; Gregory to Thomas D. McCarthy, May 1917, File 190470, NA, RG 60.

Page 34. *"Source of comfort":* Bielaski to Briggs, May 3, 1917, Frey Papers, UCLA.

Pages 34–36. *Conscription:* Woodrow Wilson, *A History of the American People* (5 vols.; New York: Harper, 1902), IV, 236; Cronon, *Cabinet Diaries,* 120, 551.

Page 36. *"Volunteer system ... relegated to the past":* Secretary of War, *Annual Report* (Washington 1916), I, 159; Roosevelt quoted in *New York Times,* December 8, 1915; Wilson quoted in Arthur Walworth, *Woodrow*

Wilson (2 vols.; New York: Longmans, 1958), II, 101; Beaver, *Baker,* 287.

Page 36. *Bill by 10:00 A.M.:* Cronon, *Cabinet Diaries,* 551.

Page 37. *"Spells my name Chowder":* Louis B. Wehle, *Hidden Threads of History: Wilson Through Roosevelt* (New York: Macmillan, 1953), 26–27; Harlan B. Phillips (ed.), *Felix Frankfurter Reminisces* (New York: Reynal, 1960), 59, 114; R. Barry, "Crowder the Genius of the Draft," *World's Work,* 36 (September 1918), 564; "Man Who is Raising the Big American Draft," *Literary Digest,* 58 (September 14, 1918), 60–66.

Page 38. *Control without interference:* John Dickinson, *The Building of an Army: A Detailed Account of Legislation, Administration in the United States, 1915–1920* (New York: Century, 1922), 191; and Crowder's classic *The Spirit of Selective Service* (New York: Century, 1920).

Page 38. *Opposition to bill:* Fiorella LaGuardia, *The Making of an Insurgent: An Autobiography, 1882–1919* (Philadelphia: Lippincott, 1948), 143; Beaver, *Baker,* 30; Cecil K. Byrd, "Selective Military Service, 1917–1918" (unpublished Master's Thesis, Indiana University, 1938), 20–24.

Page 39. *"No war for amateurs":* Wilson, *Public Papers,* V, 34.

Page 40. *Request for order:* Gregory to Wilson, April 7, 1917, Wilson Papers, LC, File II, Box 116.

Page 40. *"Crossing wires":* McAdoo to Wilson, April 16, 1917, McAdoo Papers, LC, Box 522.

Page 40. *Eliminate Post Office:* McAdoo to Wilson, April 17, 1917, *ibid.*

Page 40. *"Not the slightest":* Gregory to Wilson, April 17, 1917, Gregory Papers, LC, Box 1.

Page 41. *"Too much machinery":* Ray Stannard Baker (ed.), *Woodrow Wilson, Life and Letters* (8 vols.; New York: Doubleday, Page, 1927–1937), VII, 14; Wilson to Baker, April 16, 1917, Wilson, *Public Papers,* V, 44; Wilson's administrative policy in Arthur W. Macmahon, "Woodrow Wilson: Political Leader and Administrator," in Earl Latham (ed.), *The Philosophy and Policies of Woodrow Wilson* (Chicago: University of Chicago Press, 1958), 117; Charles Seymour, *Woodrow Wilson and the World War* (New Haven: Yale University Press, 1921), 188; H. J. Tobin and Percy W. Bidwell, *Mobilizing Civilian America* (New York: Council on Foreign Relations, 1940), 24, contains a diagram of the executive establishment in November 1918, showing the division between normal and emergency agencies.

Page 43. *Acceptance of APL announced:* United States Committee on Public Information, *Official Bulletin,* I (May 12, 1917), 4; Flynn's protest mentioned in McAdoo to Wilson, May 15, 1917, McAdoo Papers, LC, Box 522.

Page 43. *"Absolutely dangerous":* McAdoo to Wilson, May 15, 1917, *ibid.*

Page 44. *"Three straws":* McAdoo to Wilson, May 16, 1917, *ibid.*

Page 44. *"Gravest danger":* McAdoo to Wilson and McAdoo to Gregory, June 2, 1917, *ibid.*

Page 45. *"Stop it":* Wilson to Gregory, June 4, 1917, quoted in H. C.

Peterson and Gilbert C. Fite, *Opponents of War, 1917–1918* (Madison: University of Wisconsin Press, 1957), 19.

Page 45. *Arrests: New York Times,* June 2, 1917, 1:8.

Page 46. *Lists of Honor:* Wilson, *Public Papers,* III, 39.

Page 46. *One man shot: New York Herald,* June 6, 1917.

Pages 46–47. *Secret Service:* Miscellaneous memoranda and Earl F. Barrett to Briggs, May 15, 1917, Frey Papers, UCLA; George E. Greene to Briggs, July 23, 1917, New York File, H. R. Basford to Briggs, April 18, 1917, California File, NA, RG 65.

Page 47. *Volunteers:* Memorandum by Richard Levering, May 25, 1917, for Garrison, E. W. Wellington to Briggs, June 22, 1917, Frey Papers, UCLA; Clabaugh remark in *Chicago Tribune,* May 5, 1917; W. P. Hitchcock to Briggs, June 13, 1917, New York File, Briggs to Muma, April 14, 1917, California File, NA, RG 65; APL Papers, New Jersey State Library; Hough, *Web,* 286.

Pages 47–48. *Work for municipalities and states:* Bulletin No. 4, Chicago Bureau of Investigation, Frey Papers, UCLA; Hough, *Web,* 403.

Page 48. *"Not shure":* Undated letter H. A. Elson to Charles Frey, California File, NA, RG 65.

Page 48. *APL badge:* Bulletin No. 1, Chicago Division, to Operatives, and Bulletin No. 2, Chicago Division, Department of Investigation, to Captains, Frey Papers, UCLA.

Page 49. *Bulletins:* All in Frey Papers, UCLA.

Page 49. *Bastard units:* Briggs to D. White, April 26, 1917, Briggs to W. F. Fay, April 27, 1917, New York File, Briggs to Muma, July 9, 1917, California File, NA, RG 65.

Page 50. *"Should be encouraged":* Gregory to McAdoo, June 12, 1917, McAdoo Papers, LC, Box 522; Gregory to Wilson, June 14, 1917, Wilson Papers, LC, File II, Box 120.

Pages 50–51. *Reformers:* I have used "reformers" when referring to those early twentieth-century men and women who crusaded for reform and change. I have done so even though they sometimes called themselves "liberals" because the group included many who differed with later depression and post-depression reformers we usually call "liberals." Occasionally, I have used "progressives" interchangeably with "reformers." When capitalized Progressive refers to members of the political party formed in 1912 which disintegrated during the war. Since historians have not yet solved the problem of terminology, I have used "reformer" and "liberal" in the narrower sense, although in the broader sense both groups participated in the American liberal tradition. The later split over New Deal policies indicates that there was no easy transition from "progressive" reform to "liberal" reform as Otis L. Graham, Jr., shows in *An Encore for Reform: The Old Progressives and the New Deal* (New York: Oxford University Press, 1967), even if he does not completely explain the split. Christopher Lasch adopts the term "liberal" for his study of progressive reformers in

World War I, *The American Liberals and the Russian Revolution* (New York and London: Columbia University Press, 1962), then divides them into regular liberals and "war liberals." It seems to me that historians dealing with the liberal tradition in America must also adopt narrower terms to define specific groups of reformers of different periods.

Pages 50–51. *"Competition of patriotism":* Claude G. Bowers, *Beveridge and the Progressive Era* (Cambridge: Houghton Mifflin, 1932), 484; J. D. Works to T. Perceval Gerson, February 15, 1917, reveals similar attitudes toward the benefit of war in stimulating patriotism, T. Perceval Gerson Collection, UCLA; *California in the War: War Addresses, Proclamations and Patriotic Messages of Governor William D. Stephens* (Sacramento 1921), 5; Richard T. Ely, *The World War and Leadership in a Democracy* (New York: Macmillan, 1918), presented a classic statement of the progressive theory of crisis in lectures delivered at the University of California, Berkeley, in November 1917. For the *New Republic,* see Charles Forcey, *The Crossroads of Liberalism: Croly, Weyl, Lippmann and the Progressive Era, 1900–1925* (New York: Oxford University Press, 1961), 273; David W. Noble, *The Paradox of Progressive Thought* (Minneapolis: University of Minnesota Press, 1958); and Christopher Lasch, *The New Radicalism in America [1889–1963]: The Intellectual as a Social Type* (New York: Vintage, 1967), 203–204. Bourne's statement is in *War and the Intellectuals: Collected Essays, 1915–1919* (New York: Harper, 1964), 3, originally in *The Seven Arts* (June 1917).

Page 51. *"Engine of conscription":* "Morality of Conscription," *New Republic,* XIII (May 5, 1917), 7–8, reminiscent in argument of a letter endorsing conscription from Walter Lippmann to Wilson, February 5, 1917, Beaver, *Baker,* 26–27.

Page 51. *"Sinister intrigue":* Wilson, *Public Papers,* June 14, 1917, V, 61–63; Lasch, *New Radicalism,* 239.

Page 52. *Not "specially concerned":* "Conscription of Thought," *New Republic,* XIII (September 1, 1917), 128–129; Gregory to Josephus Daniels, February 19, 1924, Gregory Papers, LC, Box 2.

Page 53. *"Recognition . . . settled":* Briggs to Frey, June 26, 1917, July 11, 1917, Frey Papers, UCLA.

Pages 53–54. *Seditious publications:* McAdoo to Gregory, June 18, 1917, McAdoo Papers, LC, Box 522.

Page 54. *Gregory overwrought:* McAdoo to Wilson, July 5, 1917, McAdoo Papers, LC, Box 522; McCarthy to Tumulty, July 5, 1917, Wilson Papers, File VI, Box 73.

Page 54. *German spy system:* McAdoo to Wilson, July 6, 1917, McAdoo Papers, LC, Box 522.

Page 54. *"Hysteria":* Cronon, *Cabinet Diaries,* 173.

Page 55. *"No hysterical notions":* McAdoo to Baker, McAdoo to Wilson, July 9, 1917, McAdoo Papers, LC, Box 522.

Page 55. *"Spies are in our departments":* "The Alarm Against Spies,"

Literary Digest, 55 (July 21, 1917), 13–14.

Page 56. *"Need of counsel":* Wilson to Gregory, July 12, 1917, Wilson, *Life and Letters,* VII, 159.

Page 56. *In daily touch:* Memorandum from Warren to Gregory, July 16, 1917, NA, RG 60.

Soldiers of Darkness

Page 57. *"Agitators and anarchists":* Thomas Gowenlock, *Soldiers of Darkness* (Garden City: Doubleday, 1937), 41. An estimated 32,000 men joined the IWW between April 1, 1917, and September 1, 1917, bringing in almost sixty-four thousand dollars in initiation dues. A government accountant testified at the Chicago trial that there was absolutely no evidence of German financing. See Philip Taft, "The Federal Trials of the IWW," *Labor History,* III (Winter 1962), 57–91.

Page 58. *"Flying squad":* ibid.; Hough, *Web,* 194.

Page 58. *Socialists:* Hough, *Web,* 269–270; Ford Plant, File 186233, NA, RG 60.

Pages 58–59. *Rockford, Illinois:* Hough, *Web,* 489–490.

Page 59. *IWW:* For Tulsa see File 10110, NA, RG 165; for Pennsylvania and South Dakota, Hough, *Web,* 200, 414.

Page 60. *England:* Frank P. Chambers, *The War Behind the War; 1914–1918: A History of the Political and Civilian Fronts* (London: Faber and Faber, 1939), 258; Justice Department, Circular 703, Bureau of Investigation Circular 701, July 3, 1917, Frey Papers, UCLA.

Page 61. *Partisan purposes:* Beaver, *Baker,* 34–35; County Health Officer and Examining Physician to War Department, September 28, 1917, NA, RG 167.

Pages 61–62. *IWW's busy:* Alfred Jacques to Attorney General, January 15, 1918, File 187415, NA, RG 60.

Page 62. *Schenectady:* Report in File 10110, NA, RG 165.

Page 62. *East St. Louis:* Rudwick, *Race Riot,* 72–140.

Page 63. *Arizona:* Gregory to Warren, July 11, 1917, File 186701, NA, RG 60; reports in File 10110, NA, RG 165; Glasser File, Box 9, NA, RG 60; Felix Frankfurter, *Reminisces,* 136, for vigilantes.

Page 63. *"Great danger":* Wilson to Governor Campbell, July 12, 1917, Wilson, *Life and Letters,* VII, 160–161.

Page 64. *IWW dangerous:* Bielaski to Special Agents and Attorney General to U.S. Attorneys, July 17, 1917, Frey Papers, UCLA; Cronon, *Cabinet Diaries,* 173, 178; *New York Times,* July 17, 1917, 7:2.

Page 64. *Bell's plan:* Cronon, *Cabinet Diaries,* 178, 180.

Pages 64–65. *Civil rights:* Rudwick, *Race Riot,* 262, 133n, Karch to Gregory, July 23, 1917, 137.

Page 65. *No facts:* Wilson to Dyer, July 28, 1917, Wilson, *Life and*

Letters, VII, 198; Rudwick, *Race Riot,* 136, 140.

Page 66. *Physicals:* Bielaski to Special Agents, July 27, 1917, Frey Papers, UCLA.

Page 66. *Not "sufficient ground":* William W. Folwell, *A History of Minnesota* (4 vols.; St. Paul: Minnesota Historical Society, 1921–1930), III, 568–569.

Page 66. *"Wasted and . . . paralyzed":* Lind to Gregory, July 26, 1917, NA, RG 60.

Pages 66–67. *Conspiracy:* For Bopp and Hindu cases, Jensen, "Annette Abbott Adams," 191–193.

Page 67. *"What shall I do?":* Cronon, *Cabinet Diaries,* 184.

Page 67. *Immediate paralysis:* Folwell, *History of Minnesota,* 568–569; *New York Times,* August 2, 1917, 20:1.

Page 68. *Secret Office:* Bureau of Investigation to All Employees, August 16, 1917, Frey Papers, UCLA; Hough, *Web,* 488–489.

Page 69. *"Effective service":* Bielaski to Briggs, August 16, 1917, Frey Papers, UCLA.

Page 69. *Newspapers:* "Lynch Law and Treason," *Literary Digest,* 55 (August 18, 1917), 12.

Pages 69–70. *Oklahoma:* Charles C. Bush, "The Green Corn Rebellion" (unpublished Master's Thesis, University of Oklahoma, 1932), 12, 50; Patrick Renshaw, *The Wobblies: The Story of Syndicalism in the United States* (Garden City: Doubleday, 1967), 219; Bennett M. Rich, *Presidents and Civil Disorder* (Washington: Brookings Institution, 1941), 152.

Page 71. *Troops and labor:* Preston, *Aliens and Dissenters,* 104–105; Chief of Staff Tasker H. Bliss to Attorney General, July 27, 1917, August 10, 1917, File 15045, NA, RG 165.

Page 71–72. *Deserters: New York Times,* August 19, 1917, 3:3; Bielaski to Special Agents, August 17, 1917, Frey Papers, UCLA; U.S., Provost Marshal General's Bureau, *Second Report of the Provost Marshal General to the Secretary of War on the Operation of the Selective Service System to December 20, 1918* (Washington 1919), 283.

Page 72. *Racial violence:* Hough, *Web,* 293–302, 400–401; Beaver, *Baker,* 228.

Page 72. *Demand suppression:* Cronon, *Cabinet Diaries,* 199; Hayden to Attorney General, August 29, 1917, File 186813, NA, RG 60; Gregory to Francis H. Weston, August 10, 1917, Gregory Papers, LC, Box 1; *New York Times,* August 19, 1917, I, 5:4 and August 28, 1917, 4:4; Renshaw, *Wobblies,* 220.

Page 72. *Search for evidence:* Bielaski to Rudolph Forester, August 13, 1917, Wilson Papers, LC, File VI, Box 573.

Page 73. *Bielaski: "German Plotters Fear Him,"* 62.

Page 73. *Gregory:* Cronon, *Cabinet Diaries,* 199.

Pages 73–74. *"Meanest games":* Anderson to Gregory, August 20, 1917, File 186701, NA, RG 60.

Page 74. *Frankfurter plan:* Memorandum for Secretary of War, September 4, 1917, Baker Papers, LC, Box 1.

Pages 74–75. *IWW raid:* Ralph Chaplin, *Wobbly: The Rough-and-Tumble Story of an American Radical* (Chicago: University of Chicago Press, 1948), 227–228; *New York Times,* September 6, 1917, 1:8.

Page 75. *"Country-wide" plot: New York Times,* September 6, 1917, 1:8, 2:1.

Page 75. *"Sedition must stop": New York Times,* September 7, 1917, 4:1.

Page 75. *"We were warranted": New York Times,* September 6, 1917, 2:2.

Page 75. *"Such a varied character":* Frierson to Anderson, September 11, 1917, File 186701, NA, RG 60; Hough, *Web,* 133–134.

Page 76. *Darrow:* Chaplin, *Wobbly,* 225.

Page 76. *American press:* "Raiding the IWW," *Literary Digest,* LV (September 22, 1917), 17.

Page 77. *Reason to be grateful:* "IWW Raids and Others," *New Republic,* XIII (September 15, 1917), 176–177.

Page 77. *Radicals:* Nelles to Eastman, September 17, 1917, quoted in Walter Nelles, *A Liberal in Wartime: The Education of Albert DeSilver* (New York: Norton, 1940), 118.

Page 77. *American Union Against Militarism:* Donald Johnson, *The Challenge to American Freedoms: World War I and the Rise of the American Civil Liberties Union* (Lexington: University of Kentucky Press, 1963), 65–66.

Page 77. *"Without substantial merit":* Gregory to Wilson, September 13, 1917, Wilson Papers, LC, Box 126; Clabaugh to Bureau of Investigation, October 1, 1917, Frey Papers, UCLA; Lucille Millner, *The Education of an American Liberal* (New York: Horizon, 1954), 65.

Page 78. *"Line must be drawn":* Wilson to Eastman, September 18, 1917, quoted in Walworth, *Woodrow Wilson,* II, 113.

Page 78. *"Patriotism complex":* Lewis Mumford, "Patriotism and its Consequences," *Dial,* LXVI (April 19, 1919), 406.

Page 79. *Dissent labeled treason:* "America Infested with Spies," *Literary Digest,* LV (October 6, 1917), 9–11.

Page 79. *Disloyal "promptly hung":* "Dr. Van Dyke on Traitors," *New Republic,* XIII (November 24, 1917), 213–214.

Page 79. *"Disloyal troublers":* "Treason Must Be Made Odious," *The North American Review,* CVI (October 1917), 516.

Page 80. *Columbia University:* Richard Hofstadter and Wilson Smith (eds.), *American Higher Education: A Documentary History* (2 vols.; Chicago, University of Chicago Press, 1961), 833–844. See also Grover C. Bates, "The James McKeen Cattell Papers," *Library of Congress Quarterly Journal of Current Acquisitions,* XVII (May 1960), 170–174; Cattell recovered $45,000 in damages in a libel suit.

Pages 80–81. *Dewey:* "In Explanation of Our Lapse," *New Republic* XIII (November 3, 1917), 17.

The Bounty Hunters

Page 83. *Bounty:* War Department to Governors, September 27, 1917, Frey Papers, UCLA; David A. Lockmiller, *Enoch H. Crowder: Soldier, Lawyer, and Statesman, 1859–1932* (Columbia, Missouri: University of Missouri Studies, 1955), 153, says he didn't want them.

Page 83. *Collecting the bounty:* Bielaski to Special Agents, September 24, 1917, September 27, 1917; Gregory to U.S. Attorneys, Circular No. 744, October 8, 1917, Frey Papers, UCLA; O'Brian to U.S. Attorney, Detroit, Michigan, January 18, 1918, File 186751, NA, RG 60.

Pages 83–84. *Deserters:* Bielaski to Special Agents, October 24, 1917, and Selective Service Regulations, November 16, 1917, Frey Papers, UCLA.

Page 84. *Conscientious objectors:* Norman Thomas, *The Conscientious Objector in America* (New York: Huebsch, 1923), 81, 178; Lucille Millner, *The Education of an American Liberal* (New York: Horizon, 1954), 67–70; "Defect in the Draft Law," *Nation,* 105 (August 23, 1917), 192–193.

Page 85. *Political purposes:* Wilson to Baker, December 6, 1917, Wilson, *Life and Letters,* VII, 395.

Pages 85–86. *War Emergency Division:* O'Brian, "Changing Aspects," 149.

Page 89. *Reform:* See bulletins and memoranda in Frey Papers, UCLA; APL to H. S. Basford, January 22, 1917, California File, NA, RG 65; S. J. Graham to J. T. Amis, January 18, 1917, File 186751, NA, RG 60.

Pages 89–90. *November:* Lincoln Steffens to Laura Steffens, November 1, 1917, and November 11, 1917, Ella Winter and Granville Hicks (eds.), *The Letters of Lincoln Steffens* (2 vols.; New York: Harcourt, Brace, 1938), I, 411, 413; Wilson, *Public Papers,* V, 122.

Page 90. *Wilson silent:* Nelles, *Liberal in Wartime,* 108.

Page 90. *"Avenging government":* New York Times, November 21, 1917, 3:3.

Pages 90–91. *Chicago meeting:* Bulletin and notes for Frey speech, Frey Papers, UCLA.

Page 91. *Welcome the APL:* Gregory to Briggs, November 16, 1917, Frey Papers, UCLA; Attorney General, *Annual Report,* 1917, 83.

Page 92. *Borderland confusion:* Herbert Hoover to Todd, November 16, 1917, and Director, Bureau of War Trade to Attorney General, November 7, 1917, File 190470, NA, RG 60. For Hale incident see Wilson to McAdoo, November 19, 1917, McAdoo Papers, LC, Box 523.

Page 92. *Gregory complained:* Cronon, *Cabinet Diaries,* 237.

Page 92. *Food hoarding:* APL to Brennan, February 20, 1918, and February 25, 1918, Brennan to Connell, February 26, 1917, NA, RG 87.

Page 92. *"A bit distressed":* Wilson to McAdoo, November 19, 1917, and McAdoo to Wilson, November 22, 1917, McAdoo Papers, Box 523.

Page 92. *Attack continued:* McAdoo to Gregory, December 1, 1917, McAdoo Papers, Vol. 55; Report from Charles W. Seymour, File 186233, NA, RG 60; Gregory Memorandum to Fitts, December 10, 1917, December 13, 1917, File 190470, NA, RG 60.

Page 93. *Dangerous Austrian subjects:* Lansing quoted in Victor S. Mamatey, *The United States and East Central Europe, 1914–1918: A Study in Wilsonian Diplomacy and Propaganda* (Princeton: Princeton University Press, 1957), 157–158; Konta to Cobb, November 28, 1917, Wilson to Cobb, November 30, 1917, Wilson Papers, File II, Box 130.

Page 93. *Illegal arrests:* Frey memorandum, December 3, 1917; Clabaugh to Frey, December 4, 1917; General Bulletin, No. 3, December 5, 1917, Frey Papers, UCLA.

Page 94. *"Not Government officers":* O'Brian to Charles G. Davis, December 26, 1917, File 187415, NA, RG 60; Bielaski to Baldwin, February 9, 1917, in Johnson, *The Challenge,* 65.

Pages 94–95. *"Discord": New York Times,* January 4, 1918, 7:2; Warren to Gregory, January 5, 1918, File 190470, NA, RG 60.

Page 95. *"If I were a German spy":* McAdoo to Gregory, January 5, 1918, McAdoo Papers, LC, Box 497.

Page 95. *Central intelligence agency:* Alexander L. and Juliette L. George, *Woodrow Wilson and Colonel House: A Personality Study* (New York: John Day, 1956), 199; Mason, *Brandeis,* 523–524, for recommendation of January 9, 1918.

Page 96. *"Not disposed to continue":* Memorandum Gregory to O'Brian, January 12, 1918, File 190470, NA, RG 60.

Page 96. *ADS:* Peterson, *Opponents of War,* 18, 109, 120, 195; Norman Hapgood (ed.), *Professional Patriots* (New York: Boni, 1927), 23–24; Elting Morison and John M. Blum (eds.), *The Letters of Theodore Roosevelt* (8 vols.; Cambridge: Harvard University Press, 1951–1954), VIII, 1268n.

Page 97. *"Power ... to do harm":* Biddle to Van Dieman, October 29, 1917, Allan Forbes to Van Dieman, December 27, 1917, File 10261, NA, RG 165; C. W. Kress to APL, October 16, 1918, New York File, NA, RG 65.

Page 97. *Kill ADS activities:* Frey to Briggs, January 5, 1918, and January 7, 1918, Frey Papers, UCLA.

Page 98. *"Veblen ... in jail":* Roosevelt to L. B. Hayes, January 2, 1918, Roosevelt to R. M. Hurd, January 23, 1918, Roosevelt, *Letters,* VIII, 1267, 1276.

Page 98. *"Not ... necessary to confer":* APL Headquarters report, January 21, 1918, Frey Papers, UCLA.

Page 98. *Flynn and ADS: New York Times,* January 25, 1918, 3:5, 7:2; *New York Tribune,* January 25, 1918.

Page 99. *Rathom: World's Work,* XXXV (February 1918), 394–415.

Page 100. *"Mentally deranged":* Gregory to Albert C. Diffenbach, September 8, 1920, Gregory Papers, LC, Box 2; *New York Times,* February 9, 1918, 10:2 and February 27, 1918, 22:5, for action of Justice Department.

Page 100. *Taft: New York Times,* February 22, 1918, 4:1.

Page 100. *Greek-American chauffeur:* Interview with Dr. Francis Bacon, January 22, 1938, in Chester R. Milham, "A History of National Espionage Legislation and its Operation in the United States During the World War" (unpublished Ph.D. dissertation, University of Southern California, 1938), 277.

Pages 100–101. *"German taint":* O'Brian to Knox, quoted in Richard Drinnon, *Rebel in Paradise: A Biography of Emma Goldman* (Chicago: University of Chicago Press, 1961), 206.

Page 101. *Berkman and Tagore: New York Times,* February 25, 1918, 1:2, 4:6 and February 28, 1918, 3:3; *Official Bulletin,* II (February 25, 1918), 1.

Page 101. *Weekly meetings:* O'Brian to Gregory, March 12, 1918, File 190470, NA, RG 60; Interview with John Lord O'Brian, June 20, 1961; O'Brian, "Changing Aspects of Freedom," in *The John Randolph Tucker Lectures* (Virginia: Washington and Lee University Press, 1952), 152.

Page 102. *"Nothing will be accomplished":* McAdoo to Gregory, February 14, 1918, McAdoo Papers, LC, Box 497; *New York Times,* February 20, 1918, 5:2.

Page 103. *"The chief question":* O'Brian to Gregory, March 1, 1918, File 190470, NA, RG 60.

Page 103. *Plans for coordination:* O'Brian to Gregory, March 7, 1918, File 190470, NA, RG 60.

Page 103. *Secret Service move doomed:* McAdoo to Gregory, March 21, 1918, McAdoo Papers, LC, Box 498.

Page 104. *Danger inefficiency:* See for example the argument of former pacifist James Scherer, a member of the Council of National Defense, *Nation at War* (New York: Doran, 1918), 37.

Prompt Trials, Quick Hangings

Page 105. *Europe:* Chambers, *The War Behind the War,* 182, for Austria; Warren, "Spies," 221, for England.

Pages 106–107. *Warren:* L. H. Woolsey, "Charles Warren," *American Journal of International Law,* IL (January 1955), 50–54; Holmes to Laski, January 3, 1926, *Holmes-Laski Letters,* II, 817.

Page 107. *"One man shot":* Warren to Gregory, January 11, 1918, and John W. Davis to Attorney General, January 18, 1918, File 9-5-395, NA, RG 60.

Page 108. *"Power . . . should be given":* Gregory to O'Brian, January 12, 1918, File 190470, NA, RG 60.

Page 108. *War zones:* APL Headquarters Report, January 19, 1918, Frey Papers, UCLA: Gregory to Senator John Bankhead, January 14, 1918, File 9-5-395, NA, RG 60; Kahn speech in *New York Times,* January 20, 1918.

Page 108. *"Extension . . . inexpedient":* Gregory to John W. Weeks, January 19, 1918; Memorandum on Senate Bill No. 3387, February 7, 1918; Gregory to Wilson, February 7, 1918, File 9-5-395, NA, RG 60; Gregory to Sheppard, February 25, 1918, File 187415, NA, RG 60.

Page 109. *"Serious mistake":* Wilson to Senator Robert L. Owen, Wilson, *Life and Letters,* VII, 517–518.

Page 109. *Wilson's total economic war:* Chambers, *The War Behind the War,* 43; Wilson to Gregory, March 25, 1918, and Wilson to Grant Squires, April 1, 1918, Wilson, *Life and Letters,* VIII, 48–49, 67.

Page 110. *"German whelps":* D. D. Aitken to Senator W. A. Smith, File 186233, NA, RG 60.

Pages 110–111. *Kahn, Harding, Taft: San Francisco Examiner,* March 25, 1918, 4:2; *New York Times,* March 25, 1918, 8:4, March 4, 1918, 11:5, and April 4, 1918, 2:7.

Page 111. *Praeger:* Wilson, *Life and Letters,* VIII, 73.

Page 111. *Clamoring for action:* E. G. Ivey to Ernest Hawkins, March 12, 1918, North Carolina File and E. R. Stonaker to Briggs, April 10, 1918, New York File, NA, RG 65.

Page 112. *"Germany does not hesitate":* U.S., *Congressional Record,* 65th Cong., 2nd Sess., 1918, LVI, Part 5, 4637, 4647, 4714 for spy debate.

Pages 112–113. *Military control over spies:* Warren, "Spies," 219, 226; other discussions in L. K. Underhill, "Jurisdiction of Military Tribunals in the United States Over Civilians," *California Law Review,* 12 (January-March 1924), 75–98, 159–178 and John W. Curran, "Lincoln Conspiracy Trial and Military Jurisdiction Over Civilians, "*Notre Dame Lawyer,* 27 (November 1933), 27–49.

Page 113. *No liberals:* Roger Baldwin to Harold Evans, April 13, 1918, quoted in New York State, Legislature, *Report of Joint Committee to Investigate Seditious Activities* (4 vols.; New York, 1920), I, 1099.

Page 114. *"Zone of influence":* Elting to Mahlon R. Kline, April 9, 1918, Frey Papers, UCLA.

Page 114. *Not honeycombed with spies:* Notes on Bridgeport, Connecticut speech, copy in Frey Papers, UCLA.

Page 115. *Doing adequate job:* "Suggestions of Attorney General Gregory to Executive Committee in Relation to the Department of Justice," *American Bar Association Journal,* IV (July 1918), 305–316; "Disloyalty and Treason and Their Punishment as Provided by Federal Law," *Washington Law Reporter* (1918), 326–328.

Page 115. *"Hysteria":* Gregory to T. V. Taylor, April 15, 1918, Gregory Papers, LC, Box 1; Gregory to C. N. Ridgeway, April 20, 1918, File 190470, NA, RG 60; Gregory to James A. Frear, *Official Bulletin,* II (April

15, 1918), 4; "Boloism in This Country," *Literary Digest,* LVI (March 2, 1918), 14–15.

Page 116. *"Keep . . . heads and stop disorder":* O'Brian to Gregory, April 18, 1918, Wilson Papers, LC, File VI, Box 37 and undated memorandum O'Brian to Gregory, "Conference on Insurance Matter at Treasury Department," File 190470, NA, RG 60.

Pages 116–117. *Chamberlain: New York Tribune,* April 17, 1918.

Page 117. *Van Dieman:* Ralph Van Dieman, "Memorandum," April 8, 1949, in possession of General George W. Fisher, San Diego, California.

Page 118. *Gregory's complaint:* Baker to Gregory, June 29, 1918, File 190470, NA, RG 60.

Page 118. *Larger appropriations:* Herbert H. White to Van Dieman, August 10, 1917, File 10148, NA, RG 165.

Page 119. *Van Dieman and APL:* APL Headquarters Report, January 14, 1918, Frey Papers, UCLA.

Pages 119–120. *Waberski:* Edmund M. Morgan, "Court-Martial Jurisdiction Over Non-military Persons Under the Articles of War," *Minnesota Law Review,* 4 (January 1920), 79–116; and File 10560, NA, RG 165.

Page 120. *"Ghastly failure":* Committee on Military Affairs, *Extending Jurisdiction of Military Tribunals,* 36–37, 51, 57.

Page 120. *ADS: New York Times,* April 21, 1918, 15:2.

Page 121. *"Worst possible policy":* O'Brian to Gregory, April 18, 1918, File 189083, NA, RG 60; *New York Times,* April 20, 1918, 8:2.

Page 121. *Opposition to bill:* Wilson to Overman, April 20, 1918, Wilson, *Life and Letters,* VIII, 99; Gregory to Gordon, April 20, 1918, quoted in *Washington Evening Star,* April 22, 1918.

Page 122. *Sedition Act:* Wilson, *A History,* III, 153.

Page 122. *Volunteer Intelligence Corps:* Rolin G. Watkins to Military Intelligence Bureau, April 18, 1918, California File, NA, RG 65.

Page 122. *"Competition for efficiency":* Reichmann to Van Dieman, April 28, 1918, File 9684, NA, RG 165.

Page 123. *"Unnatural jealousy of the League":* Van Dieman to Reichmann, May 15, 1918, *ibid.*

Page 123. *Secret recruitment:* Van Dieman to Reichmann, *ibid.*

Page 123. *Reliable citizens:* O'Brian to Attorney General, June 14, 1918, June 18, 1918, File 190470, NA, RG 60.

Page 124. *Careful with civilians:* MI 3, Bulletin for Intelligence Officers, No. 11, June 3, 1918, and MI 3, Bulletin for Intelligence Officers, No. 14, June 14, 1918, Frey Papers, UCLA.

Page 124. *"Decided to supplant":* O'Brian to Gregory, June 18, 1918, File 190470, NA, RG 60; O'Brian to Churchill, June 19, 1918, copy in Glasser File, Box 9, NA, RG 60.

Page 124. *"Proper spheres":* Baker to Gregory, June 29, 1918, File 190470, NA, RG 60; Churchill to Commanding General, Camp Wheeler,

Georgia, June 22, 1918, File 10660, NA, RG 165.

Page 125. *"League will continue"*: *Spy Glass*, June 28, 1918.

Page 125. *Councils of defense:* Oklahoma, O. A. Hilton, "The Oklahoma Council of Defense and the First World War," *Chronicles of Oklahoma*, XX (March 1942), 18–42; Ohio, S. F. D. Meffley to Justice Department, October 17, 1917, File 186751, NA, RG 60; Governor of Hawaii to Provost Marshal General Crowder, March 12, 1918, NA, RG 163; California, Attorney General to U.S. Attorney, San Francisco, August 24, 1917, File 186701, NA, RG 60.

Page 126. *Massachusetts:* Elting ms. diary, January 8, 11, 17, 22, 23, 1918; Frey to Elting, March 25, 1918; Gregory to Charles F. Choate, May 3, 1918, copy, Frey Papers, UCLA; O'Brian to Hugh Bancroft, April 10, 1918, File 186751, NA, RG 60.

Page 126. *Minute Men:* William C. Fitts to Secretary of War, July 28, 1917, File 186701, NA, RG 60; reports in Thomas Burke Papers, University of Washington; APL, Minute Men Division, *American Protective League, Minute Men Division* (Seattle: Mercantile Printing, 1918), 13.

Page 127. *Need more jails:* William Stuart Forth, "Wesley L. Jones: A Political Biography" (unpublished Ph.D. dissertation, University of Washington, 1962), 406–407.

Page 128. *Merger:* APL Form 225, June 14, 1918; *Spy Glass*, June 28, 1918.

Page 128. *Supplant state councils:* Form 225, June 14, 1918, Frey Papers, UCLA; O'Brian to J. R. Welch, June 20, 1918, File 192922, NA, RG 60.

The Web

Page 130. *The Web:* Little Rock, Arkansas File, NA, RG 65.

Page 131. *State inspectors:* Lists in Frey Papers, UCLA: Tom Stout, *Montana: Its Story and Biography* (3 vols.; Chicago and New York: American Historical Society, 1921), II, 515.

Page 132. *"Separate and distinct":* Fred Voiland to S. S. Doty, May 4, 1918, S. S. Doty to Voiland, May 9, 1918, Kansas File, NA, RG 65; A. T. Bagley to APL, July 25, 1918, Frey Papers, UCLA.

Pages 132–134. *Chiefs:* G. L. Seaton to APL, March 5, 1918, *ibid.*; O. P. Adams to APL, January 9, 1919, California File; R. Wentworth Floyd to Rushmore, October 2, 1918, New York File, NA, RG 65.

Page 134. *Moral reform:* R. S. Spears to APL, December 13, 1918, and A. L. Keet to APL, July 22, 1918, *ibid.*

Page 135. *State affairs:* APL Headquarters Report, January 9, 1918, January 25, 1918; B. F. Morgan to APL, April 2, 1918, and Report on Clay Center, Kansas; S. S. Beggs to Frey, April 19, 1918, George L.

Seaton to APL, March 5, 1918, Frey Papers, UCLA.

Page 135. *Local police: Spy Glass,* June 28, 1918; A. W. Ellis to APL, December 18, 1918, and J. W. Hale to Elting, December 18, 1918, California File, NA, RG 65.

Page 137. *Errant chief:* Douglas White to APL, April 25, 1918, May 30, 1918, *ibid.;* Joseph Scott to J. P. Tumulty, May 27, 1918, Gregory to O'Brian, July 1, 1918, Gregory to Colonel Fred Feigl, July 19, 1918, File 186751, NA, RG 60.

Page 137. *Agents' recommendations:* Bielaski to Agent Hayes, March 29, 1918, Frey Papers, UCLA.

Pages 138–140. *Businessmen:* Material which follows concerning the Chicago Division is drawn from the Chicago Handbook and various other lists and memoranda in the Frey Papers. Biographies were traced in *The Book of Chicagoans: A Biographical Directory of Leading Men and Women of the City of Chicago* (Chicago: Marquis, 1917), and *Who's Who in Chicago* (Chicago: Marquis, 1923). James B. Forgan, president of the National Bank of Chicago, was one of the American financiers who brought pressure on the State Department in the summer of 1915 to revoke the ban on large-scale loans to the Allies.

Pages 141–142. *Other units:* APL Headquarters Report, January 9, 1918, for Washington, D.C., Frey Papers, UCLA; Briggs to Muma, February 19, 1918, B. Colby to APL, March 13, 1918, California File; F. L. Seely to Frey, December 25, 1917, and April 19, 1918, North Carolina File; APL to DeMille, July 10, 1918, California File; Frey to Rushmore, June 27, 1918, New York File, NA, RG 65; Douglas White to DeMille, June 17, 1918, File 10660, NA, RG 165.

Pages 142–143. *Women spies:* Hough, *Web,* 296, 256, 259, 189; James R. Mock, *Censorship, 1917* (New Jersey: Princeton University Press, 1941), 208–209.

Page 142. *"Wonderful lady detective":* Frey to Kate Marjoribanks, February 8, 1918, and form letters, Frey Papers, UCLA.

Page 142. *"Discreet" women:* General Orders No. 5, California State Inspector to Chiefs, July 15, 1918, California File, NA, RG 65.

Page 142. *"Brainy women":* W. E. Cochrane to Frey, June 1918, Frey Papers, UCLA.

Page 143. *Actresses:* Frey to Briggs, June 28, 1918, *ibid.*

Page 144. *Women not eligible:* APL Bulletin No. 15, July 1918, *ibid.*

Page 144. *Patriotism:* Morton Grodzins, *The Loyal and the Disloyal: Social Boundaries of Patriotism and Treason* (Chicago: University of Chicago Press, 1956), 5–8.

Page 144. *Peter Gudge:* Upton Sinclair, *100%: The Story of a Patriot* (Pasadena: By the author, 1920), 177.

Pages 144–145. *Obregón:* H. G. Holabird, "An Interesting Experience," California File, NA, RG 65.

Page 145. A *"talking to":* Hough, *Web,* 253.

Page 145. *"Almost . . . a lynching":* Frey to Briggs, May 14, 1918, Frey Papers, UCLA.

Page 146. *Disloyal dissuaded:* Frey Report to the War Department, File 10566, NA, RG 165.

Pages 146–147. *Vigilante groups:* Hough, *Web,* 328, 390, 401–402; W. C. Witherbee to APL, June 21, 1918, New York File, NA, RG 65; William G. Shepherd, "Ku Klux Koin," *Colliers,* LXXXII (July 21, 1928), 8–9, 38–39.

Page 147. *"Physical violence":* Spy Glass, June 4, 1918.

Page 147. *California universities:* Mock, *Censorship,* 193; Walton E. Bean, "George Creel and His Critics: A Study of the Attacks on the Committee on Public Information, 1917–1919" (unpublished Ph.D. dissertation, University of California, Berkeley, 1941), 107; White to APL, May 3, 1918, California File, NA, RG 65.

Page 148. *Books: Spy Glass,* October 1918.

Pages 148–149. *Post Office:* Elting to P. A. Erlach, April 1, 1918, Frey Papers, UCLA; APL to Douglas White, August 17, 1918, California File, NA, RG 65; Hough, *Web,* 163.

Page 149. *Telegraph:* Elting to Ralph W. Smith, June 13, 1918, Frey Papers, UCLA.

Page 149. *Minneapolis:* Hough, *Web,* 322.

Pages 150–151. *Wiretapping:* James S. Easby-Smith to Wilson, January 1917, File VI, Box 37; Annette Abbott Adams to Attorney General, November 25, 1918, Gregory to Adams, December 4, 1918; W. B. Wilson to Attorney General, December 11, 1918, Adams to Gregory, December 23, 1918, File 17844, NA, RG 60; Samuel Dash, *et. al. The Eavesdroppers* (New Brunswick: Rutgers University Press, 1959), 24, 28, 35. Fifty years elapsed before the Supreme Court applied the Fourth Amendment to wiretapping and other forms of electronic eavesdropping in *Katz* v. *United States.* See "Unconstitutional Bugging," *New Republic,* Vol. 157 (January 6, 1968), 11–12. Then Congress, in 1968, voted to exempt law enforcement agencies in certain classes of investigations from the Court's ruling.

Page 150. *Telephones:* Bielaski to APL, May 17, 1918, APL to Harry A. Melius, May 21, 1918, New York File, NA, RG 65.

Page 151. *Kansas:* Will G. Price to Briggs, December 18, 1917, Kansas File, *ibid.*

Page 151. *Federal wiretapping law:* U.S., *Statutes at Large,* 40, Part I, 1017 (October 29, 1918); Dash, *Eavesdroppers,* 28.

Page 151. *Arizona: State* v. *Behringer,* 172 P. 660 (1918). The dissent by J. Cunningham contains an early defense of the right of privacy against the use of dictaphones.

Page 151. *Dictaphones:* Major Durant Whipple, Chief, Little Rock, Arkansas, to APL, Arkansas File, NA, RG 65; Hough, *Web,* 261, 312, 322. For use of evidence so obtained to convict see *Schoberg* v. *United States,* 264 Fed. 1.

Page 152. *"Access to any house":* Will G. Price to Briggs, December 18, 1917, Kansas File, NA, RG 65.

Page 152. *Coal chute:* Hough, *Web,* 322.

Page 152. *Stealing: Gouled* v. *United States,* 255 U.S. 298 (1921).

Page 152. *Breaking and entering:* Hough, *Web,* 163.

Page 153. *Brandeis: Burdeau* v. *McDowell,* 256 U.S. 465 (1921).

Page 153. *Questioning: APL, In re Military Intelligence Investigations* (n.p., n.d.); *Spy Glass,* June 28, 1918.

Pages 153–154. *Decoys:* W. A. Capron to Colonel Seagraves, August 5, 1918, undated report re A. D. Lasker, Frey Papers, UCLA.

Page 154. *"Reproduction in a crude way":* Annual Report for King County by S. J. Lombard, September 13, 1918, APL Papers, University of Washington.

Pages 154–155. *Expansion of investigation:* Charles DeWoody to Rushmore, March 2, 1918, Frey Papers, UCLA.

Pages 155–156. *Costs:* Rushmore to Frey, April 19, 1918, New York File; S. S. Doty to Stephens, October 10, 1918, North Carolina File, NA, RG 65; Memorandum of June 11, 1918, APL Papers, University of Washington; Hough, *Web,* 184, 289; APL Headquarters Report, January and February, 1918; Elting from letter April 27, 1918, and policy letter May 22, 1918, Frey Papers, UCLA.

Page 156. *Businessmen financed:* A. Evan Wisban to APL, November 4, 1918, California File, NA, RG 65; Briggs to Frey, February 15, 1918, February 27, 1918, Frey Memoranda, January 13, 1918, April 14, 1918, May 14, 1918, August 1, 1918, Frey Papers, UCLA.

Page 156. *"Suspicion and fear":* Allan Dulles, *The Craft of Intelligence* (New York: Harper and Row, 1963), 22.

Page 157. *"Forget its details":* Wilson, *Life and Letters,* VIII, 32.

Alien, Dissenter, Citizen

Page 159. *Wilson statement: New York Tribune,* July 23, 1918, 6:3.

Page 159. *"Disgraceful evil":* Wilson, *Public Papers,* V, 238–239.

Page 159. *APL guardians: Spy Glass,* August 10, 1918.

Pages 159–160. *Alien voters:* A. J. Montague to Wilson, June 13, 1918, Wilson Papers, LC, File VI, Box 473. The states were Arkansas, Indiana, Kansas, Michigan, Missouri, Nebraska, South Dakota, and Texas.

Page 160. *Comparison of the two wars:* Chicago, Civil Liberties Committee, *Pursuit of Freedom: A History of Civil Liberty in Illinois, 1787–1942* (Chicago: Chicago Civil Liberties Committee, 1942), 118; Robert E. Cushman, "American Government in War-Time: Civil Liberties," *American Political Science Review,* XXXVII (February 1943), 53; "Treatment of Prisoners of War in France," File 28573, NA, RG 60.

Page 160. *"Without the guarantees":* Spy Glass, June 28, 1918.

Page 161. *Tageblatt case:* Thomas F. Carroll, "Freedom of Speech and the Press in War Time: the Espionage Act," *Michigan Law Review,* XVII (June 1919), 661–662; Hough, *Web,* 218.

Page 161. *Internments: Official Bulletin,* I (December 14, 1917), 3; (May 26, 1917), 1; (December 12, 1917), 8; II (June 12, 1918), 1; U.S., Department of Labor, *Annual Report* (Washington 1917), 103, 132, 177.

Pages 161–162. *"Conservative course":* Warren to Byrd, April 14, 1917, File 9–16–12, NA, RG 60.

Page 162. *"Silent and mysterious":* U.S., Congress, House, Committee on Immigration and Naturalization, *Deportation of Interned Aliens,* 65th Cong., 3d Sess., 1919, 5–6.

Page 162. *"Anarchist outbreak":* Attorney General to U.S. Attorneys, Circular No. 708, July 18, 1918, Frey Papers, UCLA.

Page 162. *"German accent":* Committee on Immigration and Naturalization, *Deportation,* 8.

Page 163. *Muck:* Bliss Perry, *Life and Letters of Henry Lee Higginson* (Boston: Atlantic Monthly, 1921), 484–490, 497, 501.

Page 163. *Warrants:* Bielaski to Special Agents, January 22, 1918, Frey Papers, UCLA.

Page 164. *Habeas corpus: Ex parte Grager,* 247 Fed. 882.

Page 164. *Parole system:* Frey Report to War Department, File 10566, NA, RG 165; *Official Bulletin,* II (April 8, 1918), 10.

Pages 164–165. *Palmer: Spy Glass,* July 12, 1918; Attorney General to U.S. Attorneys, Circular No. 790, February 9, 1918, Frey Papers, UCLA.

Page 165. *Enemy propaganda:* O'Brian to Gregory, June 6, 1918, Gregory to Palmer, June 6, 1918, File 190470, NA, RG 60; John Lord O'Brian, "Changing Aspects of Freedom," in *The John Randolph Tucker Lectures* (Virginia: Washington and Lee University Press, 1952), 157.

Page 165. *"Not content": Spy Glass,* August 10, 1918.

Page 165. *"Boche business": Spy Glass,* November 4, 1918, October 5, 1918; John Lord O'Brian, *Civil Liberty in Wartime,* U.S., Congress, Senate, 65th Cong., 3rd Sess., Senate Doc. No. 434 (Washington 1919), 8.

Page 166. *Alien regulations:* U.S. Marshal J. J. Bradley to Frey, October 9, 1917, Bielaski to Special Agents, January 10, 1918, Frey Papers, UCLA; Attorney General, *Annual Report* (Washington 1918), 25–37. The Enemy Alien Act was amended on April 16, 1918, to include women fourteen years of age and over. German male aliens were required to register on February 4, 1918, women on June 17, 1918. Over 480,000 registered.

Page 166. *Defense plants:* Hough, *Web.* 223; Committeee on Immigration and Naturalization, *Deportation,* 9.

Pages 166–167. *Employment:* Bielaski to Special Agents, January 14, 1918, Frey Papers, UCLA.

Page 167. *Special assistants:* O'Brian to Michael Devanney, July 26, 1918, File 9-16-4, NA, RG 60.

Page 167. *Plant protection:* Gregory to Bielaski, August 19, 1918, James

A. Blair to E. N. Hurley, September 9, 1918, File 190470, NA, RG 60; APL Headquarters Report, January 17, 1918, February 14, 1918, Frey Papers, UCLA.

Pages 167–168. *Naturalization:* Attorney General, *Annual Report,* 1918, 37; *Spy Glass,* June 28, 1918; Hough, *Web,* 299.

Page 168. *Denaturalization: Official Bulletin,* I (August 6, 1917), 15; *United States* v. *Raverat,* 222 Fed. 1018.

Page 168. *Cancellation:* Edmunds to Elting, April 26, 1918, O'Brian to Elting, May 3, 1918, File 186751, NA, RG 60.

Page 168. *Fraud: Official Bulletin,* II (June 6, 1918), 2, (June 14, 1918), 20; *United States* v. *Wursterbarth,* 249 Fed. 908.

Page 169. *World War II:* Cushman, "American Government," 54.

Page 169. *"Dangerous propaganda":* Undated memorandum Bettman to Frey, California File, NA, RG 65.

Page 171. *Drawing the line:* Attorney General to U.S. Attorneys, May 23, 1918, *Spy Glass,* Supplement to June 11, 1918.

Page 171. *Liberty loans: Spy Glass,* October 5, 1918.

Page 171. *Search for disloyal:* Bulletin No. 14 to Chiefs, July 18, 1918, Frey Papers, UCLA; Frey Report to War Department, File 10566, NA, RG 165: *Spy Glass,* October 19, 1918.

Pages 171–172. *New York American Liberal:* Copy in Frey Papers, UCLA.

Page 172. *"Juries convict":* Amos Pinchot to Wilson, May 24, 1918, Wilson Papers, LC, File II, Box 140.

Page 173. *Debs:* Hough, *Web,* 262; *Spy Glass,* July 25, 1918; Ray Ginger, *The Bending Cross: A Biography of Eugene Victor Debs* (New Brunswick: Rutgers University Press, 1949), 357–363.

Pages 173–174. *Russellites:* Hough, *Web,* 191; *Spy Glass,* June 28, 1918; Oswald G. Villard, *Fighting Years: Memoirs of a Liberal Editor* (New York: Harcourt, Brace, 1939), 388; *Rutherford* v. *United States,* 258 Fed. 855.

Page 174. *Irish "slackers":* Gregory to E. M. House, June 10, 1920, Gregory Papers, LC, Box 2.

Pages 174–175. *O'Leary:* Carl Wittke, *The Irish in America* (Baton Rouge: Louisiana State University Press, 1956), 284; Hough, *Web,* 202; Jeremiah O'Leary, *My Political Trial and Experience* (New York: Jefferson, 1919), 238, 417.

Pages 175–176. *Sabotage: Spy Glass,* August 24, 1918, November 4, 1918; *United States* v. *De Bolt et. al.,* 253 Fed. 78.

Page 176. *Civil service:* U.S., Committee on Government Security, *Report* (Washington 1957), 5; Elting ms. diary, January 25, 30, 1918, Frey Papers, UCLA; Paul P. Van Riper, *History of the United States Civil Service* (Evanston, Illinois: Row, Peterson, 1958), 268.

Page 177. *"Faults":* File 10560, NA, RG 165.

Page 178. *Passports: Official Bulletin,* I (November 15, 1917), 1.

Page 178. *"Close the border":* O'Brian to Gregory, April 19, 1918, Wilson Papers, LC, File II, Box 139.

Page 179. *"Semi-judicial capacity":* Bielaski to DeWoody, May 28, 1918, quoted in Alexander Eisemann, *American Protective League: Investigations for the United States Department of Justice Bureau of Investigation* (New York: Conway, 1918).

Page 179. *Passports refused:* Steffens, *Letters,* II, 439; Villard, *Fighting Years,* 362.

Page 179. *Commissions:* APL Headquarters Report, January 23, 24, 1918; *Spy Glass,* June 28, 1918; Bulletin No. 19, to Chiefs, October 2, 1918, Frey Papers, UCLA.

Page 180. *"Underground methods":* C. F. Lea to Wilson, November 30, 1918, Wilson Papers, LC, File II, Box 157.

Pages 180–181. *Vice and liquor:* Dickinson, *Building an Army,* 205.

Page 181. *Women protectors: ibid.,* 215–216.

Page 182. *"Outside influence":* APL Headquarters Report, January 4, 5, 7, 1918, Frey Papers, UCLA.

Page 182. *Prohibition:* Frey to Briggs, January 4, 1918, Briggs to Frey, January 8, 1918, O'Brian to U.S. Attorneys, January 21, 1918, *ibid.*

Page 182. *New Orleans:* Briggs to Frey, January 5, 1918, E. J. Kerin to APL, August 13, 1918, *ibid.;* Hough, *Web,* 327–329, 190; *New York Times,* March 8, 1918, 7:1; American Protective League, New Orleans Division, *A Summary of the Activities of the New Orleans Division of the American Protective League* (New Orleans 1919), 10.

Page 183. *"Hard-headed businessmen":* New Orleans Item, March 6, 1918; George D. Buckley to Briggs, March 13, 1918, Frey Papers, UCLA.

Page 183. *"Cannot be done":* Frey to Briggs, March 29, 1918, *ibid.*

Page 183. *Authority "a bit weak":* Dickinson, *Building an Army,* 217.

Page 183. *Diseased women:* Circular No. 812, Attorney General to U.S. Attorneys, April 3, 1918, and accompanying memorandum on legal aspects of proposed system, Frey Papers, UCLA.

Page 183. *"Great advance":* Elting to Mahlon R. Kline, April 9, 1918, *ibid.;* Frey Report to War Department, File 10566, NA, RG 165.

Page 184. *"News . . . spread":* Briggs to Frey, April 12, 1918, Frey Papers, UCLA.

Page 184. *Amproleague Farms:* Frey Report to War Department, File 10566, NA, RG 165; APL, New Orleans Division, *Summary; Spy Glass,* August 24, 1918.

Page 184. *Liquor:* Briggs to Frey, April 12, 1918, Frey Papers, UCLA.

Page 185. *"Psychological stimulation":* Frey Report to War Department, File 10566, NA, RG 165, mentions bulletin of January 12, 1918.

Page 185. *"Cheerful home news":* G. B. Perkins to APL, July 6, 1918, *ibid.*

Pages 185–186. *Weekly intelligence report:* Churchill to APL, July 22, 1918, File 10660, *ibid.*

Page 186. *Wisconsin:* G. P. Braun to S. S. Doty, August 1, 1918, File 9684, *ibid.*

Pages 186–187. *Intelligence reports:* In File 177, *ibid.*

Slacker Raiding

Pages 188–189. *New rules:* Bielaski to Special Agents, January 7, 1918, Frey Papers, UCLA.

Page 189. *Deputization:* Attorney General to Crowder, January 10, 1918, Crowder to Adjutant General, Illinois, January 11, 1918 (not sent), Memorandum of January 15, 1918, Illinois File, NA, RG 163.

Page 190. *"Somewhat complicated":* APL Headquarters Report, January 25, 1918, Frey Papers, UCLA.

Page 190. *"All possible authority":* APL Headquarters Report, January 23, 1918, Gregory to Briggs, January 30, 1918, *ibid.*

Pages 190–191. *Causing and apprehending:* U.S., Provost Marshal General, *Circulars and Telegrams of the Selective Service Organization* (2 vols.; Washington 1917–1919), I, 395; Bielaski to Special Agents, February 6, 1918, APL Bulletin No. 3, February 6, 1918, Frey Papers, UCLA.

Page 191. *"A government status":* Colonel Reichmann to MIB, February 26, 1918, File 9684, NA, RG 165.

Page 191. *"Safety Committee":* White to APL, July 24, 1918, Crowder to Adjutant General, California, July 26, 1918, White to APL, July 30, 1918, California File, NA, RG 65.

Pages 191–192. *Minneapolis raid:* APL Summary and Report of War Service, Minneapolis Division, Frey Papers, UCLA; Franklin F. Holbrook (ed.), *St. Paul and Ramsey County in the War of 1917–1918* (St. Paul: Ramsey County War Records Commission, 1929), 226; Franklin F. Holbrook and Livia Appel, *Minnesota in the War With Germany* (2 vols.; St. Paul: Minnesota Historical Society, 1928, 1932), II, 38.

Page 192. *Defend chief:* O'Brian to John E. Kinnane, April 5, 1918, File 186751, NA, RG 60.

Page 192. *"Must comply":* Bulletin from APL Chief, Wilkes County, North Carolina to Officers and Privates of Wilkes County Branch APL, North Carolina File, NA, RG 65.

Pages 192–193. *Number dwindling:* "Major General Crowder on the Selective Draft," *Outlook,* 118 (January 16, 1918), 245. Totals given for the first call were:

Total registrants	9,586,508
Not called	6,503,550
Called	3,082,949
Exemptions claimed (20% alien birth and nationality)	1,560,570
Rejected as physically unfit	730,756

Failed to appear	252,294
Called for examination	457,713
Exempted (60% alien)	381,168
Certified	76,545

Page 193. *Ambitious measures:* Memorandum Martin Conboy for Captain Hope, General File 17-915, NA, RG 167.

Page 193. *Summer series:* For Alabama raid see note attached to Martin Conboy Memorandum, *ibid.*; Hough, *Web,* 256; Frey Report 10566, NA, RG 165; *Spy Glass,* September 7, 1918; Carl Wittke, *German-Americans and the World War* (Columbus: Ohio State Archeological and Historical Society, 1936), 190.

Page 194. *Frenzied competition:* S. S. Doty to B. H. Stephens, October 10, 1918, for APL ruling, North Carolina File, NA, RG 65; Gregory to U.S. Attorneys, April 15, 1918, Frey Papers, UCLA; Memorandum James J. Mayes, Acting Judge Advocate General, May 22, 1918, File 17-355, NA, RG 167.

Page 194. *Bounty hunting: New York Tribune,* July 9, 1918, 11:3; July 22, 1918, 8:4.

Page 194. *Suspects held:* U.S. Attorney Caffey to Attorney General, July 23, 1918; O'Brian to Crowder, July 31, 1918, General File 17-471, NA, RG 167.

Page 195. *Extend the age group:* For congressional debate on extension of the draft see Seward W. Livermore, *Politics is Adjourned: Woodrow Wilson and the War Congress, 1916–1918* (Middletown, Connecticut: Wesleyan University Press, 1966), 177.

Pages 195–196. *Chicago raid:* Hough, *Web,* 143; *Spy Glass,* July 25, 1918, August 24, 1918.

Page 196. *"Efficiency . . . lessened":* Milton Vaughan to APL, August 17, 1918, Arkansas File, NA, RG 65.

Page 196. *"Best efforts":* S. S Doty to Milton Vaughan, August 29, 1918, *ibid.*

Page 197. *"Such little things":* Rushmore to Frey, July 3, 1918, New York File, *ibid.*

Page 197. *Darn old town:* Elting ms. diary, January 14, 1918, Briggs to Frey, January 9, 1918, Frey Papers, UCLA.

Page 197. *"Accomplished wonders":* Charles DeWoody to Briggs, April 13, 1918, New York File, NA, RG 65.

Page 198. *"100% rotten":* Frey to Briggs, May 14, 1918, Rushmore to Frey, May 25, 1918, Frey Papers, UCLA; Rushmore to Frey, May 29, 1918, Frey to Rushmore, May 26, 1918, New York File, NA, RG 65.

Page 198. *Rosenfeld:* Memorandum for DeWoody "In re Slacker Raid of Wednesday, June 6, 1918," Rushmore to APL, June 10, 1918, Frey Papers, UCLA; Clipping from *New York Telegram,* New York File, NA, RG 65.

Page 199. *"Extreme difficulties": New York Tribune,* June 6, 1918; Rushmore to APL, June 11, 1918, Lewis to Rushmore, June 10, 1918, Frey Papers, UCLA.

Page 199. *"To the limit":* Frey to Rushmore, August 22, 1918, New York File, NA, RG 65.

Page 200. *Protests:* McDermid to author, August 27, 1961; C. A. Hope memorandum for Crowder opposing countrywide raid, General File 17-373, NA, RG 167.

Page 200. *A major campaign:* Undated report on raids by O'Brian, New York File, NA, RG 65.

Page 201. *Time too short:* Kemp to Whitin, September 9, 1918, *ibid.*

Page 201. *Contacted Bielaski:* Frey to Briggs, August 31, 1918, Frey Papers, UCLA.

Page 201. *National guardsmen:* Breckenridge Jones to Crowder, September 11, 1918, New York File 17-1070, NA, RG 167.

Page 202. *Request in writing:* C. H. Sherrill, Adjutant General, New York to Crowder, September 16, 1918, *ibid.*

Page 202. *Draft boards:* Kemp to Whitin, September 9, 1918, *ibid.*

Page 202. *APL publicity: Philadelphia Public Ledger,* September 2, 1918, 6:2; *New York Tribune,* September 2, 1918, 5:1.

Page 202. *"Hold and bring":* Transcript of long distance telephone conversation between Bielaski, Rushmore, Briggs, and Boese, September 16, 1918, Frey Papers, UCLA; also O'Brian report on raids, New York File, NA, RG 65.

Page 203. *No "cossacking":* W. A. McDermid to author, August 27, 1961.

Page 203. *DeWoody and Praeger:* Sherrill to Crowder, September 6, 1918, New York File 17-1070, NA, RG 167.

Page 204. *No surprise: New York Tribune,* September 3, 1918, 1:1; *New York Times,* September 3, 1918, 8:1.

Page 205. *DeWoody rushed over:* Jones to Crowder, September 11, 1918, New York File 17-1070, NA, RG 167.

Page 205. *Conboy appeared: ibid.*

Page 206. *Wilson endorsed work:* Gregory to O'Brian, September 3, 1918, File 186751, NA, RG 60.

Page 206. *Raiding continued: New York Tribune,* September 4, 1918, 1:3; *New York Times,* September 4, 1918, 1:2, 17:3; *Philadelphia Public Ledger,* September 4, 1918, 2:1; Interview with O'Brian, June 20, 1961; O'Brian report, New York File, NA, RG 65.

Page 206. *The Tombs and Camp Dix: New York Times,* September 5, 1918, 3:1; *New York Tribune,* September 5, 1918, 7:5, 7:6, 6:1; *Philadelphia Public Ledger,* September 5, 1918, 9:1, September 7, 1918; O'Leary, *Political Trial,* 194–195; Local Board No. 1, Burlington County, New Jersey, to Adjutant General, New Jersey, September 12, 1918, New York File 17-1070, NA, RG 167.

Pages 207–208. *Senatorial critics:* U.S., *Congressional Record,* 65th Cong., 2d Sess., LVI, Part 10, 9976–9986, 10063–10068; *New York Times,* September 6, 1918, 1:2; *Philadelphia Public Ledger,* September 6, 1918, 1:3.

Page 208. *Bury it: New York Times,* September 6, 1918, 1:2.

Page 209. *"Silly to assume": Philadelphia Public Ledger,* September 6, 1918, 1:3, 2:7; *New York Tribune,* September 6, 1918, 5:3; *New York Times,* September 6, 1918, 24:1; *New York World,* September 6, 1918, quoted in Arthur E. Ekirch, *The Civilian and the Military* (New York: Oxford, 1956), 193.

Page 209. *"So much interest":* Wilson to Gregory, September 5, 1918, Wilson, *Life and Letters,* VIII, 385–386. Livermore, *Politics,* 208, fails to consider the congressional furor over the slacker raids as a factor in Wilson's cancellation of the tour.

Pages 210–211. *O'Brian: New York Times,* September 8, 1918, 9:3; *New York Tribune,* September 7, 1918, 14:1.

Page 211. *Criticism:* Charles Collman to Gregory, September 6, 1918, Hyacinthe Ringrose to Gregory, September 6, 1918, File 186751, NA, RG 60.

Page 211. *"Shameful spectacle":* Wilson, *Life and Letters,* VIII, 385–386, 405; Nelles, *Liberal in Wartime,* 154; "Civil Liberty Dead," *Nation,* 107 (September 14, 1918), 382.

Page 212. *"A whitewash":* W. A. McDermid to author, August 27, 1961; O'Brian report, New York File, NA, RG 65.

Page 212. *Raids justified:* Gregory to Wilson, September 9, 1918, Gregory Papers, LC, Box 1.

Page 213. *Presidential approval:* Frey Report to War Department, File 10566, NA, RG 165; APL Bulletin No. 18, September 12, 1918, Frey Papers, UCLA; *New York Tribune,* September 13, 1918, 5:5; *Philadelphia Public Ledger,* September 13, 1918, 10:7.

Page 214. *"Indignantly and emphatically":* Transcript of long distance telephone conversation in Frey Papers, UCLA.

Page 214. *"Hold": Casserly* v. *Wheeler,* 282 Fed. 389.

Page 215. *"Technical distinction": New York Times,* September 13, 1918, 10:2.

Page 215. *"Entirely voluntarily":* Bielaski to Special Agents, September 19, 1918, Gregory to Briggs, September 21, 1918, Frey Papers, UCLA; *Spy Glass,* September 21, 1918.

Page 217. *Fall "broken loose":* Newspaper articles in Wilson Papers, LC, Box 149.

Page 217. *"Make sure":* E. S. Underhill to Attorney General Gregory, September 30, 1918, File 186751, NA, RG 60.

Pages 217–218. *California case: Casserly* v. *Wheeler,* 282 Fed. 389.

The Danger Line

Page 219. *"Trying situation":* Frey to Briggs, September 25, 1918, Frey Papers, UCLA.

Page 219. *Discipline problems:* Burnett H. Stevens to APL, October 18,

1918, North Carolina File, J. J. MacEwen to APL, November 9, 1918, New York File, Douglas White to APL, September 24, 1918, California File, NA, RG 65; *Spy Glass*, October 5, 1918.

Page 220. *A "nut":* A. B. Colvin to APL, September 24, 1918, R. J. Kunful to Briggs, October 14, 1918, New York File, NA, RG 65.

Page 220. *Feudal barons:* Frey Report, October 4, 1918, Frey Papers, UCLA.

Page 221. *Strict enforcement:* Briggs to Frey, September 25, 1918, *ibid.*

Page 221. *"Trouble makers":* Frey Report, October 4, 1918, Elting to Briggs, September 26, 1918, *ibid.*

Page 221. *Badges overseas:* Assistant Chief of Staff, AEF to Chief MID, September 23, 1918, File 10347, NA, RG 165.

Page 221. *Lansing and New Orleans:* APL Lansing, Michigan, to Adjutant General, September 6, 1918, S. T. Ansel, Acting Judge Advocate General, to APL, September 27, 1918, Oscar Dowling to Attorney General C. C. McCrory of Louisiana, October 26, 1918, McCrory to Dowling, November 1, 1918, Dowling to Secretary of War, November 19, 1919, NA, RG 94; S. S. Doty to Frey, October 22, 1918, NA, RG 165.

Pages 221–222. *Strange activities:* American Consulate General, Christiania, Norway, to Secretary of State, August 8, 1918, O'Brian to Alvey A. Adee, September 23, 1918, New York File, NA, RG 65; Frey to Bielaski, September 26, 1918, Frey Papers, UCLA; *Spy Glass,* October 19, 1918.

Page 222. *Milwaukee:* J. W. Anderson to Attorney General, August 31, 1918, Samuel W. Randolph, U.S. Marshal to Attorney General, September 5, 1918, File 186751, NA, RG 60.

Page 222. *Cleveland:* Local Cuyahoga County Socialist Party to Gregory, September 6, 1918, *ibid.*

Page 222. *Insubordinate:* S. W. Randolph to Attorney General, September 18, 1918, *ibid.*

Page 222. *Led astray:* Bielaski to Special Agents, September 26, 1918, Attorney General to Division Superintendents and Special Agents, October 1, 1918, Frey Papers, UCLA.

Pages 222–223. *Warnings:* Bielaski to All Employees, June 24, 1918; Bielaski to Special Agents, September 26, 1918; Bielaski to Special Agents, September 10, 1918, *ibid.*

Page 223. *"Situation ... hopeless":* Kent to Wilson, October 5, 1918, Gregory Papers, LC, Box 1.

Page 224. *"Pointed questions":* Wilson to Gregory, October 7, 1918, Wilson, *Life and Letters,* VIII, 460.

Page 224. *"Orderly process":* File 10560, NA, RG 165.

Page 224. *"Why Worry":* MI Bulletin for Intelligence Officers, No. 20, August 5, 1918, Frey Papers, UCLA.

Page 224. *Treason:* Special Regulations 101, July 26, 1918, discussed in Gregory to Baker, October 23, 1918, Glasser File, Box 9, NA, RG 60.

Page 225. *Negative Branch:* Brigadier General Marlborough Churchill,

"The Military Intelligence Division, General Staff," *Journal of the United States Artillery*, LII (April 1920), 311–312.

Page 225. *"Utmost care":* Churchill to APL, September 19, 1918, File 9684, NA, RG 165.

Page 226. *Butte, Montana:* Copies of reports are in Glasser File, Box 9, NA, RG 60; originals are in File 10110, NA, RG 165.

Page 228. *Councils of defense:* John L. O'Brian, "Uncle Sam's Spy Policies: Safeguarding American Liberty During the War," *Forum*, LXI (April 1919), 414–415.

Page 229. *Minnesota:* O. A. Hilton, *The Minnesota Commission of Public Safety in World War I, 1917–1919* (Stillwell: Oklahoma Agricultural and Mechanical College, 1951), 15; Alan Reeve Hunt, "Federal Supremacy and State Legislation," *Michigan Law Review*, 53 (January 1955), 407; Zechariah Chaffee, *The Inquiring Mind* (New York: Harcourt Brace, 1928), 40–47.

Page 230. *Expansion:* Masteller to APL Directors, October 19, 1918, S. S. Doty to Frey, October 21, 1918, File 10660, NA, RG 165.

Page 230. *Take command:* O'Brian to Gregory, October 18, 1918, File 190470, NA, RG 60.

Page 230. *Defend civil liberties:* Cummings and McFarland, *Federal Justice*, 426; O'Brian interview, June 20, 1961; Walter Johnson, (ed.), *Selected Letters of William Allen White, 1899–1943* (New York: Holt, 1947), 78.

Page 230. *Chain of command:* Bielaski to Special Agents, October 23, 1918, Frey Papers, UCLA.

Page 231. *Socialists:* E. S. Wertz to Gregory, September 26, 1918, O'Brian to Wertz, October 14, 1918, File 186751, NA, RG 60.

Page 231. *Threat at home:* U.S., General Staff, Military Intelligence Division, *The Functions of the Military Intelligence Division* (Washington, 1918), 15.

Page 232. *Detention is arrest:* Gregory to Baker, October 23, 1918, Glasser File, Box 9, NA, RG 60.

Apparently the War Department never accepted the arguments of Gregory. According to Allen Woode, "How the Pentagon Stopped Worrying and Learned to Love Peace Marchers," *Ramparts*, Vol. 6 (February 1968), 47–51, "MPs can detain civilians but cannot arrest them."

Page 233. *Strict supervision:* APL to State Inspectors, October 17, 1918, Frey Papers, UCLA.

Page 233. *Office security: Spy Glass*, October 19, 1918.

Page 233. *"Labor questions":* Gregory to W. B. Wilson, October 18, 1918, File 190470, NA, RG 60.

Page 234. *Corrupt practices:* Attorney General to Bureau of Investigation, Circular 906, October 28, 1918, APL Bulletin No. 21 to Chiefs, October 31, 1918, Frey Papers, UCLA; APL to Lombard, November 1, 1918, APL Papers, University of Washington.

Page 234. *Local "bad men": Spy Glass,* November 4, 1918.

Page 234. *American way:* Frey to Elting, September 25, 1918, Clabaugh to Frey, September 25, 1918, Frey Papers, UCLA; *Spy Glass,* October 5, 1918, January 25, 1919.

Keep the Home Fires Burning

Page 235. *Influenza and hate:* Cronon, *Cabinet Diaries,* 346; Mark Sullivan, *Our Times: The United States, 1900–1925* (5 vols.; New York and London: Scribner's, 1933), V, 654.

Page 236. *Election postmortem:* Creel to Wilson, November 8, 1918, quoted in George Creel, *The War, The World, and Wilson* (New York: Harper, 1920), 146; J. Thomas Heflin to Wilson, November 12, 1918, Wilson Papers, LC, File II, Box 153; Gregory Memorandum to Charles Seymour, August 1924, Charles Seymour (ed.), *The Intimate Papers of Colonel House* (4 vols.; Boston: Houghton Mifflin, 1926–1928), IV, 223.

Page 236. *Violent and indiscriminate:* Captain H. S. Gilbertson to Colonel Masteller, August 5, 1918, File 10560, NA, RG 165.

Page 236. *Relentless battle:* Bielaski to APL, November 4, 1918, Bulletin No. 22 to all Chiefs, November 6, 1918, Frey Papers, UCLA; Johnson, *Challenge,* 47.

Page 237. *Possibilities for APL:* Clarence L. Reames to M. M. Davis, November 8, 1918, APL Papers, University of Washington; Frey Report to War Department, File 10660, NA, RG 165; *New Orleans Times Picayune,* November 10, 1918; *Chicago News,* November 11, 1918; Frey to Briggs, November 12, 1918, Frey Papers, UCLA.

Page 237. *League to continue:* Bielaski to Weinberger, November 13, 1918, Hough, *Web,* 331.

Page 237. *APL help:* Minute Men Division, Bulletin 165 to Officers, November 21, 1918, APL to S. Lombard, November 28, 1918, APL Papers, University of Washington.

Page 238. *Commendation for APL: Official Bulletin, II* (November 22, 1918), 2.

Page 238. *Irish converted:* Shielen Mahon to Gregory, November 22, 1918, File 190470, NA, RG 60.

Page 239. *President on reconstruction:* Preston, *Aliens and Dissenters,* 258; Mason, *Brandeis,* 527.

Page 239. *Patriotic wrath:* Statement by O. P. Adams, California File, NA, RG 65. Members of the new advisory group were: Henry W. O'-Melveny, head of the largest law firm in Los Angeles; Dan Murphy, president of the Murphy Oil Company and director of many other large institutions; Harry C. Chandler, owner and publisher of the *Los Angeles Times;* Reese Llewellyn, president of Llewellyn Iron Works; Dan Brownstein, president of the Brownstein-Lewis Company, wholesale clothing manufacturer; Fred Baker, president of Baker Iron Works, Los Angeles

Building Company (a concern with ninety million in contracts for war ships); J. F. Sartori, president Security Trust and Savings Bank; Stoddard Jess, president Merchants National Bank and one of the signers of the October APL appeal for funds; J. E. Fishburn, president Merchants National Bank; W. H. Holabird, for many years confidential investigator for H. Harriman and Colis P. Huntington and receiver for the California Development Company which owned and furnished water to Imperial Valley; F. W. Braun, president of Braun Drug Company.

Page 240. *No debasements:* O. P. Adams to APL, November 27, 1918, Douglas White to APL, November 29, 1918, California File, *ibid.*

Page 240. *No place for APL:* APL to O. P. Adams, November 29, 1918, December 5, 1918, California File, *ibid.*

Page 240. *Elting interview:* "Behind the Scenes at the Nation's Capital," *Philadelphia Inquirer,* December 9, 1918.

Page 241. *"A square deal":* Frey to Elting, November 26, 1918, Frey Papers, UCLA.

Page 241. *Enemies of the country: Official Bulletin,* II (December 6, 1918); Donald Johnson, "Wilson, Burleson and Censorship in the First World War," *Journal of Southern History,* XXVIII (February 1962), 56.

Page 242. *"Get in wrong":* Hough, *Web,* 196–197.

Page 243. *"Big brothers":* W. H. Wagner to Commissioner of Naturalization, November 23, 1918, File 27671/6184, NA, RG 85.

Page 243. *Americanization:* Campbell to W. H. Wagner, November 26, 1918, *ibid.*

Page 243. *"One of us":* Deputy Commissioner of Naturalization to R. A. Gunn, December 5, 1918, *ibid.*

Pages 243–244. *No new cases:* G. L. Stancliff to Department Intelligence Officer, November 24, 1918, Glasser File, Box 9, NA, RG 60; Crockett to MID, November 24, 1918, File 9684, NA, RG 165.

Page 244. *"Report if true":* Dunn to Intelligence Officer, Chicago, November 29, 1918, *ibid.*

Page 244. *MID balks:* Stancliff to Department Intelligence Officer, November 24, 1918, Glasser File, Box 9, NA, RG 60.

Page 244. *"Continue undercover":* Dunn to Crockett, December 7, 1918, *ibid.,* Preston, *Aliens and Dissenters,* 238.

Page 245. *State inspectors' reports:* Crockett to APL State Inspector, Michigan, William Judson, December 12, 1918, File 10110, Crockett to Ralph Smith, State Inspector, Colorado, December 18, 1918, File 9684, R. G. Woodruff to Director, MID, December 18, 1918, File 10660, NA, RG 165.

Page 245. *"Interested in . . . future":* Crockett to Arthur Nichols, State Inspector, Missouri, December 19, 1918, File 9684, NA, RG 165.

Page 245. *"Return . . . to normal":* Gregory to Wilson, December 14, 1918, Wilson Papers, LC, File VI, Box 473.

Page 245. *Slackers:* Attorney General to U.S. Attorneys, Circular No.

915, November 14, 1918, Attorney General to U.S. Attorneys, December 19, 1918, Frey Papers, UCLA; Cronon, *Cabinet Diaries*, 359.

Page 246. *Bielaski resignation:* Bielaski to Bureau of Investigation, December 17, 1918, Frey Papers, UCLA.

Page 246. *Decision to disband: Spy Glass*, December 21, 1918.

Page 247. *Bielaski:* Memorandum from T. K. Schmuck to Colonel Dunn, December 26, 1918, File 10566, NA, RG 165.

Page 247. *"Services ... tendered":* Crockett to Director, MID, December 18, 1918, File 9684, NA, RG 165.

Page 247. *"Scratching the back":* Memorandum from T. K. Schmuck to Colonel Dunn, December 26, 1918, File 10566, *ibid.*

Page 248. *"Question of policy":* Dunn to Crockett, December 31, 1918, File 9684, *ibid.*

Page 248. *General Staff:* Report of December 28, 1918, File 10148, *ibid.*

Page 248. *"Investigation ... stopped":* Churchill, "Military Intelligence," 313.

Page 249. *"Considerable regret":* Crockett to Director, MID, December 30, 1918, Intelligence Officer, Chicago, to Shinkle, January 7, 1919, File 10110, NA, RG 165.

Page 249. *"Thanks of Congress":* Elting to Frey, December 27, 1918, Elting to Briggs, January 4, 1919, Frey Papers, UCLA; U.S., *Congressional Record*, 65th Cong., 3d Sess., LVII, Part 1, 1002.

Page 251. *"Wonderful work":* Committee on the Judiciary, *Brewing and Liquor Interests*, II, 2251.

Page 251. *"Keen to fight":* R. M. Easly to Gregory, January 9, 1918, File 190470, NA, RG 60.

Page 251. *Seattle:* See reports 10110, 10218, 10634, Glasser File, Box 6, *ibid.*

Page 252. *Crockett and volunteers:* Crockett to Intelligence Officer, St. Louis, Missouri, January 3, 1919, Crockett to William Bobbs, January 24, 1919, File 9684, Crockett to R. C. Stall, January 14, 1919, File 10110, APL meeting, File 1–560–708, NA, RG 165.

Page 252. *Radical menace:* U.S., Conciliation Service, File 33/1913, NA, RG 280 for Texas; George R. Ford to APL, January 17, 1919, File 10660, NA, RG 165.

Pages 252–253. *Reasons for dissolution: Spy Glass*, January 25, 1919.

Pages 253–254. *Chicago meeting:* Report of final meeting, January 25, 1919, Frey Papers, UCLA.

Pages 254–256. *Gold badges:* Bulletin, November 23, 1918, *ibid.*

Page 256. *"Protecting the rear":* American Protective League, New York Division, *Report* (New York, 1919).

The Veterans

Page 257. *Minneapolis:* Committee of Thirteen to Crockett, December 11, 1919, File 10660, NA, RG 165.

Page 257. *Cincinnati:* Statement by Loyal American League, April 11, 1918, File 186751, NA, RG 60.

Page 258. *Tacoma:* U.S., *Congressional Record*, 65th Cong., 3d Sess., 1919, 57, Part 3, 2872–2873.

Page 258. *Seattle:* APL Papers, University of Washington, Report of February 18, 1919.

Page 259. *"Revolution":* Robert L. Friedheim, *The Seattle General Strike*, (Seattle: University of Washington Press, 1964), 101; Preston, *Aliens and Dissenters*, 198.

Page 259. *Rumors:* Dunn to Captain F. W. Wilson, February 7, 1919, Glasser File, Box 6, NA, RG 60; Kate Claghorn, *The Immigrant's Day in Court* (New York: Harper, 1923), 336.

Page 259. *Rebellion:* Sullivan to MID, February 7, 1919, Glasser Files, Box 6, NA, RG 60.

Pages 259–260. *Volunteer informants:* Acting Director MID Dunn to F. W. Wilson, February 24, 1919, Wilson to MID, February 26, 1919, Glasser File, Box 7, NA, RG 60; also see reports in File 10110, NA, RG 165.

Page 260. *Gregory's record:* Gregory to Henry H. Glassie, June 2, 1922, Gregory Papers, LC, Box 2; Statement quoted in Chicago Civil Liberties Committee, *Pursuit of Freedom*, 87; Gregory to Wilson, March 1, 1919, quoted in Johnson, *Challenge*, 67.

Pages 260–261. *From outside:* "Mr. Gregory Resigns," *Public*, 22 (January 18, 1919), 54; "Impressive Record," *Nation*, 108 (January 25, 1919), 112–113; "War Statutes," *Harvard Law Review*, 32 (February 1919), 417–420.

Page 261. *Palmer accusations:* Committee of the Judiciary, *Brewing and Liquor Interests*, I, iii-iv.

Page 261. *Indian National Party*, O'Brian to Palmer, February 8, 1919, NA, RG 60.

Page 262. *"Still at war":* A. Mitchell Palmer, "Germany's Industrial Army on American Soil," *Central Law Journal*, 87 (1918), 61; A. Mitchell Palmer, "The Great Work of the Alien Property Custodian," *American Law Review*, 53 (January 1919), 52, 63; *Spy Glass*, November 22, 1918.

Page 262. *"This disturbs me":* Wilson to Tumulty, January 31, 1919, Tumulty Papers, LC, Box 6.

Page 262. *"Party . . . dispirited":* Tumulty to Wilson, February 1, 1919, *ibid.*

Page 263. *Constant vigilance:* O'Brian to Yates, March 6, 1919, File 186751, NA, RG 60.

Page 263. *No private detectives:* United States Bulletin, I (April 3, 1919), 1; *Minneapolis Journal, Minneapolis Tribune*, April 3, 1919; Arch C. Klumph to E. S. Wertz, April 11, 1919, File 186751, NA, RG 60.

Page 264. *Loyal American League:* William M. Yanacek to Palmer, April 4, 1919, *ibid.*

Page 264. *No "affront":* O'Brian to Wertz, April 14, 1919, *ibid.*

Page 264. *Indignant:* Arch C. Klumph to E. S. Wertz, April 11, 1919, *ibid.*

Pages 264–265. *O'Brian unmoved:* O'Brian to Wertz, April 14, 1919, O'Brian to Clifford Gildersleeve, April 29, 1919, *ibid.*

Page 265. *Palmer reasonable:* Johnson, *Challenge,* 114.

Page 265. *"Further assistance":* Gunn to Churchill, April 22, 1919, Churchill to Gunn, April 26, 1919, Churchill to Crockett, April 28, 1919, File 10660, NA, RG 165.

Page 265. *"District No. 8":* I. D. Berg to Crockett, April 30, 1919, Crockett to Berg, May 5, 1919, File 94-38, *ibid.*

Page 266. *Louisiana:* Memorandum from J. S. Easby-Smith, Baker to Dowling, November 27, 1918, Crowder to Dowling, March 6, 1919, NA, RG 94.

Page 266. *Ohio:* O'Brian to Palmer, April 30, 1919, Palmer to Cox, April 30, 1919, File 186751, NA, RG 60.

Page 267. *"No . . . menace":* Thomas Watt Gregory, "How the Rear of Our Armies Was Guarded During the World War," North Carolina Bar Association, *Proceedings,* XXI (1919), 17.

Page 267. *"Eternal vigilance": ibid.*

Page 268. *"A creditable job":* Half the commutations occurred under Gregory, half under Palmer. Memorandum O'Brian to Palmer, April 30, 1919, File 186701, NA, RG 60.

Page 268. *"Between ourselves":* Holmes to Laski, March 16, 1919, Mark DeWolfe Howe (ed.), *The Correspondence of Mr. Justice Holmes and Harold J. Laski, 1916–1935* (2 vols.; London: Cumberlege, 1953), I, 190; Chaffee, *Free Speech,* 80.

Pages 268–269. *O'Brian's defense:* "Uncle Sam's Spy Policies," 407, 413; *Civil Liberties,* 3–4, 6, 11.

Page 269. *O'Brian's foundation:* "Changing Aspects," 158.

War Plans White

Page 270. *Defending Stars and Stripes:* Robert K. Murray, *Red Scare: A Study in National Hysteria, 1919–1920* (Minneapolis: University of Minnesota Press, 1955), 76.

Pages 270–271. *"Bomb fiends":* G. V. R. Mechin to Palmer, May 2, 1919, File 186751, NA, RG 60.

Page 271. *Gard resolution:* U.S., *Congressional Record,* 66th Cong., 1st Sess., 1919, 58 Part 1, 25.

Page 271. *Web publicity:* For example in the *Chicago Tribune,* May 26, 1919.

Page 271. *Hough:* Edwin W. Gaston, Jr., *The Early Novel of the Southwest* (Albuquerque: University of New Mexico Press, 1961), 273.

Page 271. *Renew the battle:* Hough, *Web,* 471.

Page 272. *Crockett invitations:* Department Intelligence Officer, Chicago to H. H. Seaman, former APL State Inspector for Wisconsin, File 10110, NA, RG 165.

Page 272. *"Thee and thou":* James Roosevelt and Sidney Shalett, *Affectionately, F.D.R.* (New York: Harcourt, Brace, 1959), 59–61.

Page 272. *APL antiradical:* New York Legislature, *Seditious Activities,* I, 812; *New York Call,* June 2, 1920.

Page 274. *Recall the APL: Washington Post,* June 3, 1919; B. M. Brigman to Palmer, June 7, 1919, File 186751, NA, RG 60; Berg to Campbell, June 4, 1919, File 94-38, NA, RG 165.

Page 274. *Encourage veterans:* Campbell to Berg, June 5, 1919, *ibid.;* Crockett to MID, June 9, 1919, in Glasser File, Box 7, NA, RG 60; Crockett to J. Boyle, Crockett to Director, MID, June 16, 1919, File 9684, NA, RG 165.

Pages 274–275. *Minneapolis:* Davis to Newton, September 3, 1919, File 196751, NA, RG 60.

Page 275. *Lusk raids:* New York Legislature, *Seditious Activities,* I, 21; Lawrence H. Chamberlain, *Loyalty and Legislative Action: A Survey of Activity by the New York State Legislature* (Ithaca, Cornell University Press, 1951), 10–12; Chaffee, *Free Speech,* 309.

Page 275. *A giant drive:* Preston, *Aliens and Dissenters,* 211, 214.

Pages 275–276. *High cost of living:* Stanley Coben, *A. Mitchell Palmer: Politician* (New York and London: Columbia University Press, 1963), 155–170; H. H. Rush to Wilson, August 25, 1919, C. B. Ames to H. H. Rush, August 29, 1919, J. H. Atwood to C. B. Ames, December 1, 1919, File 186751, NA, RG 60.

Page 276. *Churchill:* "The Military Intelligence Division," lecture given at War College September 4, 1919, NA, RG 165.

Page 276. *Resurgent MID:* Intelligence Officer, Northeastern Department to all Intelligence Officers, September 30, 1918, Glasser File, Box 7, NA, RG 60.

Page 277. *"A going institution":* Blackwood to Frey, August 24, 1919, September 2, 1919, Frey Papers, UCLA.

Page 277. *Noncommittal:* Frey to Blackwood, August 26, 1919, Frey to Blackwood, September 10, 1919, *ibid.*

Pages 277–278. *Radical search:* John B. Campbell to Intelligence Officer, Camp Pike, Arkansas, and to Intelligence Officer, Fort Omaha, Nebraska, October 2, 1919, Glasser File, Box 7, NA, RG 60.

Page 278. *"Behind this strike":* U.S., Congress, Senate, Committee on Education and Labor, *Investigation of Strike in Steel Industries,* 66th Cong., 1st Sess., (2 vols.; Washington 1919), I, 14.

Pages 279–280. *Steel strike:* Reports and summary in Glasser File, Box 9, NA, RG 60.

Page 280. *"Radical rebel groups":* APL reports from Cincinnati, November 24, 1919, for example, File 10110, NA, RG 165; Confidential memorandum for Officers, Intelligence Reserve, Frey Papers, UCLA.

Page 280. *APL files:* Palmer to Nelson, August 29, 1919, R. P. Stewart to Walter H. Newton, October 10, 1919, File 186751, NA, RG 60.

Page 281. *American Legion:* Richard Seelye Jones, *A History of the American Legion* (Indianapolis and New York: Bobbs-Merrill, 1946), 29, 363; *New York Times,* May 11, 1919, 20:2.

Page 281. *Four points: Evanston News-Index,* October 13, 1919.

Page 281. *November raids:* Murray, *Red Scare,* 195–196; Johnson, *Challenge,* 137.

Page 282. *"Silent Army": New York Evening Telegram,* November 25, 1919; H. L. Jackson to Palmer, November 25, 1919, File 186751, NA, RG 60.

Page 282. *Correspondents:* A. B. Coxe to Intelligence Officers, December 2, 1919, File 10660, NA, RG 165.

Pages 282–283. *Secret collectors:* See letters in File 10660, *ibid.*

Page 283. *Chiefs respond:* Davis to Crockett, December 11, 1919, O. P. Adams to Crockett, December 13, 1919, Crockett to Director, MID, December 16, 1919, Circular 65, December 30, 1919, *ibid.*

Page 283. *"Eternally vigilant": Abrams et. al. v. United States,* 250 U.S. 616 (1919).

Page 284. *Palmer raids:* "The Anderson Decision," *New Republic,* Vol. XXIII (July 14, 1920), 189–191.

Page 284. *Hoover and Churchill:* Preston, *Aliens and Dissenters,* 225.

Page 284. *O'Brian and Anderson:* "Keepers," *Survey* (February 7, 1920), 538.

Page 285. *Thirty thousand spies:* Sheppard to Palmer, February 26, 1920, Palmer to Sheppard, March 3, 1920, File 186751, NA, RG 60.

Page 285. *Qualms:* Memorandum Gardner L. Harding to Churchill, March 13, 1920, File 10560, NA, RG 165.

Page 286. *"Had to stay":* Churchill, "Military Intelligence Division," 313.

Page 286. *"War Plans White":* Preston, *Aliens and Dissenters,* 245.

Page 286. *Wilson:* Johnson, *Challenge,* 181.

Page 287. *"In no way responsible":* Baker to Senator Joseph Ransdell, April 30, 1920, NA, RG 94.

Page 288. *Bureau of Investigation:* Carroll H. Woody, *The Growth of the Federal Government, 1915–1932* (New York and London: McGraw-Hill, 1934), 91; Johnson, *Challenge,* 172–175.

Page 288. *"Evil reputation":* Walter C. Sweeney, *Military Intelligence: A New Weapon of War* (New York: Stokes, 1924), 208.

Page 289. *No discharge:* L. O. Rice to Justice Department, March 25, 1927, File 186751, NA, RG 60.

Pages 289–290. *Ku Klux Klan:* Shepherd, "Ku Klux Koin," 8–9.

Page 290. *Klan investigations:* Charles G. Alexander, *The Ku Klux Klan in the Southwest* (Lexington: University of Kentucky Press, 1966), 59–60, 76.

Page 290. *Civil Legion:* Hapgood, *Professional Patriots,* 188–189.

Pages 290–291. *Bogus medals: Chicago American,* June 16, 1923, *Chicago Tribune,* June 17, 1923, *Chicago Evening Post,* July 16, 1923, July 18, 1923, *Chicago Tribune,* January 11, 1924, *Chicago Herald-Examiner,* January 11, 1924.

Legacy of the League

Pages 292–293. *Conspiracy:* Charles Crowe, "The Emergence of Progressive History," *Journal of the History of Ideas,* XXVII (January-March 1966), 109–124; William T. Hutchinson, "The American Historian in Wartime," *Mississippi Valley Historical Review,* XXIX (September 1942), 163–186.

Page 293. *Necessity for APL:* O'Leary, *Political Trial,* 238; Florence Kelly, *What America Did: A Record of American Achievements* (New York: Dutton, 1919), 333–334.

Page 293. *"Desolating and repulsive":* Carl Becker to William E. Dodd, June 17, 1920, quoted in Phil L. Snider, "Carl L. Becker and the Great War: A Crisis for a Humane Intelligence," *Western Political Quarterly,* IX (March 1956), 1–10; *Nation,* 111 (November 2, 1920), 489; Harold Stearns, *Liberalism in America: Its Origin, Its Temporary Collapse, Its Future* (New York: Boni and Liveright, 1919), 109.

Page 294. *War a hoax:* Warren I. Cohen, *The American Revisionists: The Lessons of Intervention in World War I* (Chicago and London: University of Chicago, 1967), 75, 79.

Page 294. *Radicals:* Upton Sinclair, *The Brass Check: A Study of Journalism* (Pasadena: by the author, 1919), 381; Louis Adamic, *Dynamite: The Story of Class Violence in America* (New York: Viking, 1929), 279–280; John Dos Passos, *1919* (New York: Harcourt, Brace, 1932), 16.

Pages 294–295. *Main business:* Charles and Mary Beard, *The Rise of American Civilization* (2d ed. rev.; New York: Macmillan, 1934), 642–644.

Page 295. *Politicians:* Oscar W. Underwood, *Drifting Sands of Party Politics* (New York: Century, 1928), 357.

Page 295. *Fear of subversion revived:* W. C. Pope to Attorney General, August 15, 1932, File 186751, NA, RG 60.

Pages 295–296. *"Untrained and undisciplined":* Swisher, "Civil Liberties," 344.

Page 296. *"Sore as a pup":* F. H. Timson to Cummings, December 31, 1935, File 186751, NA, RG 60.

Page 296. *Hoover and APL:* Whitehead, *F.B.I. Story,* 189; McDermid to author, August 14, 1961.

Page 296. *Preparation for another war:* Richard W. Rowan, *The Story of the Secret Service* (Garden City: Doubleday, Doran, 1937), 87; Jesse Clarkson and Thomas Cochran (eds.), *War as a Social Institution: The*

Historian's Perspective (New York: Columbia University Press, 1941), 177, 187; Tobin, *Mobilizing*, 28.

Page 297. *World War II:* Cushman, "American Government," 49–50.

Pages 298–299. *FBI volunteers:* John Caughey, *In Clear and Present Danger: The Crucial State of Our Freedom* (Chicago: University of Chicago Press, 1958), 58.

Page 299. *World War I:* Max Lowenthal, *Federal Bureau of Investigation* (New York: Sloane, 1950), 22–23.

Page 299. *O'Brian:* "Changing Aspects," 154.

Page 299. *Vigilantes:* Whitehead, *F.B.I. Story*, 38–44.

Page 300. *"Gap in our defenses":* Undated brochure published by the American Security Council, Chicago, Illinois.

Page 300. *"The American Vigilante":* Tristram Coffin, *The Armed Society: Militarism in Modern America* (Baltimore: Penguin Books Edition, 1964), 113–115.

Page 301. *Christian Anti-Communist Crusade: ibid.,* 115, 222–223; *CACC Newsletter,* April 1962, has complete text of Mosk's television speech.

Page 301. *"A rare Red":* San Diego Union, January 23, 1952, 3:4–5, B2:2.

Page 302. *250,000 file cards: San Diego Union,* March 2, 1962, A24:3, February 20, 1962, 15:5; February 18, 1962, 15:6.

Page 302. *Three governors: San Diego Union,* March 2, 1962, A24:3; February 20, 1962, 15:5; February 18, 1962, 15:6.

Page 302. *"A hazard and liability":* San Diego Union, February 20, 1962, 15:5.

Page 303. *"Unpatriotic acts":* "The Home-Front War," *Newsweek,* Vol. 69 (May 8, 1967), 31–36.

Page 303. *"Crystallized the thinking":* "The Right to Answer Dissent," *Life,* Vol. 62 (May 12, 1967), 4.

Page 303. *"Propaganda bludgeoning":* "War on the Third Front," *Nation,* Vol. 204 (May 15, 1967), 610–611.

Page 304. *"Infiltrated": Los Angeles Times,* November 18, 1967, 12:7–8. The Administration had 25,000 troops ready if the October protests got out of hand, *New York Times,* November 22, 1967, 9:1.

Page 304. *"Can the Republic endure": San Diego Tribune,* November 22, 1967, A3:3; *New York Times,* November 16, 1967, 2:4. The October 25 directive was not made public until November 21. The October 26 directive was not made public for over a week. *New York Times,* November 9, 1967, 2:4, 3:1 carried text of this directive.

Pages 304–305. *"Less than patriotic": Sunday Ramparts* (San Francisco), March 12–26, 1967, 1:5, 6:6.

Page 305. *"Lowering the morale":* Edward F. Sherman, "Dissenters and Deserters," *New Republic,* Vol. 157 (January 6, 1968), 23–26.

Page 306. *"Growing their hair long": The Daily Pilot* (Costa Mesa, California), undated clipping supplied by university student. For selection of Negroes on draft boards see *New York Times,* January 14, 1968, 1:7.

Page 306. *Plastic lapel buttons:* Aryeh Neier to Editor, December 11, 1967, *New York Times,* December 14, 1967, 46:3.

Page 307. *"Honest mistake":* New York Times, December 8, 1967, 12:1.

Appendix

Page 308. *Records closed:* Wittke, *German-Americans,* 177.

Pages 308–309. *APL and nativism:* John Blum, "Nativism, Anti-Radicalism and the Foreign Scare, 1917–1920," *Midwest Journal,* III (1950–1951), 46–53; John Higham, *Strangers in the Land: Patterns of American Nativism, 1860–1925* (New Brunswick: Rutger's University Press, 1955), 212, 223.

Page 309. *APL "converted":* Murray, *Red Scare,* 12.

Page 309. *APL "blessed":* Harold M. Hyman, *To Try Men's Souls: Loyalty Tests in American History* (Berkeley and Los Angeles: University of California Press, 1959), 271–297.

Pages 309–310. *Gregory and Palmer:* Donald Johnson, "The Political Career of A. Mitchell Palmer," *Pennsylvania History,* XXV (1958), 350; Harry N. Scheiber, "A. Mitchell Palmer: A Comment," *Pennsylvania History,* XXVI (October 1959), 377–379.

Page 310. *Record "deplorable":* Harry N. Scheiber, *The Wilson Administration and Civil Liberties, 1917–1919* (Ithaca: Cornell University Press, 1960), 43, 47, 49.

Page 310. *Enigma:* O. A. Hilton, "Freedom of Press in Wartime, 1917–1919," *Southwestern Social Science Quarterly,* XXVIII (1947), 358.

Page 310. *"Ritual patriotism":* Richard P. Longaker, *The Presidency and Individual Liberties* (Ithaca: Cornell University Press, 1961), 21–23.

Page 311. *Amateurism: ibid.,* 98.

Page 311. *"Lynch mob":* John P. Roche, *The Quest for the Dream: the Development of Civil Rights and Human Relations in Modern America* (New York: Macmillan, 1963), 43–44, 64.

Index

Butler, Nicholas Murray, 80
Byrd, R.E., 162

C

Calder, William, 207, 208
California State Council of Defense, 125
California, 301–303; University of, 147–8
Campbell, John, 274, 277, 280
Canada, 11, 234
Capital Democrat, 70
Cattell, James McKeen, 80
Cavell, Edith, 106
Censorship, 148–9, 241
Census Bureau, 45
Central Electric Company, 140
Central Intelligence Agency, 297–8; bureau, 95–6, 103
Chaffee, Zechariah, 268
Chamberlain, George, 39, 55, 98, 112, 116, 120, 121, 208
Chaplin, Ralph, 74
Character investigations, 176–80
Chicago, 138–43, 220–1, 242–3, 247–8, 253–4
Chicago and North Western Railway, 138
Chicago American, 291
Chicago Daily News, 76
Chicago Evening Post, 87
Chicago Real Estate Board, 138
Chicago Tribune, 196
Choate, Charles F., Jr., 126
Christian Anti-Communist Crusade, 301
Christian Herald, 100
Christian Science Monitor, 115
Church, Frank, 303
Churches, 148

Churchill, Marlborough, 124, 185–6, 225, 226, 231, 238, 248, 265, 274, 280, 284, 285–6
Cincinnati City Club, 263
Cincinnati Enquirer, 263
Citizen's Bureau of Investigation, 146, 289
Citizen's Protective League, 63
Citizenship, 159–60
Civil Legion, 290
Civil liberties, 65, 71ff, 84, 90, 101, 108, 111–12, 113, 147, 148, 151–2, 207ff, 229, 260–1, 262, 268–9, 297, 298, 309ff; *see also* American Civil Liberties Union; National Civil Liberties Bureau
Civil Rights Congress, 302
Civil Service Commission, 176
Clabaugh, Hinton D., 17ff; 47, 59, 66ff, 74, 77–8, 93–4
Clark, Speaker, 39
Cleveland Chamber of Commerce, 264
Cleveland News, 265
Cleveland Plain Dealer, 79, 248–9
Cleveland Press, 249
Cobb, Frank I., 14, 93, 211
Cobb, Irwin S., 97
Cochrane, W.K., 143
Coffin, Tristram, 300
Colcord, Lincoln, 51
Collier's Weekly, 87
Columbia University, 80
Comerford, Frank, 290
Committee of Thirteen, 257, 274, 280
Communism, 298ff; *see also* Bolshevism
Communist Labor party, 273
Communist party, 281, 284–5
Conboy, Martin, 199ff, 205
Concentration camps, 161–5
Confiscation of property, 164–6
Conscientious objectors, 77, 84–5, 281, 297

Conscription, 34, 38, 45, 51, 58, 60, 65, 69ff, 80, 83, 85, 100, 153, 188ff; deferments, 188–9; "deserters," 83–4, 189; raids, 189–213, 215–18; slackers, 189–213, 215, 245–6
Cooksey, George R., 102–103
Coolidge, Calvin, 276
Corrupt Practices Act, 234
Council of National Defense, 72, 127, 128, 130, 228–9
Counterespionage, see Investigations, official; Volunteer forces
Covington, J. Harry, 72, 74
Cox, James, 266
Coxe, Colonel, 282
Craft of Intelligence, The (Dulles), 156
Creel, George, 101, 179, 222, 236
Creel, General George, 304
Crockett, Thomas B., 25, 243–5, 247–9, 251–2, 265, 273, 274, 277, 278, 280, 283
Crowder, Enoch, 36ff, 51, 61, 66, 71, 83, 84, 99, 113, 124, 188ff, 224, 227, 238
Cummings, Homer, 296
Czechoslovakia, 235

D

Dana, Henry Wadsworth Longfellow, 80
Daniels, Josephus, 23, 36, 182
Darkow, Martin, 161
Darrow, Clarence, 76
Daugherty, Harry M., 288–9
Daughters of the American Revolution, 300
Davis, Charles D., 275
Davis, Dwight F., 288
Davis, John W., 107

Dayal, Har, 100
Deal, R.L., 190
Debs, Eugene, 76, 173, 268, 286
Defense, councils of, 125ff, 131
Defense of the Realm Act (England), 105–106
Defense plants, 167
DeMille, Cecil B., 28, 141, 296
Dent, Hubert S., 38
"Deserters," see under Conscription
DeSilver, Albert, 265
Detroit Free Press, 76
Detroit Patriotic Fund Committee, 156
Dewey, John, 51, 80–1
DeWoody, Charles, 197, 199ff
Dictaphones, 151–2
Dissent, 65, 71ff, 81, 90, 110ff, 147, 169, 173, 175, 283ff, 293, 297, 298, 303
Dos Passos, John, 294
Doty, S.S., 132, 230
Dowling, Oscar, 266
Draft, see Conscription
Draft boards, local, 61, 69, 71–2, 83–4, 85, 198, 304, 306
Duke University, 304; Chronicle, 305
Dulles, Allen, 156
Dunn, John M., 248
DuPont, T. Coleman, 198
Dyer, L.C., 65

E

Easby-Smith, James S., 150
Easly, Ralph M., 251
Eastland, 18
Eastman, Max, 77, 78, 172
Edmunds, Sterling, 168
Eisner, Kurt, 235
Eliot, Charles W., 179

137, 145, 147, 167, 170–1, 174,
178, 188–9, 190, 200, 207–208,
209ff, 228, 230, 236ff, 245, 256,
260ff, 267, 284, 309, 311, 312,
315

Grodzins, Morton, 144
Gruening, Ernest, 303
Gunn, R.A., 242–3, 254, 265, 279,
280

H

Haan, William G., 280
Hale, William Bayard, 91
Hand, Learned, 175
Harding, Gardner, 285–6
Harding, Warren G., 111
Hardwick, Thomas R., 270
Hart, Philip A., 304
Hartman, Cornelia G., 315
Harvard Law Review, 260
Harvey, George, 79–80
Hatch, Charles B., 182
Hatfield, Mark, 303
Hayden, Carl, 72
Hayes, L.B., 97
Haywood, Bill, 67, 72, 74, 76
Henderson, Theodore, 148
Hershey, Louis B., 304
Higham, John, 308–309
Hill, Roderick, 302, 303
Hillman, Sidney, 74
Hillquist, Morris, 122
Hilton, O.A., 310
Hindenberg, Paul von, 9
History of the United States (Wilson), 36
Hodges, W.F., 278
Holmes, Oliver Wendell, 107, 268,
283
Home Rule, Irish, 174
Homestead Strike, 278
Hoover, Herbert, 86, 91–2

Hoover, J. Edgar, 275, 282, 284,
288, 295–6, 298–9
Hough, Emerson, 149, 152, 158,
241, 271–2, 293, 313
House, Edwin M., 14, 52, 89, 95,
179, 267
House Committee on Military Affairs,
180
Huddleston, George, 38
Hughes, Charles Evans, 16
Humes, Major, 250
Hurd, Richard, 98
Huston, David F., 23
Hyman, Harold, 310, 313

I

Immigration Bureau, 269
India, 18, 21
Indian National Party, 261
Industrial Workers of the World,
56–81, 127, 172, 225–8, 244, 246,
267, 271, 275, 278, 310
Inflation, 276ff
Inglis, Agnes, 100
Insull, Samuel, 25
Internal Security Act, 298
International Bible Students' Association, 174
International Brotherhood of Bookbinders, 259
Interstate Commerce Commission,
126
Irish radicals, 174–5
Italy, 82, 235

J

Jacques, Alfred, 61–2
Jancke, Kurt, 119

Lombard, Sumner J., 128
Longaker, Richard P., 310–11
Los Angeles, 239
Louisville Times, 76
Lowden, Frank O., 27
Lowenthal, Max, 299
Loyal American League, 257–8, 264, 270
Loyal Citizens Vigilance Committee, 146
Loyal Legion of Loggers and Lumbermen, 127
Loyalty oaths, 96
Ludendorff, Erich von, 9
Lusitania, 9, 153
Lusk, Clayton, 131, 275; Committee, 282, 285
Lynn, John D., 47
Lyons, Albert, 175

M

McAdoo, William, 11ff, 20, 21, 23, 30, 39, 40, 43–5, 48, 52–6, 90, 91, 94–6, 102–104, 193, 290, 315
MacArthur, Arthur, 117
McCarthy, Joseph, 297, 299
McCarthy, Thomas D., 54, 172, 198–9
McDermid, William, 131, 275, 315
McGee, J.F., 53, 120
McGinnis, W.P., 70
McGovern, George, 303
McNamara, John J., 76
McReynolds, James C., 15, 16
Mahon, Shielen, 238
Mann Act, 181
Mann, Congressman, 249
Marjoribanks, Kate, 142
Martin, Charles H., 72
Maryland Casualty Company, 148
Massachusetts League, 126
Masses, The, 77, 171

Masteller, K.C., 225
Mata Hari, 106
Mellon, Andrew, 291
Midway Oilfields Protective Committee, 47
Midwest Journal, 308
Military conduct, 180–2
Military Intelligence, 86, 103, 108, 109, 117–20, 122, 123–5, 149, 151, 176, 179, 181–2, 185ff, 191, 224ff, 231–2, 241, 243ff, 248, 251ff, 259, 273, 274, 276ff, 305, 314, 315; Negative Branch, 225, 230, 282; Military Morale Subsection, 185; Plant Protection Section, 118, 167
Military jurisdiction, 102–105, 107, 108, 112ff, 305–306, 307
Millner, Lucille, 84
Minnesota Commission of Public Safety, 53, 66, 117, 120, 125, 229
Minute Men, 125, 126–9, 154–5, 237, 258, 315
Moffett, Cleveland, 97
Montgomery Ward, 138
Morton, Louis, 18
Mosk, Stanley, 301
Mowry, George, 296
Muck, Karl, 163
Mumford, Lewis, 78–9
Murray, Robert, 309
Myasoedev, Colonel, 106

N

Naked Communist, The (Skousen), 300
Napora, 227–8
Nation, The, 179, 211, 260, 293, 303
National Association for the Advancement of Colored People, 65
National Civil Liberties Bureau, 84, 211, 231, 265, 294, 309

41, 42, 45, 46, 50, 51, 55–6, 60, 63–4, 65, 67, 72, 77, 78, 82, 85, 89, 90, 92–3, 104, 109, 121, 128–9, 156–7, 159, 165, 209ff, 235ff, 262, 275, 276, 277, 285, 292, 293, 295, 306, 307, 310–12, 315

Winterbotham, John H., 128

Wiretapping, 149–51

Wisconsin Council of Defense, 117, 125

Wisconsin Defense League, 25

Wittke, Carl, 308

Wood, Leonard, 27, 84, 96, 195, 279

Woodrow, Fitzwilliam McMaster, 36

Woodruff, B., 177

Woolley, Robert, 40, 41

Working-Class Union, 69

Workmen's Loyalty League, 63

World War I, 82, 235ff, 310ff; *see also* Conscription; Espionage, German

World War II, 296–7

World's Work, 99

Wursterbarth, Frederick W., 168

Y

Yale Law Journal, 107

YMCA, 133, 168, 176–7

Yates, Edward, 263

Youth Against War and Fascism, 305

Yugoslavia, 235

Z

Zimmerman, Arthur, 21; telegram, 22

Printed in the U.S.A